LITERARY VALUE AND SOCIAL IDENTITY
I[illegible] *ES*

Literary authors, especially those with other occupations, must come to grips with the question of why they should write at all, when the world urges them to devote their time and energy to other pursuits. They must reach, at the very least, a provisional conclusion regarding the relation between the uncertain value of their literary efforts and the more immediate values of their non-authorial social identities. Geoffrey Chaucer, with his several middle-strata identities, grappled with this question in a remarkably searching, complex manner. In this book, Robert J. Meyer-Lee examines the multiform, dynamic meditation on the relation between literary value and social identity that Chaucer stitched into the heart of the *Canterbury Tales*. He traces the unfolding of this meditation through what he shows to be the tightly linked performances of Clerk, Merchant, Franklin, and Squire, offering the first full-scale reading of this sequence.

ROBERT J. MEYER-LEE is Associate Professor of English at Agnes Scott College. He is author of *Poets and Power from Chaucer to Wyatt* (Cambridge University Press, 2007), as well as numerous articles on Chaucer, fifteenth-century poetry, and literary value published in journals such as *Speculum, Studies in the Age of Chaucer, New Literary History, The Chaucer Review, JEGP*, and *Exemplaria*.

CAMBRIDGE STUDIES IN MEDIEVAL LITERATURE

This series of critical books seeks to cover the whole area of literature written in the major medieval languages – the main European vernaculars, and medieval Latin and Greek – during the period c.1100–1500. Its chief aim is to publish and stimulate fresh scholarship and criticism on medieval literature, special emphasis being placed on understanding major works of poetry, prose, and drama in relation to the contemporary culture and learning which fostered them.

Recent titles in the series

Sarah Elliott Novacich *Shaping the Archive in Late Medieval England: History, Poetry, and Performance*
Geoffrey Russom *The Evolution of Verse Structure in Old and Middle English Poetry: From the Earliest Alliterative Poems to Iambic Pentameter*
Ian Cornelius *Reconstructing Alliterative Verse: The Pursuit of a Medieval Meter*
Sara Harris *The Linguistic Past in Twelfth-Century Britain*
Erik Kwakkel and Rodney Thomson (eds.) *The European Book in the Twelfth Century*
Irina Dumitrescu *The Experience of Education in Anglo-Saxon Literature*
Jonas Wellendorf *Gods and Humans in Medieval Scandinavia: Retying the Bonds*
Thomas A. Prendergast and Jessica Rosenfeld (eds.) *Chaucer and the Subversion of Form*
Katie L. Walter *Middle English Mouths*
Lawrence Warner *Chaucer's Scribes*
Glenn D. Burger and Holly A. Crocker (eds.) *Medieval Affect, Feeling, and Emotion*
Robert J. Meyer-Lee *Literary Value and Social Identity in the "Canterbury Tales"*

A complete list of titles in the series can be found at the end of the volume.

LITERARY VALUE AND SOCIAL IDENTITY IN THE *CANTERBURY TALES*

ROBERT J. MEYER-LEE
Agnes Scott College

CAMBRIDGE
UNIVERSITY PRESS

CAMBRIDGE
UNIVERSITY PRESS

University Printing House, Cambridge CB2 8BS, United Kingdom

One Liberty Plaza, 20th Floor, New York, NY 10006, USA

477 Williamstown Road, Port Melbourne, VIC 3207, Australia

314-321, 3rd Floor, Plot 3, Splendor Forum, Jasola District Centre, New Delhi - 110025, India

103 Penang Road, #05-06/07, Visioncrest Commercial, Singapore 238467

Cambridge University Press is part of the University of Cambridge.

It furthers the University's mission by disseminating knowledge in the pursuit of education, learning and research at the highest international levels of excellence.

www.cambridge.org
Information on this title: www.cambridge.org/9781108707435
DOI: 10.1017/9781108757621

First published 2019
First paperback edition 2021

A catalogue record for this publication is available from the British Library

ISBN 978-1-108-48566-1 Hardback
ISBN 978-1-108-70743-5 Paperback

In memory of
Lee Patterson, 1940–2012
and
Robert Lee, 1928–2016

Contents

Acknowledgments

Given how long this book has been stewing, I cannot hope to thank here everyone who in some fashion helped me to reach this point, but I will attempt to recognize those to whom I owe particular debts.

This book's origin lies in my experiences, now more than a dozen years ago, leading a pair of seminars on the *Canterbury Tales* at Goshen College, in which remarkably accomplished students prompted many of its essential ideas. Two of these students – Benjamin Miller Jacobs and Claire Swora – contributed to the initial research as part of the college's wonderful Maple Scholars program. At a crucial juncture during this time, Holly Crocker offered much-needed encouragement, without which the quite incipient project may well have languished. After many years of fiddling with possible recipes, I began to pull ingredients together with the assistance of grants from the Indiana University New Frontiers program and Indiana University South Bend, and with time provided by a sabbatical from the latter institution. An appointment as Visiting Scholar at University of Notre Dame's Medieval Institute greatly facilitated my research. Much of the final stage of writing was completed during my time as Dabney Adams Hart Distinguished Visiting Humanities Professor at Agnes Scott College.

Key interlocutors over the years have been Susanna Fein and David Raybin, who also invited me to present a précis of the project at their 2016 NEH seminar, at which the participants, along with others at the talk, formed the ideal audience for a test run. Leah Schwebel, her students, and others in the audience at a later presentation at Texas State University helped launch the project into completion. Matthew Giancarlo lent his sharp eye to the book proposal. Thomas J. Farrell braved readings of some initial drafts and provided enormously helpful feedback, as did, later, the anonymous press readers, and series editor Daniel Wakelin. At CUP, along with Dan, I have been honored to work with Emily Hockley, her predecessor Linda Bree, and the entire production team. Ardis Butterfield,

Robert Epstein, Alexandra Gillespie, James Goldstein, Lee Kahan, Kathryn Kerby-Fulton, Ashby Kinch, Tim William Machan, Jill Mann, David Matthews, Mark Miller, Stephen Partridge, Thomas Prendergast, Catherine Sanok, D. Vance Smith, Paul Strohm, Kyoko Takanashi, and the participants in the 2007 and 2012 Medieval Writing Workshops offered essential guidance and support. Lucas Meyer-Lee lent his amazing design skills to a mock-up of the book cover. My journey with Chaucer began in 1993 with Derek Pearsall, who remains inspiring in so many ways. No one besides me, of course, deserves blame for anything amiss in the pages that follow, and I apologize to the many whose assistance has gone unrecorded.

I must also apologize to Gabriel, Jackson, and Lucas – who became young adults over the course of my work on this book – for too often being a distracted dad, and express my deepest gratitude to Elaine, for being all that I could ever imagine a life partner to be. The book's dedicatees shaped its most profound concerns in ways that I have only begun to understand.

An early version of a portion of Chapter 1 appeared as Robert J. Meyer-Lee, "Literary Value and the Customs House: The Axiological Logic of the *House of Fame*," *The Chaucer Review* 48 (2014): 374–94.

Abbreviations

CLR	Crow, Martin M. and Clair C. Olson, eds. *Chaucer Life-Records*. Oxford: Clarendon Press, 1966.
MED	*Middle English Dictionary Online*. http://quod.lib.umich.edu/m/med/.
MR	Manly, John M. and Edith Rickert. *The Text of the* Canterbury Tales: *Studied on the Basis of all Known Manuscripts*. 8 vols. Chicago: The University of Chicago Press, 1940.
OED	*Oxford English Dictionary Online*. www.oed.com/.
Variorum GP	Andrew, Malcolm, Charles Moorman, and Daniel J. Ransom, eds. *The General Prologue*. The Variorum Chaucer. Vol. 2, parts 1A and 1B. Norman: University of Oklahoma Press, 1993.

Unless otherwise indicated, all quotations of Chaucer's works are cited by line number in *The Riverside Chaucer*, gen. ed. Larry D. Benson, 3rd ed. (Boston: Houghton Mifflin, 1987). For the Hengwrt manuscript, I have relied on *The Hengwrt Chaucer Digital Facsimile*, ed. Estelle Stubbs (Scholarly Digital Editions, 2000); and, for Ellesmere, *The* Canterbury Tales: *The New Ellesmere Chaucer Monochromatic Facsimile*, ed. Daniel Woodward and Martin Stevens (San Marino: Huntington Library, 1997). All Chaucer manuscripts other than these two are cited by the sigla in *MR*.

Introduction
Canterbury Tales IV-V and Literary Value

This book represents, in some ways, a relatively straightforward literary critical endeavor, one that focuses on explicating a sequence of four pilgrim performances in the middle of Chaucer's *Canterbury Tales*: those of the Clerk, Merchant, Squire, and Franklin. For some readers, this sort of monograph will require no explicit justification, but I suspect that, at this stage in the history of the study of British literature, others may harbor reasonable reservations about its value. Some may wonder what I have to contribute to the centuries-old project of *Canterbury Tales* criticism that does not merely retread much-worn tires. More skeptical readers (if they get even this far) may question my assumption that the project of Chaucer criticism – by which I mean interpretation of Chaucer for its own sake – is itself still worthwhile, even if I do have something new to add to it.

The first reservation is considerably easier to address than the second. In offering a reading of the sequence of tales that make up so-called Fragments IV and V, this book redresses an oversight in the critical tradition that derives from two of its very longstanding features. First, a mid-nineteenth-century editorial error divided the four tales between two fragments, thereby discouraging subsequent readers from considering the sequence as such – in the way that, say, Fragment I has been considered. When the tales have been read together, they are almost invariably analyzed as two pairs or as a component of some larger literary structure. Second, one such larger structure – the so-called marriage group – early in the twentieth century became perhaps the single most pervasive topos of modern *Canterbury Tales* criticism, thereby further discouraging focus on the sequence as such. For these reasons, despite the long and close critical scrutiny that the *Tales* has attracted, there has been no extended study (as far as I am aware) of the IV-V sequence as a unit. And in light of the manuscript evidence, this lack is all the more conspicuous, given the fact that, among the many intractable uncertainties surrounding Chaucer's composition of and intentions for the *Tales*, the stitching together of these particular pilgrim performances to form a four-part sequence appears to represent a very definite and striking artistic decision.

The trail of these preliminary justifications, moreover, has led me to adopt a pair of approaches to the sequence – one methodological and one conceptual – that has made this project somewhat less straightforward, more novel, and broader in its implications than it may initially appear. First, in honoring the fact that the basis of my claim for the unity of IV-V lies in recognition of the manuscript evidence in this regard, I have taken, so to speak, the bad with the good. I have accepted the limits that my understanding of this manuscript evidence imposes upon interpretation along with the interpretive vistas that the evidence opens up, limits that concern especially the kind of claims that can be made about the unity of the component parts of the tale-telling performances: the pilgrim portraits, prologues and epilogues, and narratives. Second, in considering what the IV-V sequence is about (in addition to, obviously, marriage and the status of women in the late medieval English patriarchal imagination), I have found it to be pervasively and centrally preoccupied with an oft-noticed career-long concern of Chaucer's, his anxiety about the value of his writing and of literary fiction in particular; and I have found that this concern – when viewed not just as a feature of each of the individual tales but also as the subject of a conflicted conversation staged by the sequence of pilgrim performances – becomes inflected in a way that requires a more fluid approach to literary value than has been typical of Chaucer criticism on the topic. Accordingly, drawing upon scholarship from the last few decades on the general matter of cultural value, I have developed a conceptual approach to Chaucer's agon with literary value in IV-V that, while by no means unprecedented, is at least unusual.

The subsequent two sections of this introduction present these methodological and conceptual approaches in turn, explaining their bases, rationales, and implications; indicating how they inform the chapters that follow; and supplying definitions of the terms that I use across the book. Next, after briefly touching on the relation between the focus of this book and the body of criticism on the IV-V tales that has been devoted to marriage, women, gender, and sexuality, I return (also briefly) to the more difficult reservation about this project: the question of what justifies, well into the first quarter of the twenty-first century, a book devoted to an investigation of the meaning and achievement of one portion of an uber-canonical work like the *Canterbury Tales*, regardless of the insights about that work thereby achieved. Both of these latter sections also provide some further glimpses of what is to come.

Before launching into these matters, however, let me offer a preliminary sketch of the book's argument about IV-V. When we put this sequence back together, three of its features emerge as especially striking. First, Chaucer has collected within it the very four pilgrims whose social identities most overlap with those several identities that characterized his own social experience (discounting the pilgrim Chaucer, for whom the author does not provide such an identity). For, as has been often pointed out independently for each of the pilgrims, Chaucer was a squire and sometime courtier; his father was a merchant, and he himself worked for many years among merchants on the Wool Wharf; he resembled the Franklin at the time that he was writing the *Tales*; and, though not technically a clerk, he held clerkly jobs and represented himself, in such efforts as the *House of Fame*, as clerk-like. Second, Chaucer has arranged the sequence's pilgrims to alternate youthful (or at least quasi-youthful) tellers with ones who represent more experienced, mature, and paternal (or quasi-paternal) perspectives. Third, and most obviously, when the tales are set side by side, one recognizes the overwhelming number of points of contact among them – close similarities of narrative, characters, and structure; apparent verbal echoes; thematic continuities; and generic duplication or inversion – along with their overriding concern with tale telling and fiction: a concern that explicitly suffuses the links and is as well, in one fashion or another, central to each narrative. Considering all these features together, this book argues that the IV-V sequence stages a dialectical grappling with the problem of literary value. More specifically, it contends that IV-V enacts a dynamically unfolding, conflicted meditation on how literary value may be construed in a way that justifies the time, energy, and expense devoted to the writing of fiction – a justification made in respect to other activities pertaining to other values, especially to economic value in the sense of making a living. Or, more colloquially, this book reads IV-V as a meditation on the conflict between writing and Chaucer's day jobs, with the latter understood to encompass the nexus of values associated with the specific normative masculine occupational identities of clerk, merchant, squire, and franklin.

In the chapters that follow, in describing the character of the IV-V dialectical trajectory and its provisional resolution, I necessarily encounter myriad local and often longstanding problems of *Canterbury Tales* interpretation, on some of which I take novel or at least atypical positions that I hope may further the understanding of the *Tales* in smaller ways. But what I most claim to offer in this book is neither this collection of incidental interventions nor the overall argument, but rather a detailed account of how the IV-V dialectic unfolds. Hence, whether readers find the journey through this book worth the effort will ultimately depend not on its beginning or its end but on the collective effect of the changing scenery that they encounter along the way, an encounter conditioned by the vehicle – my approach – in which they ride. I turn now to the two most distinguishing features of that approach.

The IV-V Sequence and the Work Room

That the division of the IV-V tales into two fragments was a simple editorial error – for which the redoubtable Frederick Furnivall, in his over-enthusiastic embrace of Henry Bradshaw's ideas, was largely responsible – is an argument that I have pursued in detail elsewhere, and which to this point has received no challenge, as far as I am aware.[1] Here I briefly mention the three major points of this argument most relevant to this book's purpose and then consider their interpretive implications. In subsequent chapters I review the claims in this regard that are related to the respective component parts of IV-V and introduce any additional pertinent evidence.

First, as has been no secret to all the Chaucer editors familiar with the manuscript variations pertaining to the IV-V tales (including Furnivall), the passage that Furnivall divided to form the *Merchant's Epilogue* and the *Introduction to the Squire's Tale* – which he then used, respectively, to terminate Group E (Fragment IV) and begin Group F (Fragment V) – never appears so divided in the manuscripts (discounting a couple of nonexceptional exceptions). Rather, it constitutes a single, unbroken linking passage. To be sure, in this linking passage's variant versions the tales that it joins are not always the *Merchant's* and the *Squire's* (most notably, in Hengwrt the passage joins Merchant and Franklin). Yet the strongest reading of this evidence, by far, is that the version that joins Merchant and Squire represents the passage's original rendering.

Second, despite many variations, the three links that form the IV-V sequence – in addition to the Merchant-Squire passage, the Clerk-Merchant link (i.e., the *Merchant's Prologue*) and the Squire-Franklin link (i.e., the Franklin's words to the Squire at the end of the *Squire's Tale*) – travel together in the manuscript traditions. For example, in all fifteen manuscripts in which the Squire-Franklin link joins the tales of those two pilgrims, the Clerk-Merchant and Merchant-Squire links appear as such; and in all twenty-two manuscripts in which the Squire-Franklin link instead joins Squire and Merchant, the Clerk-Merchant link is absent and the Merchant-Squire link is either also absent or joins tales other than those of Merchant and Squire. Again, as with Merchant-Squire link, the strongest reading of the evidence by far is that the variations in the other two links that involve other tales represent scribal adaptations.

Third, the best explanation of the peculiar disposition of the links in Hengwrt and of the nature of the variation in this regard across manuscript traditions is that Chaucer composed all three links independently of and sometime after composing the tales that they join and, indeed, after composing most and perhaps all the rest of what survives of the *Canterbury Tales*. In Hengwrt, both the Merchant-Squire and the Squire-Franklin links are copied in the same light yellowish ink that contrasts dramatically with the darker ink of the text that surrounds them; the Squire-Franklin link has been squeezed into the space left on folio 137v following the final couplet of the *Squire's Tale*, while the inclusion of the Merchant-Squire link required the insertion of a new leaf (f. 153) between the already copied *Merchant's* and *Franklin's Tales*. In the process, both links were textually adapted to fit the exigencies of the already copied context into which they were squeezed, with Merchant-Squire altered to join Merchant and Franklin, and Squire-Franklin altered to join Squire and Merchant.[2] And the Clerk-Merchant link – which does not appear in Hengwrt – was either not received in time or was deemed unadaptable to any of the remaining gaps where it might have been inserted. Revealingly, when the Hengwrt scribe later copied Ellesmere, he addressed all these problems, placing all three links where we are used to encountering them, and repairing the text of the first two.[3] Altogether, this evidence suggests that the links were composed on single leaves separately from main body of the *Tales* materials, and, as Simon Horobin observes, this physical disposition, combined with the links' belated receipt by the Hengwrt production team and the confusion generated by the Man of Law's Endlink, accounts for the significant variations of the order of the IV-V tales in the manuscripts.[4]

In summary, the three links "form a single, if variant, textual intervention into the *Canterbury Tales*."[5] This intervention we must either reject, as a whole, as inauthentic even in its original form, deeming all three links, following Norman Blake, to represent an instance of the scribal desire to complete that which Chaucer left unfinished; or accept, in the form shared by the manuscripts of Manly and Rickert's type *a* tale order group, as enacting one of Chaucer's post-hoc artistic decisions regarding the ever-developing structure of the *Canterbury Tales*.[6] And if we choose the latter (as the vast majority of readers do, albeit tacitly, by accepting the divided

IV-V sequence as authentic), we must also contend with the implications of the signs of hasty, retroactive adaptation in such an otherwise carefully copied manuscript as is Hengwrt. These signs, along with the fact that in Ellesmere the Hengwrt scribe returns the links to their authoritative places, support the view that Chaucer's writing of these links – and thus his construction of IV-V – was one of his *final* artistic decisions for the *Tales*. Although it is obviously possible that Chaucer had conceived the thematic and structural implications of the links long before he actually wrote them, it seems more plausible, given what appears to have been – from the evidence of his other tinkering – the evolving nature of the *Canterbury Tales* project, that much, if perhaps not all, of what the links accomplish represents Chaucer's retroactive realization of the artistic potential of such a sequence of tales.[7] It is this retroactive realization that this book seeks to describe.

As much as manuscript evidence enables my interpretation of IV-V as a unified authorial composition, therefore, it also compels me to acknowledge as likely what Donald Howard long ago dismissed as the "work-room" view of Chaucer's composition of the *Tales*: the view that emphasizes the status of the semi-linked collection as a work in progress, one guided by plans that evolved, probably opportunistically, in the course of composition, as Chaucer added to and altered the work in dialogue with his own creative process, and thus a work that was subject to open-ended revision at global and local structural and thematic levels right up until he gave up on it (or died). To the question, "how does one account for the presence of the General Prologue, for the work's overriding structure, for the dramatic interplay among the pilgrims, for the way the tales reflect the characters of their tellers – in short for the work's unity and complexity," I answer: critics are adept at finding the complex unities that they assume to be present.[8] This is indeed the essence of what we do in a nutshell, even when the unities that we find are so complex that they are not really unities at all. And any such assumptions – even those that put aside authorial intention, whether of the new critical, poststructural, or historicist variety – are necessarily grounded on an imagined primal scene of composition: a scenario that posits which parts of the work were written when and with what other parts in mind, and what degree of global revision was performed once all the parts were put together.

For the vast majority of *Canterbury Tales* criticism on the tales of IV-V (as well as more generally), the imagined scenario is a totalizing one that posits that every component of each pilgrim performance (portrait, tale, and link) was written or at least revised with every other component in mind, and so each component is to be understood against the informing background of the other two. Each therefore may serve in practice as a kind of interpretive key for the others, so that, for example, the tale of Dorigen, Arveragus, and Aurleius may be understood to reflect the Epicureanism that the Franklin's portrait attributes to the teller, while, conversely, that tale's failures (so runs one avenue of interpretation) signal Chaucer's disapproval of the teller as his portrait describes him; and the Squire-Franklin link conveys both the nature of the tale's failures and of the moral or spiritual weaknesses of the teller, neither of which are fully evident on their own. This kind of totalizing assumption is virtually unavoidable for the kind of dramatic readings that were in fashion in Howard's day, but it is also typical of any study that finds intricate thematic connections among portrait, tale, and link – which is to say, most studies of the IV-V performances, by far.

To Howard's credit, he articulates this assumption explicitly as the ground upon which his monograph rests, whereas most studies of the *Tales* – before *and* after – just tacitly accept it.[9] To be sure, for some pilgrim performances, such as that of the Pardoner, the totalizing scenario does not seem unlikely, and in this book I make no assumptions about Chaucer's composition of any portion of the *Tales* other than IV-V. But for that portion, most basically because of the manuscript evidence pertaining to the prologues and epilogues that alone identify the tellers of its four tales, I find that the totalizing scenario does not adequately account for the significant degree of uncertainty about whether Chaucer ever thought to associate these tales with these pilgrims before authoring those prologues and epilogues.[10] I recognize that this degree of uncertainty is itself uncertain, and that it varies among the four pilgrim performances. By no means, therefore, am I claiming that manuscript evidence definitively indicates that Chaucer did not preplan the pilgrim/tale assignments in these instances. I am claiming, rather, that the uncertainty is ample enough to demand a position-taking on relative probability. And in my view – especially for the latter three tales, for which the pilgrim assignments rest wholly upon what seems a very late structural innovation – the more probable scenario is that Chaucer had not yet determined to associate the respective portraits and tales at the point at which he authored them in the form in which they have come down to us. Specifically, I am claiming that the most probable scenario – the one that most accords with the manuscript evidence – is that Chaucer determined the pilgrim assignments, especially those for the latter three tales, in the same late creative act that produced the IV-V sequence, and that before that moment Chaucer had portraits and tales but no definite plan for which pilgrim would tell which tale.

For those used to understanding the four tales of IV-V as eminently suited to their tellers in global and minute ways – from overall themes and narrative treatment to individual narratorial characteristics – this position may seem simply wrong, impoverishing of Chaucer's artistry, and oddly self-defeating for a book that proposes to offer a reading of a sequence of four pilgrim performances as such. These objections merit individual responses.

Subsequent chapters present the specific evidence for each performance that, at the very least, casts some doubt on whether one may simply dismiss my position as wrong. Again, critics are adept at finding what they go looking for, and if we assume that Chaucer wrote, say, the *Merchant's Tale* with the Clerk-Merchant link in mind, it is not difficult to fashion an interpretation that would appear to provide a definitive demonstration of this artistic unity of parts, when in fact it is the prior assumption of that unity that makes that interpretation possible. Moreover, for each of the IV-V performances there exists a longstanding minority critical tradition that has pointed toward certain inconsistencies among portrait, tale, and link – inconsistencies that other critics, under the sway of the totalizing scenario, have either ignored or understood as subtle artistic effects, typically species of irony. The ensuing chapters consider the merits of the claims of this tradition for the respective performances. Here I simply observe that among the few things about which most scholars of the *Tales* agree is that Chaucer compiled into this collection some earlier efforts that he had completed sometime before he conceived of the enclosing work – certainly before he wrote the *General Prologue* – and that he did so with very little adaptation to the new literary context. And, even more certainly, we know that when Chaucer wrote the *General Prologue* he did not have tales for all the portraits that he included, since some (e.g., the Yeoman's) never received one. Given, therefore, that Chaucer wrote some number of tales without a teller in mind, and some number of portraits without a tale in mind, and some number of both tales and portraits without the links in mind that associate them, we can conclude that the totalizing scenario does not apply across the board for the pilgrim performances, and hence we have *a priori* reason to doubt it when there is evidence to the contrary.

About whether these assumptions about the composition of IV-V impoverish Chaucer's artistry, my best response is this book itself, whose premise is that the intricate artistry of this four-tale sequence deserves a monograph-long explication. But, more specifically, I would counter that the totalizing scenario has its own impoverishing effects, from its tendency to understand portrait, tale, and link as interpretive keys for one another. For example, readings of the *Squire's Tale* that seek to understand that tale as the preplanned utterance of the pilgrim Squire as he is described in the *General Prologue* tend to limit themselves to what seems consistent with that portrait: hence, the long tradition of reading that tale as a dramatization of youthful, amateurish, and perhaps faulty tale-telling. But if we instead imagine tale and portrait as originally independent compositions, our readings of them are open to the wide range of possible meanings that they encompass on their own (or, in the case of the portrait, also within the literary context of the *General Prologue*). As virtually any seasoned reader of Chaucer would acknowledge, his writings tend to explore simultaneously many different subjects in complex ways that are not always easily assimilable to each other and that frequently possess more-or-less underdetermined conclusions. Resisting the impulse to make portrait, tale, and link wholly consistent with one another, therefore, helps us to compass this characteristic capacious open-endedness. Rather than explain away the apparent discrepancies in this consistency, we can follow where they lead.

It is this alertness to the independent meanings of each component of a pilgrim performance that, rather than scuttling this book's project at the outset, serves as one of its justifications. In my imagined primal scene of composition, the IV-V sequence arose as a kind of cento, the product of Chaucer's rereading of his own work – his looking over of some of the material that he was considering incorporating into the *Tales*, or material that he had written for the *Tales* but without final plans for how he would situate it.[11] In this scenario, IV-V was the result of a specific insight that Chaucer had about his own, already-composed work, a singular inspiration regarding which of these tales he should assign to which tellers, in what order the performances should appear, what thematic through-lines the links should enact, and what thematic contact points the links should activate between each of the tales and portraits, and among the four performances. It is this inspiration, this insight that Chaucer had about the relations among his own, already-composed work, for which this book seeks to account, and it is this book's basic contention that this inspiration is, by itself, a spectacular artistic achievement that reaches deeply into the heart of one of Chaucer's career-long concerns, one indeed fundamental to the literary enterprise then as now.

This inspiration of Chaucer's constitutes the informing idea of IV-V, but it is an idea that depends upon, rather than is foreclosed by, the workroom view of the *Tales*. For, according to my scenario for the primal scene of composition, Chaucer enacts this inspiration like the final layer of a parfait: it does not, by itself, alter what lies underneath (i.e., what was already written), but produces a final result that, on the one hand, may still be relished in each of its separate parts and, on the other hand, is something other than the sum of those parts.[12] Or, to use the more historically apt analogy that Robert Jordan long ago proposed for Chaucer's artistry generally, the form that Chaucer's idea for IV-V took was that of the gothic cathedral, in which "[t]he mode of relationship between whole and parts can be one which does not at any time rob the parts of integrity and completeness within their formal outlines"; and in which, conversely, the part, "in its wholeness and complexity" does not "detract from the integrity of the whole."[13] The totalizing scenario tends to occlude appreciation for this mode of relationship; it hampers our perception of how the different components of the tale-telling performances that constitute IV-V are at once independent compositions and constituent parts of an overall, if post hoc, artistic design. By insisting on harmonious consistency among the parts, the totalizing scenario obscures those parts' distinctiveness and thus also how that very distinctiveness (especially as it is carried by those aspects of tale, portrait, or link that are not easily assimilable to the other parts) contributes to the belatedly assembled whole.

Throughout this book, therefore, while my focus is on this artistic design, I impose upon myself the interpretive limit that disallows readings that depend on Chaucer's having a portrait in mind when he wrote a tale, a tale in mind when he wrote a portrait, or a link in mind when he wrote portrait or tale. (For some of the tales – the *Merchant's* in particular – I do allow for the likelihood that he had in mind one or more of the other tales.) This self-imposed limit has implications, obviously, for how I approach that perennially vexed question of *Tales* interpretation: the nature of the relation between pilgrim and tale. I must of course *a priori* preclude the so-called dramatic approach, in which one assumes that a tale is primarily designed to convey in some fashion the character of its teller. This mode of interpretation, dominant through much of the twentieth century, received in the second half of that century trenchant critiques from many quarters.[14] Nonetheless, although it has since faded as a critical orthodoxy and is now very rarely practiced in the bald manner most exemplified by R. M. Lumianksy, it remains, as A. C. Spearing has shown, to a significant degree an enabling principle in much – and perhaps most – criticism on the *Tales*, well into the twenty-first century.[15] As I review in subsequent chapters, while critics do not often anymore argue directly that a tale discloses a teller's character, they nonetheless typically understand aspects of the teller's depiction in portrait and/or link (whether those aspects are thematic, as in the Clerk's Aristotelianism; or psychological, as in the Merchant's bitterness; or historical, as in the Squire's campaigning in Flanders) as informing the tale, and conversely they understand the tale as disclosing the significance of the thematic, psychological, or historical details of that depiction. The typical dependencies within the conceptual structure of critical reasoning, therefore, remain akin to those of the dramatic approach.

I will not take the time to rehearse the critiques of that approach but instead simply acknowledge my acceptance of them, especially Spearing's, in their general contours, if not in all their details. I have significant reservations, however, about their alternative proposals for the relation between teller and tale, or, more generally, the relation between tales and dramatic frame. For, despite the variety of the critiques, they share the tendency to depreciate the thematic significance of the frame and especially of the assignment of pilgrims to tales. For David Lawton, for example, pilgrim assignment merely reflects the social protocols of literary kinds. The suitability of pilgrim and tale does not extend to "the nuances of portraiture and characterisation found in the General Prologue or in the links, but to what might in such circumstances be expected of a typical knight, lawyer, prioress and monk. It is a literary version of social hierarchy: a matter of decorum."[16] Yet, while decorum is plainly a factor in pilgrim assignment, "the nuances of portraiture and characterisation found in the General Prologue or in the links," and the specific manner in which these resonate with their associated tales, are nonetheless crucial to understanding the overall import of each of the IV-V performances and the unfolding significance of the sequence. Critiques like Lawton's, in throwing out the bathwater of totalizing dramatic readings, tend also to throw out the baby of the import of the interactions among the *Tales'* composite layers.[17] These interactions represent distinct artistic decisions, even if Chaucer made each of those decisions independently, at disparate points in time, and in ignorance of those that would come later.

To return to my parfait analogy, critiques of dramatic readings affirm a structure of independent layers, but then they emphasize the bottom layers over the top, considering the latter to be relatively unimportant and even discardable. To begin to account for the artistic achievement of IV-V, however, we must recognize – as, presumably, Chaucer did, when he constituted the sequence – the powerful effect achieved by the juxtaposition of all the specific details of all the independent layers. Again, I do not extend this claim for the significance of this composite structure to the entirety of the *Tales* (although it seems obviously applicable to, say, Fragment I), and indeed I believe it to be unlikely that Chaucer himself followed any single structuring principle in his evolving work on the collection. But for IV-V, the final layer of the parfait – the links – produces a post hoc orchestration of parts in which the nuances of those pilgrims' depictions do have essential bearing on the stories they tell, and vice versa, albeit within the interpretive limits that I have stated. As I hope subsequent chapters demonstrate, rather than disabling interpretation, these methodological limits help to bring into view relations that are otherwise difficult to see.

Axiology

The thematic focus of this book – Chaucer's concern with literary value and especially the value of his own imaginative writing, in the sense of whether such writing is *worthwhile* – is, as I have mentioned, scarcely unusual in Chaucer studies. Within twentieth-century criticism, its most obvious precedent is perhaps Alfred David's *The Strumpet Muse*, although, as many readers will have already gathered, its most inspiring conceptual touchstone is Anne Middleton's seminal essay "Chaucer's 'New Men' and the Good of Literature in the *Canterbury Tales*," in which she explores the relation between the social identities of a set of pilgrims and their respective, distinctive formulations of literary value. Indeed, Middleton amply demonstrates that the tales of IV-V in particular may be fruitfully considered along these lines, as her essay includes brief but perspicacious readings of three of them. As we all know, however, in the field of literary study generally, in the same period in which David's and Middleton's studies appeared and increasingly thereafter, literary value itself became an increasingly fraught and contested topic. Studies such as Barbara Hernstein Smith's *Contingencies of Value* put into question all attempts to ground literary value upon, say, aesthetic or ethical criteria; and, especially in the 1990s, many in the field embraced the formulations of sociologist Pierre Bourdieu, in which literary value functions as the currency of a semi-autonomous field of cultural production, the activities and products of which also serve the purposes of social distinction and hence economic advantage.[18] Not surprisingly, in the wake of this self-critique, various movements within the field – e.g., new formalism, new aestheticism, the "ethical turn" – have sought to reestablish something akin to an aesthetic or ethical ground for literary value, even while this self-critique continues to haunt such efforts.[19] In this context, a study like the present one that purports to consider Chaucer's agon with the problem of literary value must at the very least offer some clarification of its own thinking in this regard.

Elsewhere, I have sought to develop a theory of literary valuing that, building upon the work of Bruno Latour and Georg Simmel, understands literary value not as some essence or some misrecognized form of capital but rather as a multifarious activity, one that settles to some degree into predictable patterns but is always in motion. According to this theory, literary value emerges within a network of value-ascribing actors, both human and non-human, within which network every actor's literary-value-ascriptions are performed in relation to (or, in Latour's terms, as translations or mediations of) other actors' literary-value-ascriptions, as well as in relation to ascriptions of other kinds of value, for example, economic and spiritual.[20] This incipient theory supplies the conceptual infrastructure of the present book, although most of its details will not require rehearsal. For this book's purposes, most important is the basic point that any ascription of literary value necessarily occurs as a mediation of other ascriptions of value. Inasmuch as this book's object of inquiry is Chaucer's ascriptions of literary value – which is to say, the implicit or explicit claims about literary value that pertain to the components of IV-V, to the sequence as a whole, to the evolving *Tales*, and to the category of literary fiction generally – the theory encourages a scrutiny of the value ascriptions that these ascriptions of Chaucer's mediate, and especially of how those mediated ascriptions enable the articulation of literary value through supportive or competitive relations, or, more typically, some uncertain and unstable combination of the two.

As an illustration, we may imagine a simpler case: that of the lyric poet with a day job as an hourly contracted web programmer.[21] To produce any verse at all, this poet must, however consciously, ascribe some value to that verse, in the very act of choosing to write rather than not. This ascription of value will emerge as mediations of other ascriptions of literary value (say, of Keats's of negative capability, and of the poet's publisher's desire for something more straightforwardly confessional), and also as mediations of ascriptions of other kinds of value – most germane to present purposes, of the time and energy that the poet chooses not to devote to her income-producing activity. While some translation of negative capability and confessional poetry may well then appear in the poet's work as explicit topics of poetic reflection or as distinctive formal invention, the sacrifice of web-programming time and energy may not be so evident. Nonetheless, that sacrifice – and the competing value ascriptions that constitute the poet's temporarily suspended income-producing activity – will be necessarily and profoundly entangled with the ascriptions of value that brought the writing into being, and will therefore lie at the heart of the poet's understanding (again, however conscious) of the purpose and nature of her poetry. More pertinently, we may consider the somewhat more complicated case of Chaucer's *House of Fame*, whose whimsical, searching, ambiguous, and ambivalent meditations upon literary value are, as I suggest in Chapter 1, shaped in a pervasive if somewhat obscure fashion by the value conditions of Chaucer's then day job as controller of customs, to which the poem draws our attention near the beginning of its second book. The IV-V sequence is a massively complicated instance of these simpler cases, one which includes diverse explicit considerations of literary value but also mediations implicitly conveyed by genre, narrative organization, allusion, etc.; and one which (in effect) dramatizes a series of the author's day jobs, projecting them upon narrators comprised of carefully calibrated literary stereotypes, each of whom tells a literarily self-reflexive narrative that emerges in conflicted conversation with the others.

To facilitate the exploration of how these fluid, sometimes harmonious, sometimes fraught relations among literary value and other kinds of value (especially the values that constitute particular socioeconomic identities) occur within the complex form of IV-V, I have coined a set of interlocking terms, all of which emphasize *axiological* breadth – that is, a concern with value that encompasses such diverse domains as ethics and economics. As many readers will readily detect, the concepts that these terms denote overlap with ones that have a long history in *Canterbury Tales* criticism; I have nonetheless fashioned new ones in order to maintain important, if sometimes subtle, distinctions between those concepts and mine. These terms are of course, in name, entirely alien to the fourteenth century, but this merely reflects the gap between the literary theory current in Chaucer's day and his peculiar achievements in IV-V – a theory/practice gap by no means uncommon in writings of any age, and one that renders potentially misleading even those axiologically laden terms that Chaucer himself uses, such as *moralite, estat, worthinesse*, and *sentence*.

The most important of these terms are *axiological person, literary axiology*, and *axiological apologia*, which serve, respectively, as this book's conceptual lenses for its analyses of pilgrims, tales, and the self-justifying arguments comprised by their combination; and which hence provide the basic structure of the critical work of each of the following chapters.

Literary axiology is perhaps the simplest to explain. In discussing the IV-V narratives, I use this term to designate the specific overall character of a tale's self-ascription of literary value, considered *independently* from pilgrim portrait and link. In a narrower, more traditional sense a literary axiology corresponds to a tale's implicit or explicit theory of its own value and that of the encompassing category of literary fiction, including negative theories that deny this value. For example, the medieval commonplace, ubiquitously present in the *Tales*, that a fictional narrative serves to illustrate one or more moral precepts is a literary axiology, whether stated directly or implied; but the term additionally takes into account, say, a coinciding socioeconomic instrumentality that may also be among the purposes of a specific narrative in a specific context.

For students of the *Canterbury Tales*, much that is denoted by *axiological person* will be equally familiar, as it reconnoiters a terrain whose many earlier explorers include David and, especially, Jill Mann in her still foundational monograph on the *General Prologue*. Nonetheless, this term requires a rather more extended explanation, as it carries much of the burden of my parfait-traversing analytical methodology and in particular of how I conceive of the relations, for IV-V, between pilgrim and tale.

From David, I take the idea that the portraits serve as embodied focal points of specific, distinctive sets of values. Noting the frequent appearance of the adjective *worthy*, David proposes that the *General Prologue* leads readers to consider the particular values that constitute *worthinesse* in each instance. He emphasizes especially ethical and spiritual values, but the notion that the *General Prologue* is a meditation upon varying and competing sorts of *worthinesse* plainly also extends to the single most obvious feature of the portrait collection: that it parses its "essay in '*worthinesse*'"[22] by social identity and, more specifically, by occupation. As Mann remarks in the penultimate sentence of her magisterial study, "The society it evokes is not a collection of individuals or types with an eternal or universal significance, but particularly a society in which work as a social experience conditions personality and the standpoint from which an individual views the world."[23] Considerably more concrete than a type but less concrete than a representation of a historically specific individual, each portrait embodies a constellation of values (including, for example, social and economic as well as ethical and spiritual ones) that constitute, are necessarily implicated by, and serve as local ideals for the respective occupation as Chaucer composes his version of it from various literary and experiential sources.

Axiological person is my name for this embodied constellation of values, a name in part inspired by Elizabeth Fowler's term *social persons* – which are the "abstract figurations of the human" that form the common stuff underlying the repertoire of lived social experience and literary characters[24] – and indeed Fowler's general approach to character, alongside another basic insight of Mann's, undergirds two important aspects of my approach to the portraits. First, as Mann demonstrates, in most of the portraits, albeit to varying degrees, Chaucer has suspended the overt and even implied judgment of values that characterizes estates satire and instead foregrounds the distinctive sets of occupational values per se, with the narrator typically expressing approval for how well each pilgrim exemplifies the value constellation of his or her occupation. As Mann concludes, "the *Prologue* acts on the assumption that *all* the portraits are of 'estates ideals.'"[25] In this way, Chaucer forestalls subordination of these value constellations to the master axiological categories of morality and spirituality. This deferral enables his pilgrims to embody provisionally coherent and legitimate axiological perspectives, if ones that – again to varying degrees – the reader may ultimately understand to be deficient in one or more respects. The very abstraction of the term *axiological person* aims to emphasize this suspension of judgment, and, as a complement to the label *character*, it also aims to leave undetermined the question of whether the portraits, in addition to being embodiments of axiological perspectives, also serve to represent fictional (or historically actual) individuals with distinctive personalities and, possibly, interiors. This, then, is the second aspect of my approach to the portraits: the view that, in themselves, axiological persons do not constitute characters in the sense of implying a distinctive subjectivity or interiority. They are to varying degrees individualized, but, as constellations of values, they need not be as mimetically specific and consistent as the typical understanding of character requires. Plainly, given the paucity of description in some instances, not all the portraits represent characters in the latter sense, and thus it is self-evident that no one interpretive rule may apply across the board to the *General Prologue*. What I assume for the purposes of this book is that the primary function of the IV-V portraits, if not necessarily for all those in the *General Prologue*, is to limn characters in the sense of axiological persons, and that any other function is at most incipient and incidental to this one.

These aspects of my approach in turn have several interrelated consequences that further delineate it in respect to longstanding critical debates about the portraits. First, my approach significantly dampens the problem of ascertaining point of view within the narration of the portraits – that is, of determining where the lines fall among the perspectives of pilgrim, narrator, and implied author, and hence also of determining whether and how much irony may be present. When we assume that the primary function of these portraits is to depict distinctive value constellations, then we may understand the fluid and ambiguous shifts of points of view in the narration as serving to demarcate the contours of these constellations by providing both inside (i.e., sympathetic) and outside (neutral or even hostile) perspectives on the ascribed values. The narrator's famous combination of seeming naiveté; ambiguous slides into irony; and extensive, even intimate, but oddly still limited knowledge about the pilgrims makes sense, then, not in respect to any naturalistic view of the narrator as a character (which even already in E. T. Donaldson's seminal formulation was difficult to sustain)[26] but rather as a finely honed device for rendering a variety of at times radically differing value constellations that we are nonetheless to perceive as legitimate within their own axiological boundaries, but which we (as readers or implied author) may or may not share. Exactly what point of view is guiding us at any particular moment is not as important as the value constellation that that point of view is casting into relief.

Second, when we assume that the primary aim of these portraits, despite shifting points of view and the presence of irony, is not to pronounce *a priori* judgment upon their respective value constellations but rather to fashion those constellations per se, then there is no need to determine whether, in each case, a portrait is on balance more satire or idealization. And in fact to do so actually occludes many other kinds of useful thinking about the portraits, in this instance the role that they play in the unfolding significance of IV-V. As I review in subsequent chapters, all the IV-V portraits, like most of the others, have been the subject of rather polarized readings in this regard (albeit the balance and depth of disagreement varies). When we so separate the portraits into the goats and sheep of satire and idealization, and thereby perform the judgment that Chaucer has projected but suspended, we make our own value ascriptions, mediating the value ascriptions of the portraits, and then attribute the result not to ourselves but to Chaucer's intentions. This kind of critical foreclosure may be justifiable if the object of one's interpretation is, say, solely a single portrait, as in that case the reader's exercise of judgment, if not necessarily the specific content thereof, does in a way realize the portrait's ultimate aim. But when we consider the portraits as a series of *competing* value constellations, and those constellations as forming one layer of the artistic compound comprising IV-V's evolving series of arguments about literary value, then we must follow Chaucer and suspend the categorization of the pilgrims as goodies or baddies so that we remain open to the axiological possibilities afforded by the distinctive constellation of each portrait. Hence, even when we may reasonably suppose Chaucer either to have shared or not to have shared the balance of value ascriptions rendered by a portrait, and accordingly hear the narration as mostly in earnest or mostly ironic (and, for the IV-V portraits, such suppositions have often been overstated), we must not reduce the function of the portraits to idealization or satire. For this judgment would preempt the unfolding movement of the axiological dialectic of IV-V by preinstalling master evaluative categories. It is instead, in the first place, the distinctiveness of the axiological perspectives, rather than their positive or negative evaluation, that matters if we are to understand how that dialectic unfolds.

Third, because within the space of a portrait what is important is not whose speech or thoughts we are hearing but rather the nature of the distinctive constellation of values brought into association with the pilgrim's occupation – regardless of whether those values are conveyed from the inside or outside – we need an auxiliary term for designating the narration that constitutes an axiological person. That is, inasmuch as all the elements of a portrait contribute toward the development of a distinctive axiological focal point, irrespective of whose voice those elements belong to, we need a term to designate the *narrational space* governed by this focal point – a term other than voice, point of view, perspective, etc., that all traditionally depend upon a unity of speaker. Cued by Thomas J. Farrell's application to the *General Prologue* of M. M. Bakhtin's notion of character zone, I will name this narrational space a *characterological field*, on the analogy of a gravitational or magnetic field, with the axiological focal point the constituting force.[27] As with the notion of character zone, a characterological field encompasses all narration pertaining to a specific individual (e.g., description of that individual, direct or indirect speech of that individual, etc.), whether or not that narration is given wholly or in part from that individual's point of view. I do not use Bakhtin's term because I do not wish to invoke his concept's hierarchical aspects (in which, for example, the voice of the implied author carries the most weight), analytical precision, and political implications. A characterological field is fuzzier in its internal organization and more ambiguous in its overall effect than is a character zone. As Farrell's study shows, character zones still lead us to authorial judgment, whereas characterological fields crystallize an axiological person while leaving that judgment suspended.

This addition to my set of terms is not so important as to require the sort of accompanying narratological systematization that Farrell and Spearing admirably achieve in their studies. But even in its vaguely formulated state, it suggests how my approach to value in the portraits dovetails with what I elaborated in the preceding section about the principles and limits of the artistic design that govern the relation of the portraits to the links and tales. For the links, the concept of characterological field allows for discrepancies and inconsistencies in characterization that perhaps derive from the differing original purposes of portrait and link, and from the lapse of time between Chaucer's composition of them, while still providing a principle of unity – the function of axiological integration – for the two components. Inasmuch as a link registers cognizance, in some fashion, of the portrait of its respective pilgrim, it does so *not* primarily toward the end of drawing upon and further developing the *character* of that pilgrim (in the traditional sense of that term) but rather as a means of bringing the portrait's axiological person to bear on the interaction among the literary axiologies of the tales and the other axiological persons involved in the link. We need not expect the characterizations evoked by a link, therefore, to be consistent in respect to the personality or psychology conveyed by a portrait, and so we need not develop a character-based explanation for the sort of inconsistencies that we encounter with, say, *Lenvoy de Chaucer* and the *Merchant's Prologue*. Instead, we may understand these passages as extensions of the characterological fields of the respective pilgrims into an environment that includes the literary axiologies of the tales previously told and that serves as an axiological frame for the subsequent tale. The axiological person – not the personality – of this pilgrim governs this extension of the characterological field, and it is also further developed by this extension. What is important about the sober Clerk's sudden joviality or the reserved Merchant's sudden loquaciousness, then, is not what these apparently abrupt personality changes seemingly reflect about their characters, but rather the manner in which they articulate a specific literary axiology as the expression of a distinctive occupational constellation of values.

We may likewise understand the narration of the tales as extensions of characterological fields. My assumptions about the primal scene of composition for IV-V precludes understanding this narration as development of the characters of the pilgrims as they appear in the *General Prologue*; but, again, characterological fields need not be internally consistent in a manner that requires that each contribution to them be written with the other in mind. Instead, any passage positioned in a manner so as to be understood as governed by a particular axiological person belongs to some degree to that axiological person's characterological field. Chaucer, simply by naming the pilgrim who tells a tale, thereby places the entire narration of that tale within a characterological field and hence under the sign of the respective axiological person – regardless of the original purposes of the narration and thus of how much the narration appears unrelated to and even in some contradiction with the manner in which the portrait imagines the teller. In investigating the contribution of a tale to the unfolding axiological dialectic of IV-V, what is most important is not the nature of the narration's imagined speaker (or, in the more theorized vein of H. Marshall Leicester and Elizabeth Scala, the desiring subject constituted by the narration's language), however fruitful that may be for other purposes, but instead the narration's evaluative attitude at any given point, and hence the collective character of the value ascriptions the narration enacts. As we will see, in this regard analysis not just of narrational style but, especially, of tone is crucial.[28] Although, on the one hand, my approach disallows the assumption that Chaucer originally calibrated the details of narrational style and tone for the axiological person that comes to govern the tale, on the other hand my approach compels an investigation of how those details, once placed under the sign of an axiological person, contribute to the overall performance. This contribution is, after all, precisely what I am claiming that Chaucer himself belatedly perceived about the artistic potential of the portraits and tales that he eventually assembled into IV-V.

With this account of the axiological interaction of tales and portraits, I have already provided the gist of my third and culminating key term, *axiological apologia*, which is my label for the literary self-justification Chaucer articulates in each stage of the IV-V sequence precisely by placing the literary axiology of a tale under the sign of an axiological person with whom he shares some amount of social overlap. The aim of the subsequent chapters is to define the distinctive axiological apologia constituted by each of the IV-V performances. Each chapter, that is, shows how the association – enacted by prologues and epilogues – of a tale's literary axiology with a portrait's axiological person, in combination with a partial overlap of the latter with a specific facet of Chaucer's own social experience, articulates a distinctive ascription of value to Chaucer's literary fiction. Traversing the parfait-like literary structure while keeping in view the biographical resonance between pilgrim and author, each chapter describes the manner in which Chaucer uses an axiological person to ground a tale's literary axiology in a concrete social scenario of literary authorship, thereby providing that authorship some amount of social legitimation (even when a largely negative one) by means of the axiological person's standing as a normative masculine socioeconomic identity. And each chapter explores how a performance's axiological apologia dialectically arises in response to that of its predecessor and yields to that of its successor, until reaching its provisional conclusion with the Franklin's performance.

Two less important terminological habits also merit some initial comment. In the analysis of portraits as well as tales, to refer to specific constellations of values in proximate mediation with the value ascriptions on which I am focusing, I use the term *axiological environment*. In a more static, less Latour-influenced sense, this term corresponds to institutional or institutionalized contexts of diverse kinds, such as the university or the genre of romance.[29] To refer more generally to a set of values possessing a particular overall character, I use the noun *axiology* by itself, as we use *philosophy* in such locutions as "my philosophy of life."

Besides the regular appearance of the terms defined in this section, for the most part I have confined the theoretical details of my approach and its rationale to this introduction, with locutions such as "mediation of other value ascriptions" left mostly implied rather than continually reiterated. Moreover, notwithstanding these terms' unfamiliarity, readers will find much in the subsequent chapters that engages more conventionally with the critical tradition on this portion of the *Canterbury Tales*. Although I seek to be consistent with my self-imposed methodological rules and conceptual principles, my more basic aim is simply to contribute to this tradition.[30]

Fathers and Sons

A large portion of the critical tradition on IV-V, as all students of the *Tales* know, focuses on marriage, the status of women, and, more recently, gender and sexuality. To be clear, this book is in no sense claiming that literary value is actually the more important or central topic of the sequence; it is simply one that has not received the scope of attention that it demands. Moreover, many aspects of the former topics, along with the criticism that elucidates them, necessarily come to the fore in this book's consideration of the details of this sequence and especially of its father-son dynamic – or, more precisely, its thematically fraught series of interactions between a figure of some type of normative masculine maturity and a figure of some type of normative masculine adolescence. As we will see, this dynamic shapes the conflict among the axiological apologias of the IV-V performances, combining with the biographical resonances between axiological persons and author to infuse the unfolding of IV-V with the thematic energy, if not overt narration, of a psychobiographical developmental trajectory. What plainly underlies this dynamic – what is crucial to the distinctions among its masculine social identities and hence what is essential to its depiction of their competition with one another – are the gender identities produced through the concepts and practices of marriage and actual and imagined relations with the female Other.

A brief recollection of Chaucer's depictions of these masculine identities and their associated performances makes this dependency patently evident. IV-V begins with an unmarried narrator of uncertain age but whom the Host and the *General Prologue* portrait depict as a kind of eternal student, contentedly self-suspended in a kind of endless adolescence, who tells a tale about a marriage that he concludes by offering various suggestions for what that marriage may represent. Answering this performance is then the recently and unhappily married Merchant, whose social identity necessarily, if coyly, evokes Chaucer's paternal heritage, giving an oblique son-father cast to the relation between performances. In light of his opening exchange with the also unhappily married Host, this second IV-V narrator tells a tale that, while also entertaining various possibilities for what marriage may represent, appears founded on the contrasting aim of depicting marriage as it really is. This tale, having by its conclusion apparently reinforced the Host's marital unhappiness, next inspires the group's leader to turn to the unmarried, youthful, amorous Squire to tell a tale about love, a narrative that, in striking contrast with the preceding one, insists on its categorical unreality, its status as fantasy. This tale's abortive termination, then, provokes the unmistakably paternal (and perhaps paternalistic) compliment of the presumably married Franklin, who declares his wish that his own son were like the Squire. Yet this final IV-V narrator, while he goes on to tell a tale also self-labeled as fantasy, in fact provides a story that resembles in several ways the one told by the Merchant – a story that features an unmarried, youthful, amorous squire who desperately wishes for an adulterous liaison with a (happily, in this case) married woman.

The prominence of the father-son dynamic within the IV-V dialectic entails, therefore, that Chaucer's concern with literary value is not separate from but wholly imbricated with his obvious concern with marriage, the status of women, gender, and sexuality, which is indeed what we should expect given the occupational and quasi-biographical lens through which the sequence meditates upon literary value. For in Chaucer's day (as well as in many other ages, before and after) normative masculine adulthood, for most estates, involved both marriage (or the institutional equivalent for the clerisy) and securing a livelihood. And fatherhood, however little actual parenting it involved, entailed responsibility (again, for most estates, to different degrees) for the son's achievement of both of these, especially the latter.[31] IV-V hence raises the question of whether poetry-making is compatible with manhood, or, more specifically, whether the activity of ascribing value to fiction may be reconciled with the value-ascribing activities that constitute a socially legible form of adult masculinity, along with the specific relations to marriage and women that necessarily define that form. In this regard, the sequence's trajectory – from an impoverished celibate without a benefice to a prosperous landowning father, and from a story about absolute masculine authority in marriage, which may not in the end be about marriage at all, to one that famously features a paean to companionate marriage – would seem to suggest progressively more practicable articulations of a place for fiction-making. How problematic or qualified this culminating articulation may yet remain will become evident as the following chapters unfold the details of the IV-V dialectic.

(Self-) Justifications

This characterization of IV-V as a dynamic, fitfully progressive attempt to define a practicable social justification for fiction-making returns us, finally, to the second reservation about this book's project that I voiced at this introduction's outset: the question of what justifies today the activity of documenting the attempt of one particular, relatively prosperous, fourteenth-century Englishman to justify his activity of creating fiction. In some quarters, no such justification will be needed, even for a book that possesses as tight a primary-text focus as this one.[32] For these readers, it remains an institutionalized given that this particular Englishman's writing is valuable enough, *in itself*, to serve as the object of considerable investments of time, energy, money, and other resources. But for other readers, at this point in the history of literary study, even if Chaucer's writing continues to serve in practice (in some places and to varying degrees) as such an object of investment, the notional status of Chaucer's writing as self-evidently valuable in itself, and more so than most other writing in English (i.e., as self-evidently canonical), may no longer be accepted axiomatically.

I will not take the time to rehearse the familiar critiques of the last several decades that argue this latter view, some of which I have elsewhere reviewed in their relation to Chaucer studies (and ones with which, despite the apparent evidence otherwise, I sympathsize).[33] It suffices instead to observe that this book's conceptual approach to Chaucer's writing suggests that its own justification must necessarily consist of ascriptions of value to that writing that are mediations of the value ascriptions of an endlessly receding array of other actors, most obviously the institutions that have employed me, those in which I have been a student, my several teachers of Chaucer, my own students, my perceived readership, the Chaucer editions on which I rely, the critical tradition that stretches back (at least) to Lydgate and Hoccleve, and, of course, Chaucer himself. Moreover, the mediations of value within this axiological network, and across interlinked networks of value, are for me, as they were for Chaucer, both supportive and competing. Every sentence that I type requires an ascription of value to Chaucer's writing that is defined not only by what values this ascription serves or is served by (e.g., the value of the professional status that I hope to maintain), but also by its necessary sacrifice of other kinds of value (say, the pedagogical value that would be obtained by developing a more cogent syllabus for a first-year seminar, the economic value of researching retirement investment funds, the political and civil value of resisting the policies of the US president as of this writing, the recreational value of watching the latest Avengers film, *ad infinitum*). These supportive and competing value-ascription-mediations are inextricable elements of this project's necessary ascription of value to Chaucer's writing, and – at great temporal distance but in relatively close proximity of axiological relevance – they include mediations of the supportive and competing value ascriptions that Chaucer himself mediated with every line of verse that he inked. To adapt Derrida's famous formulation, there is no outside-axiology. Thus, any insight that this project achieves regarding Chaucer's axiological agon is enabled by the distinctive character of its own constituting axiological agon, and, by that same token, its depiction of Chaucer's axiological agon cannot help but also be, to some degree, a distorted projection of its own.

To put this point more straightforwardly: this book, by tracing Chaucer's dynamic, conflicted self-defense of his writing, necessarily also interrogates its own justification. Not surprisingly, then, while this book represents the four positions on literary value that the IV-V dialectic articulates as fourteenth-century literary axiologies that Chaucer at one point either entertained himself or considered compelling enough to require a response, these four positions are also legible as more-or-less familiar claims for or critiques of literary value that, in one form or another, have currency today. The first position, the literary axiology of the Clerk's performance, corresponds ultimately to a version of an art-for-art's-sake apology for literature. But it is a claim for an autonomous literary value that is refracted through what twenty-first-century readers will recognize as a poststructuralist, *mise-en-abyme* lens, in which the value of the Clerk's particular kind of fiction is the peculiar contemplation of competing axiologies that it enables by putting into play, but leaving unresolved, various non-autonomous definitions of its value. This literary axiology has some general affinities with such formulations as Paul de Man's in *Allegories of Reading* (or at least with how the rather elusive formulations in that volume have subsequently been simplified) and, in a less deconstructive vein, with such more recent meditations on literary distinctiveness as Derek Attridge's *The Singularity of Literature*. The Merchant's performance articulates in response a critique of all claims for a distinctive literary value, seeing literary discourse as one species, among many others, of a mystifying and/or mystified instrument of desire in a world whose most fundamental imperative is to gain advantage over others, whether socially, economically, libidinally, or otherwise. This position is a kind of crude, though still trenchant, version of Bourdieu's and later elaborations thereof, such as that by John Frow in *Cultural Studies and Cultural value*.[34] The Squire's performance similarly understands literary value as reflective and hence productive of elite social status. Yet at the same time it also conceives of literary fiction as possessing a more egalitarian, even utopian value as a distinctive discourse of the marvelous that may provide social and personal renewal. In this latter aspect, the Squire's literary axiology has general affinities with such diverse formulations as those of Wolfgang Iser's *The Fictive and the Imaginary*, Martha Nussbaum's *Poetic Justice*, and Gregory Jusdanis's *Fiction Agonistes* (as well as, at some points, Attridge's *The Singularity*).[35] In its long tradition, it stretches back through Sir Philip Sidney's *Defense of Poesy* and well before. Finally, the Franklin's performance achieves provisional resolution of the IV-V dialectical debate by incorporating elements of each of the previous positions – that is, those of autonomous value, instrumental value, and what might be called romance or fantasy value – in order to formulate a literary axiology in which an affirmation of literary value rests upon an underlying skepticism.

In traversing Chaucer's axiological agon in IV-V, therefore, this book also stages my own wrestling with current debates about literary value, and, in fact, as my conceptual approach to value mandates, it may do nothing else. Accordingly, the position that the Franklin takes in the culminating performance of this agonistic drama inevitably resembles something like my own, at least as of this writing. For these reasons, the book ultimately possesses no external justification, but rather argues its own justification, and scrutinizes that very argument, from beginning to end. What justifies this book, or not, is its implied, self-questioning, gradually culminating defense of literary value, a defense that it offers at a moment in history in which, as we all know, that value has been subject to doubt in many quarters, both inside and outside the academy. If the Franklin's position is a convincing one – or, even if it is not, but some other position is, one missing from the IV-V sequence but for that very reason disclosed by it – then this attempt to describe that position and its dialectical predecessors must be a worthwhile activity, regardless of whether anyone remains invested in the value of Chaucer's writing per se.

It is therefore the resonances of IV-V with the problem of literary value today that have informed this book's writing and constitute at least one of the reasons why I am typing this very sentence instead of doing something else. Nonetheless, because the choir to whom I preach likely already has faith in these matters (indeed, perhaps stronger than mine), in the chapters that follow I have mostly left these resonances for readers to infer, and have focused my efforts on piecing together what the IV-V sequence meant for Chaucer.

CHAPTER I

Clerk

Because of the vastly different natures of their respective content and form, the Clerk's performance in the *Canterbury Tales* has not often been considered alongside the *House of Fame*.[1] But in this chapter, I argue that the axiological apologia of the latter, the most clerkly and poetically self-conscious of Chaucer's dream visions and his most explicit engagement with *trecento* poetic ambition, corresponds in some fundamental ways to the axiological apologia of the former, a poetically self-conscious performance by a clerk who takes his tale from "Fraunceys Petrak, the lauriat poete" (IV.31). More precisely, it corresponds to the axiological apologia of that aspect of the Clerk's performance that defines the initial position of the IV-V sequence, as that position crystallizes within the characterological field of the Clerk. As I propose below, the *House of Fame* develops a literary axiology conceptually legible within the axiological environment of Chaucer's then occupation as controller of customs. With the Clerk's performance Chaucer begins a more general exploration of the possibilities for literary value within the imagined axiological environments of a series of masculine occupations that adjoined or overlapped with his own life experience. The *House of Fame* in this way serves as prompt and starting point for IV-V, over the course of which sequence Chaucer interrogates four possibilities for literary value from occupational perspectives with which he had at least some partial coincidence.

To pursue this argument, after providing an account of the axiological apologia of the *House of Fame*, I examine the literary axiology developed by the concerted effect of the *Clerk's Prologue*, the *Clerk's Tale*, and the performance's unmarked epilogue (the return to the dramatic frame that includes *Lenvoy de Chaucer*), an axiology that I contend comprises, like that of the former work, contemplation of competing literary axiologies – that is, it is profoundly meta-axiological. I next explore the question of why Chaucer associates this literary axiology with the axiological person of the Clerk, as he limns the latter in the *General Prologue*, an explanation that involves some historical reconstruction of this axiological person and a consideration of its overlap with Chaucer. I avoid, as I describe in this book's introduction, a reading of the performance that depends upon Chaucer having in mind the portrait of the Clerk when he originally composed his version of Petrarch's tale of Griselda (or vice versa), although in this instance, unlike as for the other three components of IV-V, the manuscript evidence does not especially argue for or against this scenario. But because it is not implausible that Chaucer produced an initial translation of Petrarch before he envisioned the *Tales*, and to avoid the interpretive foreclosure of a reading of the *Clerk's Tale* that requires close calibration with a reading of the Clerk's portrait, I assume the Clerk of the *General Prologue* to be Chaucer's premeditated narrator only in the tale's prologue and epilogue, that is, only in that portion of the performance that stitches the tale of Griselda into the fabric of the *Tales*. I seek then to describe how the axiological person of the Clerk, in orchestration with the prologue, tale, and epilogue, comprises the inaugurating axiological apologia of IV-V. I conclude this chapter by pointing out some key vulnerabilities of this axiological apologia that, latent in the very device of having this particular clerk relate the tale of Griselda in the manner that he does, become more acute in the Merchant's response.

Controller Axiology

Some time before Chaucer's active appointment as controller of wool customs ended in 1385, he spent a number of evenings composing the *House of Fame*, which would become the most sustained interrogation of the nature and value of literary discourse in his oeuvre, and which also happens to be the only place that he refers explicitly to his nonliterary "labour" – the "rekenynges" of his work as controller (653–60). This is no coincidence: Chaucer's formulation of what we will see to be a qausi-autonomous literary axiology in the *House of Fame* is inseparable from the social, ideological, and practical circumstances of his controllership. To be sure, the poem is, as most critical accounts describe, a kind of boomerang response to Chaucer's initial contact with *trecento* authors and especially with Dante's *Commedia*.[2] But if we widen the axiological environment in which we consider the poem, we see that Chaucer's professional home in the customs house, and accordingly his relative distance from his previous home in the English court, was just as crucial an influence on the peculiar axiological apologia of the *House of Fame*.[3]

Within the axiological environment of the English court, the normative literary models were, of course, primarily French. How Chaucer sought to adapt his English verse to these is a familiar story, and is readily evident in the *Book of the Duchess*. In this poem, as is well known, he draws on the works of French contemporaries to align his poetry with the fourteenth-century *dits amoreux*. Aimed at an elite audience, the *dit* proffers the literary value of its reflection of noble interiority. At the same time, the *dit* in the hands of, say, Guillaume de Machaut and Jean Froissart was cultural work performed by an intellectual in service to the court, which matched well Chaucer's social location as an esquire of the household – a location that, as Richard Firth Green has so well detailed, was fully recognizable as one from which refined verse about secular love might legitimately be produced.[4] Idiosyncratically learned, the *Book of the Duchess* features a narrator whose cluelessness serves as a humility topos that enables the poem's claim to authority, namely that the lower-born, intellectually talented esquire Chaucer has something to say to his higher-born implied audience. The poem thereby succeeds in mimicking a normative axiological apologia. It articulates its literary value in a manner legible with respect to its author's social position, and, in principle at least, it garners its author distinction by the ways that the work conforms to extant literary models.

When Chaucer came to write the *House of Fame* some years later, however much his own sense of literary value had changed, that of the English court was largely the same. His personal challenge, therefore, was doubtless in part to mediate a *trecento* sense of literary value in a manner that would be legible within the axiological environment of the English court. Yet we must also consider this challenge in the context of the more immediate one of Chaucer's altered circumstances. For while still nominally an esquire of the household, Chaucer was no longer, in practice, a courtier, but instead, as controller of the wool customs, a lay civil servant. And, for Chaucer at least, this position was no sinecure. Documentary evidence makes plain that, except when he was on temporary leave, for ten and half years Chaucer labored daily at the customs house on the Wool Wharf, responsible for writing and sealing, with his own hand, over a thousand documents per year, as well as appearing in person at the Exchequer for audits once or twice a year.[5] This work was hardly characteristic of aspiring courtiers. As Lee Patterson observes, the London controllership had been filled not with men like Chaucer but with clerks in the king's service, who constituted Chaucer's five immediate predecessors.[6] In this occupation, Chaucer was no longer, in a very practical sense, among the courtiers who had played such a key role in the early formation of his identity as poet; rather, he was back in the mercantile world in which he had been born. He was, that is, no longer in a position that was at that time a socially legible one for a poet writing for the English court.

The exact social valence of Chaucer's movement from court to customs house is impossible to reconstruct and indeed was likely to have been ambiguous to Chaucer himself. It was perhaps something more significant than, as Olive Coleman describes, "a modest office for modest men" or, in David Carlson's more slighting depiction, "a defenestration, a setback or stall in [Chaucer's] social ascent"; yet, as Paul Strohm observes, it was also likely "not one he would have dreamed up or sought for himself. It substituted a stringent daily routine and profit-driven associates for the relatively free and easy circumstances of court life."[7] Given that no one of Chaucer's status had occupied the position before him, the appointment likely reflected some combination of royal desire to evolve this fiscally key position into one reflective of the status of an esquire of the household, and of the perception that the relatively lowly but learned Chaucer, with his family connections to the mercantile community, suited this traditionally clerical role.

As Robert Baker has shown, since the initiation of the wool customs in 1275, the office of controller was conceived as the key to the effective production of royal revenue (from a tax that held, in the late fourteenth century, "absolute pre-eminence" among sources of revenue).[8] Controllers were responsible for ensuring that the collectors of customs recorded the proper tax, an accounting task that relied on two basic methods: the creation of a duplicate set of records and the use of one-half of the double-faced "cocket seal," which, along with the other half in the keeping of a collector, authenticated all customs receipts.[9] Because the collectors were most often powerful merchants, frequently wool traders themselves, and often royal creditors, they had many motivations beyond general greed to be less-than-dependable agents of the king in their recording of sums to be deposited in royal coffers. "From the outset," Baker notes, "the ministers of Edward I had been aware that collectors might take improper advantage of their positions."[10] Hence, the controller was not so much an active agent of revenue collection as an observing agent of redundant tasks, who ensures thereby that the revenue collection actually works. Rather like the check-sum in an electronic transmission, the controller was a redundancy that ensures the accuracy of the information transmitted – that is, of the money due the Crown.

Yet from the very start the controllership at best only intermittently and quite imperfectly fulfilled its function, and the reasons for this had much to do with the social profiles of those who occupied the post. A controller must have the technical training that the post demands, he must be willing and able to be present in the customs house and perform the required labor, and he must be loyal to the king, especially when there is (as there frequently was) a divergence of interest between the Crown and the merchant oligarchs who dominated the collectorships. The difficulty in meeting these criteria lay in the fact that those most qualified in respect to the requisite training and loyalty – king's clerks sent to the ports from Westminster – were also those most likely to be drawn away into other service, for personal and institutional reasons, thereby leaving the controllership in less reliable hands, if in any hands at all. For example, Chaucer's eventual successor John de Hermesthorpe, a chamberlain of the Exchequer and later confessor to the king, abandoned the post as soon as he could, leaving a deputy in his place (despite the usual official prohibition of that practice); and Chaucer himself, although long-serving and dutiful, was more than once called away to perform the king's business.[11] As a remedy, the strategy for staffing the office, especially outside London, at times shifted to individuals local to the port with connections to the mercantile community, but of humbler wealth and status in comparison with the collectors. Such individuals were more likely to remain active in their positions during the course of their appointments, yet – beyond the question of whether they possessed the requisite skills – their loyalty to the king, given their connections to the mercantile community, was quite fragile. Compounding these problems, moreover, was the fact that, as a salaried office, the controllership was easily conceived as analogous to a benefice or property: from Edward I on, all English kings, to varying degrees, used controller appointments more as an object of largesse than as a tool of fiscal practice, which is evident in their tendency to make life appointments to the post. As a result, absenteeism, incompetence, and outright corruption were more common than not, leading to frequent demands – and less frequent actual attempts – to reform the process of appointments.

As Strohm in his consideration of the vexed status of the controllership has so much helped us to see, Chaucer's appointment to the office – given his specific qualities and the socially unprecedented nature of his appointment – offered a compelling solution to these problems.[12] He was an esquire with many years in royal service and could thus be expected to be loyal; yet he was also in effect a local man with long-standing connections to the wool trading community. And through some means (whether his poetry, other writings, or just learned conversation), he had proven himself a clerkly layman, more than able to take on the responsibilities of the controllership. It remains unclear, however, whether the appointment was considered to be a promotion, demotion, or lateral move; it likely fell to Chaucer to demonstrate the position's significance by the manner in which he occupied it. Although we have no way of knowing how consciously Chaucer pursued such social signification, we may assume that he would at least have wished to maintain the social status that he had attained prior to the appointment. Accordingly, since writing poetry was part of his identity as courtier and an expression of his distinctive occupation of that position, then, naturally, Chaucer would want to continue this activity in his new position. In addition to whatever personal fulfillment writing poetry provided, the activity would link the controllership's new duties with his prior role at court.

But herein must have lain a dilemma. If Chaucer were to continue to write poetry in the manner of the *Book of the Duchess*, he would be invoking an axiological apologia that depended upon the axiological environment of the English court; his composition of further English *dits amoreux*, rather than socially elevating his position, might then call attention to the mismatch between that position and the normative one for the authorship of courtly verse. To put it colloquially, he would risk appearing as a poser, and thus in effect make his movement out of court look like a demotion. At the same time, to produce writing more socially legible in respect to his new, traditionally clerical position – to produce something, that is, like the *Parson's Tale*, with an affinity with Latin rather than French models, and with didactic and spiritual frameworks rather than expressive and erotic ones – would heighten the social distinction between his old and new positions. As a non-cleric, he would again risk appearing as a poser, and would still be, in effect, publicizing his demotion.

It is impossible to know how directly Chaucer perceived this dilemma. If, as I suggest in this book's introduction, all authors must necessarily ascribe value to their writing that justifies the sacrifice of time and energy that writing requires in respect to both competing proximate socioeconomic values and extant normative literary axiologies, then at the very least Chaucer's writing would register some response to this dilemma as a matter of course. And if Chaucer perceived simply that the change in his socioeconomic location increased the distance – both physical and social – from the English court, this perception might have been enough to urge him to remediate the problem in poetry. Regardless, the distance effected by the appointment left him with the project of producing literary work that was recognizable in respect to extant literary axiologies, as well as in respect to the institutionally bestowed authority of his new position, and was coherent in this combination. In other words, he needed a poetry that cast him as an authentic literary producer with respect to the axiological environments of both the court and the traditionally clerical civil service, rather than as a poser with respect to both. Ideally, this poetry would, in responding to both environments, articulate a literary value that was at once recognizable and unique.

For legibility within the axiological environment of the court, the *House of Fame*'s formal resemblances to the French dream vision would in part have served this purpose. These have often been remarked upon, but they have typically been construed in terms of the internal trajectory of Chaucer's poetic career – as, for example, the transitional residue of his so-called French phase in a poem that inaugurates his Italian era. But these resemblances must also be understood as markers of conformity with the normative literary axiologies of the court. Hence, we should not be surprised when Queen Alceste, in the prologue to the *Legend of Good Women*, cites "the bok that highte the Hous of Fame" as the very first of Chaucer's works with which he "hath maked lewed folk to delyte / To serven [the God of Love]" – giving it the place of honor before the more obviously Eros-centered *Book of the Duchess, Parliament of Fowls*, and "love of Palamon and Arcite" (G 403–408; compare F 415–20). Self-identified as a species of courtly romance, and marked as such by its formal conventions, the *House of Fame*, in order to be recognized as such within the axiological environment of the court, must also be perceived as proffering the literary value of an idealizing mirror of aristocratic emotion.

In this respect, the story of Dido is pivotal. As many commentators have pointed out, and especially Christopher Baswell, the *House of Fame*'s rendering of the Dido story falls in line, in several ways, with the long tradition of romance adaptations of the *Aeneid*.[13] As in other romance treatments, Chaucer emphasizes not Aeneas's eventual transcendence of past political trauma but the immediacy of erotic trauma, the noble, internal suffering that literature turns into an art object by means of a verbal portrait of keenly felt emotion. In this regard, the poem offers the same matter as the *Book of the Duchess*. Nevertheless, taken as a whole, the *House of Fame*, despite Alceste's generous characterization of it, hardly qualifies as a work that leads its readers to praise the God of Love. Eros is, instead, in the form of "tydynges / Of Loves folk" (644–45), what the narrator is promised but never receives – a narrator who is not coincidentally identified as a maker of "bookys, songes, dytees / . . . / . . . in reverence / Of Love" (622, 624–25), that is, as Chaucer the esquire, a poet within the axiological environment of the English court. Rather than love, the *House of Fame* is more extensively concerned with what its authorially bestowed title would lead one to expect: fame. And it is so not just when the narrator reaches Lady Fame's court in the third book, but from the first book's account of Dido, where the conflict between fame and love is precisely what produces the emotion of her complaint against "wikke Fame" (349).

Fame is, of course, what epic proffers as literary value: it is what epic poets bestow on their heroes and typically, in this way, on the epic hero's contemporary political doppelgänger; and it is what poets thereby garner for themselves. Chaucer unmistakably invokes the epic tradition in his rendition of the *Aeneid*'s opening lines (143–48), but then he appears to become more sympathetic to Dido and even hostile to Aeneas. Many readers understand him to be developing a generic opposition in this way, signified by the apparent irreconcilability of the two sources that he so nonchalantly juxtaposes: "Virgile in Eneydos / Or the Epistle of Ovyde" (378–79). Although opinions vary, most readers understand Chaucer to side with Ovid and romance over Virgil and epic.[14] In my view, however, Chaucer evokes the idea of opposition ultimately only to evade it, signaling instead an allegiance that is best understood as lying with both and neither. Notably, at the end of Book 1, the hero of Chaucer's poem, like that of the *Aeneid*, leaves Dido behind. Despite the Ovidian sympathy he shows for her, Chaucer follows Aeneas by setting off, divinely compelled, in search of fame, and he follows Virgil in his willingness "to excusen Eneas / Fullyche of al his grete trespas" (427–28), and then in the redaction of the rest of the *Aeneid* (433–67).[15] Indeed, the Eagle's description of the reward offered to Geffrey for his service to Love – new matter for poetry in the form of "tydynges" of lovers that consist of "Both sothe sawes and lesinges" (676) – unmistakably recalls the Fama who effectively kills Dido.[16] In other words, the fame offered Geffrey both literally and implicitly in the structure of the poem – like the fame won by Aeneas and Virgil, and, indeed, by Chaucer – depends on the "wikke Fame" attached to Dido.

We might thus be tempted to conclude that the poem's response to the dilemma caused by Chaucer's movement out of court was the signification, through the use of the Dido story, of a turn away from the *dit* in favor of something like a romance-ironized pocket epic. After all, if Chaucer's status as a non-clerical civil servant would have cast a shadow of inauthenticity over English verse modeled solely on either contemporary French or clerical Latin literary models, then it would not be so surprising if an adaptation of classical Latin emerged as a viable route through this generic Scylla and Charybdis. After all, classical Latin was at once the fountainhead of much courtly verse (especially that deriving from Ovidian models) and had, in Virgil, the ultimate secular clerkly *auctor*. Yet the parallel with the *Aeneid*, of course, falls apart in many key ways, two of which are that Chaucer's hero, as an alter ego identified as Geffrey in the poem, plainly does not easily function as the doppelgänger of a contemporary political authority, even a romance-ironized doppelgänger; and this hero has not in fact embarked on a journey in pursuit of fame, but rather has been granted a vision in which the nature of fame will be disclosed. Chaucer's relatively close (but tellingly altered) translation of the *Aeneid*'s opening lines thus registers a *rejection* of epic as the solution to his dilemma, a rejection conditioned at least in part by the fact that the axiological environment of the early Ricardian court was not a propitious one for contemporary vernacular poets as producers of epics, serious or otherwise. Hence, instead, the poem remains within the orbit of the dream vision but extends the reach of this genre by taking cues from Dante's response to the *Aeneid*, which reconfigures the epic journey as a visionary one, in which the hero is the poet and the destination is revelation.

Yet the *House of Fame* is obviously no more an adaption of the *Commedia* than it is of the *Aeneid*; such an adaptation would be even less legible in the axiological environment of the English court. Despite its structural and verbal debts to Dante and its intertextual nods to apocalypse visions more generally, Geffrey's vision is not a sacred one.[17] He does not, in the end, confront the face of God but rather the distribution center for tidings, understood as the matter of all writing. As is explained to Geffrey and as he sees himself, sound floats upward to its "kyndelyche stede" (829), the House of Tidings, and becomes embodied there as discrete vessels of information, next traveling to the House of Fame, where Lady Fame

> . . . gan yeven ech hys name,
> After hir disposicioun,
> And yaf hem eke duracioun,
> Somme to wexe and wane sone,
> As doth the faire white mone,
> And let hem goon. (2112–17)

Long ago Alfred David offhandedly likened the House of Tidings to the customs house, and by extending this insight and placing it alongside the generic gymnastics we have so far witnessed, we may glimpse the axiological apologia of the poem.[18] For it is not just the House of Tidings that parallels Chaucer's work environment, but rather the whole tidings/fame complex. The customs house was the central point where raw materials (wool) converge from many directions to be given discrete quantity (bagged and weighed on the ground floor) and then discrete value (taxed on the upper floor) before moving outward, in many directions, eventually to become cloth.[19] Likewise, the tidings/fame complex is the central point where raw materials (sound) converge from many directions to be given discrete quantity (embodied in the House of Tidings) and then discrete value (the "disposicioun" and "duracioun" bestowed in the House of Fame) before moving outward, in many directions, eventually to become (among other things) poetic compositions.

If this analogy seems far-fetched, we may recall the fact that the *House of Fame* is the *only* poem in which Chaucer explicitly refers to his nonliterary "labour," and we may review the context of the well-known passage in which he alludes to the "rekenynges" that he performed at the customs house. As mentioned above, just a few lines before this allusion the Eagle describes Geffrey as a maker of "dytees . . . in reverence / Of Love" – that is, a member of what Green has dubbed the court of Cupid, a professional courtier producing verse in happy mediation with the axiological environment of the English court. Next, immediately before the "rekenynges" passage, the Eagle explains to Geffrey that Jupiter's reward (of the trip to the House of Fame) is recompense for the fact that Geffrey has not had "tydynges / Of Loves folk," neither of those "fro fer contree" nor of his "verray neyghebores" (644–49). Putting this all together, we understand that it is precisely because of Geffrey's "labour" at the customs house that he is no longer able to author "dytees . . . of Love" as a member of the court of Cupid. In recompense, he will receive a trip to the House of Fame, a trip that – when read alongside the distinctly uncourtly, jokingly monastic self-description as solitary scholar that concludes the "rekenynges" passage (655–60) – promises to lead somewhere other than back to the court of Cupid. Again not at all coincidentally, only a few lines later the Eagle addresses Geffrey by his given name (729, the only time in all Chaucer's writing that he so names himself), thereby fusing narrator and author and, with the preface of the "rekenynges" passage, ensuring that the socioeconomic identity of the narrator/author cannot be mistaken.

Crucially, Chaucer does not depict his narrator at the tidings/fame complex as producer or carrier of fame. He is rather an observer of the process of its creation, valuation, and dissemination. He has not "come hider to han fame" (1872), but he is nevertheless, as author of the poem, the individual who enables this process to succeed in this instance, by making public both the nature of fame and his own name. Likewise, as controller, Chaucer was effectively a paid observer, not an integral part of the process but nonetheless essential to its success. The tidings/fame complex, positioned "Ryght even in myddes of the weye / Betwixen hevene and erthe, and see" (714–15), is at once marginal and central – as was Chaucer, in economic space as controller, both marginal and central in his position among wool merchants, customs collectors, and the Crown.[20] So too was Chaucer positioned in social space somewhere "even in myddes of the weye / Betwixen" gentle, clerical, and mercantile.

Taken together, these parallels suggest that the distinctive value of this particular poem is in fact *pendant* on the poet's failure to possess a normative social status for the authorship of courtly or clerical writing. Positioned between romance, epic, and sacred vision, the *House of Fame* partakes of but does not really participate in these genres, instead observing and taking account of their axiological relations, that is, the dependencies and distinctions among the kinds of literary value they proffer. Chaucer as poet, like his narrator Geffrey, belongs neither fully outside the court, like the entertainers outside Lady Fame's castle, nor fully inside the court, like the *poetae* standing on pillars around the goddess herself; but he rather moves among and around all positions, describing and accounting for their structure and value. The literary value extended by the *House of Fame*, then, is the value of the accounting for literary value itself, a meta-value that presupposes, and therefore authorizes, the value of the literary accountant. As readers have readily perceived, behind the comic self-depiction of the "noyous" Geffrey (574) stands the master-poet manipulating the strings of his narrator, the implied author who possesses the valuable intellectual and compositional abilities – married to a paradoxically marginal and central positionality – that are required to perform the poem's act of accounting. And it is these implied valuable abilities and positionality, finally, that constitute the common ground shared by the poem's literary meta-value and a controller's economic meta-value: both the *form* and the *intensity* of the labor required by the *House of Fame*'s accounting of the stuff of all kinds of poetry are not just parallel to, but exactly those required by, Chaucer's effective accounting of the wool customs.

In this light, we may understand Geffrey's apparent assertion of an autonomous literary axiology – "I wot myself best how y stonde" – as also an expression of controller ideology. Here is the entire, well-known passage:

> I cam noght hyder, graunt mercy,
> For no such cause [i.e., "to han fame"], by my hed!
> Sufficeth me, as I were ded,
> That no wight have my name in honde.
> I wot myself best how y stonde;
> For what I drye, or what I thynke,
> I wil myselven al hyt drynke,
> Certeyn, for the more part,
> As fer forth as I kan myn art. (1874–82)

As a poet, he is like a good controller in that he does not desire the proffered value (fame or money, respectively) of the system in which he is present as observer ("I cam noght hyder") but instead asserts autonomy by accounting for that value ("Sufficeth me, as I were ded") and accepts complete responsibility for the effects of this autonomy ("For what I drye"). In this fashion, an autonomous literary axiology – an understanding of literary value as not dependent on other kinds of value – arises here as a projection onto the artistic plane of the conceptual form of the controllership that, in the socioeconomic plane, is the poem's inaugurating problem. Moreover, the wry qualifications in this seemingly assertive passage (e.g., by naming himself in this poem, Chaucer has ensured that future readers, after his death, must necessarily have his "name in honde") stand also as markers of where controller ideology comes up short against controller practice. Neither the poet nor the controller is, in fact, autonomous.[21] From this perspective, the skepticism that most readers have found pervading the poem's meditations on poetry reflects not just Chaucer's literary, theological, and philosophical dispositions, but also his socioeconomic experience of the vitiation of ideals within a system that, as Carlson has quipped, "was corrupt by design."[22]

Let me be clear: in calling attention to these several interlocking parallels, I am *not* arguing that they disclose some sort of quasi-allegorical, socioeconomically self-referential commentary that is the true meaning of the poem. The analogies are not so developed as this; they resonate more than they symbolize. Instead, I am arguing that these parallels create a socioeconomic framework for what are very much literary concerns – the poem's inscrutable, poetically self-referential content. And it is the combination of framework and content that constitutes the axiological apologia of the *House of Fame*: the fusion of values at the level of form and intensity of labor means that the proffering of literary meta-value and the proffering of economic meta-value become mutually affirming, and hence the poem and Chaucer's controllership become mutually legitimating. Whether present as a reflexive or more active response to his circumstances, in this poem literary and socioeconomic axiologies blend and affirm each other in a generalized assertion of the value of the exceptionally literate and marginally central (and so theoretically autonomous) accountant of value.

This axiological apologia, we know with the benefit of hindsight, was an effective one: despite what seems to have been the limited circulation of the poem, it encouraged Chaucer to keep writing, and his readers to keep reading, notwithstanding his distance from court. Nonetheless, as the remainder of this chapter argues, Chaucer ultimately found it inadequate. As we will see, in bestowing a similar axiological apologia on the Clerk's performance, Chaucer at once celebrates its artistic power and identifies its weaknesses, and this in turn creates the artistic space for the IV-V sequence.

The Meta-Axiological Clerk's Performance

Compared to the critical response to the *House of Fame*, the response to the Clerk's performance, like that to all the IV-V performances – has been considerably more polarized.[23] Crucial interpretive questions have provoked diverse, mutually exclusive answers. Critics divide, for example, over whether the performance as a whole is antifeminist or anti-antifeminist (and, relatedly, whether it counters or complements the Wife of Bath's performance); whether Chaucer's version of the Griselda story complicates Petrarch's (supposedly) more straightforward version or whether it recognizes and extends the complexity already present in its sources (and relatedly, whether the Clerk's or Chaucer's attitude toward Petrarch is favorable or unfavorable); whether the *Clerk's Tale* is best understood as allegory, exemplum, allegorical exemplum, or something else; whether or not Chaucer's version reflects knowledge of Boccaccio's, and, if so, whether that knowledge is general and memorial or intimate and verbal; and whether or not the version of the Griselda story told by the Clerk is, overall, artistically successful, and, if not, whether the fault lies with the Clerk or with Chaucer.

While some of these questions will necessarily enter into the discussion below, my emphasis here is not so much on resolving them but rather on recognizing, along with what I take to be the majority of current scholars, that the performance's interpretive challenges are not merely anachronistic projections of modern critics keen on identifying difficulties upon which they can demonstrate their expertise. Green, K. P. Clarke, and William Rossiter, among others, have made clear that medieval readers and writers of the tale of Griselda in its many versions found the tale difficult, for reasons both similar to and different from those argued by modern critics; and Charlotte Morse has documented the long critical tradition that has painstakingly identified the elements of the Clerk's performance that not just reproduce these difficulties but in fact compound them.[24] Like many others, then, I contend that at least part of the point of the Clerk's performance is to manifest – indeed, to foreground – this very interpretive difficulty, to underscore the multiplicity of possible interpretations, and thereby (I will add) to represent a meta-axiological posture: that is, to reflect on, from an apparently non-committal position, the different literary axiologies encompassed by this multiplicity.

For this chapter's purpose of establishing the function of the Clerk's performance as the inauguration of a four-part sequence, there is no need to review the inventory of the many features of the Clerk's performance that compound an already interpretively difficult tale. It will suffice to consider a few aspects of three especially prominent such features: the ambiguity of the Clerk's attitude toward Petrarch in his opening exchange with the Host; the nature of the changes that Chaucer makes to his principal sources in an otherwise close translation (for which I will discuss just one repeated, consistent change in wording involving the verb *tempten*); and the effect of the explicitly voiced alternative and competing interpretations of the tale that accompany its transition back to the dramatic frame.

"heigh stile"

Other than the Clerk's mention of Petrarch, in all the *Canterbury Tales* the only instance in which a pilgrim names the author of his or her source is the Physician's four-word aside, "as telleth Titus Livius" (VI.1), and the differences between these instances highlight the distinctiveness of the Clerk's naming of his *auctor*. First, of course, the Physician's identification of Livy is at best misleading, as Chaucer's principal source for the tale of Virginius and Virginia was the *Roman de la rose*, whereas Petrarch's *Historia Griseldis* in *Seniles* 17.3 (along with an anonymous French crib, *Le Livre Griseldis*) was indeed Chaucer's principal source for his version of Griselda – making the Clerk's naming of Petrarch the only place in the *Canterbury Tales* in which a pilgrim correctly names his or her source author.[25] This singularity underscores the even more revealing differences between the manners in which the Physician and Clerk respectively identify their sources. For the Physician, Livy is simply the identity of an ancient text, the esteem accorded to which he formulaically borrows to bestow authority on his own, quite idiosyncratic telling of a putative historical event. In contrast, for the Clerk Petrarch is very much a (recently deceased) person, one whom he has supposedly met, of whose career and stature he has direct knowledge:

> I wol yow telle a tale which that I
> Lerned at Padowe of a worthy clerk,
> As preved by his wordes and his werk.
> He is now deed and nayled in his cheste;
> I prey to god so yeve his soule reste!
> Fraunceys Petrak, the lauriat poete,
> Highte this clerk, whos rethoryke sweete
> Enlumyned al Ytaille of poetrie,
> As Lynyan dide of philosophie
> Or lawe, or oother art particuler;
> But Deeth, that wol nat suffre us dwellen heer,
> But as it were a twynklyng of an ye,
> Hem bothe hath slayn, and alle shul we dye.
> But forth to tellen of this worthy man,
> That taughte me this tale, as I bigan,
> I seye that first with heigh stile he enditeth . . . (IV.26–41)

Mentioning first how the Clerk "[l]erned" the tale from Petrarch and, just thirteen lines later, repeating that Petrarch "taughte" him the tale, this initiating piece of the dramatic frame notably echoes (albeit with different denotation) the "gladly wolde he lerne and gladly teche" (I.308) that concludes the Clerk's own *General Prologue* portrait. Indeed, this passage seems at first to reproduce the artistic design of the *Tales* itself, with the Clerk providing a (brief) portrait of the individual whose tale he will then repeat, and with the epithets "worthy clerk" and "worthy man" serving to recall the *General Prologue*'s characteristic descriptive language. As an *apparently* idealizing portrait of Petrarch, lacking any straightforwardly determinable satire – as with the apparently idealizing *General Prologue* portrait of the "worthy knyght" (I.65), or for that matter the Clerk's own – the passage serves to hypostatize literary authority, to present a flesh-and-blood individual who personally carries the *auctorial* esteem of merely textual figures like Livy.

In other words, like Chaucer's translation of the *Aeneid* and his use of Dante in the *House of Fame*, this passage carries the premise of remarkable poetic ambition, an auspicious vision of what English poetry might become and of the status an English poet might achieve, as a laureate serving the public as moral and cultural authority, illuminating all England "of poetrie." Yet as many have noted – and, I would add, in precisely the same fashion as in the *House of Fame* – Chaucer seems to undercut this ambition in the very gesture of suggesting it, most prominently in this instance by supplying, alongside his ushering of the idea of laureate into English poetry, a repeated, acute declaration of what gives the lie to any human ambition: the ineluctable leveling force of "alle shul we dye." The degree of this undercutting, or even its presence, however, is uncertain. What makes all the difference in our understanding of these lines is the texture of the voice that we imagine speaking them; that is, the key to gauging the passage's attitude toward Petrarch and Petrarchan ideas about poetry is discernment of its tone. But with the passage's unstable conflation of assertion and deflation, and the virtual absence of obvious tonal signifiers, its tonal possibilities are broad and ambiguous. Critical reactions to this uncertainty predictably bifurcate, polarized between detections of wry critique and celebrative litotes, with the two camps exemplarily represented by the influential accounts of the Clerk's performance by, respectively, David Wallace and Anne Middleton.[26]

The continuation of this passage, through the end of the *Clerk's Prologue*, intensifies and deepens this ambiguity, paradoxically by offering an explicit evaluation of one aspect of Petrarch's *Historia*. Here the Clerk supplies the oft-observed *occupatio* in which he loosely translates Petrarch's "prohemye" (IV.43) despite his later, retroactive report that he will skip over it:

> I seye that first with heigh stile he enditeth,
> Er he the body of his tale writeth,
> A prohemye, in the which discryveth he
> Pemond, and of Saluces the contree,
> . . .
> The which a long thyng were to devyse.
> And trewely, as to my juggement,
> Me thynketh it a thyng impertinent,
> Save that he wol conveyen his mateere;
> But this his tale, which that ye may heere. (IV.41–56)

At the outset of this *occupatio*, the Clerk notably repeats the literary critical term "heigh stile" that the Host has just used, negatively, to define the kind of tale that he wants from the Clerk:

> Telle us som mury thyng of aventures.
> Youre termes, youre colours, and youre figures,
> Keepe hem in stoor til so be ye endite
> Heigh style, as whan that men to kynges write. (IV.15–18)

As Middleton has noted, the Host here appears to refer to the curial style of such professional letter-writers as Philippe de Mézières (whose late fourteenth-century French version of the Griselda story, *Le Miroir des Dames Mariées*, Chaucer may have known) or, we may add, to the style marking the professional bureaucratic work of Chaucer's clerkly disciple Thomas Hoccleve: the style one uses when writing formal, necessarily flowery addresses to kings (or when adapting this epistolary style in literary works, like the *Regiment of Princes*, that address royalty).[27] In this regard, the Host's demand that the Clerk keep such devices of curial style "in stoor til so be ye endite / Heigh style" suggests that the Host wants him to leave aside this style not only until another occasion but also until he is engaged in a professional activity in which that style is appropriate (which is how I read the implication of the intrusive "so be"): that is, when he would, like so many of his fellow Oxford students, take up a post in a royal, baronial, or ecclesiastical office that involved penning formulaic letters to the king. In turn, this implication recalls what we know from the *General Prologue*: that the Clerk neither possesses, nor wishes to possess, such "worldly" "office" (I.292).

As in the aforementioned echo of "gladly wolde he lerne and gladly teche," however, this internal allusion is not an instance of a dramatized character referring to the details of the *General Prologue* narrator's description of the Clerk, but it is rather a narratological device that points toward the axiological person that that description develops and thereby signals its relevance to this context. I consider this axiological person later; for now it suffices to point out that the Clerk's lack of interest in worldly office evident in the *General Prologue* reemerges here in more positive fashion in his silent relocation of the term *high style* into a different discursive domain: the domain signified by the term's use, as Chaucer mistakenly believed, by Petrarch as his own description of the *Historia*'s style.[28] Specifically, this relocation redirects the term *high style* from instrumental curial writing to the very differently intended lofty Latin eloquence of Petrarch's *Historia*, which was written not in professional service as a flowery address to a king but rather as an expression of what we would now call high culture, directed toward an elect group of writers and readers that Wallace names the "Petrarchan Academy." One reading of just lines IV.41–43, then, would understand the Clerk as insinuating, in response to the Host's demand, that he would never put his writing to such curial, instrumental use, but that he instead strives to emulate the imagined "Petrarchan man of letters, leading a life wholly 'in bokes' and in 'poetrie' . . . [one who] professes a stylish and grave, but wholly secular, *contemptus mundi*, which means in his case only and exactly what it says: a distaste for present worldly life, and a corresponding sense of companionship with the mighty dead in books."[29]

But, of course, at the end of this *occupatio* – when we discover, belatedly, that it was indeed an *occupatio* – any hint of this positive attitude toward Petrarch seems swept away by the Clerk's "juggement" of the latter's high style as "a thyng impertinent." If read as if spoken in earnest, this passage becomes not only the sole consideration of a source *auctor* in the *Tales* but also the sole disparagement of a source, as well as a relatively rare instance, across all of Chaucer's writings, of stylistic literary evaluation. It would seem, therefore, that Chaucer is signaling the distinction of his version of the Griselda story from Petrarch's, and perhaps even a degree of hostility to what he understood to be Petrarch's poetic and professional career; as Wallace puts it, Chaucer signals "that the translation to come will be actively critical rather than passively faithful," or, as Leah Schwebel remarks, his "wholesale repudiation of Petrarch as a literary *auctoritee*."[30]

Yet, again, how one reads the tone of IV.52–56 makes all the difference. The Clerk's declaring Petrarch's prohemium a "long thyng . . . to devyse" after actually having concisely summarized most of it may be taken as Chaucer's private joke, underscored by the fact that no other fourteenth-century translation of the *Historia*, including Chaucer's French crib, includes the prohemium, making Chaucer's version uniquely closer to Petrarch in this regard.[31] Moreover, many critics have detected a note of irony in the Clerk's apparently negative judgment of this example of Petrarch's high style, understanding that judgment to be a superficial acquiescence to the Host's command that masks and thereby enables a resistance to, even a subversion of, the Host's authority. The Clerk has, after all, declared the prohemium irrelevant *except* for its function of introducing the story ("*Save* that he wol conveyen his mateere") only *after* having in fact introduced his version with this unique translation of the prohemium – suggesting that that function may not be so insignificant. Many readers have noted the parallels between this strategy of resistance-through-acquiescence with what they perceive to be the nature of Griselda's response to Walter's authority and, in a more complex manner, of the Wife of Bath's mimicry of clerical antifeminist discourse. And perhaps "impertinent," inasmuch as it signifies a lack of relation, suggests a value in and of itself, that is, the very autonomy of literary discourse that is the impossible dream of laureate poetics: "a thyng impertinent" may not be a bad "thyng," but rather a backhand pointer to a poetic ideal.[32] Like the dead-on-arrival appearance of the laureate in English poetry, and like the *House of Fame*, this passage simultaneously seems both to affirm and to turn away from Petrarch's high style and what it represents. Whether or not the passage's inscrutable tone can be persuasively deciphered in one direction or another, Chaucer has clearly made such determination difficult, and has therefore made this ambiguity of attitude toward the Petrarchan ideal a prominent element of the characterological field of the Clerk.

"tempted in assay"

At the very least, we can say with certainty that the Clerk's stated "juggement" about the prohemium signals to the reader that the Clerk does not feel obligated to repeat Petrarch's *Historia* verbatim, in contrast with the *General Prologue*'s narrator's attitude toward the tales that he relates. This seeming difference incurs the further irony – disclosed to readers who have access to the marginal excerpts from Petrarch's *Historia* that accompany the *Clerk's Tale* in Hengwrt, Ellesmere, and other manuscripts – that this tale is in fact among Chaucer's closest translations; apparently, Chaucer found little else impertinent. And if Chaucer did originally produce the translation independently of the *Clerk's Prologue*, the irony – indeed the whole riff on the prohemium – adds another instance to the collection of private jokes that no doubt permeate the *Tales*. Nevertheless, as close as the translation is, J. Burke Severs long ago exhaustively demonstrated that Chaucer departs from his source in key places, most typically by addition but also by significant changes in wording. And while Severs found Chaucer's changes to be relatively unproblematic improvements to the tale, resulting in an "almost magical transformation" of his source material, most readers since – especially in the wake of Elizabeth Salter's study – have found them to heighten the interpretive difficulties already present in Petrarch's version in whatever degree (about which critics vary widely).[33]

Here I will consider the nature and implications of just one of Chaucer's changes to his source: his response to the problem of the distinction between the notions of tempting and testing (or proving). This distinction is of course doctrinally crucial, since tempting, in the sense of enticing someone to evil (*OED tempt,* v. 4a), is an action that God may permit but does not himself perform, whereas the action of testing, when performed by God, nurtures and enables one to demonstrate spiritual strength, and thus is a spiritual benefit that God bestows out of his grace. Hampering the effort to make this distinction, however, is that the Medieval Latin verb *temptare* (or *tentare*), as is evident in its varied uses in the Vulgate, held both senses, as did the French and English verbs that descended from it, and as indeed did the Greek verb (and its associated noun forms) that the Vulgate sought to translate. Indeed, the trickiness of this lexical breadth is a rather prominent feature of Jerome's rendering of the passage in the first book of the Epistle of James from which Petrarch draws his moralization:

> [2] omne gaudium existimate fratres mei cum in temptationibus variis incideritis [3] scientes quod probatio fidei vestrae patientiam operatur . . . [12] beatus vir qui suffert temptationem[:] quia cum probatus fuerit accipiet coronam vitae quam repromisit Deus diligentibus se [13] nemo cum temptatur dicat quoniam a Deo temptor[:] Deus enim intemptator malorum est ipse autem neminem temptat [14] unusquisque vero temptatur a concupiscentia sua abstractus et illectus

> [2] My brethren, count it all joy, when you shall fall into divers temptations; [3] Knowing that the trying of your faith worketh patience . . . [12] Blessed is the man that endureth temptation; for when he hath been proved, he shall receive a crown of life, which God hath promised to them that love him. [13] Let no man, when he is tempted, say that he is tempted by God. For God is not a tempter of evils, and he tempteth no man. [14] But every man is tempted by his own concupiscence, being drawn away and allured.[34]

As Bishop Challoner's note to verse 2 remarks, "The word temptation, in this epistle, is sometimes taken for trials by afflictions or persecutions, as in this place: at other times, it is to be understood, tempting, enticing, or drawing others into sin." Thus, in verses 2–3, "temptationibus" is evidently synonymous with "probatio," and in verse 12 "suffert temptationem" is equivalent to "probatus fuerit"; and by themselves these verses could serve as the simplest abstract of the moral of Petrarch's *Historia.* But verses 13–14 seem to consider temptation in its more malevolent sense. While before we were told that it is a blessing to fall into temptation, now we are told that God does *not* tempt, on the rationale "Deus enim intemptator malorum est," which is rendered by the Rheims translators as "[f]or God is not a tempter of evils," that is, God is not an inciter to sin, taking "intemptator" as a negated noun, a "not-tempter."

Petrarch and Chaucer likely understood verse 13 in essentially the same manner, if the Wycliffite bible may be taken as representative of the fourteenth-century construal of the verse – "No man whanne he is temptid, seie, that he is temptid of God; for whi God is not a temptere of yuele thingis, for he temptith no man."[35] But whatever their precise understanding of the passage, the specter of God prodding humans toward evil has been invoked, and we are suddenly in the deep waters of theodicy. Accordingly, the burden of the next verse is to identify explicitly the only possible agent of evil temptation: original sin, here given as human *concupiscentia.* (As the Parson puts it: "And whan the soule is put in oure body, right anon is contract original synne; and that that was erst but only peyne of concupiscence, is afterward bothe peyne and synne" [X.334].) By this point, however, we seem to have come a long way from *temptationibus* of verse 2: clearly we are not to "count it all joy" when we are "drawn away and allured" by our "own concupiscence." Medieval exegetes consequently took pains to elaborate the nature of the two senses of *temptare*. Thus, for example, for verse 13 *Glossa Ordinaria* comments, "Exteriorem tentationem immittit Deus ad probationem suorum, interiorem vero, qua saepe concipitur furtum, adulterium, homicidium, non immittit Deus" (God sends external temptation for man's proving, whereas internal temptation – which often conceives theft, adultery, and murder – God does not send). And for the following verse, it clarifies, "Duo sunt genera tentationum: unum quod probat, secundum quod tentavit Deus Abraham. Aliud quod decipit, secundum quod Deus neminem tentat" (There are two kinds of temptations: the one which tests, as when God tempted Abraham; the other which deceives, and God tempts no one in this way).[36]

In practice, this neat division between Godly external testing and sinful internal tempting can be difficult to maintain, especially when, as in the story of the temptation of Christ, there is an external evil *temptator* (Matthew 4:3), namely, the *diabolo* (Matthew 4:1), who seeks to provoke internal *concupiscentia* in the Son of God (or, analogously and more pertinently, in the story of Job).[37] Hence, given the romance structure of the Griselda tale that Petrarch inherited from Boccaccio, the spiritual dimension that Petrarch sought to layer into the story would plainly be more easily digestible if he consistently referred to Walterus, Griselda's husband and father of her children, as a testing agent rather than a tempting one. And indeed Petrarch's adaptation of James 1:13 in his moralization would seem to establish the terminology for precisely this distinction. Citing "Iacobus . . . Apostolus," he asserts, almost verbatim from verse 13, that God "intemptator malorum sit, et ipse neminem temptet," but then immediately adds, "probat tamen" (yet he proves) (400–1), using the Epistle's lexis to distinguish, more rigorously than the Epistle itself, *temptare* from *probare*.[38] However much Petrarch had in mind this distinction during the composition of the Griselda story itself, he did tend to avoid *temptare* and derivative forms in the applicable places in the narrative, using it, as the table below indicates, only twice: in the narrator's accounts of Walterus's initial decision to test Griselda (following the birth of her daughter) and of Walterus's later decision to pretend to divorce her. Petrarch's much more common term, used in some form six times, is *experientia* or *experimentum*, which more neutrally denotes "test" without the malevolent taint of *temptatio*; he also uses once a form of the neutral *probare*. *Le Livre Griseldis* follows Petrarch in this regard, and, as the table shows, actually tips the balance of usage further toward neutral terms. Providing the same distinction of terminology in the moralization ("[Dieu] ne tempte nul, mais bien appreuve" [428–29]), it uses *tenter* only in the two places Petrarch uses *temptare*; elsewhere it five times uses *essaier* ("to try"), five times uses *approuver* ("to test"), and three times uses *experiment* ("test"), often combining these terms in phrases.

Like *Le Livre Griseldis*, Chaucer supplies a close translation of Petrarch's distinguishing terms in his rendering of the moralization, even repeating the neutral term:

> For greet skile is he preeve that he wroghte.
> But he ne tempteth no man that he boghte
> As seith seint Jame, if ye his pistel rede;
> He preeveth folk al day . . . (IV.1152–55)

But as the tabular comparison makes evident, Chaucer's lexical choices in the narrative strikingly contrast with those of his sources: Chaucer uses *tempten* and its related forms considerably more often in his rendering of the story, repeating it seven times, not only in both places that Petrarch uses *temptare* but also in three others where Petrarch and *Le Livre Griseldis* avoid the term. Indeed, the only places where Chaucer avoids the term are in Walter's direct speech and at the end of tale in referring, unlike his sources, to Walter and Griselda's son's treatment of his wife rather than to Walter's treatment of his father-in-law. To be sure, Chaucer makes frequent use of neutral terms as well – *assayen* (eight times), *preeven* (twice), and *experience* (once) – but these often accompany use of *tempten*.

Table: Comparison of the lexis of testing between the Clerk's Tale *and its sources*

Place in narrative	Petrarch	*Le Livre Griseldis*	Chaucer
Introduction of the first test	"experendi" (194), "**retemptandi**" (194)	"essaier et approuver" (160), "experimenter et essaier" (163–64), "essayee et approuvee" (164–65), "**tenter**" (165)	"**tempte**" (452), "t'assaye" (454), "assayed" (456), "**tempte**" (458), "assaye" (461)
Introduction of the second test	(no word for test)	(no word for test)	"**tempte**" (620), "**tempted** in assay" (621)
Narratorial comment between second and third tests	"experimenta" (272–73), "experiendique" (289)	"experimens" (264)	"assayes" (694), "preeve" (699), "**tempte**" (707), "**tempte**" (735)
Introduction of the third test	"**retemptaret**" (298)	"approuver" (276), "essaier et **tenter**" (296–97)	"**tempte**" (786)
Walter's words signaling tests are complete	"experimenta" (378)	"approuvé (401)	"assayed" (1054)
Walter's explanation to the people	"experientem" (383), "probasse" (384)	"appouver et essaier" (408)	"t'assaye" (1075)
Explanation for Walter's neglect of his father-in-law	"experiencie" (393)	"experiment"	"assay" (1138) (but referring to Walter and Griselda's son)

Chaucer's distinctiveness in this regard, moreover, is even more striking when one juxtaposes the fuller lexical contexts of the three versions of the passages listed in the table. Perhaps the most dramatically differing passage is the narrator's account of Walter's decision, after the birth of his son, to renew his testing of Griselda:

> . . . quo nutricis ab ubere post biennium subducto, ad curoisitatem solitam reversus pater, uxorem rursus affatur . . . (239–40)

> When the child stopped nursing after two years, however, the father returned to his former inquisitiveness, and spoke to his wife again . . .

> Lequel enfant puis qu'il ot deux ans et qu'il fut sevré de la nourrice, le marquis de rechief vint a sa femme et lui dist . . . (219–21)

> When the child was two years old and had finished nursing, the marquis once again came to his wife and said to her . . . .

> Whan it was two yeer old, and fro the brest
> Departed of his norice, on a day
> This markys caughte yet another lest
> To tempte his wyf yet ofter, if he may.
> O nedelees was she tempted in assay!
> But wedded men ne knowe no mesure,
> Whan that they fynde a pacient creature. (IV.617–23)

Neither Petrarch nor *Le Livre Griseldis* even bother to name the action that Walter plans; Petrarch merely provides the motive of *curoisitatem*, and even that much narratorial comment the French author skips. In contrast, Chaucer's significant expansion incurs a telling lexical redundancy with its account of Walter's initial decision to test Griselda (IV.449–62; also much expanded in respect to the Latin and French), recalling the identification of the action there (as in the two sources) as one of temptation. And, most prominently, with the narrator's added lament of IV.621, Chaucer not only repeats the verb *tempten* in consecutive lines, but he also apparently goes out of his way to distinguish its denotation from that of *assayen*: for if the phrase "tempted *in* assay" is meaningful beyond simple tautology (in contrast with the common emphatic redundancy of "tempted *and/or* assayed"), "tempted" here must carry some shadow of its malevolent meaning.

Chaucer's usage of the term elsewhere in his writings, furthermore, strongly supports the likelihood of this shadow of malevolence. For, despite the fact that the neutral meaning was current in his day, Chaucer's other twenty-two recorded uses of the term, in both its verbal and nominal forms, *without exception* clearly carry the malevolent meaning; the explicit or implied tempting agent in all these other uses is either the devil or human concupiscence.[39] As one might expect, the term appears most frequently in the *Parson's Tale*, which accounts for seventeen of the thirty total instances (including those in the *Clerk's Tale*, which contains the next greatest number). And indeed the densest cluster of usage – seven instances across the twenty-three sentences of X.335–57 – occurs in the very passage where the penitential treatise seeks to explain the relations among an external tempting agent such as the devil, the internal tempting agent of concupiscence, and culpability, quoting James 1:14 as its authority.

Given this lexical evidence, and given that Chaucer (perhaps unlike Petrarch) knew in advance the terminological distinctions of Petrarch's moralization, it strongly appears that Chaucer systematically calibrated his lexis of testing not just to question Walter's motives but also to cast a dark theological shadow over them. This conclusion, of course, is very much in line with how many have characterized some of the more obvious changes that Chaucer made to his sources. But what this more subtle lexical adjustment helps to clarify is that Chaucer readily perceived the specifically *hermeneutic* difficulties and, indeed, contradictions already present in Petrarch's *Historia*, and that he sought to bring these difficulties more into the foreground in both prominent and intricate ways. For Chaucer's lexis of testing does not simply label Walter as demonic or the personification of concupiscence;[40] rather, it exploits a lexical ambiguity that insinuates such meanings without insisting upon them, meanings that cut across the grain of the moralization without thereby rendering it a mere non-sequitur, increasing the tension between narration and *sentence* without fully splintering them apart.

"nat so strong"

Because Chaucer's translation continues past the end of the narrative proper to include Petrarch's moralization of the tale, in a strict, compositional sense, the return to the pilgrimage frame begins with the original material that he added, perhaps some time later, directly following that moralization, with the line "But o word, lordynges, herkneth er I go" (IV.1163). Discursively, if not tonally, however, this perhaps retroactive stitching of the translation into the dramatic frame is virtually seamless, for when the narrator earlier dispels the fictional world of the tale by stating "And herkneth what this auctour seith therfoore" (IV.1141), we hear that line as the Clerk speaking to the pilgrims, and thus we hear the ensuing moralization as the Clerk's proffering of an initial interpretation of the tale that he has just told. As a result, the effect of this epilogue's ultimately and notoriously polysemous conclusion to the Clerk's performance is to compound the hermeneutic difficulties provoked by the prologue/tale combination, and to do so precisely where readers look for closure.

With the "And herkneth" line, the narrator refers to his "auctour" in a conventional authorizing gesture, seemingly introducing a passage that enacts the typical form that authoritative closure takes. And perhaps indeed the line originally played merely this conventional role, albeit as a masquerade of sorts, given what we have seen to be the nature of the preceding translation. But dropped into the context of the Clerk's performance, it also recalls the ambiguous matter of the prologue, as it introduces auto-interpretive commentary that names for a second time the Clerk's laureate "auctour" "Petrak" and the latter's "heigh stile" (IV.1147–48).[41] One might contend, therefore, that Chaucer supplied his ambiguous prologue to the Clerk's performance because he knew that the concluding moralization would neatly clarify simultaneously both the tale's *sentence* and the opening ambivalent attitude toward Petrarch: if the moralization strikes us as applicable, valuable, and authoritative, then our hermeneutic puzzle is solved in the same moment in which we recognize (i.e., positively evaluate) Petrarch's wisdom and literary prowess. Yet, as we know and will shortly revisit, the actual pilgrimage frame material that follows the moralization, at the very least, renders the status of the moralization uncertain, and as we have seen, the lexis of the preceding tale has already preemptively problematized the distinction of *tempten* from *preeven* upon which the moralization depends. Moreover, in the stanza immediately prior to the moralization that concludes with the directive to "herkneth" to the tale's "auctour" – a stanza that is largely original to Chaucer – the narrator appears to ensure this preemptive problematization of the moralization, albeit, as with the tale's conflation of *tempten* and *preeven*, in a subtle and enigmatic fashion.

This stanza serves as kind of reflective ramp up to the full break in the fiction at IV.1141. Speaking of the future of Walter and Griselda's son, the narrator remarks that he

> . . . fortunat was eek in mariage,
> Al putte he nat his wyf in greet assay.
> This world is nat so strong, it is no nay,
> As it hath been in olde tymes yoore,
> And herkneth what this auctour seith therefoore. (IV.1137–41)

Using the neutral term "assay," the narrator explains that the son chooses not to emulate his father in his domestic behavior, not because such behavior was, say, demonic, but because "[t]his world is nat so strong" as it used to be. But what does the wide-ranging adjective *strong* mean here? The *MED* gives "spiritually or inwardly strong" (*strong*, adj. 5a), which sense suits the subsequent moralization, although it still leaves open the question of the character of Walter's testing (i.e., the nature of the agency against which Griselda's spiritual strength is manifested). More problematically, it casts an oddly pessimistic didacticism over the moralization, making the latter virtually self-canceling: on the one hand, we are told that like Griselda we ought to receive "all in gree that God us sent" (IV.1151); but, on the other hand, we have already learned that it is futile to try to emulate her, since the spiritual strength of this world, in contrast with that of Griselda's, has waned.

Furthermore, other meanings of *strong* are possible and indeed perhaps more likely, such as "sturdy" (*MED* 3a) or "fortified" (*MED* 4a), both of which would imply a quite different, much more literal understanding of the tale – viz., that Walter and Griselda's son chooses not to test his wife simply because women in his day (which has presumably continued to the narrator's present) are not as sturdy, in respect to uxorial *assay*, as they were in the past. Offering support for this reading of *strong* is how it seems closely to anticipate the narrator's remarks at the beginning of the post-Petrarchan pilgrimage frame material, which we encounter as the Clerk's second beckoning to his auditors to hearken, immediately after he completes the moralization:

> But o word, lordynges, herkneth er I go:
> It were ful hard to fynde now-a-dayes
> In al a toun Grisildis thre or two;
> For, if that they were put to swiche assayes,
> The gold of hem hath now so badde alayes
> With bras, that thogh the coyne be fair at ye,
> It wolde rather breste a-two than plye. (IV.1163–69)

With Chaucer perhaps retroactively elaborating his earlier preemptive strike on the moralization, the Clerk here explicitly offers a literal understanding of the tale, in which women today, like the future Marquis's wife, are so unsturdy that if "they were put to swiche assayes" they would "breste a-two." If this comparison holds, Petrarch's moralization becomes sandwiched between two instances of an alternative reading in which Griselda figures precisely in the way that Petrarch (according to Chaucer) says she does not. That is, despite the narrator's pronouncement that "This storie is seyd nat for that wyves sholde / Folwen Grisilde" (IV.1142–43), the story (according to this reading) *does* actually conceive of Griselda as a literal, if no longer obtainable, domestic exemplum for wives.

In fact, Chaucer did not invent this tension between literal and spiritual application; it is already present in both the Latin and French, and indeed – given the manner in which Chaucer rendered his own translation – we may fairly suppose that it was among the features of the story that most attracted him to it in the first place. Notably, both the Latin and French moralizations phrase the rejection of literal application in distinctly less absolute terms than does Chaucer: respectively, "non tam ideo, ut matronas nostri temporis ad imitandam" (not *so much* to urge the matrons of our time to imitate; 396–97); and, hedging even more, "non pas tant seulement que les femmes qui sont aujourd'uy je esmeuve a ensuir" (not *only* so that I might stir the wives of today to imitate; 423–24).[42] Moreover, as has been frequently noted, *Le Livre Griseldis*, like other French renderings of the *Historia*, explicitly introduces the story as this sort of literal exemplum, "a l'exemplaire des femmes mariees et toutes autres" (as an example for married women and all other women; 2). As with his use of *tempten*, then, Chaucer – with his more absolute negation and perhaps with his anticipation of the literal exemplum after the conclusion of the translation proper – has heightened an interpretive difficulty. Furthermore, as we saw in the consideration of *strong* as spiritual strength, Chaucer presents uxorial sturdiness as (mostly) lost to the past and so has oddly undone the applicability of the literal exemplum in the very moment of suggesting it. And, in this case, this self-canceling gesture opens up the additional possibility of irony, or the question – seized upon by those critics who wish to see the Clerk (or Chaucer) as the friend of women – of whether the Clerk (or Chaucer) *seriously* means to suggest such a lost domestic ideal ever existed or was even ever desirable, or whether he means something like the opposite.[43]

Such an ironic and potentially anti-antifeminist reading of this stanza gains some anticipatory support in a different fashion from yet a third possible meaning for *strong*: as "fierce" (*MED* 6a), with the "world" in this case referring not to women but to men like Walter, the men who rule the world. That is, the narrator may be saying that Walter and Griselda's son does not test his wife like his father tested his mother because the world today is – to borrow the words of another notorious ruler-father – a kinder, gentler place: a presumably desirable improvement. Although seemingly the least plausible of the three options, this sense of *strong* may be understood to echo the oft-noticed negative commentary regarding Walter's behavior that, scattered throughout the tale, the narrator imposes upon his narration (and most of which Chaucer has added to his sources). And, at least initially, this sense of *strong* does not so much create tension with the moralization as just a distraction from it, or rather a representation of such a distraction, of an undue attention to the letter of the tale provoked by Walter's apparently outrageous, sadistic behavior – a reaction typical of not just modern readers but also, as recorded in the studies mentioned above, many of their medieval counterparts, including the narrator Dioneo in Boccaccio's original. Chaucer may have then, perhaps later, expanded this distraction by the letter into the full, ironic, anti-antifeminist counter-moralization of the narrator's second hearkening request, which (according to this reading) accelerates into the deeply ironic song "for the Wyves love of Bathe" that follows, for yet a third time, the narrator's command to his audience to hearken (IV.1170, 1176). Perhaps, indeed, this song's description of "archewyves" as "strong as is a greet camaille" (IV.1195–95) winkingly redirects this sense of *strong* as "fierce" from the men who rule to those whom they oppress, following the upside-down logic of carnival that seems, to many, to be the song's animating spirit (although admittedly the more likely sense in this instance is "sturdy").

Others have, of course, read the irony of the concluding song very differently – as, for example, the more straightforward irony of stating the opposite of what is meant, that is, that "noble wyves" (IV.1183) *should* take Griselda as a literal exemplum. My point has not been to argue for one reading or another; rather, I have traced the several paths leading out from the ambiguity of the sense of *strong* in order to limn the spider-web-like polyvalence of the conclusion of the Clerk's performance, and more specifically to suggest how this polyvalence serves as the culmination of the ambiguity, interpretive difficulty, and literary self-consciousness of the entire performance. The crucial observation, for present purposes, is that this culmination, in extending polyvalence to the *application* of the tale, makes the performance as whole not just meta-hermeneutic but also meta-axiological. The Clerk, that is, offers not just varying possibilities for understanding the *meaning* of the tale but also for understanding its *value*, in the sense of how the tale ought to be used, whether (to list just some of the possibilities) as spiritual exemplum, domestic exemplum, antifeminist discursive weapon, the more interpersonal discursive weapon of *quiting* of the Wife of Bath, or an act of anti-antifeminist resistance to the authority of men like the Host (and Petrarch). Obviously, not all readers detect all these possibilities, and indeed most will readily discard some of them as largely critical inventions or (less kindly) mere error – "cultural solipsism," in the words of one critic.[44] But what my scrutiny of the ambiguity of such terms as *heigh stile, tempten*, and *strong* has sought to establish is that, on the surface at least, the Clerk quite unmistakably entertains the possibility of some number of multiple, conflicting conceptions of the value of his tale.

Furthermore – and just as important – the Clerk, again at least on the surface, does not himself choose from among these possibilities, nor does he, in the mode of the *demande* that concludes the *Franklin's Tale*, ask his auditors to choose. Instead, he offers an unresolved set of juxtapositions, abruptly terminating his performance with a song in some uncertainly ironic key. As Howell Chickering has put it, the end of the performance "creates not a final irony nor dramatic closure, but rather stabilizes the double ironies and undecidables of interpretation *as* undecidables."[45] To be sure, some critics, seeking to discard some of the juxtaposed possibilities, have sought to determine which of this set Chaucer really intends to offer, and indeed the ambiguity of the juxtaposition does not preclude an obscured singular intent. But any such detection of intent must first confront the multiplicity that hides it, and in the process must also explain that which accompanies that multiplicity in the performance's finale and is in fact even more jarring: the sudden, unanticipated, and apparently radical personality change of the narrator.

"lat us stynte of earnestful matere"

The Clerk, as we know, was before (according to the Host) "coy and stille" (IV.2); he responded "benignely" (IV.21), if perhaps secretly ironically, to the Host's boorishly jovial, half-mocking command to take his turn at tale-telling; and he was the kind of man who (according to the *General Prologue*) spoke "[n]ought o word . . . moore than was neede, / And that was seyd in forme and reverence" (I.304–5). But now the Clerk is suddenly gregarious, loquacious, openly (if enigmatically) ironic, whimsical, witty, and, most succinctly, playful – proposing, just before his concluding song, "lat us stynte of earnestful matere" (IV.1176). Some critics (especially earlier ones), befuddled by this personality change, and taking note of some inconsistencies among the manuscripts in how many of the epilogue's parts appear and in the order of its stanzas, have accused Chaucer of just fudging the ending, slapping on his own *tour-de-force* envoy despite its inconsistency of tone.[46] Others, however, have convincingly explained this manuscript variation as the product of scribal error, and, unlike as elsewhere in IV-V, Hengwrt betrays no signs of retroactive reconfiguration at this point.[47] Hence, although I would not preclude the possibility that the narrator of the Griselda story, through the end of the Petrarchan moralization at IV.1162, was a feature of a pre-*Canterbury Tales* translation of the *Historia* (in fact, I find it at least plausible), there is no concrete reason to doubt that Chaucer meant the speaker who addresses the group of "lordynges" at IV.1163 and who shortly refers to "the Wyves love of Bathe" (IV.1170) to be the Clerk whom the Host names at the beginning of the prologue.

To be sure, immediately subsequent to the Wife of Bath stanza as *Riverside* prints the epilogue, the intrusion of the rubric "Lenvoy de Chaucer" does create some confusion about the speaker's identity. This rubric in various forms with an attribution to Chaucer heads the following song in most of the earliest and best copies of the *Tales* (see *MR* 3.534–35), but its significance remains uncertain. In Hengwrt, the scribe wrote "Here is ended the tale of the clerk of oxenford" before the rubric (f. 190v), a sort of tale-*explicit* which is eventually followed by an *explicit* proper subsequent to the song and before the so-called Host's stanza, in which the Host responds to the tale of Griselda (f. 191r). To some, these features suggest that "Lenvoy de Chaucer" signals a shift in voice from character to author, just as the later *explicit* signals a shift in voices. But in Ellesmere presumably the same scribe waited until *after* the song, and indeed after the Host's stanza, to write the almost identical tale-*explicit* "Heere endeth the tale of the clerk of oxenford"; there is no other *explicit*, and the Host's stanza is headed by the rubric "Bihoold the murye wordes of the hoost" (f. 102r). The effect is ambiguous, to say the least, but because (in both manuscripts) the speaker in IV.1176 introduces the song *before* the rubic ("Herkneth my song that seith in this manere"), we have good reason to suppose (especially in Ellesmere) that the voice of the Clerk continues across the "Lenvoy" rubric and persists through the end of the song.

Indeed, some scholars, following the widespread assumption that the "Lenvoy" rubric is scribal, understand it not as signaling voice at all but rather authorship, seeing it as the scribe's attempt to indicate where the translation of Petrarch ends.[48] This view, however, does not adequately account for the position of the rubric, its very presence, or the differing placements of the tale-*explicit*. For if the scribe felt the need to mark the place where Chaucer leaves Petrarch behind, he would have done so in the actual place that this occurs, which is clearly two stanzas *before* the beginning of the song. But in fact I do not see why the scribe would have felt this need, or provide any sort of paratextual marker for the song, since it is already unmistakably introduced by the narrator in IV.1175 and then further emphasized by the abrupt change in stanza form. Instead, it seems more plausible that the scribe's confusion about the status of the song, reflected in his placing the tale-*explicit* in different manuscripts both before and after it, derives from the presence of the "Lenvoy" rubric in his exemplar, so that, like us, he was uncertain about what this rubric indicates regarding the song's relation to the Clerk's performance. That is, the most plausible explanation of the presence and position of the rubric is that Chaucer himself put it there, and hence I am suggesting that along with Clerk's designation of the song as his own in IV.1175, the rubric signals not an abrupt intrusion of an authorial voice but rather Chaucer's temporary identification with the Clerk, a possibility to which I will shortly return.[49]

Most readers of this passage have not worried much if at all over these issues and have instead tacitly embraced the view that it is the Clerk – as he is characterized in both the *Clerk's Prologue* and the *General Prologue* – who is the speaker of the entire epilogue; and they have then attributed the Clerk's apparent personality change to some aspect of his psyche or interactions with other pilgrims (especially, of course, the Wife of Bath), fleshing out a full character from the few details that we have.[50] As I have contended in this book's introduction, however, such psychological or dramatic explanations of these sorts of inconsistencies in characterization between portrait and link, as insightful as they have been, involve assumptions that are, at least, not self-evidently warranted. In this book's approach, I do not assume that Chaucer's artistic aims in the pilgrimage frame material for IV-V necessarily included psychological or dramatic coherence. Instead, I assume that Chaucer seeks in these passages to reflect on the different axiologies of different tales, especially those tales' articulations of their own literary value, and on how those articulations relate to the constellations of values that the pertinent pilgrims embody.

This approach has the benefits of putting aside the awkward and probably irrelevant issue of the realism of the Clerk's personality change and, more important, of explaining the coincidence of this sudden shift in tone with the Clerk's tacit refusal to choose among the array of literary self-valuations. For, indeed, it is this very shift in tone that *enacts* this tacit refusal: the sudden playfulness signals both the Clerk's awareness of the multiplicity of self-valuations and his gleeful embrace of the absence of any reconciliation among them – that is, the playfulness serves as formal device to signal that this literary self-consciousness is an aspect of the characterological field of the Clerk. Accordingly, the shift in tone suffuses that characterological field with the distinctive perspective of a tale-teller who has both mastered these various literary applications and risen above them all to convey, in the end, just the fact of that mastery. At the end of the performance, the literary value of the tale of Griselda does not rest with any one of its possibilities but rather with the transcendental perspective on literary value that their playful collision produces.

This perspective is very similar to the one that emerges over the course of the *House of Fame*, which in that case is the perspective of the accountant of literary value, whose literary axiological meditations become themselves the poem's proffered literary value. Not surprisingly (indeed, for Chaucer probably axiomatically), these similar perspectives are conveyed by equally similar tones. The implied author of the *House of Fame*, as we have seen, is a puckish bookworm who tells us that to find out more about the story of Dido, simply consult "Virgile in Eneydos / Or the Epistle of Ovyde," knowing that we know how these versions of the story radically differ; and who asserts that he does not wish any "wight" to have his "name in honde," in the very poem in which he has a Dantean Eagle name him for posterity. Surely this poet is much the same as the one who offers a tale by the laureate clerk Petrarch but concludes by singing to the Wife of Bath, with inscrutable, self-reflexive irony, to "lat no clerk have cause or diligence / To write of you a storie of swich mervaille / As of Grislidis" (IV.1185–87).[51] For this sort of poet, the distinction between earnest and game, and thus between their predictable literary values, appears to collapse under the weight of self-conscious irony – irony of some undecidable degree aimed at some undecidable target.

That the wry puppet master of the *House of Fame* – so closely associated in that poem, as we have seen, with the flesh-and-blood Chaucer – reappears in the epilogue to the Clerk's performance may well be the point of the enigmatic rubric "Lenvoy de Chaucer." In this book's approach to such moments, we need not decide, as I do not think Chaucer did, whose specific voice we are hearing in the ensuing song. The perspective and tone of the epilogue in the two stanzas before the song – that is, after IV.1162 – are consistent with what follows and, in Ellesmere at least, the entire epilogue is formally marked as within (and as the culmination of) the characterological field of the Clerk. Characterological fields are always open to one or more of the author's voices (of which, in a work like the *Canterbury Tales*, there are many). Such authorial voices may be more or less hostile to, sympathetic with, or, as here, the secret sharer of the voice of the character. Given the similarity in axiological perspective between the *House of Fame* and the Clerk's performance, we may fairly suspect that Chaucer conflates his voice with the Clerk's at this point in IV-V to signal to us that the literary axiology of the Clerk's performance was once – and perhaps to some degree still is – his own. The literary value of accounting for literary value reemerges in the Clerk's performance displaced upon the figure of an Oxford student (which, as the next section explores, alters it in important ways), but Chaucer, in his playful rubric, indicates that the stakes of this proposal for a literary axiology are that of the sacrifices that he himself has made in the past (and perhaps also at this very moment) in order to write at all.

In the *House of Fame* an axiological apologia emerges through the orchestration of the poem's literary axiology with the characterological field of the narrator/poet, which refracts the axiological environment of

Chaucer's occupation as customs controller. The question, therefore, to ask about the Clerk's performance is how an axiological apologia emerges through an orchestration of the literary axiology of the prologue, tale, and epilogue with the characterological field of its narrator/poet, which in this case refracts the axiological person of the Clerk's portrait, and the axiological environment that the Clerk's occupation in turn mediates.

Axiological Person

The evidence suggests that Chaucer's assignment of the Clerk to the tale of Griselda was a decisive one. Although we have no way of knowing whether he had this assignment in mind whenever he first translated the *Historia*, the manuscripts suggest that when he compiled the story into the *Tales* the assignment was firm.[52] And at first glance, the rationale for the assignment seems obvious enough: the Clerk clearly seems an apt teller for a (supposedly) spiritually edifying story taken from the famous clerk Petrarch. Yet, of course, Chaucer need not have written the prologue in such a manner to so identify the story, and he was certainly capable of assigning (supposedly) spiritually edifying narratives to seemingly less suitable pilgrims, such as the Physician. The rationale for the assignment, then, likely possesses significance beyond mere social and professional appropriateness.

Ever since Kittredge (and to some degree before), one ready explanation has been that the Clerk, offended by the Wife's depiction of her clerical fifth husband Jankyn, as well as her general usurpation of clerkly authority on the matter of female sovereignty, counters with the tale of uber-passive Griselda.[53] Others have conceived the portrait as a kind of embodied thematic signaling device for some clerkly idea to be found within the tale. For example, Laura Ashe contends that Griselda models the Clerk's Augustinian reading habits.[54] More commonly, however, even those who look elsewhere than the marriage debate still conceive the portrait to be a depiction of a more-or-less dramatically coherent individual (although in recent studies, perhaps wary of the Kittredgean tradition, they do so usually tacitly and sometimes alongside explicit demurrals otherwise). These sorts of studies find a rationale for the pilgrim assignment in the Clerk's dramatically rendered personal intentions, psyche, institutional conditioning, and/or personal historical context; and this rationale typically supports readings that assign the tale's interpretively problematic elements to one or more of the Clerk's dramatized peculiarities, as in the otherwise rather different studies by Peggy Knapp, Lee Patterson, Carolyn Dinshaw, and Warren Ginsberg.[55]

I have considered in this book's introduction the assumptions, limits, and potential pitfalls of these kinds of approaches, as well as the similarities and differences between them and mine. Following the principles that I outlined there, I propose only that at some indefinite point in the compositional process Chaucer chose to associate the portrait of the Clerk with the tale of Griselda, and proceeded then to author the prologue and (the non-Petrarchan portion of) the epilogue that enact this choice, perhaps even completing the latter, with its reference to the Wife of Bath, some considerable time after the former (i.e., late in his work on the *Tales*, after he had developed the organization that has come down us). Under these diminished assumptions, I follow those critics who see the rationale for the assignment as primarily thematic rather than dramatic, but I do not also then presume, as most do, that tale and portrait are mutually calibrated to one another. Rather, I contend just that Chaucer wished readers to encounter the literary axiology of the Clerk's performance through the lens of the axiological person of the Clerk's portrait, even if he may have originally written tale and portrait as independent compositions.

In fleshing-out this contention and ultimately, thereby, defining the axiological apologia of the Clerk's performance, I focus on two key questions. First, I briefly consider why Chaucer, in the passage that associates tale and portrait, also announces that tale as one by the laureate poet Petrarch (recalling, again, that he was under no obligation to name his *auctor*, and does so unprecedentedly here in the *Tales*). Second, at greater length, I explore how the teller's depiction as an impoverished university student shapes how we are to evaluate the performance's literary meta-axiology. The latter question has some bearing on the first, since, while the Clerk's general learnedness makes him more akin to Petrarch than any other pilgrim, in other ways he is an unapt choice as spokesperson for the laureate. As is well known, British scholasticism, Aristotelian logic, and many aspects of the fourteenth-century university in general, to all of which the Clerk's portrait alludes, were anathema to Petrarch. Although we do not know how much Chaucer knew of "Petrarch's distaste for the kind of learning that the Clerk ostensibly represents," it seems likely at the very least that Chaucer's notion of what it meant to be a "lauriat poete" who "[e]nlumyned al Ytaillle of poetrie" was not merely a lofty version of what it meant to be a poor fourteenth-century Oxford student.[56] Rather, what must have been important to Chaucer is the relation between what these two different kinds of clerks represent.

Petrarchan Ideal

Middleton has provided a penetrating account of what Chaucer may have glimpsed in Petrarch's laureate ideas about the poet and poetry, and of how he sought to situate these ideas in respect to the axiological environments of English courtly and clerkly writing. The laureate ideal that Chaucer detected, according to Middleton, imagines a poet who "holds no office or place; the community within which he acts has no institutional location, living only in the pages its members exchange and share."[57] The hidden negotiation between the sort of tale that the Host asks from the Clerk and what the latter actually provides thus enacts Chaucer's negotiation between the laureate ideal and the options for literary practice available in late fourteenth-century England:

> The interplay between Harry's instruction and the Clerk's "obeisant" narration is a confrontation of the Petrarchan Clerk as an emanation and creation of his own books, a man wholly of letters, with the more familiar socially-embodied French and English sense of the Clerk as speaker in his writing, a corrective voice and public presence, whether in exhorting the layman to repentance or the king to a proper view of his office and duties. As the tale closes, it successively gives standing to each of the competing views of clerkly eloquence and its role in the world, then, with the Envoy, adds one more: that of the courtier-poet and recreative counsellor to the noble.[58]

What occurs across the course of the Clerk's performance, in other words, is, first, a confrontation with "the more familiar" set of options for literary value that the Host presents (some of them negatively) in his command to the Clerk: homiletic ("precheth nat, as freres doon in Lente" [IV.12]), politically advisory ("whan that men to kynges write" [IV.17]), and recreative ("Telle us som murie thyng of aventures" [IV.15]). Second, by way of the Clerk's occulted response to this command, Chaucer posits the alternative of an ideal of literature as a value in itself (of benefit spiritually, morally, etc., but not reducible to the function of providing those values), thereby also positing the occupation of the poet as valuable for its own sake, "an emanation and creation of his own books, a man wholly of letters." Yet – whether because of Chaucer's awareness, as Wallace argues, of Petrarch's role as a literate lackey of despots; because of skepticism about the laureate ideal for other spiritual or ethical reasons; or because the laureate ideal was simply impossible to achieve within the English fields of cultural production – Chaucer in the Clerk's performance affirms neither the Petrarchan, nor the other literary axiological options. Instead, as we have seen, in the culminating move of the Clerk's performance,

Chaucer juxtaposes several possibilities for the value of the fiction that the Clerk relates, providing, as Middleton puts it, a "playfully enigmatic" "guided tour of several specifically secular literary canons and ideals current at the end of the fourteenth century."[59]

In this very playfulness, as I have just claimed, Chaucer in fact posits a meta-axiological value for the fiction of the *Clerk's Tale* and for the poet who tells it, a value more or less the same as the one that in the *House of Fame* emerges as the value of accounting for literary value. In this manner, he circles back to the opening confrontation with the Host and offers a somewhat different response to the options that the latter presents. Wishing to escape the confines of available axiological environments – or, as we saw with the *House of Fame*, actually also requiring such an escape because of his socioeconomic position – Chaucer shows us the laureate ideal not as a real proposition, but as an alien analogue that helps to clarify what may be possible in England: the more constrained, limited, betwixt-and-between autonomy of the accountant of literary value. Petrarch appears at the opening of the Clerk's performance, then, for much the same reason that Dante appears in the *House of Fame*: not only do they serve, respectively, as those works' source *auctores* (Dante more loosely, of course), but also they stand for a *trecento* literary ideal toward which Chaucer expresses skepticism even while he seeks to translate it, at least in part, into his own circumstances. With the Clerk's performance, therefore, Chaucer presents a version of the same solution that the *House of Fame* offers to the problem of determining the value of the occupation of the kind of poet that Chaucer wished to become within the constraints of his axiological environment. And, as this solution is one that he formulated *prior* to the *Canterbury Tales*, it accordingly serves here as a starting point, the initial position in the IV-V sequence.

Clerkly Chaucer

In bringing this solution into the framework of the *Tales*, however, Chaucer obviously incurs one very large difference: he swaps out the axiological environment of the occupation of controller of customs for that of an Oxford University student. And this difference takes us to the second key question about the pilgrim assignment: why Chaucer chooses the latter occupation as the social identity of the teller for this particular tale. In this regard, we may first observe that the occupational difference between Chaucer as controller and the Clerk as university student – or the difference between their social identities more generally – is not as large as it may initially seem. Some affinity between author and character is already evident at the level of literary representation. The bookish, introverted self-image that Chaucer evokes in the very *House of Fame* passage that identifies his occupation – when, for example, the Eagle accuses Geoffrey, "Thou goost hom to thy hous anoon, / And also domb as any stoon, / Thou sittest at another book / Tyl fully daswed ys thy look; / and lyvest thus as an heremyte" (655–59) – seems to reappear in the portrait of the Clerk as one for whom it was "levere have at his beddes heed, / Twenty bookes . . . / . . . / Than robes riche, or fithele, or gay sautrie" (I.293–95). To be sure, this latter description serves to provide an anticipatory contrast with that other Oxford clerk, "hende Nicholas," and in the *House of Fame* the Eagle's wry conclusion to his portrait of Geoffrey, "Although thyn abstinence ys lyte" (660), does not so well match the Clerk. Nonetheless, as many have noticed, in addition to the Clerk's general similarities to Chaucer's bookish self-representations, even within the *Canterbury Tales* itself there are parallels between Chaucer and the Clerk, as in the Host's accosting of the Clerk as riding "coy and stille" (IV.2) and his later accosting of Chaucer, "Thou lookest as thou woldest fynde an hare, / For evere upon the ground I se thee stare" (VII.696–97).[60] Such similarities in dramatized personal dispositions seem then doubled by a similarity in implied authorial dispositions; in addition to the return of the *House of Fame*'s puppet master in the epilogue of the Clerk's performance, we have, for example, the ironic playfulness that permeates *Sir Thopas*. For these reasons, a long critical tradition has detected at least a partial authorial self-portrait in the Clerk, however circumscribed by other more predominant aspects of the character. Indeed, on the further evidence of Chaucer's ample learnedness, early biographers like John Leland were often convinced that Chaucer must have spent some time at university (a supposition rejected by all modern biographers).[61]

Moreover, and for present purposes more important, in addition to these admittedly broad similarities in literary representation, Chaucer's actual social identity overlapped with a clerkly one in several, socially palpable ways. As M. T. Clanchy has shown, the term *clericus* in late medieval England carried a rather diffuse set of denotations, referring in some cases specifically to men in orders but often merely to someone who could read Latin.[62] The Middle English *clerk* accordingly possessed a similar semantic range, although, as the organization of the *MED* entry for the noun suggests, there was perhaps more distinct division into the three occupational categories of: (1) clergyman; (2) someone who possesses an identity broadly similar to what we now call an intellectual; and (3) someone whose occupation involves extensive work with documents, such as town clerk. Chaucer – as both translator of Boethius and controller of customs required to produce a steady flow of documents *manu sua propria* – clearly qualifies as *clerk* in the latter two senses.[63] Furthermore, in the eyes of the *MED* editors, the occupation of university student was a subcategory of the second branch (i.e., *MED* 2c), and this semantic affiliation is indeed not merely a reflex of the requirements of lexicographic form. As Katherine Zieman and others have observed, of men who went to university, the number who did not later become clergyman but instead used their training in some documentary capacity (thereby falling also into the third category of *clerk*) was proportionally large – likely, in fact, the majority.[64] Since these occupations were also increasingly held by men who, like Chaucer, received an education elsewhere than the university, the socially salient distinction between the university-trained clerk and the intellectual who lacked this academic background was in many contexts not very pronounced. Indeed, that Chaucer's predecessors in the London controllership were king's clerks, and thus almost certainly university men, suggests just how indistinct the social difference was. Gower's famous epithet for Chaucer, Venus's "owne clerk," hence was perhaps not merely a literary conceit but also carried the wit of resonance with what Gower perceived to be Chaucer's social identity as a secular clerk.[65]

Oxford

Nonetheless, whether or not one went to university (and received at least the first tonsure) was, obviously, still a socially legible difference, one which Chaucer, precisely because of the proximity of his social identity within the shared categories of intellectual and documentary laborer, no doubt had occasion to feel more or less acutely within the variety of circles in which he moved, from those including Oxford logician Ralph Strode to those including aristocrats like Sir Lewis Clifford. In this light, then, it is particularly telling, on the one hand, that Chaucer fashions the social identity of the Clerk to cast into relief his own *difference* from the pilgrim – for the latter is throughout, and from his very first appearance, defined as a "Clerk ... of Oxenford" (I.285) – but also, on the other hand, that Chaucer emphasizes this difference against an internally represented and externally understood background of their similarity. If the similarity provides the basis for the translation of the controller meta-axiology of the *House of Fame* into the Clerk's performance in the *Canterbury Tales*, then the difference signals the essential distinction of the new context. It signals, in other words, what the axiological environment of the university, rather than the controllership, makes possible for the literary axiology of the *House of Fame* – or, as we will see, what the new environment discloses about that axiology.

At first glance, the translation would appear promising, since as an institution Oxford was about as autonomous – in the sense of free from the control of town government, baronial or royal dominion, or episcopal or papal authority – as any medieval institution could be, or at least it was locked in a constant struggle to achieve such autonomy, achieving enough success to keep the ideal alive.[66] Then as now, universities were the place where (in theory and according to some) the mastery of diverse branches of knowledge became itself a valuable endeavor, whatever may be the specific utility of those branches of knowledge. As universities were "essentially masters' guilds that were governed by the teaching masters solely in the academic interests of their own members," the institutional autonomy they sought was, at least in part, aimed at insulating this meta-axiological endeavor from the interference of those who had an interest in the utility of the knowledge that they housed.[67] In contrast, therefore, with the controllership – which held no actual institutional autonomy but only the fraught, notional autonomy paradoxically achieved through multiple, conflicting allegiances – the university would seem to offer an institutionally grounded inward-oriented axiological environment that would be the ideal nursery for a meta-axiological poetics. Within this environment, the poet's mastery of the diverse branches of literary value would simply duplicate more narrowly the enclosing institutional meta-axiology. The axiological apologia of the *Clerk's Tale* would thus emerge homologously as a clerkly poet's literary meta-axiology within the enclosing more general meta-axiology of the institution that provides for that poet occupational legitimacy.

To be sure, the university as fundamentally meta-axiological is only one way to imagine it, among many others, and most of those who favor this vision would admit that it is an ideal to which to aspire rather than a condition easily or fully achievable in practice.[68] Nonetheless, Chaucer appears to have thoroughly calibrated his *General Prologue* portrait of the Clerk to emphasize this vision to the exclusion of all others; indeed, the Clerk here is virtually the vision's personification. Jill Mann long ago perspicaciously identified this peculiar manner in which Chaucer renders the estate of the student, noting the Clerk's "ivory tower" "remoteness from the world of social ends," with "Chaucer's admiration . . . directed towards the Clerk's proficiency in his professional functions [i.e., learning and teaching], not towards the purpose [i.e., instrumental value] of those functions." In a word – the portrait's own word – the Clerk is not "worldly" (I.292), which in its context does not mean that he has instead chosen a path of spiritual contemplation but rather, as Mann remarks about the general impression of the portrait, that he has taken the road of "the eternal student."[69]

Crucially, however, whatever desirability this status may have had for Chaucer or his audience, it was in practice quite far from the social norm. Whether Chaucer imagines the Clerk as working toward his baccalaureate or toward a higher degree (an unanswerable question that has long vexed literal-minded critics), the occupation of university student was even more normatively temporary than it is now. For the vast majority, the socio-economic and spiritual rationale for attending university was to receive training that qualified one to work outside of it. As Guy Fitch Lytle writes,

> Universities existed primarily to train youths for careers in the church and state. That training produced the necessary qualified personnel to staff royal, noble, and ecclesiastical administrations, to serve the sundry needs of the church and to ply the emerging professions in an increasingly complex society. A university degree that led to such employment and promotion also offered a promising avenue of social mobility and a chance to create or to augment personal and familial fortunes great or small.[70]

This utilitarian motivation, given the social background of the typical English undergraduate, is neither surprising nor something most students would seek to disguise. For in the late fourteenth century, Oxford was not, as it would come to be in the Early Modern period, a conveyor of great symbolic capital. The wealthy – whether noble, gentle, or mercantile – did not frequently send their sons to university (and when they did, those sons usually focused on law); the majority of students instead seem to have been "sons of rural farmers and small holders."[71] In comparison with undergraduates at southern European universities, English students were "less mature, less socially elevated and less experienced in worldly affairs."[72] Furthermore, as mentioned above, many students, perhaps the majority, did not stay to earn a degree, and there was no stigma attached to early departure. Some amount of training could qualify one as enough of a *clericus* to obtain employment in the church or in civil service positions like those held by Chaucer.[73] While some students did indeed attend university for motives resembling that of the Clerk – a group

R. N. Swanson refers to as that of the "committed student" – and some attended merely to escape some other undesirable situation, Swanson concludes, "The majority of students . . . went to university largely as an investment: education paid off."[74]

Even the employment that we may fairly imagine as the Clerk's aspirant occupation, that of university scholar-teacher – that is, the late medieval regent master – was a temporary one, imposed for a few years upon those earning a Master's degree.[75] Financially dependent as it was on student lecture fees (i.e., lacking a salary or system of tenure), this position paid rather poorly, and in England, unlike some places on the Continent, regent masters did not obtain in compensation very lofty social status. While the financially self-sustaining system of lecture fees did help to maintain an axiological environment of some autonomy, so that "[r]egent masters were free to pursue lines of intellectual enquiry that were independent of the siren call of crude market forces," most did not possess that motivation but rather left as soon as their regency was complete or, following that, as soon as a better opportunity arose – a noteworthy exception being John Wyclif, with his some thirty years at Oxford.[76] There are records of a few college fellows with extended stays at university, one for as long as fifty years, but such individuals also were very far from the norm.[77] As William Courtenay summarizes, "For the majority of medieval scholastics, it is fair to say that they did not expect (and may not even have desired) to make a home and career for themselves in the world of ideas."[78] While the aim of the university was, at least in part, to achieve institutional autonomy, the vast majority of the individuals who read and lectured in its halls did not share a corresponding personal aim. And while this difference between the institution and its members may have been contradictory, it was no more so then than now, for the university has always justified its relative insulation from society as a necessary condition for its service to society.

With Chaucer's Clerk, however, we have an almost total and indeed seemingly active refusal of this contradiction, which is to say that the axiological person constituted by the Clerk embodies simultaneously an affirmation of the meta-axiological university ideal and a negation of the "worldly" or instrumental value of the training that the university bestows upon its members. And in fact only this sort of axiological person could serve as a promising occupational vessel for the literary meta-axiology imported into the *Tales* from the *House of Fame*, because, as welcoming as the autonomy of the university may be to this meta-axiology, the latter would quickly splinter upon any demand to put literary value to some use.

"A Clerk ther was of Oxenford"

The details of the Clerk's *General Prologue* portrait evoke this affirmation/negation dynamic from top to bottom. In its second line, the narrator tells us that the Clerk "unto logyk had longe ygo" (I.286). Although critics have often read this remark as a cue to associate the Clerk specifically with this particular subject (and have quibbled about how long "longe ygo" means),[79] the line's mildly figurative locution, with its sense of traveling somewhere, suggests that "logyk" is better read here as a synecdoche for the insular world of the university generally, as demarcated by the arcane (and hence non-instrumental) nature of its curriculum, and in particular of the arts course. In fourteenth-century Oxford, logic, and Aristotelian logic specifically, dominated the arts course – "overwhelmingly so in the first two years" – and much of rest of the curriculum as well.[80] For the same reason, the later reference to "Aristotle and his philosophie" [I.295] does not by itself make the Clerk an emblem for Aristotelianism, but merely aligns his desire for books with precisely those an Oxford student would need. The "technical language of logic that was used in all fields of study," as Ruth Mazo Karras explains, served as a "private language" for university members (even more private than the Latin they were required to speak at most times), "an academic jargon" for which "there was no pretense that it was intended for the general public."[81] Whatever the actual utility of the arts curriculum for the positions students eventually sought to gain outside the university (about which historians differ), within the institution the value of its mastery was, as we might expect, defined entirely in institutional terms.[82]

Most pertinently, a facility with logic was tested and recognized within the academic ritual of public disputation. Held at various times and involving virtually all members of the university, whether as participants or spectators, the disputation was the heart of the university in respect to its meta-axiological ideal, the place where questions were debated for no other purpose than to debate them. It was especially prominent in the final stage of undergraduate training, in which "the student had to respond at least one year in 'sophistical' disputations (*de sophismatibus*), during which time he was known as a *sophista*. These public disputations concerned particularly difficult or enigmatic problems arising from propositions in grammar or logic, including the paradoxes (*insolubilia*)."[83] The Host's accusation in the prologue to the *Clerk's Tale*, "I trowe ye studie aboute som sophyme" (IV.5), evokes these sophistical disputations, bringing them thereby into the Clerk's characterological field, regardless of what the accusation may or may not say about the Clerk's stage of study.[84] And in light of the ensuing nature of the Clerk's performance, we may conclude that, indeed, the Clerk had been meditatively contemplating (*MED studien* v. 3a) "som sophyme": namely, Petrarch's *Historia*, which by the culmination of his performance emerges as a species of literary *insolubilia*. I do not mean this supposition dramatically, of course, but rather axiologically: the Host's use of the term *sophyme* connects back to the portrait to help establish a meta-axiological perspective, in which the value of the *Clerk's Tale*, like that of a *sophyme*, is precisely the value of considering its value. In recalling the portrait, *sophyme* in one breath translates a literary axiology like that of the *House of Fame* into the axiological environment of the university.

Critics have long understood the anti-materialism of the portrait's next six lines – e.g., regarding the Clerk's "leene . . . hors" and "thredbare . . . courtepy" (I.287, I.290), which culminate in the statement about his desire for "[t]wenty bookes, clad in blak or reed" (I.294) – as a kind of negative image of the materialism of other clerical pilgrims, such as the Monk. Yet as the couplet that explicitly denies his worldliness suggests – "For he hadde geten hym yet no benefice, / Ne was so worldly for to have office" (I.291–92) – these lines also specify the worldly *cost* of the Clerk's embodiment of the university's meta-axiology, of his having long gone "unto logyk." Like many of those who attended Oxford in Chaucer's day, the Clerk is evidently barely able to cover the costs of his education, and perhaps we are meant to think of him as one of the *pauperes* whose financial straits entitled them to forgiveness of all or part of the university's entrance fee.[85] But unlike the actual typical poor scholar, the Clerk does not seek to parlay his university training into the "office" that would produce a return on the investment in his university education.

To be sure, the phrasing "hadde geten hym yet" implies a neutral-to-positive attitude toward the less worldly but still remunerative option of a benefice (which would be especially attractive to the Clerk if, like Wyclif's, it enabled him to stay at Oxford). Nevertheless, the syntactic logic of this line's conjunction with it rhyming partner implies the perception that, in fact, a benefice was not just provisionally unavailable but also not likely forthcoming – i.e., the preemptively rejected alternative of "office" is entertained at all because its rhyme pair, "benefice," is doubtful. Such a perception, in fact, is no mere idiosyncrasy of this portrait. As Lytle has argued, there was a "crisis in patronage" for university students in this period that led to significantly fewer benefices granted to them. Although historians continue to debate the extent, duration, and sources of this crisis, for present purposes what is most important is that contemporary recognition of the problem and a perception of its severity were widespread.[86] If we may fairly suppose, then, that the not-yet-obtained benefice is to be understood as unlikely, then the Clerk's impoverished condition threatens to be persistent; and if his only avenue of remedy is "worldly . . . office," then that persistence is a direct consequence of his refusal of the latter. Although such images of poverty as these lines depict are highly typical in accounts of the estate of the university student, those accounts often present them as a sign of society's misguided values – its lack of appreciation for the meta-axiology of the university.[87] With the Clerk and his refusal of "office," that image of poverty becomes instead an emblem of that meta-axiology.

The nature of this emblem, already evident in the remark about the Clerk's having long gone "unto logyk," emerges unmistakably in the lines that contrast his poverty with his desire for "Twenty bookes, clad in blak or reed, / Of Aristotle and his philosophie," which would be "levere" to him than "robes riche, or fithele, or gay sautrie" (I.293–96). As mentioned above, "Aristotle" here is best read not so much in a specific sense but rather as a synecdoche for the university's arts curriculum, as most of the books that Oxford students in the arts course used in Chaucer's day were either by Aristotle or commentaries on Aristotle.[88] The couplet thus weighs the Clerk's devotion to this curriculum against worldly distractions, signified here by the worldly ways in which he (like that other Oxford clerk, Nicholas) might spend his meager allowance. And, indeed, the tricky syntax of these lines heightens the parallel between the Clerk's rejection of "robes riche, or fithele, or gay sautrie" with his earlier refusal of worldly "office," since the introductory clause "For hym was levere" (I.293) seems at first to offer an explanation for the preceding line's "Ne was so worldly"; and because of the lingering conjunctive force of "For," this confusion is not entirely cleared away by the belated appearance of the actual objects of comparison three lines later. The overall effect is to emphasize the Clerk's inward orientation, an unmaterialistic unworldliness that is identified with the non-instrumentality of the arts course, the meta-axiological heart of the university. Indeed, the punning joke in the couplet that follows these lines – "But al be that he was a phiosophre, / Yet hadde he but litel gold in cofre" (I.297–98) – neatly condenses this worldly/unworldly binary into one word, with the alchemical "philosophre" standing in here for a worldly, (putatively) remunerative intellectual "office" in contrast with immersion in "Aristotle and his philosophie."

The explicit consideration of the Clerk's finances that follows powerfully reinforces this inward orientation, defining the necessary economic interface between worldly and unworldly in a way that wholly subsumes the former into the latter:

> But al that he myghte of his freendes hente,
> On bookes and on lernynge he it spente,
> And bisily gan for the soules preye
> Of hem that yaf hym wherewith to scoleye.
> Of studie took he moost cure and moost heede. (I.299–303)

It was quite typical for university students to be funded by friends and family, and the fact that the Clerk spends all those funds on his education seems straightforwardly virtuous, in comparison to what else we might imagine (e.g., the escapades of the Cambridge clerks in the *Reeve's Tale*). But the verb *hente* here is odd. Chaucer's most common use of this word, by far, is in the sense of "to seize" (*MED henten* v. 1a), and the action is usually an aggressive and often violent one, as when – to choose just a few particularly vivid instances of many possible examples – Symkyn in the *Reeve's Tale* "hente hym [Alayn] despitously" (I.4274), the "cursed Jew" in the *Prioress's Tale* "hym [the "litel clergeon"] hente" (VII.570), and, most pertinently, the sergeant in the *Clerk's Tale* "hente" both of Walter and Griselda's children (IV.534, 676), which are the only two uses of the verb in the tale.[89] If we thus translate lines I.299–300 as "And all the money that he might aggressively seize from his friends he spent on books and instruction," what before seemed straightforwardly virtuous now appears rather obsessive, even manic, an impression that the no-longer-fully-innocent emphatic statement of the Clerk's dedication to "studie" of line I.303 seems to underscore. Although Chaucer's use of *henten* here is probably not this extreme, his habitual usage suggests that we are to hear at least a hint of aggression. Narrowly driven, the Clerk energetically secures an inward flow of money, a source of worldly value that does not return to the world in the form of "benefice" or "office" but only in the other-worldly form of the Clerk's prayers for his investors.

The famous line that concludes the portrait, "And gladly wolde he lerne and gladly teche" (I.308), represents a similar inward orientation. Teaching, as I have mentioned, was not a true career at late fourteenth-century Oxford but rather more of degree requisite, and indeed to my ears the repetition of the adverb "gladly" flattens the distinction between the two verbs it modifies: together they denote the essential, inward-oriented activities of the occupation of the particular kind of late medieval university student embodied by the Clerk.[90] Even if it does also suggest a future career as regent master, the line communicates a non-normative desire to remain within the university, to continue in a condition that is intended to be a temporary suspension from the world. However noble the sentiment may be, it is – like the refusal of worldly office – nonetheless suggestive of the Clerk's thoroughgoing embodiment of the university's meta-axiology, to the exclusion of the more instrumental axiology of both actual students in the university and their benefactors outside of it.

E. T. Donaldson long ago detected a note of bourgeois, materialist anti-intellectualism in the *General Prologue* narrator's attitude toward the Clerk, which attitude he then ascribed to the character of Chaucer the pilgrim, who in regard to "the Clerk's failure to make money" reflects a "typical . . . half-patronizing, half-admiring *un*understanding that practical men of business display toward academics."[91] As is usually the case, Donaldson's ear for the nuances of Chaucer's poetry is trustworthy, even if his theory of a dramatically coherent Chaucer-the-pilgrim character (which in this instance obviously betrays his own axiological commitments) may not be sustained. For the attitude Donaldson detects is indeed the sort of counter-academic axiology that he describes, and, as such, regardless of how much it may characterize the narrator, it serves as a crucial contribution to the characterological field of the Clerk. Latent in the very tension between the Clerk's unworldliness and what Chaucer and his audience knew to be the more normative career predilections and actual career paths of university students, the attitude helps to define, by implied contrast, the very distinctive embodiment of the meta-axiology of the university that constitutes the axiological person of the Clerk.

The axiological apologia of the Clerk's performance emerges, then, through the association of this axiological person with Chaucer's rendering of the tale of Griselda and the meta-axiological, quasi-autonomous position of the poet that the epilogue to that tale eventually manifests. As we have seen, the Clerk's portrait depicts an occupation of non-instrumental intellectual labor. Spiritual and moral value are, on the horizon, the legitimating values of this occupation, but they stand at arm's-length from the Clerk's academic activities, lending them a sheen of autonomy, a value in itself. By associating the tale of Griselda with this portrait in the manner that he does, Chaucer recalibrates the meta-axiology of the *House of Fame* to fit the imagined, idealized axiological environment of the university. In this environment, the particular value of English literature and of the occupation of literary author that he conceived in that earlier poem would be fully legible socially and more stable institutionally. With the Clerk, in other words, Chaucer imagines the university as a nurturing institutional home for the kind of English poet that the *House of Fame* projects: he imagines, in short, poetry-making as a legitimate masculine occupation in itself. And yet, in the very process of translating this axiological apologia from the customs house to Oxford, its limits become evident.

The Clerk's Adolescence

The Clerk's approximate age is nowhere explicitly mentioned, and yet most readers carry away the impression that he is a young man, and they do so despite the stubborn efforts over the years by a few critics to steer them in the other direction, or at least to call attention to the ambiguity in this regard.[92] In fact, inasmuch as Chaucer meant the Clerk to be typical of his estate in respect to age, then, notwithstanding the portrait's ambiguity, his contemporary readers likely did assume a vague youthfulness. According to Alan Cobban, the age of matriculation at late medieval Oxford seems to have been "between 15 and 17," and, as discussed above, most men, even those who stayed to study for a higher degree, left the university as soon as a desirable professional opportunity became available.[93] Even the faculty tended to be on the young side, with many of the lecturers in the arts course "only in their early to mid-twenties."[94] Of greater importance than such literal considerations, however, is the more general and more striking impression of the Clerk's being somehow not fully matured. In part, this impression derives from the Clerk's non-normative desire to stay within the boundaries of the university for as long as possible, which in effect defers his inevitable entrance into the workforce, whether through a "benefice" or "office." As Ann Astell writes, the Clerk's portrait "depicts someone who is 'unfinished,' *in potentia* ... he could become a schoolteacher, a secretary to a lord, a civil administrator, a physician, or even a lawyer." For Astell, this state makes him "uniquely potent," but inasmuch as he does not desire any of the latter offices (but would rather seize his friends' money and spend it on books by or about Aristotle), we may just as accurately conclude, vis-à-vis his professional potential, that he is uniquely impotent.[95]

Impotency, in a somewhat more literal sense, is also part of what is behind the impression of youthfulness. For as Karras has described, although the various estates had specific protocols for achieving masculinity, the normative, most unambiguous path from adolescence into full, unequivocal manhood in the late Middle Ages was through marriage and then legitimate procreation, or at least through having "the potential" for the latter. For the celibate clergy, this gender ideology obviously presented a challenge; as Karras writes, "One could indeed make a case that such men were never fully adult or fully masculine." In practice, the further one traveled up the clerical hierarchy, the less problematic this gender conundrum became, as, for example, priests "took the title of 'Father,' and as representatives of God they had as much or more authority as a head of household."[96] In the Clerk's case, however, the benefice that would support his joining the priesthood seems doubtful, and the more "worldly" path into secular office – in which occupation he could marry, as did Chaucer's clerical fellow civil servant Thomas Hoccleve – he has refused.

To be sure, as Karras also shows, university men had their own protocols for masculinity, ones that were premised on their distinction from women by the very fact of their being members of the university, and in which achievement of masculinity was measured through intellectual competition with other men, preeminently in disputation.[97] Nonetheless, however much clerical masculinity we might imagine the Clerk as having earned in this respect, that these protocols had little purchase outside the university is evident in the manner in which the Host addresses him. In both instances, as many have noted, the Host unmistakably feminizes him: at the end of the *General Prologue*, when he exhorts both the Prioress and the Clerk to "lat be [their] shamefastnesse" (I.840) and draw straws, and, more pointedly, when he calls on the Clerk to tell his tale, describing him as like "a mayde / . . . new spoused, sittynge at bord" (IV.2–3) (thereby proleptically associating him with Griselda – and thus also with May, Dorigen, and even the Merchant's new wife). The Host perhaps means no offense, since, as Mann notes, a maidenly disposition was an estates ideal for sober, chaste university clerks; and notably, the Clerk appears at this point to accept (however ironically) this gendered interpellation by "benignely" responding to the Host, "I am under youre yerde."[98] However much disputative acumen the Clerk's performance illustrates, it does not appear to translate into a perception of his manhood by those outside the university, and thus the university from that vantage point appears as an insular place where male adolescents, no matter what age, are not yet men.

In this light, it is striking that Chaucer assigns the Clerk a tale centered upon a marriage relationship. Inasmuch as the tale is, as Salter terms it, a "religious fable," the nature of the fabular vehicle is not especially important, and yet, as Salter also cogently shows, it is the refusal of the literality of that vehicle to give way completely to moralization that makes the tale so difficult to interpret.[99] The Clerk's ironic treatment of this literality in the epilogue of his performance folds that literality into the tale's overall meta-axiology, but in the process he necessarily calls attention to this literality and hence also to his very difference from, say, Jankyn, the Wife of Bath's clerical fifth husband. In a manner of speaking, the return of the Wife of Bath – who in the dramatic conceit of the linking passage stands for a flesh-and-blood woman, in contrast with the figurative Griselda – is the return of the repressed: not something repressed within the psyche of the teller, but what the Clerk as axiological person, as constituted by his portrait, represses (rather poorly) about the temporary, liminal, insular status of the university's meta-axiology. In embodying this axiology, the Clerk cannot but appear, to those outside the axiological environment of the university, as an adolescent, as one who has not yet entered either the occupational or sexual economy, and who thus lacks the Wife's "experience." The Merchant, as we will see in the next chapter, acutely perceives this precise failing. The Clerk's performance, when considered independently, is without question stylistically sophisticated, narratively complex, and thematically wide ranging. But in its function as an articulation of an axiological apologia that would legitimate the writing of poetry as a masculine occupation, and in its position as the first sally in a four-part axiological meditation, it appears as an ambitious but ultimately youthful, even naïve, experiment.

CHAPTER 2

Merchant

This chapter argues that the Merchant's performance functions in the IV-V sequence as a symbolically paternal rebuke to the axiological apologia of the Clerk's performance. The latter, as argued in the previous chapter, imagines the university as a meta-axiological institution in which the question of the value of fiction may be endlessly deferred because it is endlessly debatable, and which consequently supplies a notional space for a quasi-autonomous occupation of secular poet. For the *Tales*-era Chaucer, such an axiological apologia, as a close cousin of that of the *House of Fame*, represented in the compressed timespan of his poetic career a youthful, optimistic, somewhat overly clever imagined harmonization of literary and occupational systems of value. For Chaucer looking back, it was an adolescent axiological apologia, embodied in the figure of the indeterminately aged but still somehow – through an implied economic and marital inexperience – not-yet-matured Clerk. Chaucer's Merchant is a figure of volte-face contrast, defined almost wholly by his experience in exactly these two realms, and telling a tale that (in effect) replays the Clerk's as a grand fable of discursive instrumentality, one that exposes the stories that we tell about the values that we hold to be mere smokescreens – or means – for ineluctable and inexplicable desire. With the Merchant's performance, Chaucer shows us the same axiological scope that the Clerk's performance ascribes to fiction but now conceives of that scope as illusive for the hearer and a means of deception for the teller, thereby condemning the Clerk's attempt (which is to say Chaucer's own attempt) to evade fiction's instrumental essence. Directed by a voice of masculine experience toward a figure of masculine adolescence, this condemnation declares that the axiological apologia of the Clerk should, so to speak, grow up and face reality.

This account of the Merchant's performance, although inflected toward my specific ends, aligns at a very general level with the views of a number of critics. Yet in order to fill in the relevant details of the performance's rich, multifaceted response to the Clerk's, and of its position in the IV-V sequence, I must wade into the roiling waters of several of the most contested, longstanding debates about the Merchant and his tale, on some of which I take atypical positions. The initial sections of this chapter reconsider these critical problems; subsequent sections examine the *Merchant's Prologue* and key moments in the tale in light of the positions that I take. The chapter then explores the significance of the tale's assignment to the Merchant, elaborating the axiological person that the pilgrim constitutes and the axiological apologia of the Merchant's performance as a whole. The chapter concludes by suggesting how the particular kind of paternal rebuke enacted by the Clerk-Merchant sequence so comprehensively clears the literary axiological ground that some sort of re-idealizing axiological response appears necessary to continue to write at all.

Masterful Negation

Oddly, behind the most chronic disagreements about the Merchant's performance is a pair of impressions about which there has been unusually broad and longstanding agreement. The first is that the tale is a masterpiece of comic narrative craft, a *tour de force* by a poet easily confident in a distinctive idiom that mixes together an astonishing array of generic and allusive ingredients in a pungently ironic sauce, producing an inimitable stew in which each element is both immediately isolatable and perfectly combined. As Helen Cooper puts it, "In its conflation of high and low style, idealism and cynicism, Christian and animal, romance and fabliau, the Merchant's Tale is one of the virtuoso pieces of the *Canterbury Tales* ... It is one of the most allusive stories in the whole collection, surpassed only by the Nun's Priest's."[1] Very few have judged the accomplishment of the tale's craft otherwise but instead have relished the wit of such moments as the sudden intrusion of a domestic squabble between pagan gods into an otherwise naturalistic setting, with Proserpina, in a wonderful burst of syncretically self-cancelling righteous indignation, hailing the virtue of women who "dwelle in Cristes hous" (IV.2282) and derogating the authority of Solomon because he built "a temple of false goddis" (IV.2295). Although it is possible to see "confused discourse" in such moments, and the tale more generally as an intentional representation of a "bad narrator," the vast majority of critics have found it instead a remorselessly and seemingly effortlessly clever, learned, and trenchant mash-up.[2]

The second point on which most critics agree – although in this case the group of naysayers has been larger and more persistent – pertains to the narrator's attitude toward his material. Most find this attitude to be profoundly corrosive, involving a wholesale negation of human values. As Robert Edwards contends, "The Merchant's Tale is by most accounts Chaucer's bleakest and most savagely ironic story in the *Canterbury Tales*."[3] The problem that arises, then, is how to explain this apparent conjunction between narratorial mastery and all-negating savagery. "The elegant wit of the poem does not surprise us," Jay Schleusener remarks, "but its meanness does, and we are especially surprised because we could not have expected anything of the sort from Chaucer."[4] It is in accounting for this surprise – in identifying the bridge between the wit and the meanness of the Merchant's performance – that there has been wide and sometimes contentious critical disagreement.

In the heyday of Kittredgean dramatic readings, critics found a ready bridge in the tale's purported function as an extended portrait of the apparently deeply troubled interior of the narrator, who contributes to the so-called marriage group a revolting depiction of a coupling that responds both to the Clerk and Wife of Bath, and that reflects his own domestic disappointment. Emerson Brown, defending this position in a two-part article in the late 1970s in the wake of a series of doubters, succinctly captures it in his suggested "generic title" for the tale: "Fabliau About an Old Blind Husband and a Fruit Tree . . . As Told by a Clever but Loveless and Cynical Misogynist."[5] In its essentials, this explanation of the tale's meanness has had great staying power, despite the waning of the dramatic approach in its most dogmatic guise, although, to be sure, the explanation has taken considerably more sophisticated forms, especially with regard to the theorization of human interiority and the scope of the Merchant's agency over his narrative materials. Thus, for example, Elaine Tuttle Hansen and, more recently, R. Jacob McDonie draw on psychoanalysis to explore, in different ways, the interiority of the narrator, while Robert Edwards draws on medieval rhetorical theory to anatomize the manner in which the tale characterizes its teller.[6] All three critics also suggest (as indeed Brown does) how the vast array of materials that the Merchant includes conveys meanings beyond his conscious intent, even meanings antithetical to his narratorial desire.

Critical unease with this view, apart from more general skepticism directed at the dramatic approach, arises from the feeling that the narrator's apparent unhappiness does not adequately account for the brilliant capaciousness of the tale's corrosive intensity. C. David Benson objects, for example, that "the painful bitterness in the poem, so well described by dramatic critics, is trivialized by being attributed only to the domestic frustrations of a disappointed husband."[7] Whether or not explicitly responding to this challenge, many critics who still locate the key to the tale in the figure of the Merchant move beyond domestic disappointment and find also (or just instead) some affective manifestation of Chaucer's own critical scrutiny of mercantile values or the historical position of merchants. Studies such as those by R. A. Shoaf, Lee Patterson, Glenn Burger, and Roger Ladd have dug deeply into the historical and theoretical complexity of fourteenth-century mercantile ideology and subjectivity, seeking to chart the interior of the Merchant against specific aspects of late medieval mercantile mentality.[8]

Nonetheless, because the tale of January and May is not, on its surface, a mercantile fable (in the way that the *Shipman's Tale* obviously is), all readers who see it as exhibiting some sort of mercantile mentality must confront the fact that so much of the *Canterbury Tales* may be read in this fashion (e.g., as evidence of proto-bourgeois subjectivity, or of the commodification of human relationships). The performances of the Wife of Bath, Friar, Franklin, Pardoner, Cook, and Canon's Yeoman, among others, may be fruitfully considered in this manner.[9] The "commercial language and commercial outlook" that, in an influential article, Patricia Eberle identifies as pervading the *General Prologue* is also evident in many other places in the *Tales*. As Eberle points out, this language and outlook are by no means automatically pejorative but in some cases may merely reflect a perspective on the world that Chaucer shared with his audience.[10] If so, then the claim that the distinctive negative force of the tale of January and May reflects Chaucer's scrutiny of a specifically mercantile mentality (rather than scrutiny of something else) must rest on more than the presence of mercantile ideas, language, and imagery; and in this regard the assumed significance of the assignment to the Merchant is crucial. That is, the association of the negative force of the tale with a mercantile mentality rests on the assumption that Chaucer designed the features of the tale that make up this negative force with the unhappy character of the Merchant in mind – even if Chaucer's intention in doing so was not, as the dramatic approach claims, simply to illustrate this character.

As I discussed in this book's introduction, the assumption that any of the IV-V tales were written with their tellers in mind is subject to doubt, and in this particular instance that assumption has been vociferously challenged. The debate has especially focused on the problematic status of the 32-line *Merchant's Prologue*, which provides both an identification of the narrator that the tale itself would otherwise leave obscure and a characterization of that narrator as (seemingly) volatilely distraught and bitter that stands in stark contrast to the (seemingly) reticent, "worthy man" (I.279) described in the *General Prologue*. Although few now question, as Norman Blake has, the authenticity of the *Merchant's Prologue*, a steady stream of scholars has continued to hold, from manuscript and internal evidence, that this link was a very late invention of Chaucer's, which he appended to a tale already written either for another pilgrim or without any definite narrator in mind.[11] I will take my own position on this issue shortly; for now, it suffices to observe that this brief passage of questionable status has indeed carried a great deal of weight in support of readings that exhaustively plumb the tale that follows for the intricacies of the Merchant's tortured psyche and/or of the specifically mercantile mentality that he represents.

Many of those skeptical of these kinds of readings nonetheless still find the tale dominated by the bitter voice of its narrator and thus seek to explain the source of that bitterness in another fashion, most often as some sort of effort at cathartic purgation – whether of a dark tendency in Chaucer's own writing, of a dark tendency in his readers, or both.[12] Many of these studies are quite compelling within the interpretive parameters that they set for themselves, and yet they all require us to grant *a priori* their ultimate claim that Chaucer intended the tale to purge this darkness: for while the darkness may be evident, its purgation is nowhere obviously represented (e.g., by an outraged response of the pilgrim audience). Having put aside the crutch of the *Merchant's Prologue*, these readings instead rely on their faith in Chaucer's good intentions. A small number of critics avoid this problem by taking the further step of questioning the supposedly self-evident presence of darkness and the bitter tone typically felt to convey it. These critics see the tale instead as essentially comic – as, for example, an exercise in "traditional anti-feminist japery" or even as an affirmation that "in nature's original plan . . . the young seek out each other for life to continue" – and argue that the bitterness others perceive is either wholly an effect of the prologue (and thus justifiably ignored) or has been exaggerated in its extent and is inessential to the more fundamental emphases of the tale.[13]

Differing perceptions of the *Merchant's Tale*'s tone (and hence the nature and source of the tale's negative force) and differing assumptions about the status of its prologue (and hence the relation between teller and tale) therefore underlie many of its critical disagreements and, in particular, the various explanations for how its negative force (if even present) may be reconciled with its narrative mastery. Of course, questions of tone and of the chronology of Chaucer's compositional process do not admit of definitive answers; at best, one may make a case for the relative probability of one's assumptions and then limit oneself to their interpretive space. In what follows, I present cases for, first, the *Merchant's Prologue* as most likely enacting a belated assignment of the Merchant to an already written tale, and, second, for the tone of the tale, as well as that of the prologue, as having been misconstrued as bitter. While I consequently follow the minority traditions in these regards, however, the conclusions about the Merchant's performance that I then draw on the basis of these positions do not, for the most part, follow those traditions, but more resemble (in a general way) those of the critics who take the opposite positions. For in my argument about the function of the *Merchant's Tale* in the IV-V sequence, I claim that the comic tale is in fact a dark one, although not because it reflects the troubled interiority of its narrator or a critique of the mentality that he represents. And I claim that the tale's assignment to the Merchant is crucial for its understanding, but again not in the way the implications of that assignment have typically been understood.

Textual Matters

Answers to the question of the status of the *Merchant's Prologue* have often been polarized, as is well illustrated by a pair of influential mid-twentieth-century studies. One may either see the prologue, with E. Talbot Donaldson, as an interpretive barometer of the tale, or one may believe, with Bertrand Bronson, that it is best ignored.[14] But like most textual questions about the *Tales*, this one cannot really be answered so absolutely; instead, the most prudent response probably lies in the murky middle ground. As I reviewed in the introduction, the case for simply ignoring the prologue is weak: the corpus of manuscripts indicates that all three IV-V links – this prologue, the Merchant-Squire link, and the Squire-Franklin link – are of a compositional piece, and the strongest reading of the manuscript and literary evidence is that all three links are authentic. Nonetheless, this same manuscript evidences also suggests that all three links were very late compositions, written sometime after the tales that they join and the *General Prologue* that describes those tales' tellers. Hence, Donaldson, in his rebuttal to Bronson's depreciation of the interpretive value of the *Merchant's Prologue*, too easily dismisses the implications of the evidence of late composition by claiming that such evidence is only "significant" "if, as a literary fact, the tale failed to fit the narrator as he is characterized in its prologue[.]"[15] Whatever a "literary fact" may be, the question the evidence raises is not the simple one of the presence or absence of "fit" between the narrator of the tale and the Merchant of the prologue, because if we accept the prologue as Chaucer's final intention, then obviously we must assume *some* sort of fit. Rather, the question is of the *scope* of that fit – whether, that is, we may also assume that every literary element of the tale potentially reflects "the narrator as he is characterized in the prologue" (i.e., what I call in this book's introduction the totalizing scenario) or whether we may only assume that the fit, rather than being so intricate and pervasive, consists of a more general, conceptual relationship between the two components of the Merchant's performance. In my view, while we can never know for certain whether or not Chaucer had a definite narrator in mind while writing the tale of January and May, the evidence of the prologue's very late composition at the very least casts reasonable doubt on the likelihood that he had in mind the Merchant specifically and even stronger doubt on the supposition that he had by then conceived the characterization of that pilgrim as rendered by the prologue.

Those who have taken such a doubting position, however, often then go too far in dismissing the significance of the tale's narratorial assignment. For example, Bronson's theory that Chaucer did not foresee the effect that the prologue would have on the tale (and thus presumably would have written it otherwise if he had) is, as Donaldson points out, far-fetched and unsupportable.[16] And, more recently, John Finlayson's critique of readings that fail to recognize "the possibility that the connection between the Merchant and his tale may not even be by Chaucer, and is, *at best*, a matter of second thoughts" is misleading both in the equal footing it gives to the rather unlikely possibility of the inauthenticity of the prologue and in its downplaying of the significance of the "second thoughts" that appear to have been Chaucer's final intentions regarding the narrator and position of the tale.[17] However long elapsed between Chaucer's composition of tale and prologue, and whatever inkling he had about the identity of the narrator when he wrote the tale, at some point it struck him that the Merchant should not just be the tale's teller but also that the Merchant should offer the tale – by means of the prologue's famous echo of the last line of *Lenvoy de Chaucer* – as the most tightly linked response to a preceding tale in the entire work.[18] Clearly, these "second thoughts" form a crucial part of the overall meaning of the Merchant's performance, even if one does not assume that they pervade the tale at a fine level of detail.

Some scholars have also suspected for the tale a different original teller, based upon narratorial remarks that appear to indicate a clerical speaker.

The remark invariably cited as the most revelatory in this regard occurs at the end of the first sentence of the tale:

> Whilom ther was dwellynge in Lumbardye
> A worthy knyght, . . .
> . . .
> And folwed ay his bodily delyt
> On wommen, ther as was his appetyt,
> As doon thise fooles that been seculeer. (IV.1245–51)

The argument is that the reference to "thise fooles that been seculeer" must mean that the speaker was not himself part of this group and hence a churchman. This rather blunt reading requires us to hear in the line straightforward, self-congratulating contempt for the entire class of heterosexual laymen, which, while not implausible, is scarcely in character with the clever, intricate irony that runs through the rest of the tale, however we gauge its tone. Moreover, as Germaine Dempster long ago showed, Chaucer's use of a demonstrative before a class of person does not at all preclude the speaker's inclusion in that group, as evident when the "olde wyf" in the *Wife of Bath's Tale* urges the knight to tell her what he seeks, since "Thise olde folk kan muchel thyng" (III.1004).[19] Hence it is entirely possible – and, I believe, more consistent with the rest of the tale's narration – to read IV.1251 as ironically self-mocking, that is, as the narrator saying, "as do these fools, *like me*, who are secular." And if the line thus identifies the speaker as explicitly *non*-clerical, it further enables us to hear a nudge in the ribs of the narrator's clerical auditors, whose implied presence is then required for the distinguishing reference to those "that been seculeer" to have pragmatic motivation. In this way, the self-mockery slyly (and characteristically) winds its way backward against those implicitly less manly men who do not take "bodily delyt" in "wommen." Furthermore, if the speaker has the Clerk in particular in mind, the remark conveys a subtle but trenchant accusation of the latter's hetero-erotic inexperience and hence of the absurdity of a churchman-in-the-making telling a preposterous tale about a marriage. Indeed, as Patterson suggests, we may plausibly hear, in the emphasis the enjambment of IV.1249–50 places on the speaker's intrusive, explicit designation of the sexual orientation of January's and his own "appetyt," a semi-occulted suggestion of the Clerk's sodomitic practices.[20]

But this possibility of narratorial aggression directed specifically toward the Clerk brings us back into the muddy waters of the question of what tale order Chaucer had in mind, if any, when he wrote the tale of January and

May. We may be sure, at the very least, that Chaucer did have other tales in mind, some of which he meant the tale of January and May to follow. To cite only two well-known and unmistakable indicators of inter-tale dialogue, Justinus's sardonic (and the narrator's witty diegetically boundary-crossing) nomination of the "Wyf of Bathe" as an authority on marriage (IV.1685–88) clearly puts the *Wife of Bath's Prologue* in the rearview mirror, and the narrator's cutting recontextualization of the *Knight's Tale*'s "pitee renneth soone in gentil herte" as a description of May's decision to "love [Damian] best of any creature" (IV.1984–86; cf. I.1761) sets that earlier tale in the crosshairs. Scholars have inventoried many other shared elements between the tale of January and May and those two other performances, as well as with tales that have no bearing on the question of order, especially *Melibee* but also, more provisionally, the tales of the Monk, Miller, Man of Law, and Prioress.

Over and above these various kinds of nods to other performances, however, the tale of January and May possesses deep and sustained parallels with the *Clerk's Tale*. These have been described by many, and in especial detail by Jerome Mandel.[21] Here I simply point out the obvious similarities of plot: both tales center on a Lombard aristocrat's decision to marry, and they both focus initially on the process of his choosing a wife; both men reject or ignore the advice of others in this regard and choose a low-born woman entirely on the basis of their own private judgment; both tales involve the subsequent stripping of the chosen woman; and, from this point on, both tales revolve around the manner in which the wife is subjected to specifically articulated demands of the husband, demands that at the resolution of both tales give way to some different kind of relationship. Such striking similitude of narrative framework, obviously, serves then to highlight the vast differences between, say, the natures of Walter's and January's respective demands and the manner in which Griselda and May respectively negotiate them, with result potentially being, as David Wallace has termed it, a "comprehensive critique" of the Clerk's performance.[22]

Hence, however many other tales the story of January and May targets – and it seems to me it is quite catholic in this regard – one of its primary interlocutors appears to be the *Clerk's Tale*. It is therefore a relatively safe assumption that Chaucer had in mind the latter tale when he began the one that he eventually assigned to the Merchant, although from this assumption it does not necessarily follow that he wholly conceived the story of January and May as an *immediately* rebutting, "comprehensive critique" of the story of Walter and

Griselda, on the model, as Wallace suggests, of the Knight-Miller pairing.[23] That one tale plainly offers a response to another does not, in the *Canterbury Tales* schema, in itself require the juxtaposition of those tales, as the Franklin's seemingly virtual rewriting of the *Merchant's Tale* witnesses (with the *Franklin's Tale* similarly possessing multiple interlocutors).[24] In this instance, the manuscript evidence of late linkage makes probable Chaucer's determination of this sequence only after his completion of the tale of January and May, when he was struck by the pairing's artistic potential, as well as by the architectural requirements of IV-V as a whole. Whether or not the late composition of the *Merchant's Prologue* was itself triggered by Chaucer's perhaps belated expansion of the epilogue of the Clerk's performance beyond its Petrarchan moralization, as some scholars have suggested, we have no way of knowing.[25] Given the manuscript evidence, all we can be relatively confident of is that, sometime after having put the Clerk's performance in its final form, he appears to have finally settled on a narrator for the tale of January and May, and composed the *Merchant's Prologue* to link tightly with *Lenvoy de Chaucer*.

To summarize: my assumptions are that Chaucer wrote the tale of January and May, initially without its prologue, as a rejoinder to the Clerk's tale of Griselda, but also to the *Wife of Bath's Prologue* and to the *Knight's Tale*, and perhaps to some degree to other tales, without, necessarily, a clear initial sense of exactly where he would place it; that he most likely imagined a secular speaker for the tale – and therefore the "seculeer" reference of the first sentence is probably a backhand swipe at the Clerk – but that his more specific intentions regarding the tale's narrator may have been more or less formulated; and that the *Merchant's Prologue* reflects both his belated recognition of the potential of the tale's placement immediately after the Clerk's performance and his belated final determination of the Merchant as the tale's most apposite narrator.

Tonal Matters

As on the issue of the textual status of the *Merchant's Prologue*, about which my position divides across both sides of the debate, on the question of the tone of the Merchant's narration my position, in its ultimate formulation, is similarly split, although I must first appear to be more partisan. Such initial side-taking is necessary in part because, in this case, one side has tended to dominate the discussion, which has had the effect of hardening a possible set of readings into *données*, and also in part because a full account of the tale's tone requires a consideration of the use to which Chaucer puts it, and this task will only be complete at the chapter's end.

Most critics of the *Merchant's Tale* over the past half century or so, including the majority of the most influential ones, hear the voice of the narrator as unrelentingly bitter. Even those who, like C. David Benson, reject a dramatic reading still find, for example, that "the reader must struggle to avoid being overwhelmed by its bitter pessimism."[26] Skeptical as they are of the interpretive significance of the *Merchant's Prologue*, such critics nonetheless tacitly agree with their opponents in hearing tonal continuity between the remarks of the Merchant in the prologue and his narration of the ensuing tale. And yet, the manifest wit of such moments as Proserpina's mention of "false goddis" – or indeed of the entire Pluto and Prosperina exchange – is not in fact easily read as bitterly narrated, and such moments, far from unusual, are regular occurrences in the tale.

In my exploration below of the tale's axiology, I consider a selection of such occurrences, the full intricacy of which is more plainly evident when they have been liberated from bitter voicing. At this point I offer just a single example, the narrator's apostrophe to Martianus Capella at the culmination of his densely mythographic description of January and May's wedding feast:

> Hoold thou thy pees, thou poete Marcian,
> That writest us that ilke weddyng murie
> Of hire Philologie and hym Mercurie,
> And of the songes that the Muses songe!
> To smal is bothe thy penne, and eek thy tonge,
> For to descryven of this mariage.
> Whan tendre youthe hath wedded stoupyng age,
> Ther is swich myrthe that it may nat be writen. (IV.1732–39)

Here, in one of the grandest instances of the narrator's wit, Chaucer imitates the convention of the poetic boast more directly that anywhere else in his corpus. If he were doing so ingenuously, he would, as Karla Taylor suggests, be vying with Dante by imitating Dante's gesture of vying with the ancients.[27] But of course the boast, and the entire mythographic passage, is superbly disingenuous: Chaucer shows us that he knows what vying with Dante would look like, but by applying the boast to a description of a wedding between "tendre youthe" and "stoupyng age," he winkingly undercuts this expression of poetic ambition in the very instant of voicing it. This passage provides, that is, a comic but trenchantly ironic nod to *trecento* poetics that is similar to the attitude that pervades the *House of Fame* and that reappears, as we saw in the previous chapter, in the

Clerk's ambivalent celebration of Petrarch in the prologue to his tale. The voice is thus a characteristically Chaucerian one, although here given within the characterological field of the Merchant. To read this passage as an instance of bitter sarcasm is to miss the playful (if biting) wit that it shares with many moments elsewhere in Chaucer's work.

Those critics who have recognized this aspect of the tale's narration have offered various explanations for it. Donald Howard cordons off these instances of wit from the voice of the Merchant, naming them moments of "unimpersonated artistry."[28] Others, like Helen Phillips, have emphasized the apparent instability of the tale's tone, seeing it as shifting "dizzyingly between registers."[29] But if we try to put the *Merchant's Prologue* out of our minds and hold the narrational style of just the tale of January and May up to that of other tales, I believe that most readers would find that that style – with its ironic apostrophes, playful erudition, and, as Patterson terms it, clever generic *bricolage* – possesses an underlying consistency in its variety, one that most resembles that of the *Nun's Priest's Tale*, whose thoroughly undramatized narrator has widely been identified as characteristically Chaucerian.[30] This similarity has not gone unnoticed, but few who have done so have thence been willing to give up the perception of an initial and sustained bitterness, with John Hines, in his study of the English fabliau, one of the more noteworthy exceptions.[31]

Those who hold the bitter view may counter that it surely makes no sense to consider the tone of the tale independently from that of the prologue, since the predominance of the Merchant's voice in the brief space of the latter indicates that Chaucer intended it as a kind of tonal key for the narration of the ensuing tale, even if it was a belated, retroactive such key. That is, even if the narration of the *Merchant's Tale* originally was akin to the *Nun's Priest's Tale*, at some point Chaucer chose to alter that tone by framing the tale with the present characterization of its narrator. In response, one may simply point out that the tale is as much a tonal key for the prologue as vice versa, and that it is more likely that Chaucer wrote the prologue to match the tone of the tale's narration rather than to alter or contrast with it. Moreover, one may also point out that to hear bitterness in the prologue requires us to understand the Merchant as sincerely describing his emotional turmoil, despite the fact that the tale provides an abundance of evidence to suggest that its narrator is almost uniformly insincere; and, again, Chaucer more likely intended a match rather than contrast between prologue and tale in this respect. In sum, to read the tone of the prologue backward from that of the tale – that is, to read it in compositional order – is to see the prologue, with Hines, not as the confession of a bitter man but rather as essentially a pose, "a confident performance by an able raconteur."[32]

The Merchant delivers the prologue, I thus contend, with the same wink that accompanies the aforementioned poetic boast and numerous other passages in the tale: the prologue's tone is bitter, but only superficially; its actual, underlying tone is perhaps best termed jocular, with a misogynistic edge. It is no accident, for example, that the prologue's climactic moment – the narrator's interruption of his own eruption of apparently heartfelt despair to address the Host and reveal the actual brief duration of his tortuous marriage – occurs across a line break:

> A, goode sire Hoost, I have ywedded bee
> Thise monthes two, and moore nat, pardee . . . (IV.1233–34)

In the context of the performative nature of the address to the Host, the enjambment here, if allowed a slight pause, and the subsequent metrical stress that especially falls on the pre-caesural "two" enact (and therefore signify) expert comic timing, producing a self-deprecating joke between two men at the expense of a woman, and women in general.[33] This revelation of the mere two months' duration of the Merchant's marriage, after the build-up of the preceding lines, is consequently not, as some critics have claimed, a joke on the Merchant – a disclosure of the "extent of his foolishness" – but rather the Merchant's joke, which at once self-mockingly discloses his prior lament to be humorous hyperbole and insinuates that the honeymoon period before the evils of women emerge is short indeed.[34] In fact, the Host, with his response to the Merchant, succinctly doffs his hat to this joke by reiterating it as the rationale for him to tell the next tale:

> "Now," quod oure Hoost, "Marchaunt, so God yow blesse,
> Syn ye so muchel knowen of that art
> Ful hertely I pray yow telle us part." (IV.1240–41)

The "art" to which the Host ironically and jocularly refers is the "cursednesses" (IV.1239) of wives, about which the Merchant's extensive knowledge derives from rather brief experience – which is nonetheless more than enough, the Host suggests, to justify an elaboration for the pilgrim audience. It is certainly no coincidence, as we will see in the next chapter, that the Host uses a similar rationale when turning to the Squire to tell the next tale.

The nature of the Merchant's joke, moreover, suggests the *Wife of Bath's Prologue* as another tonal key. Given that, as has been frequently observed, both the Wife of Bath and the Merchant begin their prologues by asserting authority in the matter of marriage on the basis of tumultuous personal experience,[35] it is no stretch to hear the *Merchant's Prologue* as a highly compact version of the Wife's winkingly comic, ambiguously veracious first-person confession of domestic travail framed within the larger discourse of antifeminism. Yet the more proximate and, for Chaucer, likely more prompting tonal key for the *Merchant's Prologue* is the one hiding in plain sight: the Clerk's concluding *Lenvoy de Chaucer*, the final line of which the Merchant's prologue echoes so tightly. Almost all readers find the tone of the envoy playfully, if bitingly, ironic, yet most then find a rather contrasting earnest despair in the Merchant's echo.[36] But to maintain this perception of tonal contrast, we must imagine Chaucer sandwiching thirty-two lines of earnest, bitter ineptitude between the playful, witty irony of *Lenvoy* and what strikes me as the equally (although not identically) playful and witty irony of much of the tale of January and May. As I have suggested, it seems far more likely that, even if Chaucer composed the prologue from some temporal distance from the tale, he would have sought to create matching rather than contrasting narrational tones between the two. That is, it seems likely that, with his echo of the conclusion of the Clerk's performance, the Merchant is matching the latter pilgrim's ironic wit with his own, becoming a knowing participant in the game that the Clerk has inaugurated – and, indeed, seeking to take over that game.

On balance, therefore, I join the minority critical tradition and find that there is more evidence in favor of an ironic, mordantly playful, consciously performed tone for the prologue and tale of the Merchant than there is for a pervasively and earnestly bitter tone. If the tone is heard as the former – and thus in his prologue the Merchant is knowingly taking up the pose of a bitter, henpecked husband – then, contrary to the requirements of a dramatic reading, the diegetic veracity of the Merchant's domestic experiences and emotional life is not determinable and, more importantly, largely beside the point of this pseudo-autobiographical outburst. Rather, the point of the latter is – as its tight link to the conclusion of the Clerk's performance suggests – to establish a basis for a refutation of the axiological apologia of that prior performance and for the establishment of a contradistinguishing alternative. In this way, the prologue enacts the first dialectical turn in the axiological meditation of IV-V. The earnest bitterness typically heard in the prologue has obscured the intricacy of this turn; if we hear instead winking irony, we are in better position to understand the prologue's function in the sequence, as well as that of the ensuing tale. Nevertheless, in my consideration of these functions in the following sections, I rejoin the majority critical tradition in detecting an underlying darkness to the Merchant's performance. But I argue that this darkness permeates the performance not *despite* its jocular tone, but to a significant degree *by means* of its characteristic Chaucerian wit.

Clerk-Merchant

The Merchant's response to the Clerk in the *Merchant's Prologue* is best understood as triangulated through the Host's response to the Clerk in the so-called Host's stanza (IV.1212a-12g). But because this stanza has so often been judged to have been canceled by Chaucer in favor of that prologue, we must pause briefly to consider another textual matter before examining the interaction between the Clerk's performance and the two responses that follow it.

The first editor to print the Clerk-Merchant sequence as such was Tyrwhitt, who also then began the tradition of suppressing or otherwise bracketing the Host's stanza. Tyrwhitt prints the stanza in his notes, remarking,

> Whatever may be thought of the genuineness of these lines, they can at best, in my opinion, be considered as a fragment of an unfinished *Prologue*, which Chaucer might *once* have intended to place at the end of the *Clerkes* tale. When he determined to connect that tale with the Marchant's in another manner, he may be supposed, notwithstanding, to have left this Stanza for the present uncancelled in his MS. He made use of the thought, and some of the lines, in the Prologue which connects the Monkes Tale with Melibee, ver. 13895–13900.[37]

The same sentiments, with greater or lesser degrees of confidence, and more or less elaboration, appear throughout the subsequent editorial tradition up to the present, with many also noting the stanza's awkward return to rhyme royal between the six-line stanzas of *Lenvoy de Chaucer* and the couplets of the *Merchant's Prologue*. Yet all editors from Tyrwhitt on have also been aware that, despite the fact that the stanza is only present in about half of the fifty-or-so more-or-less complete copies of the *Tales*, manuscript evidence does not offer strong support for the supposition of intended cancellation. In particular, of the thirteen manuscripts that contain the IV-V sequence as such, ten contain the stanza (including Ellesmere), one is missing a leaf at this point, and only two certainly lack it.[38] (And of those manuscripts without the IV-V sequence, the single most crucial one, Hengwrt, contains the stanza, and hence the Hengwrt-Ellesmere scribe included it in both of his copies of the *Tales*.) Thus, in the very set of manuscripts that contain the Clerk-Merchant transition (complete with *Lenvoy de Chaucer* and the *Merchant's Prologue*) that the Host's stanza supposedly interrupts, that stanza is nonetheless amply attested. Therefore even if the stanza represents an earlier, pre-IV-V termination of the Clerk's performance, the scribes who copied the late revision of the *Tales* that includes IV-V overwhelmingly seemed to believe that the stanza survived that revision.[39] The presumption that we know what Chaucer meant to do and what would make for a better Clerk-Merchant transition consequently seems a weak justification for the editorial elimination of an entire stanza from one's base manuscript, whether that manuscript is Hengwrt or Ellesmere. Rather than assume that the stanza, although present, is not meant to be part of the Clerk-Merchant transition, I instead assume that because it is present it is meaningful. And I further assume, since the *Merchant's Prologue* did not make it into Hengwrt while the Host's stanza did, that Chaucer wrote the former after the latter.

As Anne Middleton points out, the Host responds to the tale of Griselda as the French translators of the tale did, understanding it as an exemplum for actual, present-day wives:[40]

> This worthy Clerk, whan ended was his tale,
> Our Hoste seyde, and swoor, "By Goddes bones,
> Me were levere than a barel ale
> My wyf at hoom had herd this legende ones!
> This is a gentil tale for the nones,
> As to my purpos, wiste ye my wille;
> But thing that wol nat be, lat it be stille." (IV.1212a-12g)

For the Host, the *Clerk's Tale* is a "legend" well suited to a "purpos" that he does not identify, but presumably to the disciplining of his own "wyf at hoom"; and, in the simple brevity of this reaction, his reduction of all other possible meanings is not just akin to but even more radical than that of the French translators. The effect is to offer something of a rebuff to the axiological apologia of the Clerk's performance, however dramatically unwitting we are to understand this rebuff. For if the Clerk seeks to create a space for an autonomous literary value through a meta-axiological performance that resists, through multiplication and self-cancellation, any specific determination of the value of fiction, the Host's reduction sweeps away this complexity and identifies the value of fiction as a straightforward instrument of uxorial discipline, an enforcer of patriarchal domestic norms. And if the Clerk's performance stages Chaucer's own earlier literary axiology, the Host's response expresses Chaucer's realization that no matter how he conceives of the value of his writing, readers are free to ascribe whatever value their shaping environments and personal axiologies determine; and, consequently, that whatever notional autonomy his earlier literary axiology established, in the actual practices of literary production and reception that autonomy was chimerical.

Furthermore, inasmuch as Harry Bailly and his wife were as much actual individuals as Chaucer was, and inasmuch as readers would have been aware of this, the stanza dramatizes, through Harry's telescoping of the Clerk's fiction to the utility of a "legende" for his "wyf at hoom," the supremacy of the category of the real over that of fiction.[41] The implication is that the value of fiction is merely and entirely in its function as an instrument to obtain some non-literary value (in this instance uxorial obedience) in the real world. Yet at the same time, because the stanza *dramatizes* this supremacy, Chaucer leaves open the back door, so to speak, for the return of a more expansive, less determinate literary value. For example, whatever amusement readers may find in the stanza lies precisely in their perception that Harry's value ascription is comically misconceived, as well as in (for Chaucer's contemporary readers) their perception of the differences between this fictional Harry and the real one (as in the presumably comic differences between the "popet" Chaucer and the author). If we laugh at the stanza, we are implicitly rejecting the Host's definition of the value of fiction and of the character of the Host as anything more real than a clever parody. And, in fact, in the stanza's final line, Harry himself seems to reproduce the self-canceling value ascriptions that characterize the conclusion of the Clerk's performance, retracting his hopeful earlier account of fiction's instrumental value because the real-world value that it is supposed to provide is not obtainable in reality: it is a "thyng that wol nat be." Useless in the real word, the *Clerk's Tale* must, by implication, have some other kind of use.

With the *Merchant's Prologue*, Chaucer reworks the strategy of the Host's stanza with an equally comical intent but toward a larger and ultimately more severe thematic end. In effect, regardless of its textual status, the Host's stanza serves dramatically as a prompt for the Merchant, who in a baldly homosocial gesture joins the Host in collective lament over uxorial wickedness. Middleton accordingly pairs the interpretive mode of the Merchant's response to the *Clerk's Tale* with that of the Host's: "Both of these hearers pursue the paradigmatic usefulness of the tale, rather than its paradoxical delight ... In doing so, they are responding within the French rather than the Italian tradition of the tale."[42] Notably, however, unlike the Host the Merchant does not in fact propose a "paradigmatic usefulness" for the tale of Griselda. Instead, he inserts himself into the fictional world of the Clerk's envoy, becoming the "hym" of its final line, the one whom "strong" "archewyves" cause to "wepe, and wrynge, and waille" (IV.1195–96, 1212). Rather than first imagining, like the Host, his wife's reformation under the yoke of the Griselda exemplum before wistfully withdrawing that possibility, the Merchant skips to a stark assertion of its impossibility, recasting the envoy's ironic contrast between the "archewyves" of the present and the Griseldas of the past as the absolute, unbridgeable difference between the Clerk's fiction and his own real experience: "Ther is a long and large difference / Bitwix Grisildis grete paceience / And of my wyf the passyng crueltee" (IV.1223–25).

As with the Host's stanza, then, in the *Merchant's Prologue* the category of the real emerges in opposition to the category of the fictional. But in this instance the resulting status of the category of the fictional (whether it is, e.g., recuperated or rejected) is not clear, and it is exactly this ambiguity that the tale of January and May will go on to amplify and, ultimately, dissipate. To detect that ambiguity at this point, however, depends much on the question of tone. For if one hears the tone as sincerely embittered, then the ready conclusion is that the Merchant is rather simplistically and naively asserting the category of the real, impelled by an inner turmoil awakened by the envoy (and perhaps also the Host's remarks) into an emotional, confessional complaint about his domestic situation. Yet if we read the tone of the *Merchant's Prologue* instead in the same spirit as *Lenvoy de Chaucer*, then the category of the real emerges not as naïve error but as part of a much more sophisticated, wily cooptation of the Clerk's game. The Merchant presents his real domestic situation as precisely aligned with that which is implied by the envoy, as seen from the husband's perspective, but he does so as an element of a comic performance. Hence, although the comic effect depends upon a surface distinction between his earnestly described reality and the ironic fancy of the envoy (so that the Merchant's joke has the form of "you think you're joking, but you're describing my real life"), the ability to make this distinction wavers inasmuch as we are aware that the earnestness is part of a pose, that it is itself a fiction, whose correspondence with reality is not determinable. Indeed, inasmuch as we perceive the hyperbole of the Merchant's performance as an intentional effect rather than unguarded foolishness, that very hyperbole signals the likely difference between what the Merchant says and what actually is.

The hierarchical opposition between the actual and the fictional thus seems short lived. As in the Host's stanza, the opposition is invoked to evoke humor, which in turn dissipates it. Yet in the case of the Host's stanza we laugh, with Chaucer, at the Host, or more precisely at the *Tale*'s representation of the Host, and whatever challenge his instrumental application of the *Clerk's Tale* possesses for the Clerk's literary axiology evaporates in this instant. In contrast, in the case of the *Merchant's Prologue*, the joke issues from the characterological field of the Merchant: if we laugh at all, we laugh with him, and his targets include himself, women, and – somewhat obliquely but, for the IV-V sequence, most importantly – the Clerk. For in the latter's song, before the address to "noble wyves" (IV.1183) that occupies the final five of the song's six stanzas, the Clerk first addresses any "wedded man" in his "open audience," exhorting him not to be "so hardy . . . t'assaille / His wyves pacience in trust to fynde / Grisildis, for in certain he shal faille" (IV.1179–82), and the *Merchant's Prologue* goes on to draw unusual attention to the fact that the Merchant responds exactly as such a "wedded man."

This emphasis is most apparent in the context of his full speech:

"Wepyng and wayling, care and other sorwe
I knowe ynogh, on even and a-morwe,"
Quod the Marchant, "and so doon other mo
That wedded been. I trowe that it be so,
For wel I woot it fareth so with me.
I have a wyf, the worste that may be;
For thogh the feend to hire ycoupled were,
She wolde him overmacche, I dar wel swere.
What sholde I yow reherce in special
Hir hye malice? She is a shrewe at al.
Ther is a long and large difference
Bitwix Grisildis grete pacience
And of my wyf the passing crueltee.
Were I unbounden, also moot I thee,
I wolde never eft comen in the snare.
We wedded men lyven in sorwe and care.
Assaye whoso wole, and he shal fynde
That I seye sooth, by Seint Thomas of Ynde,
As for the moore part – I sey nat alle.
God shilde that it sholde so bifalle!
A, goode sire Hoost, I have ywedded bee
Thise monthes two, and more nat, pardee;

And yet, I trowe, he that al his lyve
Wyflees hath been, though that men wolde him ryve
Unto the herte, ne koude in no manere
Tellen so muchel sorwe as I now heere
Koude tellen of my wyves cursednesse!" (IV.1213–39)

Because the initial lines of this speech clearly establish the basic premise that the Merchant speaks, as the Wife of Bath puts it, "of the wo that is in marriage" on the "auctoritee" of his experience (III.1–3), the two additional explicit reiterations of his marital status in the brief space of the passage seem targeted toward some additional end. What is more, all three indications of this status appear prominently at the head of lines, with the leading position of the second ("I have a wyf") requiring syntactical contortion, making it initially seem oddly redundant of the Merchant's just-mentioned first indication of his marital status, until we belatedly realize that the statement pertains to the quality of the wife; and the third ("We wedded men") closely echoing the Clerk's "No wedded man." The point of these reiterations becomes evident in the conclusion of the Merchant's speech, in his sidelong address to the man who "al his lyve / Wyflees hath been," who consequently "koude in no manere / Tellen so muchel sorwe as I now heere / Koude of my wyves cursednesse." Here the indication of *unmarried* status at the head of the line serves to emphasize the contrast with his own reiterated line-leading claims to speak as a "wedded man" (even if one of only "monthes two"); and this concluding contrast, combined with the echoes of *Lenvoy de Chaucer* that place the Merchant in the role of the envoy's generic "wedded man," thrusts the Clerk into the complementary role of "he that al his lyve / Wyflees hath been."[43] We might paraphrase the speech's conclusion, therefore, as "You, Clerk, who have no experience of marriage, cannot even approach, through your fictions, the knowledge of real pain that I, a married man, could relate (even if you were stabbed through the heart)." As I have suggested above, the early mention in the tale of January and May of "thise fooles that been seculeer" who take their "bodily delyt / On wommen" (IV.1249–51) then reiterates this challenge with the same sort of jocularly biting, half-self-mocking irony as in the prologue – or, given the likely compositional sequence, the prologue, conversely, elaborates the speaker's jab at the Clerk into a fuller characterization of an identified narrator.

The category of the real, although part of the Merchant's pose (and hence itself a fiction), thus does not evaporate as it does in the Host's stanza. Framing the entire prologue, it gathers force at the end of the Merchant's speech as the principle of a half-direct, humorously delivered, but nonetheless trenchant challenge of the authority of the Clerk as a maker of fictions. The implication is that the Clerk's presentation of multiple, contradictory applications for fiction, and the corresponding suggestion of fiction's indeterminate value for the real world, constitute a euphemistic reformulation of the fact that fiction has no claim on the world at all – that the meta-axiology of the Clerk's performance is merely a sleight of hand that presents us literary value as the suspension of instrumentality while concealing in its palm the fact of literature's uselessness. In sum, in his pose as the Clerk's "wedded man," the Merchant uses a fiction of the real to challenge the axiological apologia of the Clerk's performance.

The Fabliau Real

The opposition between the fictional and the (fiction of the) real in the *Merchant's Prologue* reappears in the tale of January and May but plays out on a much larger discursive stage with much higher stakes. Here the real is signified not only by the claim of experience but also by an entire value system (or axiology), and the fictional is not just the useless tale of Griselda but any other value system and the discourses with which those systems are articulated and maintained. Such a capacious and profound opposition is the effect of the basic artistic strategy of the tale of January and May, a strategy that is readily apparent to most readers: starting with a fabliau broth, Chaucer creates a richly ironic narrative stew by deftly blending in several other generic ingredients, including sermon, debate, and, above all, courtly romance – a "dizzying conjunction of widely disparate literary materials," as Patterson puts it.[44] Chaucer avoids a potential mess of clashing flavors by thoroughly coating each ingredient in the fabliau broth, by which I mean that what unifies the myriad elements of the tale of January and May is neither plot (which, as many have pointed out, forms a relatively small part of the tale), nor any particular set of conventions, but rather the fabliau value system through which all other generic ingredients are encountered. Hence, while we may unhesitatingly agree with Cooper that the tale of January and May is "a fabliau dressed up as a romance," it is nonetheless both less and more than this.[45] On the one hand, it is hardly a fabliau at all (in comparison with, say, the narrative *tour de force* of the *Miller's Tale*). On the other hand, it is considerably more complex than a fabliau parody of romance: it is, rather, a portrait of fabliau values as an all-encompassing axiological universe, in which an array of other value systems, in their association with the various generic elements of the tale, appear to some degree as illusive or deceptive, always ironically undercut by the underlying fabliau axiology.

This axiology has been variously defined, but the general consensus has been well articulated by Cooper:

> in the fabliau, men and women leave all ideals far behind, and act with an eye to instant gratification that allows no postponement of the reward to a distant happy ending [as in romance] or to life after death [as in a saint's life]. The ruling code in the fabliau is animal instinct. The physical functions of the body, especially sex . . . provide the primary plot motifs.[46]

Similarly, and even more succinctly, Pearsall writes, "In this case, the common understanding of author and reader is that there are no values, secular or religious, more important than survival and the satisfaction of appetite."[47] As apparent in both of these definitions, a fabliau value system is conceivable as such only in relation to other, competing value systems (as is indeed the general rule for all value systems), and in this competitive relation, fabliau values claim the category of the real – they claim that the demands of the body, and the law of desire that these demands follow, are, so to speak, the facts of life, more primary, more "actual," than the cultural or psychological ideals of, say, chivalry, or the otherworldly ideals of penance and martyrdom.[48]

Any particular fabliau narrative, of course, may represent this axiological competition more or less fully, with more or less commitment to, and articulation of, a strictly fabliau axiology. What marks the tale of January and May in this regard, therefore, is – with its far-ranging generic and topical excursions – how expansively it represents this axiological competition and how relentlessly its commitment to a fabliau axiology ironically undercuts the competing axiologies it manifests. This expansiveness and undercutting occurs repeatedly across the course of the narrative through a series of set pieces that function like diastolic/systolic heartbeats. On each occasion, the narrator ushers into the narration elements of one or more other value systems, often with a pronounced emotive charge, thereby seeming to expand the tale's axiological and thematic scope, and then – whether by steady deflation through constant ironic pressure or by sudden sardonic puncture – inevitably contracts that scope to disclose again the hard ground of fabliau axiology.

In various ways and toward many different ends, critics have long recognized this expansion/contraction dynamic, and they have analyzed its operation with great sophistication in respect to the several medieval discourses of value that the narrator brings into the tale. Predictably, however, their conclusions about the outcome and significance of its operation tend to vary according to their positions on other, more contested aspects of the tale, especially those that I have considered above: the quality of the tale's tone and the bearing of the *Merchant's Prologue* on the tale's narration. For example, those who read the prologue's relation to the tale according to the dramatic theory understand the dynamic as recording the breadth and depth of the corrosive worldview prompted by the narrator's inner turmoil.[49] Others, focusing on the tale as an expression of mercantile mentality or ideology, see in the dynamic Chaucer's searching interrogation of the condition and worldview of the English merchant class.[50] Still others, less reliant or even hostile to the interpretive significance of the *Merchant's Prologue* but still hearing the tale's tone as bitter, understand the dynamic as striving toward its own transcendence, reaching toward, for example, "a series of images that assert the possibility of love, beauty, and salvation."[51] Interestingly, those few critics who have deemphasized the tale's supposedly bitter tone or have heard it otherwise have in comparison struggled to provide a persuasive rationale for this dynamic, which they nonetheless do perceive in some fashion. For example, in his magisterial study of the tale's calendrical imagery, V. A. Kolve concludes, "Despite the cynicism of its judgments and the satiric nature of its characterizations, *The Merchant's Tale* thus emerges, on some deeper level, as oddly affirmative," without then attempting to explain the presence of cynicism and satire, or to describe why we may simply ignore them in favor of the affirmative movement.[52]

The positions that I have taken on the narration's tone and the prologue lead me in a different direction than any of these approaches. Because I understand the prologue as having bearing on the tale, but as an articulation of the tale's function vis-à-vis others and especially those of IV-V, rather than as an initial disclosure of the psyche or mercantilism that the rest of the tale was designed to adumbrate, I do not ascribe the dynamic to the narrator's inner turmoil or to the vicissitudes of the historical position of late medieval English merchants. Because I hear the tone of both prologue and tale as, at base, one of jocular, biting, knowing irony, upon which various other tonal poses are strategically assumed, I understand the narrator as always in control of this dynamic, and – despite whatever extremes of emotion he appears to express, and whatever shifting judgments he seems to level against characters and events – always engaged in the same, darkly comic, puckish vanishing act of value systems. I do not therefore detect any affirmation of values escaping this vanishing act, and indeed the argument for affirmation strikes me as a reflex of the critical wishful thinking that not surprisingly accompanies the understanding of the tale's perspective as embittered, reflecting the belief that our congenial Chaucer could not himself possess such a worldview, at least not in the end.[53] Finally, I see the tale's jocular tone not as inconsistent with the negative force of the dynamic but rather as its very instrument: I see that tone as a sign of the confidence invested in the tale's assertion of the fabliau real against the parade of axiological fictions that it ironically entertains. For if the tone is not bitter, one does not have the option to marginalize the tale's implications by assigning it to an embittered consciousness, and hence the jocular manner in which the narrator reduces so many value systems to the law of desire is exactly that which makes the fabliau axiology of the tale of January and May so powerful – and such a match for the Clerk's literary axiology.

Hoolynesse or *Dotage*

Two instances of this dynamic must suffice to corroborate my contentions about its outcome and significance, one at the beginning of the tale and one toward the end. The first is in many ways the most straightforward, paradigmatic instance, yet it is also the one for which the narrator provides the most sustained elaboration: the so-called marriage encomium, which occupies lines IV.1267–1392. This passage has been thoroughly scrutinized, perhaps more so than any other in the tale. Scholars have fruitfully inventoried its sources, anatomized its structure, traced its generic affiliations, catalogued its rhetorical devices, and debated its inner consistency, degree of irony, and the basic question of who speaks it.[54] In what follows I glance sidelong at some of these debates, but my focus falls not so much on the encomium as on the twenty-two-line opening passage that leads into it. My contention is that in this passage the narrator efficiently establishes not only the tale's setting and basic premise, but also his narrational *modus operandi.*

Here is the entire opening passage, including the first two lines of the encomium:

> Whilom ther was dwellynge in Lumbardye
> A worthy knyght, that born was of Pavye,
> In which he lyved in greet prosperitee;
> And sixty yeer a wyflees man was hee,
> And folwed ay his bodily delyt
> On wommen, ther as was his appetyt,
> As doon thise fooles that been seculeer.

And whan that he was passed sixty yeer,
Were it for hoolynesse or for dotage
I kan nat seye, but swich a greet corage
Hadde this knyght to been a wedded man
That day and nyght he dooth al that he kan
T'espien where he myghte wedded be,
Preyinge oure Lord to graunten him that he
Mighte ones knowe of thilke blisful lyf
That is bitwixe an housbonde and his wyf,
And for to lyve under that hooly boond
With which that first God man and womman bond.
'Noon oother lyf,' seyde he, "is worth a bene,
For wedlok is so esy and so clene,
That in this world it is paradys."
Thus seyde this olde knyght, that was so wys.
And certeinly, as sooth as God is kyng,
To take a wyf it is a glorious thyng . . . (IV.12455–68)

As generations of readers have noticed, the tale opens by immediately signaling its relation to the *Clerk's Tale* by its choice, unique in the *Canterbury Tales*, of almost exactly the same setting, as well as of a principal male character with notable shared characteristics. This resemblance appears to have no internal motivation, given the allegorical generality of the characters January and May, and the particular details are not found in any of Chaucer's possible sources.[55] Hence, whether or not Chaucer originally planned the tale of January and May to follow immediately the Clerk, this opening indicates that, since one of the tale's principal aims is to *quit* the *Clerk's Tale*, the tale's full significance will unfold in dialogical relation with the Clerk's performance. Indeed, given what we saw in the previous chapter to be the axiological significance of the Clerk's longwinded, disingenuous decision not to repeat Petrarch's high-style account of the tale's setting in "West Lumbardye" (IV.46), the brevity here may be an indirect comment on the Clerk's entertainment of laureate poetics, however ambivalent that is – by which I mean that the brevity may reflect Chaucer's own scrutiny of his attraction to laureate poetics. In any event, the lines following the initial scene-setting, as I have argued above, more definitely and specifically target the Clerk, introducing very soon into the tale the category of the fabliau real in the form of the shared, heterosexual "appetyt" of January and the narrator, and thereby also setting the Clerk and his fable of Lombard marriage in a different category through the implied charge that the Clerk lacks this experience. This reading obviously depends upon hearing the winking tone that I have claimed characterizes the prologue and the entire tale, and rather than belabor this point, I simply suggest – with unavoidable circular reasoning – that this remark, in fact, sets that tone. It signals, retroactively, that the narrator's cooptation of the setting of the *Clerk's Tale* is no mere coincidence, and it indicates how we are to hear the narration that follows.

Thus, when the narrator next pauses to speculate very briefly on the source of January's sudden desire to become "a wedded man," I detect in the jocularity of this remark the initial instance, in miniature, of the tale's characteristic expansion and contraction dynamic. The clause order of, and line break between, "Were it for hoolynesse or for dotage" and "I kan nat seye" comically emphasizes the verbal irony of the latter declaration. Gentler and more humorous than simply stating that January's desire comes from "dotage," the remark nonetheless determines to communicate this fact even before revealing the object of his desire. Moreover, with the joke requiring for its effect an alternative explanation for this desire, the narrator uses the opportunity to invoke, with the quip "for hoolynesse," a vague set of spiritual values that points toward an axiological attitude beyond the blunt fact of January's "appetyt." But since the joke functions by canceling this expansion in the very instant of offering it, the result is the implication that January's unbridled libido is his real motive, and that his "dotage" consists of his delusion that the Church's sanction of marriage is one and the same as a sexual sanctuary for old age.

This implication quickly becomes explicit and ramifies in the lines that follow. After a witty (and antifeminist) threefold pun on "corage" – meaning at once "heart" in the sense of emotive disposition (*MED* 1a), "sexual desire" (*MED* 2b), and "valor" (*MED* 3a.), i.e., that he is brave enough to face life as a wedded man – the narrator makes use of indirect speech to elaborate January's delusion, recording his prayer to "oure Lorde" that he might experience "thilke blisful lyf" of matrimony and "to lyve under that hooly boond / With which that first God man and womman bond." Already here the narrator has evoked the Edenic allusiveness and the theological ambivalence toward marriage accompanying the story of Adam and Eve that is so important to the tale throughout, especially at its denouement. But because he attributes the word "blisful" to January, we suspect that it expresses a desire for a more corporeal sort of happiness along with spiritual blessing, a suspicion further encouraged by the narrator's pointed choice of the verb "espien" for January's pursuit of this desire, given that verb's connotations of stealth and ambush (*MED* 1a and 1b). (And the rime riche of "boond"/"bond" perhaps serves, through the emphasis that it creates, as the narrator's wry, Justinus-like comment that

January will receive more than he expects from this "blisful lyf.') The shift to direct speech in the subsequent lines – accomplishing a neatly telescoping progression of narrational modes – further reinforces this understanding of the nature of January's delusion and the according deflation of spiritual values. January's adjective "esy" has a suspiciously libidinal note (compare, e.g., Alan's pun on "esement" in the *Reeve's Tale*, IV.4179), which in turn attributes rather specific meaning to "clene," so that this adjective suggests that "wedlock" serves as a kind of laundering of the sort of ease that January has been used to. And, obviously, January's description of this scenario as an earthly "paradys" then makes explicit his already evident identification of humanity's prelapsarian condition with limitless sexual gratification, and hence of maritally sanctified sexuality as itself as a kind of salvation.[56]

Importantly, however, inasmuch as marriage is, in fact, "a ful greet sacrement" (IV.1319) – as the encomium subsequently observes – January is not simply just wrong. If that were so, then the effect of this passage would be straightforward moralistic satire, an exposure of erroneous belief by means of a caricature of a buffoonish Lombard knight. Instead, as Robert Edwards and others have pointed out, the implication and later assertion of marriage's sacramental status constitute "an orthodox expression of doctrine," one that appears as such in the *Parson's Tale*.[57] Not at all coincidentally, most resembling January's views is the Parson's identification of marriage as a "remedie agayns Leccherie," with which remedy one may realize the "chastitee and continence, that restreyneth alle the desordeynee moevynges that comen of flesshly talentes" (X.915):

> Now shaltow understonde that matrimoyne is leefful assemblynge of man and of womman that receyven by vertu of *the sacrement the boond* thurgh which they may nat be departed in al hir lyf – that is to seyn, whil that they lyven bothe. This, as seith the book, is *a ful greet sacrement. God maked it, as I have seyd, in paradys*, and wolde hymself be born in mariage . . . Trewe effect of mariage *clenseth fornicacioun* and replenysseth hooly chirche of good lynage; for that is the ende of mariage; and it *chaungeth deedly synne into venial synne* bitwixe hem that been ywedded, and maketh the hertes al oon of hem that been ywedded, as wel as the bodies. This is verray mariage, that was *establissed by God, er that synne bigan*, whan natureel lawe was in his right poynt in *paradys* . . . (X.917–21, emphases added)

The conceptual and even verbal echoes between this passage and the lead-in to the marriage encomium (and subsequently the encomium itself) are unmistakable. Regardless of whether Chaucer had this specific passage in mind when writing this portion of the tale of January and May (and the evident sources for the encomium appear to point elsewhere), he plainly was working closely with the ideas and terminology of the doctrinal positions that it voices. On close inspection, the line between January's travesty of this doctrine and that doctrine itself is difficult to draw, for that doctrine at least superficially corresponds with January's plans to mitigate the "desordeynee moevynges" of his "flesshly talentes" (i.e., his improperly excessive, habitual physical urges – see *MED disordeine* adj. a and b, and *talent* n. 2a and 3a) by means of the sacramental "boond" that "clenseth fornicacioun."

The narrator's winking rejoinder to January's assertion – "Thus seyde this olde knyght, that was so wys" – has a much darker effect, therefore, than merely remarking on the latter's travesty. By rhyming "wys" with "paradys," the obvious verbal irony attached to the former word infects the latter. While we know from the general antifeminist attitude of the passage (which the prologue belatedly makes unmissable) that in one sense the narrator is simply saying that marriage is hell, the remark draws no explicit boundaries in the subverting force of its irony: it does not appear at all hesitant to throw out the doctrinal baby with the travesty bathwater. The deeper suggestion, therefore, is that the wisdom of the doctrine itself – of the paradisiacal origin and salvific function of marriage – is ultimately a reflex of humanity's ineluctable "flesshly talentes." The joke of the line targets January, but inasmuch as we adopt the narrator's attitude toward the character, we also grant – for most readers, unwittingly at this early juncture – the implied deflation of spiritual values in confrontation with the ground of the fabliau real.

When the tale's opening is read in this fashion, the narrational status of the encomium – which begins after the narrator's remark on January's wisdom with the observation, "And certeinly, as sooth as God is kyng, / To take a wyf it is a glorious thyng" – presents no difficulty. The encomium plainly continues in the same vein as the initial twenty-two lines, functioning discursively and thematically in precisely the same fashion. It lauds marriage by expanding upon the range of values that marriage holds – especially spiritual ones, as in the aforementioned line about its sacramental status, and in such comments as "A wyf is Goddes yifte verraily" (IV.1311), but also including such practical values as a wife's provision of "good conseil" (IV.1362) and her management of the household ("A wyf is kepere of thyn housbondrye" [IV.1380]). But throughout one perceives a constantly deflating counter-pressure, most often through coy, indirect subversion, but at least twice – in the verbal equivalent of physical winks – through the same kind of unmistakable verbal irony as "that was so wys."

One of these verbal winks occurs roughly midway through the encomium (IV.1316–18), immediately before the assertion "Mariage is a ful greet sacrement," and the other, appropriately, at the encomium's termination: "They [Housbonde and wyf] been so knyt ther may noon harm bityde, / And namely upon the wyves syde" (IV.1391–92). In effect, the encomium replays the opening passage as a virtually standalone set piece that possesses magisterial amplitude of allusive erudition, rhetorical elaboration, and hortatory style. It brings the narrative to a standstill, which is to say that its principal purpose is the twin one of widening the axiological range within the narrator's sights and showing the narrator to be the equal of any Oxford clerk. Hence, whether it is to be imagined as a direct record of January's thoughts, the narrator's account of January's thoughts, the narrator's own remarks, an instance of unimpersonated artistry, or even some sort of authorial interposition, does not in the end much matter. In the encomium's clear continuity with what has come before, it is unmistakably expressed from within the characterological field of the Merchant, whoever also happens to be occupying that field in this instance.

Lewed Wordes

The second instance of the tale's characteristic narrational dynamic that I will consider – January's Canticles-inspired serenade to May and, especially, the narrator's rejoinder – possesses a similar axiological target as that of the encomium (in contrast with, say, the romance values invoked in the passages describing Damian and May). But this instance is more compressed, more discursively complex, and, ultimately, even severer in its ramifications. The passage occurs between the moment when May – in response to the now constant physical surveillance of suddenly blind and hence obsessively jealous January, his "hond on hire alway" (IV.2091) – determines to copy January's *clyket,* and the moment when she puts her plan into action, making a sign to Damian to proceed into January's garden by means of the duplicate *clyket* and wait for her "under a bussh" (IV.2155). Like the encomium, then, this passage constitutes a tellingly egregious interruption of the narrative:

> . . . unto his May seith he:
> "Rys up, my wyf, my love, my lady free!
> The turtles voys is herd, my dowve sweete;
> The wynter is goon with alle his reynes weete.
> Com forth now, with thyne eyen columbyn!
> How fairer been thy brestes than is wyn!

The gardyn is enclosed al aboute;
Com forth, my white spouse! Out of doute
Thou hast me wounded in myn herte, O wyf!
No spot of thee ne knew I al my lyf.
Com forth, and lat us taken oure disport;
I chees thee for my wyf and my confort."
Swiche olde lewed wordes used he. (IV.2137–49)

In its very superfluity, January's speech calls attention to itself as an instance of the narrator/Chaucer showing off, weaving a pastiche of Canticles imagery into an elegant, charming, standalone love poem – what one of Chaucer's most perceptive readers has judged "a passage of unsullied poetic lyricism" – and at the same time intensifying the tale's kaleidoscope of garden allusions and their correspondingly tangled spiritual and secular resonances.[58] And yet, because the mediating lens of the Song of Songs' exegetical tradition – in which, most typically, the male speaker is taken to be Christ and the female either the Church or the human soul – is so inculcated in modern reading practices (as it presumably was even more so for medieval ones), even those who find themselves feeling some sympathy for January at this point in the tale tend to reduce the significance of these lines by largely dismissing them as yet another instance of January's perverse conflation, or just inversion, of the carnal and spiritual. Cooper's assessment is typical: "January perverts [the Song of Songs] by applying it literally, reducing its allegorical function as the highest expression of the love of Christ and the Church back to bare sexuality, and blind sexuality at that[.]"[59]

What critics have missed about January's love lyric, however, is that it is at once simpler and, for that reason, more complex than a carnal perversion of scripture. For in fact January cannot be said to misinterpret the Song of Songs, simply because he is not represented as *interpreting* it at all, but rather as *imitating* it, or even *reenacting* it. And, indeed, how could January avoid "applying it literally," if he is to apply it all, in his particular situation? A reenactment is obviously much more fitting than a proper exegetical interpretation, since the latter requires, among other things, a male reader to cross-identify with the "lady free," or *sponsa*, so that, as *Glossa Ordinaria* prescribes, "requiescat inter brachia sponsi" (he may rest within the arms of the bridegroom).[60] Instead, since January is trying to coax May into outdoor, springtime coitus, he appropriately adopts the bridegroom position. One might object that he is thereby *mis*appropriating scripture – that by imitating it for this purpose he is sacrilegiously abusing it – but such an objection, again, moves too quickly through the mediation of the exegetical tradition. For of course the Song of Songs itself does not contain its own "allegorical function"; it is, rather, a lyrical voicing of erotic longing and beckoning. What January does, therefore, is not misappropriate scripture but rather entirely elide its exegetical appropriation, presenting to us the "naked text," as Chaucer elsewhere puts it: the text without gloss.[61] In contrast to the lead-in to the marriage encomium, in which January conflates the categories of carnal and spiritual, in this instance he presents as carnal what is in fact carnal, but which we are used to understanding otherwise. Our very discomfort with the passage – our sense of January's perversion – hence registers our own unease with the literal level of Canticles so laid bare. Lurking within the burlesque is a subtle evocation of the gaping hermeneutical distance between letter and spirit, between the two lovers and what they are supposed to signify.

It is a mistake, moreover, to suppose that medieval readers of the Song of Songs – and of the *Canterbury Tales* – would not have perceived such semiotic fissures as least as much as we do, if not necessarily in the same fashion. As Ann Astell has lucidly summarized, from at least Origen's third-century allegoresis of Canticles onward, medieval Christian readers have registered their acute awareness of the challenges that the Song poses.[62] Indeed, as Astell emphasizes, an exegetical tradition beginning in the twelfth century sought to leverage precisely the affective (and libidinal) power of the letter of the text within a nonetheless spiritualizing reading practice, and hence not surprisingly these commentators frequently remarked upon the risks that this practice's attention to the carnal may incur. For example, in the preface of *Glossa*, a proper reading of Canticles is conceived as a kind of libidinal laundering by means of an almost psychoanalytical transference effect, whereby the fiery energies of natural desire ("naturalis amoris incendium") become focused on God rather than on the body. So redirected, such energies become, in Astell's paraphrase of Hugh of St. Victor, "laudable (because God-oriented) concupiscence."[63] Yet Hugh was fully aware of the challenges of this kind of transformative reading practice, observing that the "difficulty consists . . . in reading the letter without reading *according to* the letter . . . in remembering the divine reference; in joining the letter and the spirit in an integral reading experience."[64] In theory the Song is so made "safe," but the very fact that it beckoned such a procedure points to evident awareness of the distance between the literal, carnal meaning and the received products of allegoresis. For this very reason, the Canticles preface in *Glossa* concludes (in some manuscripts) with the admonition – analogous with modern-day film ratings – that this book of the Bible may not be suitable for all readers:

> Illud uero non est omittendum quod a doctoribus nostris traditur apud Hebreos hanc fuisse obseruationem, ne cuiquam hunc librum legere permitterent nisi uiro jam perfectae scientiae et roboratae fidei ne forte per imbecillitatem infantiae et fidei imperitiam non tam erudiret cognitio lubricas mentes quam textus ad concupiscentias corporales conuerteret.
>
> Nor should we overlook what our scholars tell us was the custom among the Jews: they did not allow anyone to read this book unless he was complete in knowledge and confirmed in faith, lest perhaps on account of childish weakness and inexperience in faith study might not so much refine wavering minds as the text pervert to carnal desires. (ll. 101–9)[65]

Stitched into the very fabric of the Song's late medieval normative exegetical wrapping was this warning that those who are less than "complete in knowledge and confirmed in faith" may fall into the gap between carnal signifier and spiritual signified.

Thus, when even Astell writes that "lecherous old January . . . gives the Song a definitively literal reading when he paraphrases it for May as an invitation to marital sex that is, in intent and practice, no more than legally sanctioned fornication," she missteps, like other critics, in attributing to January a hermeneutic role rather than a mimetic or dramatic one (again, how could *January* give the Song an allegorical reading?).[66] But she also suggests the darker implication of the burlesque. If the Song is shorn of its transference machinery, then how different is it (at least the portions of it that January draws on) from "an invitation to marital sex that is, in intent and practice, no more than legally sanctioned fornication" – especially if one imagines the putative male speaker, Solomon, less as wise author of Proverbs and more as how Proserpina, not at all coincidentally, shortly represents him, i.e., as "a lecchour and an ydolastre" (IV.2298)? To be sure, notwithstanding the sympathy some feel for January at this point (which further complicates the response to his reenactment of the Song), the fabliau context in which this passage appears seems to defang this suggestion, precisely by making a joke out of it – with the humor analogous to that prompted by, say, chimpanzees wearing coats and ties and sitting around a boardroom table. But this surface defanging in turn indicates how this passage reproduces exactly the same sort of axiological deflation in the face of a fabliau real that characterizes the entire tale. For inasmuch as the chimpanzee joke may suggest that beneath the late-capitalist values defining the multinational corporation the actual values executives operate by are those of a bunch of chimps (a joke unfair to chimps, of course), the fabliau context may be perceived as disclosing the actual values of the Song. It may suggest, that is, that the Song is precisely what the author of *Glossa* fears "childish" readers may take it to be.

We are hence left suspended in uncomfortable, uncertain laughter at January's song, unsure whether it mocks January, Canticles, or both, and we look with some urgency to the narrator for clarifying judgment regarding this burlesque – which is why the narrator's terse, one-line rejoinder is so brilliantly devastating: "Swiche olde lewed wordes used he." Unfortunately, however, this line has been an especial victim of dramatic readings of the narrator and of construal of the tale's tone as bitter. Critics have suggested, for example, that the Merchant, as a man entrenched deeply in the secular world, simply does not understand the allusion; or that the line, in its knowing assessment of the Song of Songs, in all its figural scope, as "olde lewed wordes" is an expression of the narrator's deeply embittered perspective; or that the narrator, becoming a voice of clerical authority, here castigates January for his misreading of Canticles.[67] Instead, this line is better understood as continuous with the jocular tone and tightly controlled irony of the rest of the narrator's darkly comic performance. It is continuous with, indeed, the immediately preceding passage, in which the narrator apostrophizes "noble Ovyde" and alludes to the story of "Piramus and Tesbee," whose "sleighte" of "rownynge thurgh a wal" coyly doubles the *double entendre* of *clyket* and *wyket*. Heard with this tone, the narrator's comment on January's reenactment of Canticles is, in its most basic function, a means of calling attention to the allusion itself in the event that the reader missed it (since, unlike the allusion to Ovid, it is nowhere explicitly marked). The comment announces that there is something to be noticed in January's speech and, importantly, that the narrator is taking credit for it. For, although January speaks the "olde lewed wordes," the narrator's one-liner makes clear that the joke – the burlesque – is the narrator's doing. Retroactively, we understand that January's sudden adoption of such an allusively poetic biblical style is yet another one of the narrator's comic set pieces, just like the marriage encomium.

Of course, in addition to marking and taking credit for this set piece, the narrator's comment also offers a retrospective assessment. In this function, "olde lewed wordes" is, at one level, yet another obvious instance of verbal irony, and, as such, it is a signal that we are to notice that the "wordes," although indeed "olde," are scarcely "lewed" but rather those that are spoken by the mystical Bridegroom to the mystical Bride in one of the most heavily commented upon books of the Bible. At this level, the joke is merely the absurdity of the narrator's knowing application of the Song to the situation of January and May – the absurdity, analogously, of chimps in suits. Yet at a deeper level, as that analogy suggests, the comment also refuses to resolve the ambiguity of the implications of the absurdity: it does not, so to speak, let us off the hook of our uncomfortable uncertainty, but rather compounds it, compressing all its force into the boundaries of the semantic field of the single word "lewed."

For this instance of the word, the *MED* chooses the rather broad definition of "lacking in refinement, untutored, uncouth; of disposition or conduct: ill-bred, boorish, unmannerly; of form or appearance: rough, crude, ugly; of talk, stories, etc.: coarse, ill-mannered, rude; of literary works or style: unsophisticated, unpolished" (*leued* adj. 2c). But, as is typical of definitions, elements of this one overlap with others, so that, for example, "untutored" bleeds into "Uneducated, ignorant; unlettered, unable to read Latin; lay, non-clerical" (1a), while "of talk, stories, etc.: coarse, ill-mannered, rude" points toward "evil, wicked; dishonest; unchaste, lascivious" (2e). Although the latter meaning seems not to have been very common in Middle English and mostly later than Chaucer, it is so suitable to the character of January that it seems likely to be at least within the word's range of connotation here.[68] Insinuated, then, is a confirmation of what we suspected from January's speech alone: outside of the Latin, clerical context of the Song's exegetical tradition, the Song is, as the *Glossa* author fears, lascivious – or, as Augustine long before worried, a text conducive "ad libidinosae cupiditatis affectum" (to a disposition of libidinous cupidity).[69] Once again, we suspect that executives are chimps in suits.

As with the tale's opening passage, if we hear a jocular, controlled irony here, we cannot simply dismiss this implication as deriving from a warped, malevolent consciousness. We must recognize, moreover, that it reproduces the same opposition between the fabliau real – the libidinous cupidity of the human animal – and a spiritual set of values, only here the stakes are considerably larger. Not just the sacramental status of marriage but also the fundamental method of reading that finds the spiritual in the merely human is the target of the narrator's comic bite.[70] Let me be clear, however, that with this assertion I am not also claiming that the narrator (and Chaucer, inasmuch as an authorial perspective is present in the characterological field) represents a kind of proto-nihilist or, even less likely, proto-atheist. It was certainly thinkable in the late Middle Ages to deny that anything within the sphere of the human – whether the practice of marriage or methods of reading scripture – had certain connection with the divine and to assert that because the divine is by definition unfathomable, human discourse about it is always potentially delusional. This skepticism might roughly be identified as nominalist, but to do so would risk characterizing the tale of January and May as coded theological commentary, when its nature is rather different.[71] As we have seen, the tale does not seek to make any affirmations of a systematic kind, even implicitly; it does not argue for a nominalist position but instead, with its assumption of a fabliau real, classifies any systematic affirmation as fiction. Its target, therefore, is not theological but discursive.

In this regard, the narrator's easily overlooked word "used" is significant. While the primary sense of the word is obviously just the past tense of "to speak" (*MED usen* v. 4), the context also supports the secondary sense of "to use (someone else's words, the words of the gospel, one's wits, etc.), utilize (a means to an end)" (1d). There is, in other words, an instrumental sense in the narrator's account of January's speech, the notion that January sought to gain something through his reenactment of the Song – which, of course, he did, and as did the Song's original male actor. What the narrator further insinuates, then, is that allegoresis covers over not only the fabliau real but also the relationship between celebrated poetic lyricism and its instrumental motivation. January models not just the carnality of the naked Song but also the reasons why anything like the Song is ever composed.

A literary axiology thus lurks in the narrator's remark, although, for at least two reasons, it is not quite as simple as the formula that the value of literature is as a means to obtain what one desires. First, the category of fiction for the narrator encompasses not just literary fictions but, as we have seen, any system of values other than the fabliau one. On the one hand, then, the narrator gives to the category of fiction immense scope and power, in effect seeing it as pervading all dimensions of human life; but, on the other hand, he narrows its value to an instrument to realize individual desire. Furthermore, as suggested throughout the tale but as is especially evident in its conclusion, in respect to the instrumental value of any particular fiction, the narrator divides individuals into two groups: those under the illusion of the fiction, and those who use it to deceive the ones in the first group (with the possibility, as illustrated repeatedly with January, of the same individual playing both roles, living under a self-deluding illusion).

Famously – or notoriously – the tale of January and May possesses a highly equivocal happy ending, with a perhaps pregnant May convincing her husband, his sight newly restored, that he did not see what in fact he saw: she and Damian copulating in a tree. The tale concludes, in other words, with a vivid exemplification of its literary axiology, an exemplification that was to a large degree long ago articulated by David:

> Proserpine has given May her answer, a brilliant bit of fiction . . . January is only too willing to let the truth be decently hidden once more under the smock of language . . . May's statement – "He that mysconceyveth, he mysdemeth" – could be taken as the ironic thesis of the Merchant's Tale. Most men misconceive and misdeem, most men remain blind because they choose to believe the lies of women and the lies of poets. They do so in order to remain happy.[72]

The moral, so to speak, of the tale's conclusion is that fictions are a tool of deception, "the smock of language" that canny individuals like the Proserpina-inspired May use to obtain what they desire, especially the objects of the corporeal desire that the fabliau real declares to be "the truth" of the human condition. Dramatically enacted in the denouement, this moral is the oft-cited one that the narrator earlier expresses in aphoristic form in what is perhaps the sole earnest remark in his entire performance, his parenthetical comment about the dramatic fiction of obeisant respect for January that Damian enacts upon learning that his master's wife has agreed to have sex with him: "For craft is al, whoso that do it kan" (IV.2016). Those who are deluded by such fictions misconstrue their circumstances and live under an illusion – "He that mysconceyveth, he mysdemeth" – yet nonetheless, and crucially, "They do so to remain happy," as David observes.

In other words, the moral of the tale's ending does not actually offer a judgment of any moral sort, whether of normative or fabliau morality. Although January appears as the gulled fool, the narrator does not suggest that May is necessarily in any sort of inherently superior position. They both get what they desire, and it is in fact somewhat easier to imagine January living happily ever after than May doing so, which is to say that a deceiving agent, for whom the veil has fallen from the fabliau real, is not necessarily better off than the one who mistakes the veil for what it covers. Instead, what the ending most neatly dramatizes is the complementarity of these positions: in the world in which January and May live, May gets what she wants by deceiving January, and January gets what he wants by being deceived by May. Fictions, although valueless except as an instrument of deception, are thus nonetheless profoundly valuable: they are what sustain human relationships (and hence human society) despite the underlying human condition of the fabliau real, relationships that without those fictions would unravel into Hobbesian nastiness.

This point has already evoked the second complicating aspect of the narrator's literary axiology. As profoundly valuable as fictions are, they nonetheless have no value in and of themselves. In their instrumental nature, they are only valuable in relationship to what they are used to obtain. This aspect is what is ultimately responsible for the tale's negative force: because the tale extends the category of fiction to virtually all value systems, its insistence on the narrow instrumentality of fiction comprehensively negates those values as such. And this aspect is also what makes the tale so starkly contrast with the Clerk's performance. For in the latter, it is the multiplicity of fiction's applications that free fiction from any application whatsoever and give it a value *sui generis*. For the narrator of the tale of January and May, fiction has only one actual use; all its other putative uses merely draw lines of connections between one fiction and another, for example, Griselda as spiritual exemplum connects the fiction of the Griselda story with the fiction of a spiritual system of values, whereas Griselda as uxorial exemplum connects the tale with the fiction of a domestic, patriarchal system of values. To imagine that literary fiction, because it may connect with myriad other fictions, is therefore valuable in itself is, so to speak, to live in a dream world: it is to ignore the actual, single instrumental function of any sort of fiction. To compose fictions without regard to this instrumental function is thus to waste one's time – to be, quite literally, unproductive.

"Sownynge alwey th'encrees of his wynnyng"

These last formulations already begin to answer the question that will occupy the remainder of this chapter, the question of what Chaucer saw about the tale of January and May that eventually led him to assign it to the Merchant and position it immediately following the Clerk's performance. But the way is not entirely clear: my approach prohibits the easy circularity of claiming, for example, that the narrator's insistence on the productive instrumentality of fiction reflects a specifically mercantile mentality or ideology, and so instead I must address the question of the tale's assignment initially in more general terms. As I have mentioned, Chaucer does appear to have written the tale to respond to others, especially the *Knight's Tale*, the *Wife of Bath's Prologue and Tale*, and, most of all, the *Clerk's Tale*. Its original design, therefore, in large part seems to have been to serve as a dialogical counter to the strains of idealism in the first and third of those other tales (however complexly limited those strains already appear on their own) and at the same time as a kind male verso to the Wife's recto (in regard to, for example, the reflexive deployment of antifeminist discourse and dubiously happy endings). Specifically in respect to the *Clerk's Tale*, the tale of January and May, as I have argued, positions its disidealizing literary axiology in opposition to the ambiguously idealizing literary axiology that eventually emerges in the enigmatic Clerk's performance, which also represents Chaucer's own, perhaps by then lapsed, literary axiology. The tale of January and May in this way stages Chaucer's self-skepticism of this literary axiology, and for this purpose – as well as, obviously, that of responding to the *Knight's Tale* – Chaucer saw the great potential of the fabliau genre, and in particular in the nature of its claim on the real. He saw that, because of this built-in generic claim, an expansion of the axiological scope of a fabliau narrative could have a powerful disidealizing effect. The question that we must ask about tale assignment, then, is what led Chaucer to associate this disidealizing strategy and effect with the Merchant – and, in particular, the Merchant of the *General Prologue*.

As has been often pointed out, at first glance the Merchant's portrait does not in fact seem to be a likely description of the teller of the tale of January and May, as nothing in the portrait – in contrast with, say, those of the Monk or Friar, who have both been proposed as original tellers of the tale – seems an obvious cue to a fabliau. Moreover, to many the reticent Merchant of the portrait seems even further removed from the emotionally unleashed Merchant of the tale's prologue. Nonetheless, the order of portraits in the *General Prologue* does suggest that Chaucer conceived of the Clerk and Merchant as representing an axiologically counterpointing pair. Their portraits appear next to each other in the "new men" sequence of Merchant-Clerk-Sergeant-Franklin, which follows the ecclesiastical group of Prioress-Second Nun-Nun's Priest-Monk-Friar, and which is itself followed by the guildsmen, Cook, Shipman, Physician, and Wife.[73] Bronson long ago suggested that for the purposes of the *General Prologue*, "the Merchant and the Clerk were conceived and set side by side as a contrasting pair, in life and in philosophy" and that the "grounds of the anticipated opposition between Merchant and Clerk were then materialism vs. idealism ... an all-embracing world-outlook of opposing values."[74] In a general fashion, my argument about the Merchant's portrait aligns with this view, and therefore a simple answer to the question of why Chaucer gave the tale of January and May to the Merchant is that he realized that that assignment would serve to elaborate and deepen this "all-embracing world-outlook of opposing values" – even though Bronson himself understood Chaucer as writing the tale originally for much narrower aims.

The answer becomes more complicated, of course, when we seek to define the nature of these "opposing values" in respect to the axiological persons that the *General Prologue* portraits define in each case. As we saw in the previous chapter, the Clerk's idealism – which to a large degree takes the socioeconomic form of material deprivation – is far from a straightforwardly positive attribute but rather consists of a complex axiological positioning vis-à-vis the university, one which Chaucer may have found attractive but also perhaps limited or even naïvely escapist. The Merchant's materialism likewise requires some careful delineation against the historical resonances of the details of the portrait, for that materialism is certainly not simply a master category for all the supposedly negative character traits (e.g., greed, pride, usuriousness) that many, but not all, have found the portrait to catalog.

Indeed, just as with the Clerk's portrait (and the others of IV-V), readings of the Merchant's have tended to divide starkly along the axis of praise and blame, producing a bifurcated but lopsided critical response, with the majority finding the Clerk's portrait to be largely idealizing, while judging the rhetorical status of the Merchant's portrait to be satirical. For example, Nancy Reale argues that "while the Merchant comports himself as if he were a gentleman, he is in fact a fraud and a criminal whose profit is made unlawfully at the expense of others," and this claim illustrates well both the portrait's degree of resistance to a satirical reading (so that it at least appears to describe "a gentleman") and the critical desire to break through that resistance and record the author's actual judgment of the character.[75] In contrast to this view, a minority tradition has countered that the portrait's historically specific details of mercantile activity and concerns, when recognized as such in light of contemporary attitudes toward merchants and the portrait's lack of any directly condemnatory remarks, render a realistically drawn individual of this occupation that is at least neutral and perhaps laudatory. As Richard Goddard has aptly observed, in the "simple dichotomy" of this critical response, the minority view has often been taken by historians, especially "those whose main interest is in medieval financial history," while literary critics have tended toward the majority view. Being himself a historian, Goddard accordingly concludes that the portrait presents "an ideal, honest merchant, working within the law, whose work is essential to the efficient functioning of the state," and thus it "provides the modern reader with a detailed and realistic snapshot of a fourteenth-century merchant and his business."[76]

If we do not assume, however, that portraits must necessarily be, on balance, either acts of praise or blame, or exercises in either neutral realism or literary caricature, but (especially for this group of "new men") are definitions of particular constellations of values associated with specific occupational and institutional social positions, then we may draw freely from both critical positions without incurring the reductiveness of either. Or, to put this point another way, literary convention and historical allusion both have claims on these portraits, and their subtle interweaving comprises much of the fabric of the very specific axiological persons that as such necessarily serve as focal points of judgment, but without then necessarily determining the nature of that judgment. In the brief space of the Merchant's portrait, Chaucer powerfully evokes a quite specific constellation of values, which, as I suggested in this book's introduction, we cannot help but judge in respect to the networks of values in which we ourselves are situated. Hence, whether or not we judge this constellation wanting in comparison with that of the Clerk depends to some degree on our relative alignment with these constellations. Not surprisingly, then, literary critics have tended to denigrate the Merchant in favor of the Oxford student, while economic historians have been kinder to the former. Of course, Chaucer himself, as I consider later, had affiliations with both positions.

Here is the Merchant's portrait in its entirety:

A MARCHANT was ther with a forked berd,
In mottelee, and hye on horse he sat;
Upon his heed a Flaundryssh bever hat,
His bootes clasped faire and fetisly.
His resons he spak ful solempnely,
Sownynge alwey th'encrees of his wynnyng.
He wolde the see were kept for any thyng
Bitwixe Middelburgh and Orewelle.
Wel koude he in eschaunge sheeldes selle.
This worthy man ful wel his wit bisette:
Ther wiste no wight that he was in dette,
So estatly was he of his governaunce
With his bargaynes and with his chevyssaunce.
For sothe he was a worthy man with alle,
But, sooth to seyn, I noot how men hym calle. (I.270–84)

Jill Mann's elucidation of the claims of literary convention on this portrait remains among the most nuanced and penetrating studies in this vein. Reading the portrait closely against the context of the estates satire tradition, Mann shows how Chaucer has unmistakably evoked this tradition by means of verbal cues and telling selection of topics. Terms such as "bargaynes" and "chevyssaunce," while they had neutral meanings, also possessed pejorative ones that were common to estates satire descriptions of merchants, as were such topics as the Merchant's "wynnyng," his skill at selling "sheeldes" "in eschunge," and his indebtedness, even though none of these is necessarily in itself a negative judgment of his character. Chaucer's very evocation of this tradition, however, at the same time signals his striking departure from it, specifically, his total "omission of the victim"; as Mann observes, "The 'innocent' or the 'poor', who are elsewhere mentioned as the inevitable sufferers from this avarice and dishonesty [typical to estates satire accounts of merchants], are conspicuous by their absence."[77] As a result, the portrait suspends, for the moment, one's impulse toward immediate judgment and instead foregrounds – or begs additional scrutiny of – the occupational practices and mentalities that those terms and topics signify.

These practices and mentalities, as the minority critical tradition has amply documented, were in fact historically accurate for and typical of late fourteenth-century London merchants of the apparent stature of the one of the *General Prologue*. As Ladd remarks, "[E]very potentially negative detail of the Merchant's description can have, but need not have, a completely innocent explanation": almost all elements of the portrait – from the Merchant's "forked berd" to his "mottelee" garment, "Flaundryssh bever hat," focus on "wynnyng," concern for the safety of the Channel "Bitwixe Middelburgh and Orewelle," selling of "sheeldes," concealment of the extent of his "dette," and his "bargaynes" and "chevyssaunce" – have been corroborated in the historical record, not as necessary signs of mercantile vanity or corrupt practice, but as the expected fashions, attitudes, and activity of a London man of this class.[78] Yet to conclude, on this basis, that the portrait presents, as Goddard claims, "an ideal, honest merchant" goes too far in ignoring the implications of the literary context that Mann has identified and, more important, the vexed moral and social status of merchants (of which Goddard is fully aware) that informed and sustained that literary context. The tension in the Merchant's portrait between its simultaneous historical veracity and evocation of estates satire, instead of resolving itself in one direction or the other, points toward the larger ideological and sociological tensions that shaped a typical late medieval London mercantile axiology and thus also positive and negative evaluations of this axiology.

These latter tensions are especially signaled by the portrait's emphasis on profit, risk, and appearances, and the manner in which it associates these with one another. The disarmingly offhand remark of lines I.274–75 – "His resons he spak ful solempnely, / Sownynge alwey th'encrees of his wynnyng" – is, in its suggestive lexis, particularly expressive in this regard. The term "resons," with a simple primary sense here of "words, remarks" (*MED resoun* n.[2] 8a), connotes also justifications (4b), persuasions (8b), schemes (8e), principles (5a), and reckonings (8a), and was even used in some contexts as a synonym for income (6b). "Solempnely" means "in a dignified manner" (*MED solempneli* adv. c), although, because the narrator uses the term just after we learn that the Friar is "a ful solempne man" (I.209), we wonder if the Merchant's outward manner shares the pecuniarily instrumental function readily apparent in the Friar's dignified demeanor. "Sownynge" has a complex semantic field that extends metonymically and metaphorically from a basic sense of causing a sound to be made (*MED sounen* v. 1a). For this instance, the *MED* chooses "proclaiming" or "celebrating" (4a), but this seems in some contradiction with "ful solempnely" (which adverb, while it may indicate a calculated pose, is not elsewhere used by Chaucer with such simple irony) and with the general reticence the rest of the portrait seems to convey. More likely, the sense here lies somewhere amid "concerning," "according with," "producing," and "encouraging" – the very same corner of the semantic field, not at all coincidentally, evident in the pointedly contrasting echo of the usage in the Clerk's portrait: "Sowynge in moral vertu was his speche" (I.307).[79] The gerund "wynnyng" quite evidently is a synonym for profit (*MED winning* ger. 1b) or, more generally, material gain. Altogether, then, the statement conveys the Merchant's all-pervading concern, not just with profit, but with its "encrees," a concern he cloaks to some degree in his dignified manner, but to which his topics of conversation either explicitly habitually refer, or covertly unfailingly facilitate, or alternate between both of these.[80] Profit, in other words, is central to his consciousness, and his concern with its increase comprehensively instrumentalizes his strategies of appearance, from the clasps on his boots, to his "resons," to his "estatly . . . governaunce." Crucially, however, this characterization does not also, by itself, offer negative judgment of the merchant's supposedly crass materialism, as tempting as that conclusion may be to underpaid academics who would gladly learn and teach. Rather, it simply zeroes in on what was in fact at the practical heart of the late medieval merchant's economic livelihood and hence also social identity, and what was at the same time the crux of the merchant class's ambivalent moral and spiritual status.

Practically, in late medieval, precapitalist England – or, more specifically, before the means of production became costly enough so that their ownership became the primary basis of wealth – a merchant's livelihood depended upon cunning manipulation of "circulating capital in the form of materials," or, to put it simply, upon buying wholesale goods and supplies low and selling them high, however elaborated and multifarious those activities became when performed at the international level of Chaucer's Merchant.[81] As Sylvia Thrupp has well documented, one's entry into and continuance in the politically and economically dominant (for London) merchant class depended more-or-less wholly on purchasing power, both from the funds one had on hand and from those that one could raise through various means of borrowing – which is to say that one's social identity and participation in the London mercantile hegemony depended upon initial, ample financial resources and continued financial success.[82] As another of Chaucer's merchants succinctly remarks, "But o thyng is, ye knowe it wel ynogh, / Of chapmen, that hir moneie is hir plogh" (VII.287–88). This dependency made this class position far from secure. While fourteenth-century London merchants, dealing in large quantities, could amass great wealth (and thereby become the principal moneylenders to the Crown), at the same time they could suffer immense losses, resulting in a roller-coaster-like career trajectory that was particularly evident across generations. As Jenny Kermode observes, late medieval English merchants (and specifically those in London and York) "comprised a mobile and fluid class of people who quickly accumulated wealth within a single lifetime, only to see it as rapidly dispersed"; and thus, as Thrupp quips, "the curve of fortune was usually downward."[83]

For this reason, the immediate follow-up to the revelation of the Merchant's all-pervading concern with "his wynnyng" is almost inevitable: a disclosure of his anxiety about the security of his "chevyssaunce," specifically in this instance the safety of the Channel. For the loss – say, to pirates – of a ship laden with wool or cloth headed for the Dutch port of "Middelburgh" could be devastating. To turn again to the merchant of Chaucer's *Shipman's Tale*, this inherent insecurity of the occupation is the very point that he makes to his wife, when, approaching him when he is busy with his "rekenynges," she insists that he has "ynough, pardee, of Goddes sonde," and that he should therefore put aside his "bookes" and "thynges," let his "bagges stonde," and join her and "daun John" for dinner (VII.217–23). "Wyf," he replies,

> litel kanstow devyne
> The curious bisynesse [worrisome preoccupations] that we have.
> For of us chapmen, also God me save,

And by that lord that clepid is Seint Yve,
Scarsly amonges twelve tweye shul thryve
Continuelly, lastynge unto oure age.
. . .
And therfore have I greet necessitee
Upon this queynte [tricky] world t'avyse me,
For everemoore we moote stonde in drede
Of hap and fortune in oure chapmanhede. (VII.224–38, *Riverside*'s glosses)

Although the ratio of just two merchants out of every twelve maintaining success across a lifetime is likely here intentional hyperbole, the passage vividly conveys the mercantile predisposition toward "drede" because of the whims of "hap and fortune" and the consequent ceaseless vigilance the profession required.[84] And as the *Shipman's Tale* readily illustrates, these risks were of course intensified inasmuch as the merchant undertaking them funds his investment on credit. Apparently, we are to understand that this is the very habit of the *General Prologue* Merchant, given the line, following the disclosure of his feelings about the safety of the sea, about his selling shields "in eschaunge" (although historians do not agree on exactly what activity this describes), as well as the following couplet remarking upon the Merchant's concealed "dette."[85]

This volatility of mercantile wealth had several consequences, including the regularity with which merchants' sons (such as, of course, Chaucer) did not follow their parents into the profession but instead pursued careers with more stable sources of income, even if they were less remunerative.[86] For merchants, this volatility naturally encouraged them to maximize the profit of any particular transaction, since it may well need to make up for the loss of the next one. Contrary to the remark of the wife in the *Shipman's Tale*, at any given time a merchant could *never* have "ynough . . . of Goddes sonde," since tomorrow a single stroke of "hap and fortune" may destroy the financial basis of his "chapmanhede." For the late medieval London merchant – whether or not he also possessed such spiritually troublesome motives as greed or pride – simply to perform his occupation well (which is to say, simply to maintain himself in that occupation) required that he must always be vigilant about his profit margins, always be preoccupied with "th'encrees of his wynnyng." And he must also always keep up appearances, because the image of prosperity, irrespective of what it did or did not conceal, was a key factor in successful buying, selling, and borrowing: he had to look and act the part, regardless of what resources he actually had at his disposal.[87]

With these last points we arrive at the moral and spiritual ambivalence that continued to be directed toward mercantile activity in Chaucer's day, which ambivalence, simply put, derives from the difficulty of drawing the line between circumspect prudence on the one hand and greed and deception on the other. As a number of excellent recent studies have thoroughly demonstrated, this line, which as a matter of controversy goes back at least to Aristotle, lay at the heart of the Church's great concern with "market morality," about which it produced voluminous commentary, from highly abstract theological reflection to very practical homiletic advice.[88] To be sure, by the fourteenth century this commentary gave voice to, as Ladd puts it, both "residual and emergent ideologies."[89] The Church had in many ways reconciled itself to mercantile practice and had even developed a pro-mercantile discourse. Nonetheless, the clerical position – whether formulated by canonists, theologians, or authors of penitential handbooks – was consistent on one basic point: a merchant could indeed have "ynough . . . of Goddes sonde," and thus if he obtained more than "ynough" in any given transaction, as well as in general, he committed a sin. In regard to individual transactions, the "widespread formulation," as Lianna Farber observes, was that while human law (the law of *laesio enormis*) permitted merchants to make 50 percent over the just price, earning *any* amount over that price was a violation of divine law.[90] Thomas of Chobham, for example, in his influential early thirteenth-century penitential manual, offers a version of this formulation that was in fact unusually generous to merchants in the factors that it allows in the determination of just price, such as the value of the merchants' own labor. Nonetheless he was clear that "if they sell their goods for any amount above the just price," then they "are sinners."[91]

Thomas and most other writers on this subject, moreover, were not so naïve about economic practices to put forward a schema for the precise determination of just price. They well knew that the legitimate charge for anything must necessarily be a relative calculation rather than an absolute one, as it will vary according to the circumstances of the transaction. Consequently, the determination passes back to the merchants themselves, who must therefore assess in each action of buying low and selling high whether that low and high meet the requirements of divine law – whether, that is, the profit taken is no more than what they need to cover their costs and maintain their livelihood. Or, if they are unable to determine precise numbers in this regard, they must assess their own intentions – evaluate whether they truly mean to keep their profit only at the level required, as some writers put it, "to make an honest living."[92] Obviously, this requirement mandates precisely the inverse mentality of that encouraged by the merchants' practical situation: if morally and spiritually they are, for any given transaction, to be vigilant to *minimize* profit, prudence demands that they *maximize* it. As James Davis observes, the very justifications proffered to legitimate profit – "risk, instability, prudency" – also named those circumstances "that bred cynicism, secrecy and sly tactics on the borders of legality."[93]

Davis's remark indicates another source of the Church's ambivalence toward trade, which is that not only does it almost ineluctably provoke greed, but also its practices almost ineluctably involve deception. For, strictly speaking, a merchant deceives simply by knowingly buying lower or selling higher than the just price, or by knowing that he would not limit himself to the just price, whether or not he can actually determine it. He thereby conceals his knowledge or intentions from his partner in the transaction, and represents himself outwardly other than he is inwardly in order, in effect, to rob that partner of what the latter is due. And from this basis of almost structural deception (as anyone who has ever worked as a salesperson on commission is acutely aware), the impulse to maximize profit easily ramifies into an endless assortment of more concrete acts of deceit, of varying degrees of severity. Accordingly, a long tradition of Church commentary, going back at least to Ambrose, more-or-less directly equates the activity of trade with lying.[94] And even in the more merchant-friendly later Middle Ages, this suspicion persists, appearing in, most germanely for present purposes, the discussion of the "deceite bitwixe marchaunt and marchant" in the *Parson's Tale*. Here the Parson specifically allows for the legitimacy of international wholesale commerce: when one "contree" has an "habundaunce" of some commodity, it is both "honest and leveful . . . that men helpe another contree that is moore nedy. And therfore ther moote been marchantz to bryngen fro that o contree to that oother hire marchandises." Yet this same activity becomes "cursed and dampnable" when "men haunten with fraude and trecherie and deceite, with lesynges and false othes" (X.778–80).[95]

Among Middle English literary authors, it was Chaucer's contemporary Langland, of course, who most explicitly and extensively grappled with the spiritual plight of the merchant, as in the famous "Marchauntes in the margine" of Truth's pardon, which provides a soteriological counterweight to merchants' ineluctable "couetyse of wynnynge": they may "bugge boldly what hem best likede / And sethe sullen hit ayenyn and saue the wynnynges," as long as they eventually distribute those "wynnynges" across an array of public and religious charities.[96] However equivocal we are to understand this escape clause, given its context, this remedy was in fact, as Odd Langholm shows, widespread in penitential literature, and for good reason.[97] For it manages to transform the root of the merchant's spiritual problem – his obsession with maximizing profit – into a means of salvation, ensuring his place in heaven while at the same time benefitting society and the Church. It seems to offer a strategy by which Merchants can fully yield to the demands of prudence in any given transaction and then make amends by a kind of spiritual laundering of the excess profit so obtained. Yet this strategy once more puts the burden upon merchants to calculate what counts as excess profit and to determine when and how much to deplete their financial capital – their savings for that rainy day when they lose a ship to pirates – in distribution to charity. Despite the charitable sleight of hand, the line between prudence and greed, and hence also between honesty and deception, remains difficult to draw.

To what degree late medieval London merchants consciously struggled with this dilemma is difficult to gauge. Given its pervasive articulation in their confessors' handbooks, and the fact that, as Thrupp indicates, merchants were at least as pious as other lay Londoners, I believe it is fair to suppose that for many it was an active source of anxiety.[98] Such merchants would naturally seek to discover some means to reconcile the demands of prudence and morality. For example, in addition to regular charitable contributions, they might set aside, late in life when the termination of their career is in sight, a large portion of their remaining capital for the endowment of a chantry chapel; this would have the added benefit of further advertisement of their prosperity.[99] As D. Vance Smith observes about this general topic, alluding to the lexis of *Piers Plowman*, "The conflation of having and doing well sums up the moral calculations that every merchant who is interested in both financial success and salvation must make, which is to say probably every medieval merchant: how to practice an ethics of charity while pursuing a suitable mode of possession."[100] Whatever strategy a merchant chooses, its necessary accompaniment would be the adoption of a set of values governing daily life – an axiological posture – that accommodated this strategy. As Thrupp remarks, "Much of the moral teaching addressed to the young was focused upon the need of making what was considered prudent use of money."[101] It is exactly an adoption of values of this kind that the Merchant's portrait represents.

The portrait's ambiguous attitudes toward the Merchant's appearance and practices, its indication of his anxiety and concealments, and its insistence on his dignity and worthiness altogether depict the world-orientation of a man who privileges "th'encrees of his wynnyng" above everything else, not only because this privileging is what enables him to be who he is (and hence is scarcely escapable except by abandoning his occupation), but also because it is what may, in the end, save his soul. The axiological person drawn by the portrait is therefore indeed, as Bronson puts it, one of materialism, but a materialism that offers a coherent response to the practical and moral/spiritual conundrums that pervaded the axiological environment of the late medieval London merchant. It is a response that comprehends desire for material accumulation not as greed but as the expression of practical wisdom and engine of mature, responsible behavior, the conscientious enactment of which may in the end transpose sin into salvation. This axiology makes the things of this world that one has or may obtain of fundamental importance, and relegates the ways in which one may think about this world and those things – including even those ways that would subordinate them to the category of the spiritual – to an instrumental function, a means to an end.

Returning to the tale of January and May, we can now see that, by assigning this tale to the Merchant, Chaucer was able to provide a rationale for the axiology of the fabliau real that is considerably weightier than just an apt counterpunch to the quasi-literary autonomy evoked by the Clerk's performance. By itself, the tale tends to narrow the ineluctable rule of desire of the fabliau real to the second term in Pearsall's formulation of "survival and the satisfaction of appetite," which is perhaps another indication that Chaucer did not originally write it with a merchant narrator in mind. The connection to the portrait both expands the scope of this rule and charges it with historical specificity: by this narratorial assignment, the fabliau real becomes the literary extension of the embrace of worldly desire that Chaucer offers as the wholly explicable axiology of the class that held wealth and power in the city in which, for most of his life, he resided. Placed against this context, the concluding image of "glad" January – who responds to May's mini-fiction about her need to "strugle with a man" (IV.2374) to restore his sight by stroking May's "wombe" and leading her back "to his palays hoom" (IV.2412–15) – resonates with the more specific suggestion that in the axiological environment of late medieval London fictions are the grease the keeps the wheels of mercantile desire running smoothly. Whether the buyer deceives the seller or the seller the buyer, or both deceive each other, as long as they walk away from the deal contented, believing that they have profited, deal-making – and thus urban society – will thrive. Analogous with the result of May's performance (or Damian's earlier "craft"), whatever deceptive practices we might imagine the

Merchant of the *General Prologue* performing to ensure the increase of "his wynnyng," he remains, on the surface, "a worthy man with alle," holding the confidence of future buyers, sellers, and creditors, which thereby also helps to increase that "wynnyng."

In other words, with the assignment of the Merchant as narrator, this tale becomes the literary manifestation of the ethos of a class of men deeply engaged in urban life, and, as such, it offers a stern rebuke to the Clerk, who wishes to escape from economic life altogether and, in this situation, claim for literature a value in itself. Quite plainly, the axiological person drawn by the Merchant's portrait serves as a kind photographic negative of the one drawn by the Clerk's – or perhaps the more apt simile works vice versa. Both portraits are pervasively concerned with desire for things of this world, but the axiological person of the Clerk is defined by a rejection of that desire and, in its place, a university-sheltered, non-instrumental, meta-axiological embrace of ways of thinking about the world and its things: "Of studie took he moost cure and moost heede. / . . . / Sownynge in moral vertu was his speche" (I.303–7).[102] As we saw in the previous chapter, in relation to this portrait the *Clerk's Tale* and its aftermath develop a quasi-autonomous literary meta-axiology that completes the axiological apologia of the entire Clerk's performance, and, as we also saw, there are biographical reasons to understand this axiological apologia as a version of one that Chaucer had himself at one point proffered. By assigning the Merchant to the tale of January and May, Chaucer thus not only issues a rebuke to his own clerkly fantasies and lofty (if peculiar) conception of the value of his writing, but he also does so in a manner that engages his social position and background, and becomes all the more powerful because of this biographical resonance.

The Vintner's Son

As every student of Chaucer knows, Chaucer's father was a merchant, and specifically a vintner, as was Chaucer's grandfather, step-grandfather, and step-uncle; and soon after his father died in 1366, his mother married another vintner.[103] Moreover, throughout most of his adult life, Chaucer worked in close contact with merchants and especially extensively so, as we saw in Chapter 1, during his long stint as controller in the port of London, "the Mercantile hub of medieval London," as Caroline Barron calls it.[104] Although Chaucer was not himself a merchant but rather, as esquire and royal servant, a member of the gentry, it is wrong, as Thrupp makes clear, to draw heavy lines around the various segments of the urban middle strata.[105] The gentry frequently engaged in trade, and merchants frequently purchased country manors and, more generally, invested in land. The two groups interacted extensively not just in business and legal matters but also socially, as, for example, in religious fraternities. Marriages between members of the groups were common, although gentlemen marrying merchants' daughters was more typical than vice versa. Merchants' sons might become gentry, as in Chaucer's case, but the sons of gentlemen might also become merchants (as is so spectacularly illustrated by the *Tale of Beryn*). The notion that merchants formed a class of *nouveaux riches*, desperately seeking to spring into the aristocracy off the board of windfall profit, is, as Smith has cogently argued, something of an anachronism.[106] While there are cases (most famously that of William de la Pole) in which a merchant's rapid accrual of wealth did rocket him into the nobility, on the whole merchants' ambitions were more focused on money and stability than on matters of class, with most of them (and indeed many of the gentry) avoiding knighthood even when it was demanded of them because of their level of income. To be sure, social distinctions between the groups were apparent to late medieval Londoners and carried with them differences in hierarchy. Yet the exact nature of these differences depended on context, with mercantile status, for example, becoming more important in matters of city politics. In many ways, as Kermode observes, the merchant class was "at the apex of urban society," even if, as she also emphasizes, there was a great range of power and wealth among its members.[107]

It is misleading, therefore, to describe Chaucer, as Goddard does, as having "spurned his family's mercantile roots to become a royal civil servant," but then, "to support himself whilst he wrote," taking "an administrative, book-keeping job as controller," with the result that "he did not stray far from the commercial world which his family inhabited."[108] This account gives an impression of sharper class delineations and accompanying career trajectories than appear to have held in Chaucer's day. Chaucer did not spurn his mercantile heritage but, through the connections of his wealthy father – who also had served as a royal civil servant – at an early age was placed into baronial service, almost certainly because his father saw this as an opportunity for him to obtain a stable income, along with social and educational advantages. Chaucer did not take a "book-keeping job" to "support" a writing career, but he became controller because this position was the evolution of his career in service to the Crown. As I suggested in Chapter 1, whoever appointed him very likely did so because of his distinctive combination of past royal service and mercantile heritage. Moreover, the appointment was precisely the kind of salaried post that a merchant father, weary of the roller-coaster of buying and selling, might wish for his son, in the "driving search for success in any direction that for the time being held promise of economic security and good social status."[109]

In fact, the less begrudging continued affinity of Chaucer with the merchant class that this scenario suggests actually better supports Goddard's view that, while we may only speculate about Chaucer's feelings toward merchants, from what we know it seems unlikely that he would have perceived himself as their better, or to have any more marked anti-mercantile attitudes than merchants themselves. For example, rather than expressing moralistic disdain for usury in the equivocal term "chevys-saunce," Chaucer is more likely to have had the same sort of everyday ambivalence toward borrowing that a medieval merchant would have had, given that, as Goddard observes, during the period from 1388 to 1399 he was repeatedly sued by several different London merchants for failure to repay debts.[110] Hence, rather than understanding, say, the Merchant's "forked berd" as an iconic pointer to his "potentially duplicitous nature," as Reale claims, we might instead speculate on the significance of the fact that Chaucer himself wore his beard in this fashion (if we can trust the early portraits).[111]

Indeed, Brown – adding to the already-mentioned connections between Chaucer and the Merchant the fact that Orwell's location in Ipswich recalls the area from which Chaucer's grandfather emigrated and where Chaucer still had family – goes as far as to assert that Chaucer gives "the Merchant closer ties with his own life and work than . . . he gives to any other pilgrim."[112] More accurately, we may say that Chaucer's Merchant possesses closer ties than does any other pilgrim to *one* important aspect of his life and work. As we saw in the previous chapter, the Clerk possesses close ties to another, different aspect, as do, as we will see in the following chapters, the Squire and Franklin. Neither a clerk nor merchant, strictly speaking, Chaucer held occupations and social identities that nonetheless overlapped with those, making him thoroughly familiar with their orientations to the world.[113] In moving from the Clerk to the Merchant, then, Chaucer moves from one aspect of himself to another. To both of these aspects he had demonstrated commitments, and yet each involved distinct, not altogether compatible axiologies. Acting and thinking at different times according to one or the other of these axiologies, he would inevitably experience their friction.

In the ordering of the first two tales of the IV-V sequence, Chaucer organizes this friction as a mercantile axiology critiquing a clerkly one.

And, importantly, he adds ballast to this critique by insinuating into it a paternal connotation. In part, this connotation derives from the Merchant's portrait alone. Although the Merchant's mere two months of marriage disassociates him from fatherhood proper, and we are not given any obvious clues as to the Merchant's age, for merchants who were as established in their career as he appears to be, the norm was to have apprentices, and the master-apprentice relationship resembled a father-son one, especially in regard, obviously, to occupational concerns.[114] (In fact, Chaucer may well owe his surname to his grandfather's apprentice relationship with his master.)[115] Thus, the social idea of the kind of man represented in the portrait, if not any particular detail of the portrait itself, would contain a paternal element. But in part I am also simply suggesting that autobiographical coincidences within an author's fictions tend to develop thematic significances along personal vectors, so that, say, if one of my children were to write a novel whose male protagonist was a college professor, this feature would inevitably spawn meanings that resonate with personal significance in a way that a story about an astronaut would not. In choosing a merchant to embody the axiology of the Merchant's portrait, and in then assigning this axiological person to the tale of January and May, Chaucer did not just select a conceptually suitable occupation that was of great importance to late fourteenth-century England. He also chose the occupation of his paternal heritage and the source of the wealth and status that led to his own, somewhat different position in the world. Hence, while it would be crudely simpleminded to suggest that the Merchant represents some displaced version of Chaucer's father, it is no stretch to assume that for Chaucer the Merchant's axiology held a paternal aura.

If the Merchant's axiological critique of the Clerk stages Chaucer's self-critique of a literary axiology that he associates with his own youthful-like *trecento* idealism, then the Merchant's critique thus also represents the internalized voice of his paternal heritage's skepticism toward the justifications that he had developed for devoting time and energy to the authorship of English literature. It is, we might imagine, the voice that he heard at night in his Aldgate apartment when – with his controllership "labour doon" and its mandatory "rekenynges" all made – he stays up to write poems like the *House of Fame*: a voice that asked, "What's the profit in that?"[116] In the *House of Fame*, we hear this voice only implicitly, as the elided interlocutor whose urgent question the poem seeks to answer by offering a self-reflexive justification of a reflexive literary axiology. In IV-V, the latter axiology is given occupational embodiment in the form of an

Oxford clerk living in an indefinitely extended state of studenthood, in which guise that axiology appears, ultimately, not as successful justification but as escapist self-delusion. Positioned as a response rather than as prompting question, the Merchant's performance amounts to exactly the opinion that a merchant would have about the notion of eternal studenthood: "There's no profit in that." For, like most other fathers in Chaucer's day, merchants, when they did send their sons to university – which was less frequently than fathers of other occupations – they did so primarily because of the professional opportunities to which they believed it to lead.[117] From this perspective, to remain an impoverished student in order to study myriad systems of thought, not for what material value those systems may harvest, but simply for their own sake, is to live in a fantasy world and waste time. Considered in its entirety, the Merchant's performance, by opposing the fabliau real to the Clerk's literary meta-axiology, argues precisely that view, with the fabliau real carrying the force of London's powerful mercantile community and its presumed attitude toward a group of overeducated, under-employed young men vainly waiting for a benefice.

But the Merchant's performance also argues more, or has another dimension, which takes us back to the *Merchant's Prologue* and the fact that the two tales that these pilgrims tell are about marriage. In late medieval London, merchants did not usually marry before completing their apprenticeships and obtaining a livery, and these events together firmly established them as having achieved masculine adulthood.[118] In contrast, as we saw in the preceding chapter, the combination of the Clerk's unmarried and unemployed status casts him, at least to those outside the university, in the role of an adolescent, no matter how old he may actually be. The *Merchant's Prologue* thus underscores the disparity in masculine maturation between the two pilgrims by emphasizing, through its foregrounding of the Merchant's experience in marriage, the fact that the Clerk lacks this experience and the manhood that it confers, notwithstanding his telling a fanciful story about it. In turn, this disparity reinforces the sense, already evoked by the paternal connotations of the Merchant, that the Merchant responds to the Clerk in the form of father to (someone else's) son. In this respect, because the *Merchant's Prologue* associates the claims of the *Merchant Tale* on the category of the real with the masculine maturity that both prologue and portrait convey, as well as with the mercantile instrumentalism of the portrait, the Merchant's performance as a whole has the force of a father shaking the shoulders of son who refuses to grow up.

But what, exactly, would it mean to grow up? If, that is, the Clerk's adolescence figures Chaucer's skepticism toward the youthful axiological apologia of the Clerk's performance, then, beyond its critique of the latter, what does the Merchant's performance offer as an alternative – what constitutes a more mature, more realistic axiological apologia? While the tale of January and May, as we have seen, proposes great scope for the role of fiction-making in human life, it does so at the cost of denying any special status to that fiction-making: it both rejects the idea that fictions have any intrinsic value and does not privilege literary fictions, even in an instrumental sense, in any manner.[119] The result is a kind of anti-literary axiology, which may make one wonder, then, what motivates the Merchant to tell a tale at all.

This question, of course, has a ready answer, although one that is for that reason no less troublesome: because he was obligated to do so. Under the terms of the *General Prologue* contract, the Host and the other pilgrims are, in effect, buyers, and he, in his turn, is the seller. Through the assignment of the tale to the Merchant, therefore, Chaucer adds deeper significance to the narrator's already clever send off, "Now, goode men, I pray yow to be glad" (IV.2416). By itself, the remark would seem to reference the medieval justification for fabliaux, that is, the definition of their literary value, in distinction with the axiologies that they espouse within their fictional worlds: namely, the hygienic and recreational value of literary pleasure, as Glending Olson has so well described.[120] Yet in its context, the remark stands as a culminating instance of the narrator's characteristic mordant wit, as he expresses his wish, as several critics have noticed, that his listeners experience the same gladness in his fiction that they have just witnessed January experiencing in May's.[121] The message appears to be that our pleasure comes at the cost of our deception, and consequently, rather than offering a concluding literary axiology of hygienic and recreational value, the sendoff discloses that final possible axiology as simply another discursive instrument of delusion. And when we further understand the narrator to be the Merchant and his listeners the pilgrims (i.e., after Chaucer had assembled the tale of January and May into the Merchant's performance), we see that if those pilgrims experience any enjoyment at all, the Merchant has made a good deal: he has provided a fiction that in his view has no value in itself, except in what it may do for him, which in this case is to meet his contractual obligations and show up the Clerk as a naïve adolescent. If the pilgrims ride away happy, he has kept his customers content while gaining something for (almost) nothing – and perhaps he may in addition win a free supper.

But there is no reason, then, for the Merchant ever to repeat this effort, unless he finds himself in similar circumstances, which is to say that once Chaucer had completed this critique of his earlier literary axiology and formulated what amounts to an anti-axiological apologia, he should have just stopped writing – unless there was profit in it for him. Paradoxically, the literary value of the Merchant's performance lies in the manner in which it stages a rejection of the notion of literature as possessing any distinctive, intrinsic value, and instead characterizes it as merely one form of instrumental fiction among countless others, the relative importance of which lies in how effective they are at obtaining the objects of one's desires.[122] This paradox, while it may be repeated *ad infinitum*, will always amount to the same self-cancellation, and so, after its initial instance, any repetition is a waste of time – unless, again, new circumstances enable new gains.

We may easily imagine Chaucer's own perplexity at this result. Seeing before him what he must have recognized as one of his most masterful, comically satisfying compositions, he perhaps caught himself off-guard by the force of its negating implications. Self-provoked into formulating some sort of response, one that would need to be more radically literature-affirming, and probably more straightforwardly so, than the meta-axiology of the Clerk, he recalled having begun, and abandoned, a fanciful tale about a flying brass steed and talking falcon that would do just the trick. However far-fetched this scenario may be, Chaucer's belated positioning of the *Squire's Tale* as the answer to the Merchant serves as just such a radically affirming response, even if that answer ultimately falls apart.

CHAPTER 3

Squire

The *Squire's Tale*, misplaced throughout what was then its nearly 300-year print history, was finally restitched into its rightful place in an unbroken IV-V sequence by Thomas Tyrwhitt in his seminal 1774 edition of the *Canterbury Tales*. Yet less than 100 years later, in a whimsical decision that has had great consequences for the history of Chaucer criticism and editing, Frederick Furnivall broke IV-V asunder in his *Six-Text Print*, disjoining the *Squire's Tale* from its preceding *Merchant's Tale* and dividing the link between them into a *Merchant's Epilogue* and *Squire's Prologue*, despite the near total absence of a manuscript basis for doing so. This disposition of IV-V has remained the standard ever since. In this chapter, therefore – even while I necessarily revisit many longstanding critical questions – I strike out into territory virtually untrodden in modern Chaucer studies and offer a reading of the Squire's performance as the pivotal moment in IV-V, which is the function that Chaucer manifestly (if probably belatedly) intended for the performance but which the *Tales'* legacy in print has obscured.

Specifically, I consider the *Squire's Tale* and Squire's *General Prologue* portrait in concert with a reading of the full Merchant-Squire link as such, and argue that in this light the Squire's performance emerges as a two-pronged response to what we saw to be the literary axiology (or the lack thereof) of the Merchant's performance and the Merchant's socioeconomic critique of the Clerk. First, it supplies an earnest affirmation of a distinctively literary value in confrontation with the Merchant's reduction of literary discourse to one verbal instrument among others in a world of individual competitive desire. The *Squire's Tale*, as a venture in the genre that Jennifer Goodman has taught us to recognize as the composite romance,[1] promotes literary discourse as the unique arena in which the remaking or restoration of the world may be imagined, unconstrained by any preconceived notions of the real, whether that real be the Merchant's fabliau one of individual competitive desire or, say, the Church's dualism of earthly mutability and heavenly perfection. This sort of literary discourse offers, that is, what Sir Philip Sidney would later name the "golden" world imagined by the poet, who, "lifted up with the vigour of his own invention, doth grow in effect another nature, in making things either better than Nature bringeth forth, or, quite anew, forms such as never were in Nature . . . freely ranging only within the zodiac of his own wit."[2] In the *Squire's Tale*'s own terms, the proposal is that romance fiction may render the world "as fressh as May" (V.281), full of the wide-eyed wonder lacking in the fabliau real of the Merchant – a disenchanted real that the latter so succinctly captures in the ironically equivocal epithet for his protagonist, "fresshe May." Second, the Squire's performance counters the Merchant's critique of the Clerk's adolescent meta-axiology of uselessness by means of a pronounced self-consciousness regarding its genre's function as an instrument of aristocratic display. This self-consciousness serves to make sense of the distinctive literary value of romance fiction in social, occupational terms – to identify what was in fact the legible, normative place for this literary practice in late medieval English society and to claim for that practice a function that, far from being subject to the Merchant's accusation of profitless time-wasting, helps to consolidate the Squire's social dominance.

Or, more precisely, the Squire's performance *attempts* to answer the Merchant's in this dual, complementary fashion but ultimately does not succeed. As a whole, the performance stumbles because it cannot in fact reconcile its earnestness with its self-consciousness. The combination instead results in a kind of bipolar axiological apologia, in which simultaneous claims for a distinctive literary value and for the function of social distinction cancel rather than reinforce each other. For Chaucer, this self-cancellation means that the Squire's performance, seeking but failing fully to counter the mercantile paternal rebuke of the preceding performance, replays his own transpositions from merchant's son, to king's esquire, to – in his position as controller of customs – king's man among merchants. It represents, that is, a kind of generic and axiological regression, an imaginative reworking of the past that will create the space for the reworking of the present accomplished by the Franklin's performance.

With this latter claim, I may appear to be endorsing the view of the Squire's performance that through several decades of the second half of the twentieth century held near critical unanimity, and which is still common, if more polarizing, today: the view that the performance is, in some way, an intentional failure, and that its flaws are to be understood as critical commentary on its teller, its genre, or both. In fact, although

I will argue that the performance is profoundly concerned with literary value, I will be largely unconcerned with the question of its own literary value and of the significance of its possible lack thereof. Unlike as in so many readings of its failure, I do not measure the performance's breakdown on a scale of literary merit or in respect to the character of the teller. Instead, when I designate it a failure, I mean that it fails in the same general way that the preceding Clerk's and Merchant's performances do: as components of an unfolding axiological meditation that seeks to uncover a basis for a commitment to literary value within the axiological environments in which Chaucer practiced authorship. As such a component, each performance has "flaws" inasmuch as it manifests the contradictions and conceptual tensions in the project, and thereby dialectically yields to the next component. And in each case, the contradictions and tensions include those that arise through the collocation of frame material, tale, and *General Prologue* portrait, even though in each case these elements may be, to some degree, independent compositions. In the course of this chapter's discussion of the Squire's performance, as in previous chapters, I review some of the challenges involved in the typical ways that this performance has been read, in order to define the interpretive rules that bind my approach. My argument is that with this performance Chaucer draws on the most distinctively literary discourse of his day, which was also the most socially valuable such discourse, to stage a rebuttal to the Merchant's critique of literary value; and that this rebuttal, through its very *failure* in this task, dialectically yields to what in the next chapter we will see to be the more tentative, jaded, complex, and (for Chaucer) compelling axiological apologia of the Franklin's performance.

To pursue this reading, I first consider the long-overlooked linking passage between the *Merchant's* and *Squire's Tales*, establishing thereby a thematic framework for understanding the significance of the latter tale's position in IV-V and of its assignment to the Squire. I next turn to the tale, remarking upon the similarities and differences between my approach and others, before examining some key passages to elaborate the tale's bipolar literary axiology. I then consider the Squire's portrait in order to discern the axiological person that it defines and to gauge the significance of its overlap with and – importantly – differences from Chaucer's own social position. With the entire Squire's performance then in view, I conclude with a suggestion about how its regressive, bipolar axiological apologia clears a path for the final performance of IV-V.

Merchant-Squire

As I describe in this book's introduction, manuscript evidence makes clear that the link between the *Merchant's* and *Squire's Tales* constitutes a single unbroken passage. Although in its variant versions it joins tales other than those two (most notably in Hengwrt), if the link is accepted as authentic (which, since Tyrwhitt, almost all editors and textual critics have), by far the most likely scenario is that Chaucer wrote it to situate the *Squire's Tale* after the Merchant's performance. The best reading of the evidence, moreover, indicates that the three links that constitute IV-V represent a single, very late organizing innovation by Chaucer, and internal evidence suggests further that it may well have been the inspiration that the *Squire's Tale* belonged among the other three tales that prompted this innovation.

As has been so often pointed out in the marriage-group critical tradition, the three tales of Clerk, Merchant, and Franklin possess many obvious similarities of plot and theme, which suggests that whatever their order of composition the later-written tales were conceived with the earlier-written ones in mind. Clearly, for IV-V the *Squire's Tale* is the odd one out in this respect. Probably not coincidentally, the disposition of the portraits in the *General Prologue* appears likewise and relatedly significant. The juxtaposition of Merchant, Clerk, Sergeant, and Franklin represents a relatively coherent group of middle-strata commoners, and this social coherence seems to have influenced Chaucer's assignment of tellers to the respective IV-V tales. The anomaly of the *Squire's Tale* in IV-V is therefore matched by the anomaly of its teller's gentle status and accordingly earlier position in the *General Prologue*. Indeed, the very tight parallels between the *Merchant's* and *Franklin's Tales* in particular, and the fact that their assigned tellers together represent the urban/rural recto/verso of what we might anachronistically call the upper-middle class, suggest a socially pointed pairing along the lines of the Miller-Reeve or Summoner-Friar sequences, in respect to which the Squire and his tale represent a double intrusion. And this very intrusiveness, if that is what it was, underscores the importance of the Merchant-Squire link. For, if Chaucer did first conceive of a Merchant-Franklin pairing, his recognition that the Merchant's performance demanded instead the radical response of the *Squire's Tale* – which would in turn set up the more measured response of the *Franklin's Tale* – would have been all the more powerful, inasmuch as it provoked a departure from an original plan.

Regardless of what Chaucer's plans may have been, however, the nature of the response that the Squire's performance provides to the Merchant's has not been fully appreciated, simply because, for the reasons that I have mentioned, the Merchant-Squire link – the passage that sets the terms for understanding the *Squire's Tale* as such a response – has not been fully explicated. Indeed, while readings of so-called Fragment V have been plentiful, readings that relate the Squire's performance to the Merchant's have been relatively scarce. To be sure, the latter readings, while infrequent and tending to treat the relation in broad contours, have included some astute commentary. In addition to the predictable attempts to fit the tale into the marriage group, critics have emphasized the kind of dark/light contrast between the tales evident in the juxtaposition of the Merchant's "fresshe May" and the Squire's "fressh as May," and they have not missed the telling resemblances between the squire Damian and the Squire in his *General Prologue* portrait, such as that the former "carf biforn the knyght" (IV.1773) while the latter "carf biforn his fader" (I.1100), a "fader" who is, of course, also a "knyght." From these cues, for example, Joyce Peterson many decades ago suggested a dramatic scenario parallel to those of Fragments I and III, in which the Squire responds to a perceived insult, but, instead of churlishly trading discursive punches like the Reeve and Summoner do, he chooses "to correct the Merchant's picture of courtly love and to dissociate himself from Damyan by redefining the courtly lover"; and in this way he implies "that the refinements of courtly love are most properly understood by the gentil."[3] Helen Cooper, among others, has offered a similar reading, albeit more provisionally, "[i]f the scheme for following the Merchant's Tale with the Squire's does go back to Chaucer[.]"[4]

These readings certainly capture a crucial basic contrast between the performances. Yet they require a bit of interpretive sleight-of-hand, as the dramatized conflict that they perceive between pilgrims is nowhere explicitly represented, as it is elsewhere in the *Tales*. And, more importantly, they construe too narrowly the stakes of the contrast that they identify. The conflictual nature of the transition between performances is both more capacious and more profound in how it unfolds along social and generic dimensions than a strictly dramatic explanation is able to compass. That the Squire is the Merchant's social superior, and that he apparently offers in earnest an instance of the genre that Merchant treats with such severe irony, are not so much conclusions to draw about the relation between performances as the place to start. Let us then turn to the linking passage – for which the little attention that it has received has been partitioned between the two parts into which Furnivall divided it – and examine it in full.

In light of the likelihood that Chaucer conceived the *Merchant's Prologue* and Merchant-Squire link together, we may more easily see how the latter develops in essential ways within the logic of the former, as well as within that of the Host's one-stanza response to the *Clerk's Tale* that – as I reviewed in the previous chapter – precedes the *Merchant's Prologue* in almost all the manuscripts that contain the IV-V sequence as such. In that one-stanza response the Host understands Griselda as a domestic exemplum for wifely behavior, tacitly refusing the spiritualization of the tale that the Clerk, via Petrarch, offers as one of multiple options for its use. Fiction for the Host becomes an instrument for uxorial discipline, albeit one for which he does not seem to hold great confidence. In the *Merchant's Prologue*, then, the Merchant takes the further step, already nascent in the Host's stanza, of declaring his real-world wife to be an anti-Griselda, a living negative exemplum of wifehood, which has the effect of discarding all the options for the value of fiction that are on parade in the conclusion to the Clerk's performance.

In his response to the *Merchant's Tale* at the outset of the Merchant-Squire link, the Host thus in effect picks up the conversation where the Merchant left off when the latter put aside his "owene soore" (IV.1243) to relay the story of January and May:

> "Ey! Goddes mercy!" seyde oure Hooste tho,
> "Now swich a wyf I pray God kepe me fro!
> Lo, whiche sleightes and subtilitees
> In wommen been! For ay as bisy as bees
> Been they, us sely men for to deceyve,
> And from a soothe evere wol they weyve;
> By this Marchauntes tale it preveth weel.
> But doutelees, as trewe as any steel,
> I have a wyf, though that she povre be,
> But of hir tonge, a labbyng shrewe is she,
> And yet she hath an heep of vices mo;
> Therof no fors! Lat alle swiche thynges go. (IV.2419–30)

Notably, the Host does not respond here as he does to the (somewhat) more straightforward fabliau of the *Shipman's Tale*, with its adulterous wife. While he determines a moral for that tale – "Draweth no monkes moore unto youre in" (VII.442) – his initial reaction clearly registers his appreciation for the tale's humor and concluding witty word play: "Wel seyd, by *corpus dominus* . . . / Now longe moote thou saille by the cost, / Sire gentil maister, gentil maryneer!" (VII.435–37). In contrast, here he appears to understand the *Merchant's Tale* in the same fashion as the *Clerk's*

Tale, but with inverse polarity, taking May as a kind of photographic negative of Griselda, a model of the "wyf" whom men should avoid rather than the wife whom their spouses should emulate. Subsequently, as the Merchant does in his prologue, the Host identifies his own real-world wife as a corresponding living embodiment of a negative uxorial exemplum, "a labbyng shrewe" with "an heep of vices mo" (albeit, like the Merchant's wife, she is not necessarily also illustrative of May's adultery). As a result, for the Host the fabliau/exemplum of "this Marchauntes tale" emerges as a doubly useless fiction: it evokes no apparent amusement, and it has failed to "kepe" men like the Host from "swiche a wyf." And as if in recognition of this uselessness, the Host seems then to abandon his own personal exemplum: "Therof no fors! Lat alle swiche thynges go."

In one of Chaucer's wonderful evocations of mental processes, however, the Host immediately appears to change his mind, and his subsequently completed "tale," as he calls it, has the effect of consolidating in a brief, focused space the assertion of the merely materially instrumental value of fiction that is the more profound message of the Merchant's performance:

> But wyte ye what? In conseil be it seyd,
> Me reweth soore I am unto hire teyd.
> For and I sholde rekenen every vice
> Which that she hath, ywis I were to nyce.
> And cause why? It sholde reported be
> And toold to hir of somme of this meynee –
> Of whom, it nedeth nat for to declare,
> Syn wommen konnen outen swich chaffare;
> And eek my wit suffiseth nat therto
> To tellen al; wherfore my tale is do. (IV.2431–40)

This elaboration of the Host's "tale" makes evident two important aspects of the passage as a whole. First, the full lesson that the Host draws from the *Merchant's Tale* has an axiological and mercantile bite that succinctly echoes that of the Merchant's performance. The (misogynist) moral that the Host draws is not merely to avoid wives like May but in addition that real "wommen" in general, like the fictional May, tell fictions to obtain what they desire. Drawing on virtually the precise terms that the Parson uses later to define fiction (in order to reject it), the Host declares that women "from a soothe evere wol . . . weyve" ("For Paul, . . . " says the Parson, "Repreveth hem that weyven soothfastnesse / And tellen fables and swich wrecchednesse" [X.32–34]). At the same time, he incorporates a mercantile element into the language that he uses to describe women's deception, as in their "sleightes and subtilitees," their industriousness at being "ay as bisy as bees / . . . sely men for to deceive," and, most obviously, the "chaffare" that they "konnen outen."[5] In emphasizing the relations among storytelling, deception, and self-interest, the Host's retrospective comments bring the anti-literary axiology of the *Merchant's Tale* firmly into the Merchant's characterological field by declaring that the tale shows women in general to be everything that the antimercantile moralists claimed about merchants: "By this Marchauntes tale it preveth weel."

Second, the Host's completed "tale," as we saw with the *Merchant's Prologue* and the Host's stanza, appears to subsume the category of the fictional within the category of the real, and does so in an even more pointed and hence consequential manner. If we accept, with Martha Carlin, that "there can be no question that members of Chaucer's immediate audience would have been able to identify his Host, 'Herry Bailly', with the Southwark MP and innkeeper of the same name," then this diegetically complex moment – a dramatic fiction in which the fictional Host, who corresponds to the real-world Harry Bailly, cites his fictional wife as a real-world example of women like the fictional May who use fictions to deceive – threatens to become, instead, simply a real statement about real people.[6] That is, the Host's coy refusal to "rekenen" and professed inability to "tellen al" of his wife's "heep of vices" (verbs that cleverly perpetuate the mercantile lexis of the passage) in fact disclose these very vices to an audience who, knowing the historical Harry, presumably also at least knew of his wife, even if her name was not actually Goodelief.[7] In this way, this passage of dramatic fiction may just be posing as fiction; as a speech act it may devolve into a simple inform.

Moreover, and crucially, Chaucer calls attention to this possibility through his own May-like "sleight" of concealing it in plain sight, by representing the Host as giving his complaint "in conseil" to the fictional group of pilgrims and curtailing it – not soon enough, of course – lest "somme of this meynee" report it back to his wife. This "somme" of course denotes fictional pilgrims, like the Wife of Bath, who may report back to a fictional wife, but given the referential overlap in this passage it may also denote actual readers who may report back to an actual wife. Such a result may in fact be what Chaucer desired or at least expected: he may have dramatized the likely real-world result of his fiction within that very fiction.[8] In this way, it is Chaucer himself who "konnen outen swich chaffare": *he* becomes the ultimate agent for what amounts to a kind of misogynistic name-calling. In effect, he tells a fiction that lies about being a fiction in order to get what he wants (whatever that might be, vis-à-vis his audience, Harry, and Harry's wife), even while keeping his readers entertained, and in this way his own practice of fiction and his views on its value, as they are illustrated in this very passage, become one and the same as the Merchant's (and May's). Fiction, in a word, becomes simply an instrument of *chaffare*, and Chaucer, more than anywhere else in the *Canterbury Tales*, proves himself to be a merchant's son.

Yet, as clever as this maneuver may be, and however amusing despite its misogyny, its implications, as we saw with the *Merchant's Tale*, deny literary discourse any special status and restrict its value to one instrument of desire among others. These implications leave, in short, very little purpose or rationale for an author of literary fictions, whose continued activity therefore invites the response that the Host later gives to Chaucer in regard to *Sir Thopas*: "Thou doost noght elles but despendest tyme" (VII.931). In this light, the Host's immediately following abrupt turn to the Squire for a tale of "love" seems to offer a kind of diegetic, thematic, and axiological Hail Mary pass: at the very center of IV-V, this turn to the Squire – in one bold, unpredictable move – seems poised to reverse the downward trajectory of the sequence and reclaim a distinctive value for literature and hence a justification for writing. Yet, initially, from another point of view, it may instead seem merely to perpetuate the problem.

At diegetic and thematic levels, in asking for a tale about love, the Host asks for fiction about precisely that which, in the *Merchant Tale*'s travesty of courtly romance, only the duped January believes in, and which was indeed the instrument of his deception, including his self-deception; about that which, in the *Clerk's Tale*, functions as such an extreme rule of subjection that its bearing on anything in this world or the next remains, in the dramatized aftermath of that tale, confounding; and about that which, in respect to the tale of the Host's own life that he has just related, appears to be absent in his marriage, which absence Chaucer may be trumpeting to Harry Bailly's actual acquaintances. The entire sequence of IV-V pivots on this request, and indeed it pivots, as we might expect from Chaucer, on the uncertain discursive status of that request itself – whether it is made in *ernest* or *game*:

> Squier, come neer, if it your wille be,
> And sey somwhat of love, for certes, ye
> Konnen theron as muche as any man. (V.1–3)

The uncertainty revolves around the Host's added rationale, "for certes, / ye Konnen theron as muche as any man." As the Squire is unmarried and very likely the youngest man among the pilgrims, this statement, in the context of the mordant homosocial exchange between the married Host and Merchant, may be ironic in a simple way, that is, the Host may be saying, "Tell us about love, since you have the least experience with it."[9] Yet the Host may instead (or in addition) be asking for a tale about the kind of love for which squires were stereotypically known, and which from the *General Prologue* we know that this particular Squire does indeed *connen*, as "a lovyere and lusty bachelor" who "lovede" so "hoote" that "by nyghtertale / He sleep namoore than dooth a nyghtyngale" (I.80, 97–98). As Jill Mann has shown, the status of the erotic activity described in these lines from the Squire's portrait is ambiguous, teetering between a satirical implication of concupiscence and an idealizing romance stereotype.[10] If the Host's view of the Squire accords with the former, then the irony of "Konnen theron" also reaches back to "love," and what he asks for is a story about sex told by a libidinous squire. This reading gains some support from the line's echo of the more manifestly winking rationale accompanying the Host's request for a tale from the Merchant, following the latter's hyperbolic confession of his marital woes: "Syn ye so muchel knowen of that art" (IV.1241). Like the Host's response to the *Merchant's Tale*, this sort of request of the Squire would continue in the same vein as the *Merchant's Prologue*; rather than a reversal of the Merchant's performance, the Host wants merely a reiteration from a different perspective: Damian's tale.[11]

But if the Host sees the Squire instead as an idealizing romance stereotype, then his request is correspondingly earnest and expresses a longing for the paradoxically backward-looking renewal that such stories of "love" offer, in contradistinction with the trajectory of IV-V to this point. It is an earnest request for an earnest story that gives an account of a relationship between a man and woman that is, in contrast with the one depicted in the *Merchant's Tale*, earnestly idealizing: rather than Damian's tale, the Host wants a sincere version of the springtime fantasy in which, in effect, an aged January (he himself) may be revivified by a young May (the tale). Moreover, in contrast with the relationship depicted in the *Clerk's Tale*, the Host wants this fantasy to be appealing and envisionable; in contrast with that of his own life, emotionally recharging and rife with youthful passion; and in contrast with Chaucer's joke on Harry, restorative of the comfortable, productive boundaries between the real and the fictional. In short, the Host wants a fiction to escape the real that Chaucer, at this juncture in IV-V, has imposed upon him, which is to say that Chaucer stages this desire as the next dialectical turn in the sequence's unfolding axiological meditation.

Accordingly, this desire implies a specific literary axiology: the value of the proposed fiction will be exactly its explicitly marked unreality, its non-instrumental mandate to believe the unbelievable, to relish a world that never was, and thus make more bearable the world that is. In contrast with the literary axiology of the Merchant's performance, in which fiction is merely one of many discursive tools of deception used to obtain whatever one wants while keeping those one deceives content, the Host's sincere longing (if it is so) points toward a more distinctively valuable and noncompetitive means of self-deception: the suspension of disbelief that makes the unimaginable imaginable. This is the literary value that Chaucer's most literarily ambitious readers, Milton and Spenser, famously ascribe to the *Squire's Tale*, and that Thomas Warton, under their influence, so succinctly identifies at the conclusion of his enthusiastic commentary on the tale: "By such inventions we are willing to be deceived. These are the triumphs of deception over truth."[12]

The trajectory of IV-V rests upon these mutually exclusive comprehensions of the Host's meaning, which is another way of saying that it rests upon a pointedly undecidable determination of the Host's *entente*. Fortunately, in the dialogic manner in which Chaucer enacts this turn, our inability to decide this *entente* does not matter, since the nature of the Squire's response to the request will determine its effect:

> "Nay sir," quod he, "but I wol seye as I kan
> With hertly wyl, for I wol nat rebelle
> Agayn your lust; a tale wol I telle.
> Have me excused if I speke amys;
> My wyl is good, and lo, my tale is this." (V.4–8)

The target of the Squire's "Nay" here is ambiguous. If directed at the Host's "Konnen theron," it may function as a polite, genteel refusal of the Damian-like knowledge of love that the Host may be ascribing to him, or it may acknowledge what may be the Host's simpler irony – that, as an unmarried young man speaking after two tales of marriage (or three, with the Host's), he signals his recognition of his relative inexperience with "love." Or, even more simply, it may represent, as John Ganim has suggested, an aristocrat's disclaimer of one of the assets of good birth that would be boorish to claim explicitly.[13] Alternatively, if directed to the request to "sey somwhat of love," his demurral may register a refusal to continue the devolving exchange about "love" among Clerk, Merchant, Host, and Chaucer, and instead turn to an altogether different matter. But in all cases (and perhaps all cases are indeed active) the result is the same. The Squire responds earnestly to the Host's request in a manner that, whatever the actual discursive status of that request, transforms it into an earnest invitation to tell an earnest tale: he chooses the literary axiology implied by the Host's comprehension of him as an idealized romance stereotype.

My own repetition of "earnest" in this last sentence is meant to echo the most curious and hence telling aspect of this turn to the Squire, which is also that which elaborates the literary axiological significance of the Squire's choice. This aspect is, as David Lawton has pointed out, the passage's "relentless emphasis on 'wille' . . . [which is] unparalleled in Chaucer's work."[14] Repeated three times in eight lines, and reverberating also in the Squire's thrice-repeated use of the auxiliary *wol* in consecutive lines, the noun evolves through a series of phrases that together establish the axiological framework in which we are to understand the ensuing tale.

The initial use of the noun, in the Host's qualification of his request, "if it your wille be," deferentially recognizes the obvious social difference between the Host and the Squire. Although all the pilgrims have, by agreement, subjected themselves to the Host's authority in the tale-telling game, in this instance the social difference outside the liminal community of the pilgrimage is great enough to demand acknowledgement (in contrast with, say, his request of the Clerk, which has the force of a simple command: "Telle us som murie thyng of aventures" [IV.15]). In this phrase, the precise denotation of *wille* is less important than the phrase's pragmatic function, which is to effect a transfer of authority from Host to Squire, the latter of whom will determine, according to his *wille*, whether he will in fact be the next storyteller. The ensuing tale, therefore, issues from this authority of the Squire and does so under the sign of his class superiority. As polite as the Squire is in this passage, and as self-derogating as the narrator of the tale of Cambyuskan and Canacee later appears, this representation of the Squire's choice establishes tersely but unmistakably a connection between that tale and the class position of its teller.

The second instance, in the phrase "With hertly wyl," refers both backward to "but I wol seye as I kan" and forward to "for I wol nat rebelle / Agayn your lust; a tale wol I telle." In respect to the forward reference, the phrase has the effect of reinforcing the recognition of class difference. Since the statement that the Squire's "hertly wyl" is not to "rebelle / Agayn" the festive order of the pilgrimage comes as an explicit response to the query about his "wille," it tacitly acknowledges the sovereignty of his *wille*. In effect, the Squire signals that he *chooses* not to "rebelle." Such power relations form a striking contrast with Chaucer's one other use of the phrase "hertly wyl." This occurs in the Clerk's account of the reaction of

Walter's subjects to the latter's demand that they "swere" neither to "grucche ne styrve" against his "choys" of wife, and either that they "assente in swich manere" or "speketh namoore of this matere": "With hertely wyl they sworen and assenten / To al this thyng – ther seyde no wight nay" (IV.169–77). Here, after pretending to yield some of his sovereignty and agreeing to marry, Walter issues the demand that his subjects either agree to his choice of wife without any further questioning of his sovereignty or that they abandon their initial request. Obviously, whether they "assente" or say "nay," they confirm Walter's absolute authority. If instead they were to say, like the Squire does, that they will "nat rebelle" against his "lust," they would be hinting at the possibility of insurrection. Thus, while the adjective "hertly" in both instances has the primary sense of "loyal" (*MED hertli* adj. 1b), this sameness underscores the distinction between the obligatory loyalty of Walter's subjects and the chosen loyalty of the Squire.[15]

Yet in association with "I wol seye as I kan," the semantic field of the adjective widens to encompass a related meaning with a rather different implication. The verb "kan," uttered here in response to Host's "konnen," likely suggests the possession of knowledge, experience, or even mastery of some skill or topic (*MED connen* v. 3a, 4a, 5a), along with its primary denotation of the possession of ability (*connen* v. 1). With all these meanings in play, then, following his ambiguous "Nay" the Squire in effect declares, "I will (and consent to) tell a tale, to the extent that I am able and about that which I do know." In respect to this declaration, "hertly wyl," while conveying the loyalty in the Squire's action of consent, also describes the Squire's attitude toward what he "wol seye" as he "kan," that is, his attitude toward the matter of his ensuing tale. The adjective "hertly" carries in this regard the additional sense of "heartfelt, genuine" (*MED hertli* adj. 1a).[16] In thus loyally consenting to tell the next tale about a subject of his choice in a heartfelt, genuine manner, the Squire asserts his authority to change the subject matter to that which he deems suitable to his social status, and he rejects the ironic narrational mode of the Merchant, the Clerk (at least in his envoy, if not also in his entire performance), the Host, and Chaucer in his joke on Harry.

This latter implication of the second instance of *wille* becomes more explicit and further developed in the final instance. In the Squire's assertion that his "wyl is good," the noun's meaning has shifted entirely from the Host's usage. This statement refers back to his request, "Have me excused if I speke amys," which in turn qualifies his declaration, "a tale wol I telle."

Most simply, these latter two clauses form a conventional expression of humility, but in the context of the preceding Merchant's performance the adverb "amys" takes on, in addition to the basic sense of "in a wrong or mistaken manner" (*MED amis* adv. 1a), the connotation "wickedly" or "with evil intent" (*amis* adv. 3). (Although the *MED* does not give an example from Chaucer for this sense, it clearly informs, e.g., the frame narrator's warning to the reader before the *Miller's Tale*, "Blameth nat me if that ye chese amys" [I.3191], and the Pardoner's paraphrase of the Second Commandment, "Take nat my name in ydel or amys" [VI.642].) The two clauses thus convey the Squire's recognition that his auditors, having just heard the *Merchant's Tale*, may be listening for irony in the tale that he "wol . . . telle" – that they may be prepared to detect a similarly semi-obscene sabotage of courtly romance. Hence, in asserting "My wyl is good," the Squire seeks preemptively to preclude that understanding, to declare that whatever we think we hear in his tale, his intention (*MED wil* n. 5a) and his corresponding inner nature (*wil* n. 6a) are "good."

If what followed this preemptive apology and hermeneutic instruction were – as with the Parson's similar preliminary request to put his "meditacioun . . . / . . . ay under correccioun / Of clerkes" (X.55–57) – something like the Parson's "Moralitee and virtuous mateere" (X.38), then the correspondence between the good will of the Squire and the nature of his tale would be entirely unproblematic. He would be seeking to transmit, like the Parson, just "the sentence" (X.58) of his matter, and hence the goodness of his intent would be verified by the self-evident goodness of this *sentence*. But of course the tale that follows, while perhaps not the worst kind of "fables and swich wrecchednesse" about which the Parson complains, is nonetheless a quintessential species of imaginative literature, one that is devoid of obvious *sentence*, and one that, unlike a fabliau, does not even pretend to communicate a moral. The goodness of his will must consequently be attested by some other positive value, namely, the one implied by taking the Host's request for a tale about love in that request's ingenuous, idealistic, fantasizing sense: a value that is inseparable from the distinctive discursive mode of romance fiction. The Merchant-Squire link concludes, in this way, by establishing *a priori* affirmation of this literary value.

Whatever the Host may mean by his request, then, the multifaceted earnestness that results from the cascading repetition of *wille* in the conclusion of the link banishes the ill will in the mode and matter of the Merchant's performance, the Host's comments thereon, and Chaucer's convoluted conflation of the fictional and the real. And it promises as a replacement a different mode and matter that will reflect the good will of the Squire and accordingly restore a positive value to fiction. And yet this multifaceted earnestness also occurs, as we have seen, under the sign of the Squire's class superiority, which introduces a rather different literary axiology that mixes uncomfortably with that which is pointed to by the Host's longing for love.

The Tale and Its Critical Discontents

Contrary to what the last sentence may seem to imply, however, I will not argue that the much-commented-upon idiosyncrasies of the *Squire's Tale* serve as Chaucer's staging of a kind of stylistic, narratological, rhetorical, and thematic nervous breakdown resulting from the unbearable tension between these competing literary axiologies, even though this approach would align with much of the criticism on the tale over the last many decades. As mentioned above, readings of the *Squire's Tale* as an intentional failure, and particularly as a failure illustrative of the character of its teller, dominated criticism on the tale in the middle-to-late twentieth century.[17] This position, to be sure, is rarely argued as such today (having reached a state of critical exhaustion), and much of the recent work on the *Squire's Tale* has fruitfully moved on to consider such issues as the tale's construction of differences between male and female, human and animal, and East and West; as well as the cultural and psychological implications of the kind of romance narrative it instances.[18] Nonetheless, many of these studies, as well as other recent work on the tale, incorporate in some fashion the inherited view of the tale as a failure by design. To consider just one example, Kathryn Lynch, in her important, wide-ranging article on the tale's mutually informing construction of male/female and East/West differences, argues that

> the narrative logic that informs the Squire's Tale – indeed, to a fault – is a logic of the feminine East, morally relativistic, sexually deviant, building to a potentially incestuous conclusion without regard to the unities of time, place, or theme. Narrative improprieties mirror the more essential sexual improprieties that lie just below the surface of the tale.[19]

The "improprieties" that Lynch takes as evidence for the tale's construction of "the feminine East" are precisely those that the previous generation of critics identified as evidence of Chaucer's design of the tale as an exhibition of the Squire's incompetence as storyteller. Lynch's groundbreaking account of the tale, therefore, to a significant degree depends on assumptions of those older studies.

It is not my purpose to impugn studies like Lynch's, from which I have certainly benefitted. Rather, I mean only to make their undergirding assumptions explicit in order to explain the rationale of my self-imposed interpretive limits. First, a position like Lynch's must find aspects of the *Squire's Tale* self-evidently of poor literary merit. Then it must assume that these aspects are designedly poor in order to serve a greater artistic purpose, which in Lynch's case is to characterize the Squire's storytelling in a way that reflects a specific ideological conception of the East, one that is answered by the Franklin (and possibly also by the Physician). This assumption in turn depends on the further one that Chaucer wrote the tale for placement in the *Tales* (for Lynch, specifically in respect to the *Franklin's Tale*) with the character of the Squire in mind. Let me consider this most basic assumption first.

As discussed in this book's introduction, the evidence of the manuscripts and Hengwrt in particular suggests not just the plausibility but even the likelihood that the Merchant-Squire link, as well as the other IV-V links, was a very late revision to the *Tales*. This likelihood makes it improbable that Chaucer composed the tale with the link in mind, and, while it is less damaging to the supposition that he wrote the tale for the Squire, at the very least it creates room for doubt in this respect, since this link and its partner at the other end are alone what supply the identity of the narrator. Indeed, bereft of these links, nothing in the tale unambiguously declares it as a work written for the Squire for inclusion in the *Tales*. To be sure, the tale does appear eminently suited to the *General Prologue* Squire, as almost everyone has acknowledged. Yet this suitability does not entail that Chaucer initially conceived the story with the Squire and *Tales* in mind, since, of course, he may instead have created the pilgrim to match a preexisting tale, as he presumably did in the cases of the Knight and Second Nun. Moreover, even this scenario of portrait matched to tale may be too much to assume, since we have no way of knowing which tale assignments Chaucer had in mind when writing the *General Prologue*. From what we have of the unfinished *Tales*, it is virtually certain that he did not have them all planned, and thus, when he came to assign a pilgrim to the story of the brass steed and talking falcon, we may plausibly imagine him pausing between the Squire and, say, Yeoman.

Furthermore, as these speculations already indicate, following a minority tradition of criticism I accept that the tale's long-recognized transplantation of material from Chaucer's *Anelida and Arcite* suggests the possibility of a pre-*Tales* origin, as, for example, either an initial attempt to rework the stalled *Anelida* or, following the successful remaking of the latter into the story of "the love of Palamon and Arcite" (*Legend of Good Women* F 420), an attempt to salvage what was left on the cutting-room floor.[20] Notably, in the tale itself, the only apparent allusion to the dramatic frame is the brief reference to the time of day that follows upon the narrator's informing us that he will not speak of the "strange sewes" of the Tartars: "I wol nat taryen yow, for it is pryme / And for it is no fruyt but los of tyme" (V.67, 73–74). Rather than a nod toward the pilgrims' journey, however, this one-clause specification of time (which, astonishingly, was Furnivall's basis for dividing IV-V into two fragments)[21] may simply be another instance of the sort of rhetorical elaboration to which this narrator is prone. But even if we grant that it does index the dramatic frame, the couplet of which it is a part represents the kind of very minor adaptation to the context of the *Tales* that many see as similarly characterizing the revisions that Chaucer made to form the *Knight's Tale* out of "Palamon and Arcite."[22] But let me be clear that I am not in fact *arguing* for an early date: plainly, this and other evidence creates at best an inconclusive case for this position; my point is only that the case for a later date, although much more widely accepted, is no more conclusive.

About the literary merit of the *Squire's Tale*, one may readily observe that the tale's critical history, as Donald Baker and others have ably documented, serves as a veritable poster child for what may appear, especially to those outside the field of literary study, the impressionistic, historically unstable nature of literary judgement.[23] Celebrated – indeed, singled out for praise – by the vast majority of commentators for hundreds of years, the tale was systematically and comprehensively ridiculed through several decades in the twentieth century, and over the course of its subsequent uneven and contested critical recuperation, it has received antithetical judgments, sometimes about the same specific features. To consider just one example of the latter, the narrator's pun on "stile" and "style" (V.105–6) was in the 1960s pronounced "doubtless as embarrassing in the fourteenth century as it is now" by Robert Haller, but in the 1980s Goodman declared instead that there "is no doubt that he [Chaucer] employs this device for positive aesthetic effects" and that "this is a very good pun indeed."[24]

More recently, in a complex discussion of the pun, Craig Berry seems to have it both ways, and in this fashion supplies an especially nuanced version of the general argument of the mid-twentieth-century view: that what appears as bad art is in fact good, because it is an intentional component of a greater artistic design.[25] This way of reading the *Squire's Tale*, whatever its merits, is a rather totalizing one, and it has provoked trenchant critiques of its premises and circular reasoning, especially by Lawton.[26] In my introduction I have considered those elements of these critiques, as they apply generally to IV-V, that do and do not inform this book's approach to the *Tales*. In lieu of rehashing this discussion, we may instead observe the example of Derek Pearsall, who in his broadly influential 1985 monograph essentially retracts his earlier dramatic reading because he no longer grants its enabling, totalizing assumption. Still perceiving the flaws in the tale as before, however, Pearsall suggests that it was a pre-*Tales* failure that Chaucer, recognizing it as such, gave to the Squire as a convenient, but not pre-planned, way to characterize this pilgrim as storyteller: "Returning to the story he had left unfinished, Chaucer adapted it to the *Canterbury Tales* by adding an impossible scenario for its continuation and then having it 'dramatically' interrupted."[27] In effect, the tale does in the end turn out to illustrate the Squire's incompetence, just as Pearsall earlier argued, but not so much by design as by Chaucer's shrewd assessment of the merits of his earlier writing and his clever invention of a means nonetheless to reuse it. Chaucer's brilliance and the poor literary quality of the *Squire's Tale* remain compatible.

The myriad interlocking assumptions enabling such ingenious readings as Pearsall's are, I trust, clear enough by now, including one evident in the quotation of Pearsall that I have not yet mentioned: that the Franklin's response to the *Squire's Tale* constitutes an interruption. This assumption enables those readings of the tale as an intentional failure (whether planned or belatedly recognized as such) to appeal to the interrupted *Sir Thopas* as a precedent, but, as I survey in the next chapter, others have justly questioned this assumption and hence the comparison. All literary criticism, of course, relies upon some assortment of enabling assumptions, and hence, as I have said, my point here is to provide the rationale for my own, atypically limited set. Although there are aspects of the tale that do indeed strike me, along with many other readers, as both comic and unnoticed as such by the narrator (such as the moment when the falcon misses Canacee's outstretched "lappe" and falls "to grounde" [V.441, 473]), to forestall the totalizing tendency of this view, I will be largely agnostic about the tale's merits or lack thereof; and this agnosticism in turn requires me to put aside the question of the intentionality of such apparent flaws. Furthermore, taking as very likely that the tale was not written with the Merchant-Squire link at hand, accepting as plausible that it was not initially conceived with the Squire in mind, and granting as just as possible as otherwise that it was a pre-*Tales* composition adapted with little or no changes for placement in the larger work, I will limit myself to considering the tale of Cambyuskan and Canacee as a kind of self-contained puzzle piece for which Chaucer carved a space in IV-V.

The Axiology of the Marvelous

Within the circumference of these interpretive limits, two of the tale's most obvious aspects are especially significant. The first almost goes without saying, and it is worth explicitly noting primarily for its bearing on the second: the tale's genre of composite romance supplies a platform for a story that is both more and less than that which the Host's longing for a tale of love suggests. As Goodman describes it, this genre is characterized by "meticulous attention to the niceties of court life joined with an inexhaustible appetite for marvels."[28] On the one hand, then, the tale's marvel-filled faraway land of Tartary is a place where the merely imaginable becomes possible, where brass horses can take their riders "into every place" that they may wish "for to pace" within "space of o day natureel" (V.116–20), and where gold rings enable their wearers to understand birds' "meaning openly and pleyn" and speak to them in their "langage ageyn" (V.151–52). The tale – grounded as it is, with its historically based setting, in the notionally real world of the fourteenth century but copiously overflowing that world's boundaries into the realm of fantasy – offers an escape from the real that holds out the promise of the latter's future renovation.[29] For example, the four wondrous objects brought by the "strange knyght" who spoke "Withouten vice of silable or letter" are, in John Fyler's elegant formulation, "gifts from an innocent world to a fallen one: they offer the means of reintegration, of recapturing a lost world of freshness, transparency, and clarity."[30] Likewise, with the Tartary weather "lusty" and "benigne"; the birds inspired by "the sesoun and the yonge grene" to sing their joy at having "geten hem protecciouns / Agayn the swerd of winter, keene and coold"; and a ruler who is "hardy, wys, and riche, / And pitous and just, alwey yliche; / Sooth of his word, benigne, and honorable" (V.51–57, 19–21), the natural and political worlds of this tale are, at least at the outset, harmonious, complementary ideals: they offer a vision of imagined rejuvenation far more comprehensive then the restorative tale of love that the Host may be seeking to counter the axiology of the Merchant's fabliau real.

On the other hand, it is a restorative tale of love that the story of Cambyuskan and Canacee precisely lacks. In its abortive form, this story, when it finally does turn to love, provides only an account of female erotic despair (albeit one that engenders sex-specific interspecies sympathy).[31] While the narrator does promise, in the tale's concluding prospectus for what remains untold, "that this faucon gat hire love ageyn / Repentant" (V.654–55), the balance of the narrational energies of the tale's extant 672 lines are more focused on the "the niceties of court life," as Goodman puts it. These niceties include not just the many details of the events at Cambyuskan's court but also what is throughout the narrator's habit of explicitly reflecting on, or otherwise calling attention to, courtly speech, including his own speech both in specific instances and more generally as participation in the aristocratic discourse of romance. The tale's courtly concerns, that is, encompass the unusually marked narratorial self-consciousness that virtually all the tale's readers comment upon and that indeed typically serves as essential evidence for their overall arguments about the tale and its teller, no matter how widely those arguments diverge. Not surprisingly, then, this self-consciousness constitutes the second aspect of the tale that holds particular significance for its role in IV-V, and will require more scrutiny than the first.

The narrator's references to "Gawayn" (V.95) and "Launcelot" (V.287) as, respectively, paradigmatic courtly speaker and describer of courtly scenes encapsulate the manner in which this self-consciousness binds the tale's idealizing energies to its own act of narration and participation in the discourse of romance. Both references, moreover, link the romance project of revitalization to ideals of aristocratic masculinity. First, we learn that the "manly voys" and "cheere" of the "strange kynght" visiting Cambyuskan's court supersede those of Gawain, "with his olde curteisye / Though he were comen ayen out of Fairye" (V.99, 103, 89, 95–96); and we understand that the tale's narrator – with his rhetorically elaborate denial of a like ability (which includes the aforementioned "stile"/"style" pun) – implicitly affirms a renewal of this "manly voys" in the present, or at least raises the possibility of such a renewal, through the inverse logic of the humility topos. Second, we hear that he who is able to "devysen" the "revel and jolitee" of the dance at court "moste han knowen love and his servyse / And been a feestlych man as fressh as May," and that only Lancelot qualifies as such a man, and "he is deed" (V.282, 278, 280–81, 287); and we understand this assertion of singular ability to be tacitly counterpointed (whether or not convincingly) by the narrator's own elaborate astronomical periphrasis that introduces this passage.[32] Neither reference much involves idealizations of love. Rather, they enact idealizations of masculine chivalric performance, which is at once a pervasive subject matter of the tale as a whole and that which the very telling of the tale self-consciously seeks to emulate.

This sort of self-reflexive, class- and gender-specific idealization is most amply evident, and in a more complex manner, in the tale's disproportionately long concern with the "gifts from an innocent world" brought by the visiting knight, especially the gift of the steed of brass. As numerous critics have recognized, Chaucer treats these gifts in a patently meta-hermeneutic fashion, devoting a lengthy passage to a dramatization of the myriad, incorrect interpretations, by the "prees that swarmeth to and fro" (V.189), of the nature of the gifts, devoting some three dozen lines to the brass steed alone. Although there is some precedent for this meta-hermeneutic dramatization in the closest analogues, as far as we can tell Chaucer appears to have greatly expanded this element of the tale and to have included details that blatantly signal its self-reflexivity.[33] For example, in the lines leading up to the "stile"/ "style" pun, Chaucer has the narrator reflect on the visiting knight's delivery of his description of the gifts as the telling of a tale: "And for his tale sholde seme the better, / Accordant to his wordes was his cheere, / As techeth art of speche hem that it leere" (V.102–4). We may fairly imagine, I believe, the narrator to be according his own "cheere" to these very "wordes" as he speaks them.

As a self-reflexive inquiry into the nature of wondrous objects, the passage as a whole dramatizes self-scrutiny into the nature of its own encompassing narrative. Specifically, it stages an inquiry into the nature of precisely that element of a composite romance narrative in which the real gives way to the fantastic; in which ordinary objects have extraordinary, wondrous capabilities; and in which such objects, in the potency of their excess, stand for the idealization and rejuvenation of the real that, as Fyler observes, characterizes the distinctiveness of the genre more generally. In this regard, most crucial to recognize for present purposes is that the passage dramatizes the interpretive efforts of the crowd as a progressive impulse to *reconcile* the fantastic with the real, to *demystify* the very wondrous element of the narrative that gives it a distinctive character and value as a literary discourse.[34] Considering the horse, for example, the crowd first declares it a veritable epitome of the wondrous element of composite romance, naming it "a fairye" (V.201), yet then they increasingly rationalize it, comparing it successively to Pegasus and to the Trojan Horse. The former, although still a fantastic creature, provides a literary precedent; and the latter, while a marvelous contraption from the distant past, is nevertheless one with putatively actual historical veracity, whose wholly conceivable human construction potentially harbors a threat that impels at least one citizen to further inquiry: "It were right good that al swich thyng were knowe" (V.215). Finally, another citizen determines that while the horse is remarkable, it is accordant with the actual fourteenth-century human-made spectacles that characterize the court as a locus of distinction: "it is rather lyk / An apparence ymaad by som magyk, / As jogelours pleyen at thise feestes grete" (V.217–19). Subsequently, the other gifts provoke similar rationalizing explanations, which draw on natural philosophy along with literary and historical precedents, and the passage concludes by digressing from the crowd's speculations about the gifts into their more general debates on the "cause of thonder, / On ebbe, on flood, on gossomer, and on myst, / And alle thyng, til that the cause is wyst" (V.258–60).

With its broad scope of reference, this passage has encouraged critics to focus on various components of its attempted demystification in order to claim that they are revelatory of Chaucer's primary concerns in the *Squire's Tale*. Berry, for example, understands the passage's literary allusions to convey Chaucer's struggle to achieve originality in confrontation with the *poetae* of the classical past; Vincent DiMarco sees in the references to natural philosophy Chaucer's embrace of nascent late medieval empirical science; and Scott Lightsey detects in the allusions to court marvels Chaucer's disenchanting grasp of the mechanistic technology behind wondrous objects.[35] As fruitful as these approaches to the passage have been, however, they are partial readings that emphasize one component at the expense of others, and, more important, they tend to underemphasize, or simply ignore, the fact that the narrator entertains all these explanations in order to *reject* them. Referring throughout to the speech of the crowd using forms of the pejorative designation *jangling*, he either explicitly or implicitly disaffirms *all* their explanations. We may thus only align Chaucer with any of these explanations by assuming an ironic disjunction between narrator and author, and, shorn of the larger enabling assumption of the tale as an intentional failure, the basis for this presumed ironic disjunction is not straightforwardly evident.

Critics have frequently detected such a basis in the narrator's designation of the crowd as *lewed*, and this moment in the tale is indeed a crucial one that requires close examination. Following the account of the citizen who guesses that the brass steed is merely akin to a trick of "jogelours," the narrator concludes his report of the crowd's reaction to the horse with the disparaging observation,

> Of sondry doutes thus they jangle and trete,
> As lewed peple demeth comunly
> Of thynges that been maad moore subtilly
> Than they kan in hir lewednesse comprehende;
> They demen gladly to the badder ende. (V.220–24)

These lines are often taken to convey the narrator's aristocratic disdain and hence negative trait of snobbery that manifestly disassociates his views from those of the author.[36] Yet, even if we grant this reading's somewhat optimistic and anachronistic presupposition of Chaucer's social egalitarianism, it is by no means self-evident how much of a class distinction these lines are making. Although the semantic range of the adjective "lewed" does include such a class distinction, which the adverb "comunly" may here emphasize, in the context of this passage's rejection of explanations, "lewed" would seem primarily to denote "uneducated" – especially if, in accord with the interpretive limits that I have set, we do not assume that these lines were originally written to characterize the *General Prologue* Squire specifically. Moreover, while the lines do seem clearly to disparage the wisdom of the crowd as a *crowd*, the actual social status of this "prees" is never clearly indicated. Lying somewhere beneath the status of those dining with Cambyuskan and the visiting knight, the status may or may not also lie beneath whatever we are to presume to be the narrator's.[37]

Yet if "lewed" here does then primarily denote "uneducated," the potential for irony reemerges, since, as several readers have observed, the crowd actually appears to possess an impressive range of knowledge, extending from classical literature through contemporary science.[38] Indeed, at some moments – as when they "speken of Alocen, and Vituloin, / And Aristotle" (V.232–33) – they seem quite clerkly. The adjective may thus be knowingly misapplied in a manner similar to that which we saw with the Merchant's comment on January's Canticles allusion: "Swich olde lewed wordes used he" (IV.2149). But this perception of intentional misapplication would attribute the irony to the narrator, who would thereby be covertly siding with the crowd, and it would furthermore require us to open up the entire narration – from the initial description of Cambyuskan as a "doughty man" (V.11) to the abortive astronomical periphrasis involving the "chaar" of "Appollo" and "Mercurius hous" (V.671–72) – to *narratorial*, rather than (or in addition to) authorial irony. While it would be possible to pursue such a reading, there is virtually no warrant for it, in rather stark contrast with that which one finds with the Merchant's performance. And even if a pre-*Tales* version of the narration originally possessed such narratorial irony (which would help explain its other seemingly comic features), the tale's later framing with Merchant-Squire link, as we have seen, would have decisively (if belatedly) evacuated it by means of the Squire's declaration that his "wyl is good."[39]

The solution to this puzzle, fortunately, lies in plain view, perhaps so much so that it is often forgotten. The narrator is indeed accusing the crowd of ignorance, but in a very narrow sense: they simply do not know the secret of making the brass steed function, which, for the narrator, makes their attempts at explanations not so much wrong as beside the point. As he describes in the very lines that introduce his account of the *janglings* of the crowd, "Ther may no man out of the place it dryve / For noon engyn of wyndas or polyve; / And cause why? For they kan nat the craft" (V.183–85). For the narrator, the actual nature of the brass steed does not appear to matter very much; while he says that the crowd's ignorance pertains to "thynges that been maad more subtilly / Than they kan in hir lewednesse comprehende," he himself does not lay claim to any special knowledge of the actual construction of the horse (other than what the knight in his initial speech to the court cryptically mentions about its involving the same sort of arcane, clerical astrological lore, including the waiting on "many a constellacion" [V.129], that features so importantly in the *Franklin's Tale*).[40] Rather, when he returns to the subject of the "wondryng" provoked by "this hors of bras" (V.3405) following his account of the court dance, he lays heavy emphasis not on its nature but, again, on the trick that one needs to know to make it operate, and he does so in a revealingly lengthy account of a dialogue between knight and king:

> But fynally the kyng axeth this knyght
> The vertu of this courser and the myght,
> And preyde hym to telle his governaunce.
>   This hors anoon bigan to trippe and daunce,
> Whan that this knyght leyde hand upon his reyne,
> And seyde, "Sire, ther is namoore to seyne,
> But, whan yow list to ryden anywhere,
> Ye mooten trille a pyn, stant in his ere,
> Which I shal yow telle bitwix us two.
> . . .
> Or, if yow liste bidde hym thennes goon,
> Trille this pyn, and he wol vanysshe anoon
> Out of the sighte of every maner wight,

And come agayn, be it by day or nyght,
Whan that yow list to clepen hym ageyn
In swich a gyse as I shal to yow seyn
Bitwixe yow and me, and that ful soone.
Ride whan yow list, ther is namoore to doone."
        Enformed whan the kyng was of that knyght,
And hath conceyved in his wit aright
The manere and the forme of al this thyng,
Ful glad and blithe, this noble doughty kyng
Repeireth to his revel as biforn.
The brydel is unto the tour yborn
And kept among his jueles leeve and deere. (V.309–41)

The secret shared among knight, king, and narrator is in regard to the horse's "governaunce": how to make what otherwise would simply be a brass statue "trippe and daunce," and how to make it perform not just like an ideal, actual horse ("Right as it were a steede of Lumbardye" [V.193], as the narrator remarks earlier) but to exceed the real by, for example, being capable of vanishing instantly "Out of the sighte of every maner wight" and reappear whenever the king wishes "to clepen hym ageyn."[41] The secret is, in short, like the words of an incantation; it does not disenchant the mystery of the horse but rather produces that very enchantment.

Given the meta-hermeneutic valence of the entire matter of the brass steed, and given that the narrator is in on the secret and that it is this knowledge that distinguishes him from the crowd, when he says that the crowd "kan nat the craft," he thus also implies that they are insufficient to compose and even appreciate the kind of marvelous romance that his very tale instances. It is in this sense, then, the horse/romance is "maad more subtilly / Than they kan in hir lewednesse comprehende." And it is also therefore in this sense that the social connotation of "lewednesse" turns out, after all, to be relevant. Twice in the knight's exchange with Cambyuskan the knight emphasizes that the shared secret of the horse's "governaunce" is "betwixt" only himself and the king. With the obvious resemblance of the brass steed to the armored horses that virtually defined the late medieval aristocratic warrior class, there is no more perfect emblem of romance as part of the repertoire of masculine chivalric performance and aristocratic class legitimation.[42] The marvelous transcendence of the real achieved by composite romance, which the horse epitomizes, thus emerges as both signifier and instrument of aristocratic class distinction, of the mystery of the inherited nobility that justifies their possession of wealth and power.[43]

As the conclusion of the knight's exchange with Cambyuskan suggests, the marvels of composite romance serve the same function as the king's "jueles leeve and deere": as wondrous, spectacular signifiers and instruments of class distinction, properly possessed by the rich and powerful. Because rationalizations of the mystery of class distinction serve only the low-born, expressions of such rationalizations mark their expressers as such. In contrast, while a member of the nobility must learn the tricks of class distinction, he does not in the process become disenchanted but rather deepens his belief in the magic of the aristocratic aura that he learns to wield. And because the narrator lays claim to these tricks (as evident, for example, in his tacit self-comparisons to Gawain and Lancelot, in addition to the general self-referentiality of his narrational style), his own tale's "meticulous attention to the niceties of court life joined with an inexhaustible appetite for marvels" manifests the same instrumental aristocratic self-enchantment. Ultimately, then (if still over-simplistically), those of us in the disenchanted class may indeed fairly conceive of his account of the crowd's reactions to the gifts as a form of snobbery.[44]

But what, one may well wonder, was *Chaucer's* interest and motivation in representing a self-enchanted narrator staging, and then disparaging, the disenchantment of the kind of romance that he is in the process of narrating? The easy answer, of course, is that Chaucer sought in this way to characterize the Squire. Yet because it is just as possible that this aspect of the tale is precisely that which eventually inspired Chaucer to compose the link that belatedly assigns the tale to the Squire, that answer is not sufficient. Indeed, passages of literary self-consciousness, especially in respect to genre, that convey meta-hermeneutic and meta-axiological reflections are far from unique to this tale but rather one of Chaucer's most characteristic artistic tendencies. We have seen numerous such passages already in this book, and his other works – one especially thinks of the dream visions – are rife with them. Indeed, it is a commonplace of late medieval literary study more generally to pronounce this self-consciousness a feature of not just Chaucer's writing but also of the whole period. It would hence be unusually *un*characteristic for some such similar passages not to appear in the tale of Cambyuskan and Canacee. Nonetheless, the specific meditation on the literary apparatus of class distinction that arises in this tale, while not unprecedented in Chaucer's writing, is more unusual. This particular form of literary self-consciousness, if not explicable by the identity of a dramatized narrator, was instead very likely prompted by the genre of the tale itself, Chaucer's sole excursion into the composite romance.

In contrast with, say, the philosophical and classical pretentions of *Troilus and Criseyde*, or the courtly/clerical mélange of the *dit*-like dream visions, the composite romance was more narrowly courtly and aristocratic in regard to its implied audience. It was, as Goodman points out, the very kind of vernacular literature (in French) that Richard II appears to have favored.[45] Moreover, in contrast to that of *Sir Thopas*, the implied author of composite romance is not manifestly a member of the servant, minstrel class, but instead tacitly possesses a similar status, if still an ambiguous one, as the audience that he addresses. To repeat the obvious, a composite romance was at least notionally the kind of tale that a fashionable, late fourteenth-century squire like that of *General Prologue* would tell. Hence, regardless of whether Chaucer originally wrote the tale with any dramatized narrator in mind, its generic demands necessarily gave him comparably little narratorial room to maneuver, and these constraints consequently also underscored the similarities and differences between his own actual social status and that of the tale's implied author.

The significance of these similarities and differences is a topic that the next section considers in relation to the Squire's *General Prologue* portrait; here it suffices to suggest that they are responsible for the particular form that literary self-consciousness takes in the tale of Cambyuskan and Canacee. Someone in Chaucer's social position – viz., a clerkly squire who is also a merchant's son – would have had, so to speak, one foot in the dinner chamber along with Cambyuskan and the visiting knight, and one foot in the courtyard among the crowd, musing eruditely about the brass steed. Accordingly, to him, not only would the social instrumentality of composite romance have been readily apparent, but also the sincerity of his self-enchantment regarding this instrumentality would have been difficult to maintain, however much the implied social status of the narrator appealed to him. In this light, and given Chaucer's characteristic general tendency toward self-consciousness, the peculiar narratorial self-consciousness of the tale of Cambyuskan and Canacee, whether or not it was initially intended for a particular pilgrim, appears not just explicable but in fact almost inevitable.

The pair of literary axiologies that the Merchant-Squire link introduces, then, receives fuller articulation and exemplification in the tale that inspired the belated composition of that link. As in the Clerk's performance and the *House of Fame*, meta-hermeneutic passages serve to formulate a distinctive value for literature, but, in contrast with those instances, they do so in the tale of Cambyuskan and Canacee by negative implication. The passages' failure to account, for example, for the wonder of the brass steed highlights a distinctive feature of composite romance discourse – the marvelous – and its value as a real-exceeding idealization that holds out the promise of rejuvenation. At the same time, this failure also serves as a class demarcation, thereby pointing toward the additional, rather different literary value of an instrument of social distinction. And because the mystery of the brass steed ultimately proves inseparable from the mystery of inheritable nobility, what the *Squire's Tale* appears to argue is that this bipolar pair of literary axiologies constitutes the recto and verso of the enchantment of romance discourse. The progression, in the Merchant-Squire link, from the Host's deferential acknowledgment of the sovereignty of the Squire's "wille" to the Squire's affirmation of the goodness of his "wyl" turns out to evoke, quite succinctly, this contradictory, and yet seemingly mutually reinforcing pair: an earnest, and hence self-enchanted, tale of marvels is at once the discursive expression and instrument of the mystery of the Squire's social superiority.

That Chaucer apparently abandoned the composition of what became the *Squire's Tale* perhaps testifies to his discomfort with the genre and thus also his perception of the inadequacy of this bipolar literary axiology; and it is in this respect, I believe, that we may, after all, term the tale a failure. A fuller appreciation of the nature of this failure, however, requires an account of the axiological apologia of the Squire's entire performance and its role in IV-V, for which we must next turn to a consideration of the axiological person defined by the Squire's *General Prologue* portrait.

Aristocratic Display

In many respects, the portrait of the Squire in the *General Prologue* is more straightforward than those of the Clerk and Merchant. Nonetheless, like them, it has provoked commentary polarized between some who find it idealizing and others who see it as essentially satirical. Quite plainly, it is among the most thoroughly stereotyped of the *General Prologue* portraits, with whole sections, for example, indebted to Guillaume de Lorris's paradigmatically courtly portion of the *Roman de la Rose*. As Helen Phillips has remarked, the "Squire is created out of literature[.]"[46] Accordingly, whether one finds the Squire an ideal or a satire often depends on one's overall attitude toward this stereotype. Craig Taylor, for example, while alert to elements of the portrait that appear pejorative, concludes that on balance it represents an ideal of aristocratic masculinity; whereas Laura Hodges, while recognizing the correspondence of the portrait to literary ideals, ultimately adopts the attitude of the medieval moralists toward those ideals and argues that the portrait functions iconographically to represent not just Youth but also "Lecher, Pride, and Vainglory[.]"[47]

As I discuss in this book's introduction, this critical tendency to sort the IV-V pilgrims into goodies or baddies too narrowly construes the literary function of their portraits. Construed instead as embodiments of specific axiological orientations, these portraits function not as judgments but rather as the bases for making judgments. Following this approach, to identify the specific axiological orientation in this instance, we may take a cue from Taylor's contention (which echoes that of many others) that the ideal that informs the Squire's portrait, the "fashionable courtier," complements the soldierly ideal that informs the Knight's, and that they together thereby offer "a complete portrait of aristocratic masculinity."[48]

In this complementary relation, the portraits of Knight and Squire represent the bookends of the chivalric ethos, which Chris Given-Wilson has neatly defined as "militaristic, elitist, and ostentatious," with the first and last of these components supplying crucial bulwarks for the middle.[49] In personifying chivalric ostentation, therefore, the Squire embodies the set of values that underwrites aristocratic sociocultural display, or what Christopher Dyer names the aristocrats' "style of life: their clothing and horses, their houses . . . and above all their leisure[.]"[50] In performing this "style of life," aristocrats ascribe value to material splendor, ornamental cultural practices, codified expressions of passion, etc., apparently for their own sake (i.e., as autonomous values). But as this manner of valuing serves as an expression of the natural disposition of the elite, it thereby in fact becomes an instrument of their social and economic hegemony.[51] Moreover, while "[c]ourt display and the ideology of chivalry" were evident throughout the aristocracy from royalty to squires, they were, as Ruth Mazo Karras writes, especially important for the latter end of the spectrum, the "lower aristocracy[,]" as they gave those in that position "something by which to distinguish themselves from bourgeois merchants, who were beginning to wield substantial economic, and in some places [as in London] political power."[52] The aristocratic display that signified, legitimated, and produced elite social status was particularly salient for squires, since, as the vanguard of the aristocracy, they defined the borderline of their class.

The details of the Squire's portrait – from his "lokkes crulle" through his "Synynge" and "floytyng," his "sleves longe and wyde," and the "hoote" amorous passion that prevents him from sleeping "namoore than dooth a nyghtyngale" (I.81–98) – thus serve to embody the axiology of aristocratic display. Like the Clerk's devotion to the meta-axiological island of the university or the Merchant's all-pervading concern with profit, this axiological orientation may provoke extremes of positive and negative judgment. Yet, again like the former two orientations, aristocratic display is no more or less than that which the Squire's occupation demands from him. The Squire's wholesale alignment with the "fashionable courtier" stereotype is analogous to, say, the Clerk's extreme dedication to his books: as in the latter, the Squire's thoroughgoing realization of the axiological person of his social position makes manifest the challenges that such a complete dedication to this set of values entails, but it does not itself cast judgment on those values.

The very literariness of the Squire's portrait is crucial for this set of values and the axiological person that it defines. For – as the *Roman de la Rose* epitomizes – the social protocols of aristocratic display were profoundly imbricated with their literary representations. Karras provides a succinct articulation of this point:

> The literature of chivalry was widely read. The typical knightly household owned several books that quite often included chivalric literature . . . Tournaments and jousts picked up literary themes . . . . Literary tournaments also copied form real ones . . . . Literature provided entertainment, but it also affected the ideals, interests, mentalities, and aspirations, if not the actual behavior, of the knightly class in the late Middle Ages.[53]

Invented, recorded, codified, transmitted, reinforced, and at times put into question by literary representations, the protocols of aristocratic display form an instance *par excellence* of the endlessly evolving mutual determination of life and art. Hence the Squire's portrait, while a literary pastiche, is also an embodiment of the actual educational program of the noble household, a veritable syllabus, as Nicholas Orme points out, of the "aristocratic curriculum of the day[.]"[54] The Squire is at once a literary stereotype and model student, which is to say that, in this instance (unlike that of, say, the Merchant), actual ideals of social practice and contemporary literary idealizations are one and the same.

It is with this continuity between literary and social ideals in mind that two of the most frequently commented upon features of the portrait require some revisiting. The first – the Squire's participation "in chyvachie / In Flaundres, in Artoys, and Pycardie" (I.85–86) – I consider primarily for negative purposes, to explain why I see it as wholly in line with the rest of the portrait and hence why I do not follow the majority view. Ever since Alan Gaylord's 1960 article on this sole reference to the Squire's military activities, that reference has been, even for those who affirm the overall ideality of the portrait, a kind of realist fly in the fantasy ointment. Gaylord takes as his point of departure the earlier identification of the reference as an allusion to the misconceived, disastrous, broadly unpopular 1383 military misadventure led by Henry Despenser, Bishop of Norwich. He concludes, "The conjunction of the familiar romantic terms with the very unromantic [so-called Despenser] Crusade produces a subtle but nevertheless jarring discord."[55] Critics since, notwithstanding their varying views of the Squire's overall performance, have generally followed Gaylord's lead. For Fyler, for example, the reference betrays the disenchantment and even cynicism that is the flipside of the restorative fantasy of romance discourse.[56]

The identification of the Squire's "chyvachie" with the Despenser Crusade, however, is one of those felicitously probable historical claims that over the years has hardened into a certainty that it has not really earned. Indeed, Taylor, Mann, and John Pratt have each recently argued that the more likely allusion is to the 1380 expedition led by Thomas of Woodstock, Earl of Buckingham, because that expedition was, in its tactics and execution, more typically a *chevauchée* than the Despenser Crusade and because its progress through the continent aligns better with the "Flaundres . . . Artoys, and Pycardie" that the portrait mentions.[57] While Buckingham's *chevauchée* was also essentially a military failure, it was far from as notorious as the Despenser Crusade and hence, in respect to the Squire's portrait, considerably less an unequivocal fly in the ointment. For Pratt, for example, the reference may serve as a simple attestation that the Squire has actual military experience.[58]

Yet even further skepticism about the reference is warranted. We may fairly question whether Chaucer had in mind any specific campaign or, if he did, whether he meant the details of its execution or reputation to convey any special significance. The common assumption is that because the many references to military expeditions in the Knight's portrait all appear to refer to actual campaigns, the single reference in the Squire's portrait must also do so. But this assumption in turn entails the further one that Chaucer generally follows a consistent, predictable literary strategy from portrait to portrait – an assumption, obviously, that the history of the critical response to the *General Prologue* belies. If we instead suspend the critical desire to detect in "chyvachie" the significance of a historically specific allusion, we may see how the reference, rather than providing contrast, functions just like the rest of the portrait's details: it serves as a fleshing-out of the embodiment of the ostentation component of the chivalric ethos that complements the militaristic component embodied by the Knight's portrait.

In this regard, it is important to recall that however brutal we might find the tactics of the *chevauchée*, it was in the fourteenth century the normative mode of English combat in the Hundred Years War (although increasingly less so toward the end of the century). Hence, the portrait's mention of a *chevauchée* is entirely consistent with the portrait's stereotypical tendencies, as it would have been much more characteristic of a fourteenth-century English squire to have participated in such a short-term cavalry-oriented venture than in any of the Knight's far-flung religiously motivated crusades. Indeed, it is entirely consistent with – and almost an essential element of – the portrait's focus on aristocratic display. As Maurice Keen has discussed, the nature of the *chevauchée* suited that portion of the aristocratic class who were part-time soldiers, whose principal energies were domestically focused but who sought some military experience overseas for glory and wealth – which is to say to justify and financially support the horses, armor, and riding expertise that were key elements of aristocratic display; and among this group of aristocratic men, squires were numerous.[59] Moreover, and crucially, despite the fact that much of the action of a *chevauchée* consisted of burning fields and pillaging peasant villages, it provided an opportunity for a young well-born man to perform the role set out for him in romance fiction, and, like the Squire, to return to England having "born hym weel, as of so litel space, / In hope to stonden in his lady grace" (I.87–89). As Froissart documented for the Buckingham expedition and as Gower more generally complained, the *chevauchée* in Chaucer's day served as a vehicle for romance hero emulation, and in particular for erotically motivated masculine showing off.[60] Thus, the mention of the Squire's "chyvachie," rather than contrasting with the rest of the portrait, helps to realize the portrait's complementary relation to the Knight's by underscoring the display function of military activity and the opportunity it provides for life to imitate art.

The second frequently observed feature of the portrait especially relevant to this chapter – the Squire's stated status as a poet, who "koude songes make and wel endite, / . . . and weel purtreye and write" (I.95–96) – possesses a more important, complicating role in the constitution of the axiological person. As Malcom Andrew has documented, these lines have inspired a long critical tradition, dating back at least to the early nineteenth century, of seeing the Squire as a kind of portrait of the artist as a young man.[61] In Nevill Coghill's elegant formulation, the Squire "was still in the tapestry world of Chaucer's own youthful vision. Chaucer has passed beyond it into the common light of day, but it was a world he had never forgotten and could still recapture as if he had never grown old."[62] Because this view also lends itself to a dramatic reading of the tale as a well-intentioned youthful failure, it has had, in various manifestations, long critical persistence, being evident in such recent readings as that of Lindsey Jones, who concludes that "the *Squire's Tale* is a conscious statement on the trials and tribulations of the burgeoning author/poet."[63] Simply put, in this view the verses that identify the Squire as a poet signal that the Squire's performance represents Chaucer's wistful but critical recollection of his own early poetic compositions and the attitudes that he held toward them.

As many have pointed out, this view is not merely fanciful. The story that the *Chaucer Life-Records* tells us is that Chaucer, probably in his early teens, left his home in the Vintry to become (most likely) a page in the household of the Countess of Ulster, and that he spent the later part of his youth and his entire early adulthood in service in baronial and royal households. There he received, along with young men further up the social scale (including, certainly, sons of knights like the Squire), an education in what Orme terms the "aristocratic curriculum," and by his mid-twenties he was identified in official documents as an esquire.[64] While the portrait of the Squire is plainly self-consciously stereotypical, this bare biographical outline suggests that it may have been a stereotype upon which the young Chaucer modeled himself. Indeed, as we may recall, in the *Legend of Good Women* Chaucer reports that he wrote "many an ympne" for the God of Love, "balades, roundels, vierelays" (F 421–22).

Nonetheless, a more finely grained perspective on the likely conditions of Chaucer's experience in noble households yields a more complex, ambivalent biographical picture, one that suggests that the ultimate significance of the surface similarity between the Squire and Chaucer is rather to underscore the *difference* between them, and especially a difference in implied literary axiologies. The gist of this perspective is well captured by Paul Strohm's observation that in Chaucer's day, "even as the rank of esquire had only recently gained access to gentility, so had royal service of the sort performed by Chaucer only recently been established as a point of entry to the rank of esquire."[65] This observation contains two key points.

First, the title *esquire* as a denotation of social *status* was in England a fourteenth-century innovation. Prior to the middle decades of the century, the title denoted only a service occupation: as Peter Coss defines it, "a knight's servant with particular responsibility for his horses and arms." While knights' sons commonly did serve in this capacity, the role was by no means limited to boys "of gentle stock."[66] Indeed, one late thirteenth-century statute appears to indicate that the specific task of carving at the lord's table distinguished the better-born esquires from the lesser, and thus the final line of the Squire's portrait ("And carf biforn his fader at the table" [I.100]), rather than (or in addition to) conveying his humility, serves as a conservative reassurance of his gentility.[67] What appears to have led to the broadening of the semantic field of *esquire* is that over the course of the thirteenth century, as the costs of knighthood increased, the number of knights declined, creating a kind of social-status vacuum between those men who constituted the traditional aristocratic mounted warrior class and the lesser landowners who were their subjects. Subsequently, the onset of the Hundred Years War and its need for well-trained cavalry for its characteristic tactic of *chevauchée* put pressure on this vacuum, eventually bringing about the crystallization of a mounted warrior class lesser than the knighthood but unambiguously gentle: the squirearchy. As Keen observes, "Esquires in the fourteenth century were coming to do martially just those things that knights had traditionally done ... In war they were serving, in the larger companies, alongside knights in much the same armour and on much the same conditions, except in the matter of pay."[68]

Once the title *esquire* began to denote a social rather than merely service category, it naturally over time began to be applied to a broader group of men: those who, although not mounted warriors in their principal social identity, seemed to hold roughly the same social status, and in particular men in noble household service, like Chaucer.[69] And this leads us to the second important point of Strohm's observation: that by the late fourteenth century the rank of *esquire* encompassed a range of social statuses, in which there was a socially salient hierarchy of gradations. The most unambiguous evidence for these gradations is the Poll Tax of 1379, which lists three classes of esquires in decreasing order of hierarchy: those who are essentially knights, landed esquires of less wealth than the first group, and those esquires "who were landless but who were armed or in service."[70] This third group – and especially those within it who, like Chaucer, earned their title through service – was in some key ways different from the other two. Since for these men the status as esquire was tied to service rather than land ownership, it was considerably less stable, offering no assurance that their sons would hold similar title or that even they would maintain the title throughout their lives. Most important for this chapter's purposes, the title was very likely a terminal status, the furthest rung up the social ladder that these men might obtain through service alone.[71] Hence, while the son of a late fourteenth-century knight might *choose* not to incur the expense of knighthood, as it in fact had few benefits that someone of his status did not already possess, he nonetheless would have been perceived as someone that *could* be a knight – and, indeed, the Crown, by its practice of distraint of knighthood, would likely require him to become so or pay a fine. In contrast, a squire like Chaucer would have been perceived as gentle largely by association, possessing a status more definitively and permanently below that of knight.

In short, in the noble households in which he found himself as an adolescent, Chaucer was an outsider with manifestly limited potential for advancement. Coming from a merchant family, mixing with those like the Squire, achieving a status on the very fringes of the aristocracy, anyone in Chaucer's place, we may well suppose, would have readily absorbed the "aristocratic curriculum" but would also have grasped the activities of aristocratic display for precisely what they were. Limited in their efficacy for such an individual, these activities would easily be conceived more as the repertoire of a pose that one sought to adopt than as an inherent element of one's nature that one sought to cultivate. Such an individual, in other words, would be prone to disenchantment in regard to the very cultural mechanisms of his advancement.

Moreover, what sets Chaucer apart from just any such individual, of course, is his unusual poetic talent, which brings us back to the Squire's portrait's "He koude songes make and wel endite" and the young Chaucer's "balades, roundels, vierelays." On the one hand, we may suppose that for Chaucer this very poetic talent made the game of courtly making difficult to limit to the level of mere game (albeit one with socially instrumental efficacy). As, say, the *Book of the Duchess* makes obvious, he was inclined to push courtly making beyond the confines of merely one activity of aristocratic display among others. On the other hand, Chaucer's superiors – having brought a lower-born son into their household for service, and perhaps becoming aware of his talent as courtly maker – may have perceived his "balades, roundels, vierelays" as an element of his *service*, rather than (or in addition to) a demonstration of his putatively innate gentility. Hovering somewhere between the activity of a "sporting amateur" and "professional player" (to use Richard Firth Green's felicitous analogy), Chaucer's courtly making would have been, in the eyes of those of higher rank, ambiguously a mark of his social distinction or a sign of his social subjection.[72]

There was thus both internal and external pressure on Chaucer for him to conceive his literary activities, and for others to perceive them, as congruent but not wholly identical with courtly making as an instrument of aristocratic display: as something recognizable as a species of courtly display but also evidently offering service to the elite – something a socially cultivated household clerk might write for his lord's edification, such as, again, the *Book of the Duchess*. Of course, in this regard Chaucer was scarcely unique. This situation was, for example, more or less that of such French predecessors as Guillaume de Machaut. Closer to home, the kind writing this situation encourages more or less resembles the "public poetry" that Anne Middleton has taught us to see especially in the work of Chaucer's contemporaries Gower and Langland, work which in effect extends the audience for literature as service from the elite to English society as a whole (although to the degree that the latter poets were socially more distant from the court than was Chaucer, their writings were more manifestly didactic and less evidently a species of aristocratic display).[73]

Rather than any special distinction that Chaucer's situation provides, then, what is important to recognize about it is the simple fact that his poetic career, from the *Book of the Duchess* to the *Canterbury Tales*, testifies to its impact. It is, after all, a truism of Chaucer criticism that this career increasingly transcends the generic and stylistic limits of courtly making, evolving in a trajectory that culminates in the *Tales*. Hence, the very literary context of the mention of the Squire's poetic activities proclaims the stark differences between the normative literary axiology of those activities and Chaucer's attitudes toward, and aims for, his own writing. For the axiological person that the Squire represents, literary composition possesses a social value that would have been comparatively less fungible for Chaucer, and evidently also one that was, whether from the start or increasingly so, comparatively less important to him. The Squire's portrait is accordingly not a portrait of the artist as a young man, but instead a portrait of the artist as the young man whom he resembled but could not fully become, whether he wished to or not; and this very portrait, as a component of the *General Prologue*, stands as testimony to what that man became instead. What the portrait communicates, then, is that the *Tales*, in so exceeding the generic and stylistic limits of the poetry of aristocratic display, tacitly distinguishes its own literary axiology from that function; and at the same time, the portrait tacitly acknowledges the class difference between the squire that Chaucer was and the one who is privileged to carve "biforn his fader at the table."

Squire Versus Merchant

With this two-pronged import of the axiological person of the Squire in mind, we are now in position to grasp the axiological apologia of the entirety of the Squire's performance and of its placement in IV-V – to grasp, that is, the significance of what Chaucer brought about through his belated assignment, in the Merchant-Squire link, of the tale of brass steed and talking falcon to the Squire of the *General Prologue*. As discussed above, the *Squire's Tale* expresses a bipolar literary axiology, comprehending the value of literature as on the one hand distinctive and not subject to any other value, and on the other hand as a cultural instrument of social, economic, and political domination. Quite plainly, by assigning this tale to the Squire of the *General Prologue* by means of the Merchant-Squire link, Chaucer provides for this bipolar literary axiology an apt, concrete, historically specific social representation. But the significance of this assignment extends considerably further in light of the potent combination of the implied difference in axiological orientation between author and Squire, and the positioning of the tale as a response to the Merchant's performance.

In association with the Squire's portrait, the bipolar literary axiology of the *Squire's Tale* appears at first to emerge as a decisive double trumping of the axiological apologia of the Merchant's performance. On the one hand, the Squire's performance insists – contrary to the Merchant's reduction of literary discourse to merely one instrument of deception among others to facilitate individual desire – that literary discourse, in the form of the composite romance, possesses a distinctive value, one that offers psychological and social rejuvenation. On the other hand, the form of the composite romance simultaneously attests to – which is to say, helps to produce – the aristocratic status of its teller, and consequently insinuates that the Merchant's axiology is merely that of a churl. And yet, by functioning in this way as a discursive instrument that serves, as Karras puts it, especially lower-echelon aristocrats as "something by which to distinguish themselves from bourgeois merchants," this class-based trump card ultimately falters as a rebuttal to the Merchant's axiology. Indeed, since the class insinuation of the Squire's performance conceives of composite romance as an instrument of the Squire's desire to maintain his position of social dominance, that performance's obverse claim for the distinctive value of literary discourse becomes merely (from the perspective of the Merchant's axiology) the mystifying element required for this particular instrument's efficacy. The difference between the Merchant's literary axiology and the Squire's, then, lies not in how they view the instrumental function of literary value but in their relation to the mystification of this function.

In his portrait, as we have seen, the Squire's reported literary activities are thoroughly integrated into the repertoire of masculine aristocratic display, a repertoire that we are to understand to be in his nature as an aristocrat to perform. In this respect it is the Merchant-Squire link's representation of the Squire's good-faith belief in – or, as the Squire says, his "hertyly wyl" in regard to – the distinctive positive value of composite romance that in fact enables it to be socially instrumental. As we may extrapolate from the Host's later reaction to the Franklin (e.g., "Straw for youre gentillesse" [V.695]), any hint of social calculation in respect to the performance of aristocratic display serves to call the putative signified of that display – innate gentility – into doubt, especially from the viewpoint of those below the gentle class. The Squire's own framing affirmation of his good "wyl" accordingly serves to make clear that, like the narrator of his tale in respect to the brass steed, the Squire is enchanted by the very enchantment that he wields – and, in a nutshell, that is the axiological apologia of the Squire's performance. It is an argument for a literary value that is simultaneously distinctive and non-utilitarian on the one hand and merely one instrument of social domination, among others, on the other; an argument that seeks then to justify the making and maker of this literary value by conflating the mystery of social and psychological renewal with the mystery of social superiority, so that an earnest belief in the former becomes the very means of expressing, promoting, and indeed compelling an earnest belief in the latter. In stark contrast, the Merchant's performance expresses a pervasive disenchantment about these very notions. Relentlessly exposing the mystery of romance (among other discourses) as nothing more than an instrument to obtain individual desire, the aim of the axiological apologia of that performance seems to be to raise consciousness about the false enchantments of any of the discourses that conceal the fabliau real.

The question that this contrast between axiological apologias urges us toward – where do we locate Chaucer on the spectrum that they chart – is the subject of the next chapter. At this juncture we may understand that the function of the Squire's performance in IV-V is to raise this very question and, in this way, to define the parameters within which the axiological meditation of IV-V will conclude. In the Merchant's destruction of the Clerk's meta-axiology, he sweeps away what had been Chaucer's own wily claim for an autonomous literary value – one that depended on holding at arm's length all determinations of literary value. For the Merchant, this claim is an escapist self-deception, a willfully naïve denial of the instrumentality of all discourse and the actual ground of all value in individual desire. With this meta-axiology undone, the counter to the Merchant's corrosive axiology can only be a restorative axiology, one whose claim to positive value is not – like the Clerk's – merely notional but extant in actual social practice. Because in the Merchant's performance the fabliau real and the primacy of profit become an axiological doublet, the almost inevitable counter that that performance provokes is, in the context of late fourteenth-century English society, a doublet of romance rejuvenation and aura of innate social superiority. From Chaucer's perspective, indeed, this counter would have carried the inevitability of the trajectory of his own life: his progression from mercantile origins into the court of the king himself, from a world determined by financial capital into one ruled by symbolic and cultural capital. To put the biographical parallels crudely, if the Merchant's performance in effect serves as a father-figure telling the Clerk to grow up, face reality, and get a job, the Squire's performance responds by saying, "I've got a job, and it's a better one than yours." And for Chaucer, not at all insignificantly, it was a job in which writing poetry was highly valued.

Of course, as I have had several occasions in this book to observe, and as is obvious from the facts of Chaucer's biography, Chaucer's movement from the mercantile world into that of noble and royal households was a partial, vexed one. In his thirties, as controller of customs, he found himself once again in a profoundly mercantile axiological environment. Although still in service to the Crown, he worked in a quite different social context than the one that the Squire's portrait depicts. As Strohm puts it, "He had opted to become a slightly more elevated and better connected version of what his father had been before him: a participant in urban merchant culture, a habitué of the waterfront, an officer of the king charged with the honest collection of tariffs, duties, and customs."[74] Contemplating those many years on the Wool Wharf as he was composing the Merchant-Squire link, the Squire's portrait, and either the first or revised version of the *Squire's Tale*, he could not but have been powerfully aware of how differently his squirehood turned out from that of the portrait, and, accordingly, how far he was from the self-enchantments of the axiological apologia of the Squire's performance, if he had ever been subject to them in the first place. The ultimate return, within the Squire's axiological apologia, to an instrumentality akin to the Merchant's thus conceptually apes the trajectory of Chaucer's own professional career. Although, as I have indicated, the Squire's performance in itself necessarily cannot recognize that return as such, the position of this performance in IV-V – especially from the retrospective view of the Squire-Franklin link – precipitates that return for the reader.

Consequently, from this retrospective view, which is also Chaucer's point of view, the axiological apologia of the Squire's performance stands as a regression, an attempt to return to a literary axiology that Chaucer may have once entertained, or at least one that was current in the social context in which he, as a young man, wrote court poetry. And because even then Chaucer's marginal social location would have encouraged disenchantment in respect to the cultural means of social enchantment, his potential or actual embrace of that literary axiology would have threatened a kind of bad faith, a threat that would only become more trenchant as Chaucer's career evolved. In this respect, the regression of the axiological apologia of the Squire's performance is for Chaucer one drenched in *misconceived* nostalgia. Like the composite romance itself, it asks for belief in something (a literary axiology) that never was (for Chaucer); yet, unlike the romance, this fantasy leads not to a remaking of the world but rather to futile, bad-faith self-deception.

To some degree, then, my argument about the axiological apologia of the Squire's performance may ultimately seem to be just a rather elaborate version of the critical commonplace that the *Squire's Tale* reflects the youth of its teller, whose limited life experience and social location enable him to perform in good faith an internally contradictory narration. Yet in agreeing with this commonplace in a very general fashion, I am not also claiming that Chaucer seeks in this way to render dramatically the character of a young squire. I am rather arguing the reverse: that the portrait of a young squire serves to underscore and complicate that aspect of the *Squire's Tale*'s literary axiology that is youthful in a broadly figural sense. More specifically, I am claiming that by combining a representation of a young squire, a composite romance, and a link that assigns the former to the latter, Chaucer renders a tale-telling performance that possesses a springtime axiological apologia, one that dialectically responds to the chilly axiological apologia of the Merchant's performance, but which was constituted by its author in the autumn of his poetic career.

In this regard, we may consider one final feature of the Squire's portrait, the fact that uniquely among the portraits the narrator reports the pilgrim's specific age: "Of twenty yeer of age he was, I gesse" (I.82). Obviously, this specification functions as an indicator of the Squire's youthfulness. Yet not only would that youthfulness be easily evident without the specification, but also, depending on what scale one uses, the age of twenty is actually on the further end of youth. In particular, it is just one year younger than the typical age at which those eligible for knighthood were knighted.[75] This observation in turn provokes recognition of an easily overlooked and somewhat socially atypical aspect of the portrait: the fact that the Squire is traveling with his father. For while it would be unusual for a knight to travel without one or more squires, those squires were typically other men's sons: the norm for any well-to-do English family (such as Chaucer's, for example) was for boys to complete their adolescence away from home – at university, as an apprentice, or, for the knightly class, most often in an aristocratic household.[76] That the nearly grown Squire has returned to his immediate family would hence seem to be in some way significant.

The solution to this minor puzzle is straightforward enough; as Kate Mertes reports, "Children over the age of eighteen or so often returned to the parental household for a year or more before marriage, further service or entrance to religious life."[77] Chaucer represents the Squire, therefore, as in a liminal stage, returning to the nest for a brief period of nurture before leaving again permanently for the path to full manhood. In identifying the Squire's age, then, Chaucer not only creates the diegetic basis for bringing father and son together on the pilgrimage, thereby enabling all the many thematic contrasts between their respective portraits and tales that the pilgrims' relationship grounds. But he also suggests that, as for all liminal stages, the Squire needs to leave his behind. Like the Clerk's time at university, the Squire's return to his family is by design and function temporary; and hence, like the axiological apologia of the Clerk's performance, that of the Squire's represents the wishful thinking of an adolescence that must someday come to an end. The figurative son's response to the figurative father – "I've got a job, and it's a better one than yours" – turns out to possess a mystified understanding of the nature of his "job" (i.e., of the literary axiology of aristocratic cultural production), and it misconceives what a "better" job would really require (i.e., what sort of social situation may support a non-mystified but nonetheless good-faith affirmation of a literary value).

Let me be clear, however, one final time, that with this point I do not mean to claim that the *Squire's Tale,* after all, does dramatize the Squire's incompetence – for I am not arguing that there is necessarily anything inadequate about the tale as a tale. Rather, to reiterate, I am claiming that, when situated in IV-V, the Squire's performance – the assemblage of link, portrait, and tale – functions as a wholly appropriate, almost inevitable dialectical response to the Merchant's performance. But it is a response that in turn yields dialectically to the performance of the sequence's second and explicitly presented father-figure, whose profoundly ambiguous paternal response to the Squire is the subject of the next and final chapter of this book.

CHAPTER 4

Franklin

Over and above the polarizations that characterize the critical response to the first three performances of the IV-V sequence, the response to the Franklin's performance has tended toward stark bifurcation. Broadly considered, the two sides disagree about whether the tale, when read in light of the Squire-Franklin link and the *General Prologue* portrait of the Franklin, offers on balance an affirmation of the values it seems to espouse or a critique of those values. There are, of course, significant variations in both the values the performance is understood to espouse and in the particular mechanism of affirmation or critique identified as Chaucer's central literary strategy. And, interestingly, while there are some predictable patterns, the specific values and mechanism identified do not themselves determine whether the tale's actual attitude toward its governing values is read as positive or negative. For example, critics who take the tale to espouse egalitarian marriage have argued both that this view is Chaucer's own and that it is one that he is attacking; and critics who emphasize the dramatic perspective of the narrator, as it is revealed through such details as the portrait's reference to Epicurus and the Squire-Franklin link's obsession with *gentilesse*, have seen this perspective as both benignly paternal and unreflectively materialistic. Indeed, rather than any consistent correspondence between the aspects that critics focus upon and the positive or negative valence of the conclusions that they draw from them, what cuts across both views of the Franklin's performance is how frequently it provokes an unusually blunt disclosure of the critic's own axiology. Wittingly or not, those who see the performance as an affirmation of values often indicate their own espousal of those values, while those who detect a critique just as often affirm a counter set of values.

Such a betrayal of one's own values is, of course, endemic to literary criticism. Yet the Franklin's performance seems especially calibrated to encourage such a disclosure, most obviously with the tale's concluding *demande*, but also with its myriad conceptual and narratological disjunctions, such as (to cite just a single oft-mentioned example) the tale's happy denouement being precipitated by Arveragus's threatening to kill Dorigen if she ever speaks of what he has ordered her to do, despite, as the narrator reports, his earlier swearing "That nevere in al his lyf he, day ne nyght, / Ne sholde upon hym take no maistrie / Agayn hir wyl" (V.746–48). Such "textual fissures" or instances of "conflicting evidence" encourage the reader to repair the performance's disjunctions through an appeal to a supporting or contrasting system of values, against which those disjunctions appear coherent, whether as illustrations of virtue or error.[1] For David Seaman, this axiological provocation, a "mirror that can reflect the reader's own literary, social, and moral value systems," is the performance's ultimate aim.[2] And, indeed, given the critical response to the performance and its formal terminus in a *demande*, Seaman's argument appears well attested externally and internally, and wholly in line as well with what we know to be Chaucer's concern with the ethics of reader response (as in the Nun's Priest's "Taketh the moralite" [VII.3440], however playful that is).

Nevertheless, few readers have been content to suspend their inquiries into the performance's *raison d'être* with the observation that it serves to disclose their own axiologies. Because of its many complexities, and especially because of what appear to be the tale's numerous allusions to other tales and retreatments of topics those tales consider, many readers have instead, or in addition, perceived the Franklin's performance as some sort of culminating statement – a kind of provisional thematic end stop midway through (the Ellesmere order of) the *Canterbury Tales*, Kittredge's "triumphant conclusion" to "the debate on Matrimony," to cite just the most famous example.[3] This perception, as a general impression, I believe is not mistaken, although I suspect that it derives less from such vague thematic constellations as the so-called marriage group as from the much more definite terminal role of the performance in the unfolding dialectic of IV-V. Because the Franklin's performance supplies this sequence's final phase of its interrogation of literary value, it articulates at least a provisionally settled position on the matter. Although within the organization of the *Canterbury Tales* as a whole it obviously does not provide the final word on the subject (a function Chaucer allots to the so-called *Retraction*), it nonetheless quite probably represents, given the apparent lateness of the IV-V construction, a position that Chaucer at least entertained in his last years.[4]

This position on literary value, this chapter argues, encompasses the wondrous renewal of the Squire's performance, the amoral instrumentalism of the Merchant's, and the meta-axiology of the Clerk's. On the one hand, with the action at the center of the *Franklin's Tale* – involving a clerk's selling of a magical act to a squire, an illusion-making act slated to serve as the means for realizing the squire's rather sordid desire, which the latter cloaks in fantasies of *fin'amor* – the tale seems to insert into its narrative the tale-tellers of the first and third performances of IV-V in order to replicate the lesson about literary value of the second. On the other hand, the tale's denouement presents a vision of social harmony that, however illusory – and however many costs it incurs, especially for Dorigen – seems entirely in earnest, in contrast with the winking happily-ever-after that concludes the Merchant's performance; indeed, the illusion and costs seem essential to the harmony. In realizing this dichotomous literary axiology, the *Franklin's Tale* rewrites the *Merchant's Tale* as a sober, disenchanted, but nonetheless ultimately affirmative meditation on the creative power of fiction – one that recognizes fiction's instrumental value (precisely £1,000 in this instance) but insists that a paradoxically knowing mystification of this instrumentality can be the basis for a practicable ethics for living in a fallen world. It also rewrites the Squire's courtly romance, exposing the latter's social instrumentalism even while maintaining it as vehicle for romance wonder. And, in tracing the vexed vicissitudes of power, gender, and submission in a putatively ideal marriage as a means of self-reflexively problematizing its own interpretation, and in doing this toward the end of making a case for a distinctive value of fiction, the tale doubles the meta-axiological stratagem of the Clerk, albeit developing along the way a rather different literary axiology.

The polarization in the critical response to the Franklin's performance, therefore, is at least in part a reflex of its own profound ambivalence toward the value of fiction. And its axiological provocation of the reader is, at least in part, the inevitable accompaniment to its ultimate locating of the value of fiction in readers: specifically, in the willingness of readers of fiction to be deceived about the world in order to make the world other than what it supposedly really is. (Merely to entertain the concluding *demande*, in this regard, is to confirm that fiction has bearing on the world.) My argument about the performance's axiological apologia will thus in effect assume a "both/and" position in respect to the polarization of its critical tradition and a "yes, but also" position in respect to the contention, like Seaman's, that its meaning lies in its provocation of the reader.

In characterizing the *Franklin's Tale* as a *rewriting* of others in IV-V, however, I use the gerund figuratively. As I explain in the first section of this chapter, while some scenarios of order of composition seem more likely than others, my argument does not depend on any particular one. Moreover – and more of a break with the critical tradition – my argument about the performance as a whole does not depend on the assumption that Chaucer wrote the tale for the Franklin whom he depicts in the *General Prologue* and the Squire-Franklin link. The latter two components of the performance, obviously, are integral to its function in IV-V. As we will see, the axiological person that the portrait represents overlaps and contrasts with those of the Clerk, Merchant, and Squire in ways that augment the thematic import of the *Franklin's Tale*, lending it historically specific social valence and biographical resonance. And the link, in addition to deepening this augmentation, enacts the tale's role in IV-V, recasting it most immediately as a response to what we saw to be the unresolved tensions within the axiological apologia of the Squire's performance. Moreover – given that those latter tensions are themselves the product of a response to the Merchant, whose performance in turn serves to dismantle the axiological apologia of the Clerk's – the Squire-Franklin link repositions the *Franklin's Tale* as an unflinching confrontation with the Merchant's axiology that seeks to reclaim something akin to what was lost when the Clerk's envoy yielded to the *Merchant's Prologue*. Nevertheless, I do not assume that either the Franklin's portrait or the Squire-Franklin link necessarily informed Chaucer's composition of the tale. Rather, as in previous chapters, I assume that Chaucer's construction of IV-V, and in particular his writing of its links, was a very late addition to the *Tales*, and thus whatever significance the tale itself possesses in regard to its role as the terminal point in the sequence is the product of Chaucer's retroactive reframing.

The next section supplies a justification for these interpretive limitations, after which subsequent sections consider the literary axiology of the tale, the axiological person established by the *General Prologue* portrait, and the expansion of this axiological person and the thematic framing accomplished by the Squire-Franklin link. The chapter then concludes by considering the axiological apologia of the Franklin's performance – that which is effected by portrait, link, and tale in concert – in relation to the function of this performance as the culmination of IV-V, and this review of the thematic flux of the sequence as a whole also serves as the conclusion to this book.

Order and Narrator

That Chaucer wrote the *Franklin's Tale* during the *Canterbury Tales* period, and probably late in that period, seems the obvious conclusion to draw from its parallels with, seeming echoes of, and evident nods toward other tales. Most accounts of the Franklin's performance, however, tacitly further assume that the *Franklin*'s *Tale*'s position in the Ellesmere arrangement also reflects the order of composition vis-à-vis the tales that precede it, and so Chaucer had in mind the other components of IV-V (particularly the performances of Merchant and Squire), as well as (at least) the *Wife of Bath's Prologue and Tale*, when he wrote the tale of Dorigen's rash promise. Yet, while this scenario is probable, it is far from certain, for, unlike the *Merchant's Tale*, the *Franklin's Tale* does not in fact contain any unambiguous signals of its composition subsequent to the tales to which it seems to allude. In all cases, either the allusions are general enough to be potentially coincidental, or there is no definite indication of which direction the allusion originally ran. Hence, other scenarios of order of composition are at least as likely as the one commonly supposed.

In regard to the *Squire's Tale*, many readers – observing the *Franklin's Tale* to be a romance involving magic and featuring a squire whose description strikingly accords with that of the Squire in the *General Prologue* – find the *Franklin's Tale* calibrated to reconsider the themes and (as most believe) repair the deficiencies of the tale to which it is linked. Yet nothing in tale of Dorigen, Arveragus, and Aurelius unambiguously alludes to the tale of Cambyuskan and Canacee.[5] The fact of their more general, albeit considerable, generic and thematic similarities attests less definitely to their coordinated composition than to their author's sustained interest in that genre and those themes. Thus, the similarities may just as likely have been what led Chaucer to link two tales that he composed independently as to be evidence of his originally composing them together as "a unity."[6] Indeed, if we entertain the possibility, as considered in the previous chapter, that Chaucer wrote the *Squire's Tale* some time before the *Canterbury Tales* period, then the similarities between tales may have been merely fortuitous. Likewise, we have no way of knowing whether the highly stereotyped description of the Squire in the *General Prologue* serves as the basis for the repetition of some of this material in the tales of Merchant, Franklin, and Squire; whether the *General Prologue* repeats the material from one or more of those tales; or whether the repetition is merely a coincidental reflex of conventional language (although an entire coincidence seems unlikely; more probably, Chaucer conceived the description of Aurelius or that of Damian with the other one in mind, and in the *General Prologue* either draws on one or both of these descriptions, or vice versa). While this scenario of originally independent composition of the tales of the Squire and Franklin is, of course, only inductive guesswork, it is no more so than the more typical claim that the two tales were composed as a unit. Moreover, to the extent that arguments for the latter view do not simply offer their interpretations of this original unity as evidence for it, they rely heavily on the Squire-Franklin link; but, as I review below, this link has no bearing on the question of what other tales Chaucer may have had in mind when he first wrote his version of Boccaccio's story of a wife's rash promise.

In contrast, the extensive and close parallels between the *Franklin's* and the *Merchant's Tales* (which are at least as pointed, if not more so, as the parallels between the latter and the *Clerk's Tale*) do seem to provide firm evidence that their author was cognizant of one while writing the other. As numerous critics have pointed out, the two tales possess a "remarkably similar structure," with the *Franklin's Tale* "in many respects a twin" of the *Merchant's*.[7] I trust that readers of this book need no persuasion that these parallels, far from being coincidental, strongly suggest that Chaucer intended one of these tales to be, at least to some degree, a commentary on the other. What critics have largely ignored, however, is that it is by no means certain which way this commentary originally ran. All that we definitely know is that by the time Chaucer constructed IV-V he had arranged – and possibly rearranged – matters so that the Franklin's performance implicitly, but seemingly unmistakably, comments on the Merchant's. It is entirely possible that the converse originally held: that Chaucer wrote the *Merchant's Tale* not only, as I argued in Chapter 2, as a critique of the literary axiology of the Clerk's fable but *at the same time* as a kind of complex fabliau mockery of the Franklin's romance. Indeed, this latter sort of structural parallel within generic inversion accords with what we know to be Chaucer's practice with that other romance/fabliau pair, the tales of the Knight and Miller.[8]

Moreover, this scenario would also help to explain, and make more evident, a kind of inside joke involving the tales of the Merchant and Franklin and the latter's probable source: the fact that, in both of Boccaccio's versions of the rash promise story, the task that the Aurelius-figure accomplishes, with the aid of a magician, is the revivifying of a January garden into its May glory.[9] This motif seems to reappear in the *Merchant's Tale* as the rehabilitation of decrepit January's sight, within his suddenly newly visible garden paradise, by "fresshe May" with the help of the 'magical' device of her copulation with the Aurelius-figure. Given the strong likelihood that Chaucer knew one or both of Boccaccio's versions of the story and that there is no known analogue for the *Merchant's Tale* that features the names January and May or that develops the garden motif in such detail, this connection between the two stories is likely more than merely coincidental. And if Chaucer did indeed fashion such a farcical adaptation of this one element of Boccaccio's story, it also seems likely (because it would otherwise seem unmotivated) that he did so as a comment on an already composed, more earnest adaptation of the story as a whole. In this scenario, with the *Merchant's Tale* written, in part, as a fabliau *quiting* of the *Franklin's Tale*, the latter's adaptation of Boccaccio's story would serve to prompt the Merchant's recognition of the Franklin's rather striking alteration of the lovelorn suitor's task. It would underscore the Merchant's consequent restoration of the January/May motif to his version; his making it central to the characters and themes of his mockery; and not only his having his squire, unlike Aurelius, consummate his adulterous lust but also his depicting that very consummation as the means to January's renovation. Such a wonderfully witty doubly intertextual joke loses most of its force when the *Franklin's Tale* follows the *Merchant's*.

Hence, if Chaucer did decide to obscure this possible joke, that suggests just how important that order ultimately was to him. Specifically, it suggests how, with two potential targets in the Merchant's crosshairs, Chaucer finally decided that the most powerful sequencing for IV-V puts the Clerk's performance in the direct line of the Merchant's fire and situates the *Franklin's Tale* as a terminal literary axiological recuperation rather than as a position to be superseded. As I speculated in the previous chapter, subsequent to this repositioning of the *Franklin's Tale* Chaucer may then have inserted an already written *Squire's Tale* into the exceptionally tightly woven triplet of Clerk-Merchant-Franklin in order to flesh out what he realized was now the necessary romance/aristocratic response to the Merchant's performance, as well as to indicate the limits of that response – limits that the Franklin's performance will then appear to overcome precisely by embracing.

Let me be clear, however, that I am not actually *arguing* for this scenario; rather, I am proposing it as an alternative to indicate that it is just as likely (and perhaps even slightly more probable) as the much more common assumption that Chaucer wrote the *Franklin's Tale* as a response to the *Squire's* and *Merchant's Tales* (and others). For this reason, I do not make *any* assumptions at all about the order of composition of the *Franklin's Tale* and those tales to which it is linked, and consequently I break with the widespread practice of reading the *Franklin's Tale* as if it were wholly infused with an awareness of those tales. Instead, I assume only that the tale shares many of the same concerns as the others in IV-V, that Chaucer either wrote the *Merchant's Tale* with the *Franklin's Tale* in mind or vice versa, and that at some point after the composition of all four tales in IV-V Chaucer sought to deepen and complicate their shared concerns, as well as the more pointed relationship between the tales of Merchant and Franklin (and between the tales of Merchant and Clerk), by writing the links that bring the sequence into existence.

This supposition of the belated authorship of the links, as I have insisted throughout this book, represents the most persuasive reading of the manuscript evidence and particularly that of Hengwrt. The textual volatility of the Squire-Franklin link – as attested, say, by its absence in some twelve manuscripts in which we may fairly expect to find it, its linking of Squire and Franklin in only fifteen manuscripts, and its linking of Squire and Merchant in twenty-two – suggests strongly that it was some sort of late insertion. As I mentioned in this book's introduction, this pattern of volatility is closely tracked by the other two links of IV-V, and the most compelling explanation of this pattern is that Chaucer composed the three links on single leaves sometime after writing the tales that they join, and in this state they were not found by the Hengwrt production team until it was too late to use them as their author intended. If we follow this line of probability, then the links cannot stand as evidence for the compositional order of the tales of IV-V, and in particular the Squire-Franklin link cannot attest to Chaucer's having originally written the *Franklin's Tale* as part of a "unity" with the *Squire's Tale* (which does not follow the Franklin in Hengwrt). Moreover – and representing an even greater break with the bulk of critical commentary on the Franklin – since I find it probable that Chaucer had not conceived of the content of the Squire-Franklin link when he wrote the *Franklin's Tale*, I will also grant the possibility that he determined the Franklin as narrator as late as the composition of the link, sometime after completing the tale.

The more common assumption – that the Franklin as he appears in the *General Prologue* was the narrator whom Chaucer had in mind when adapting Boccaccio's story of a wife's rash promise – has very rarely been challenged. Most commentators readily find that the Franklin's personality and attitude pervade the tale's narration. Nonetheless, apart from the link, nothing in the prologue or tale signals the narrator's identity. Although suiting the Franklin, a Breton *lai* told by a self-identified "burel man" (V.716) would not be incongruous for some of the other pilgrims. For example, the persistent mercantile undertone that many commentators have detected in the tale's values (as evident in, for example, the £1,000 sale at the center of the plot), while not inappropriate to the Franklin, would obviously suit the Merchant even more aptly. Since only the link assigns the tale definitively to the Franklin, we cannot *a priori* exclude the possibility that Chaucer originally wrote the tale for a different narrator, wrote it for the Franklin but before conceiving of the latter's *General Prologue* portrait, wrote it in the voice of an authorial persona, or even wrote it without any definite speaker in mind. The tale's critical tradition, by making the tacit assumption that portrait and link were in place when Chaucer wrote the tale, has too often rather reductively used the details of those components of the Franklin's performance as interpretive keys to unlock the supposed hidden significance of the story of Dorigen's rash promise – as, for example, a disclosure of the Franklin's bourgeois values, his Epicureanism, or his desire to teach the Squire the true meaning of *gentilesse*. Instead, in the initial sections below, I consider the tale of the rash promise as an independent composition, focusing on the question of how that tale – not the Franklin – conceives of the value of fiction. In light of the answers to this question, I then follow what was most likely Chaucer's own creative process, and establish first the axiological person represented by the Franklin and then explore the significance of his assignment of the tale's literary axiology to that axiological person.

"Thise olde gentil Britouns . . . "

My consideration of the richly multivalent *Franklin's Tale* must of necessity be highly selective. Largely ignoring some of the tale's most prominent concerns (such as marriage), I focus on just three of the tale's features that bear most heavily on its literary axiology: its explicit signaling of its genre in its prologue; the nature and implications of the promises it represents, especially Dorigen's rash promise; and the relations it suggests between magic and fiction.

In regard to the tale's genre, we have, of course, unusual access to authorial thinking. Not only does Chaucer have his narrator in the tale's introduction declare it to be a Breton *lai*, but also – assuming that he was working from one or more of Boccaccio's versions of the story – we know that he has imposed this generic category on source material that did not possess it. Once we try to press this interpretive advantage, however, we quickly run into roadblocks, as it has proven difficult to determine exactly what this generic label meant to Chaucer. There is general agreement that it is unlikely that he knew the twelfth-century *lais* of Marie de France and that he instead almost certainly encountered the term in association with the Middle English lays in the Auchinleck manuscript or a like source, whether or not he also came across it in his reading of French poetry.[10] Yet the lays in Auchinleck by no means themselves comprise a very definite genre, resembling each other, and hence also the *Franklin's Tale*, only in rather general ways; and some critics, moreover, have plausibly suggested that the *Franklin's Tale* is in many respects closer to Marie's original literary renderings of the genre (the variety of which also does not easily lend itself to a distinctive definition) than to the minstrel-flavored Middle English versions.[11] Given this uncertainty, it is perhaps safest to follow Susan Crane in assuming that for Chaucer the Breton *lai* would not really have been "generically distinct from short romances," and thus does not necessarily point to a very specific literary model.[12] Accordingly, we may also follow Laura Hibbard Loomis in concluding that the tale's self-labeling prologue represents not so much Chaucer's indication of the precise nature of his generic reshaping of his source material as, more simply, his decision to append onto the front of Boccaccio's story an adaptation of the prologue that he found at the opening of a Middle English romance such as (so Loomis further claims) Auchinleck's *Lai le Freine* and, perhaps, on the now missing leaf heading *Sir Orfeo*.[13]

Even within these restricted parameters, however, Chaucer's generic designation demands further inquiry, for the narrower question remains of why Chaucer chose to append the Middle English lay prologue to Boccaccio's story. Most answers to this question assume that Chaucer wrote the prologue with the character of the Franklin and/or the Squire's abortive tale in mind, and thus explain the generic designation as a characterization device (e.g., as expressing the Franklin's desire to tell a tale suiting his self-perceived social station) and/or as a means to distinguish the nature of his supposedly ancient Celtic yarn from the Squire's *au courant* composite romance.[14] Certainly, in its context in IV-V, the adapted Middle English prologue possesses both of these functions, and yet its amenability to this role is just as likely to have been among the already composed features of the Boccaccio adaptation that eventually inspired Chaucer to write the link that assigns the tale to the Franklin and places it last in the sequence. Rather than presume that Chaucer originally named the genre of the *Franklin's Tale* primarily, or at all, to characterize the Franklin or to form a contrast with the *Squire's Tale*, we are on firmer ground simply to read it in light of what we know about the import of Chaucer's other meta-literary passages in IV-V and elsewhere.

Shorn of all assumptions about intended narrator, order of composition, and generic distinctiveness, the implication of the Middle English lay prologue is so basic and self-evident that its significance is easy to underestimate, or just overlook: by declaring the tale a Breton *lai*, Chaucer explicitly defines it as a kind of romance and thereby brings into the reader's foreground the tale's status as a species of that most distinctively literary of secular discourses, which as such was "the inevitable jousting ground," as Melissa Furrow puts it, "for medieval ideas about literary value and meaning."[15] While all romances to some degree bear the burden of this axiological contestation, most of course do so implicitly (and probably very often unwittingly) simply by their manifest generic affiliation. Chaucer's explicit designation in effect makes a response to this axiological challenge part of the tale's self-proclaimed *raison d'être*. Such, indeed, is the effect of this kind of prologue in general, no matter how conventional or unthinkingly derived from Marie's nuanced originals, and therefore the implication is all the more pointed in a dramatic context in which tales are to be evaluated according to the quality of their *sentence* and quantity of *solas*. In this instance, the prologue declares that in judging this tale we will be judging romance and hence determining whether, how much, and in what way secular fiction, as a distinctive discursive category, may be valuable – questions with which, of course, Chaucer was concerned throughout his career and especially in the *Tales*.

Hence, regardless of its other, perhaps belatedly acquired functions, Chaucer's decision to append the Breton *lai* prologue to source material that was not so generically flagged registers his abiding interest in the question of the value of secular fiction and his decision to frame his adaptation of Boccaccio's rash promise story with this question. Among its several ramifications, this framing instructs the reader to consider the possibility of the tale's distinctively literary value and thus to defer the presumption that literary discourse has value only as a mediation of other, more important values, such as spiritual ones. Accordingly, with Kathryn Hume we can affirm that Chaucer's explicit designation of the tale as a species of romance serves for an English audience "to minimize the religious implications of certain elements in the story."[16] But we may add that the reason that Chaucer seeks to minimize these implications is not simply because (as Hume suggests) his English audience would be offended by material that Boccaccio's Italian audience took in its stride, but also, more importantly, to open up a space in which the value of secular fiction may be assessed without simply being trumped by established spiritual and moral givens. Another ramification of tale's prologue, therefore, is that the many moralizing readings that the tale has received (which have not entirely gone out of fashion), while rightly noticing the presence of these givens within the tale's capacious thematic scope, appear as unapt foreclosures of the very possibility that the prologue signals we are to keep open.[17]

Nevertheless, inasmuch as such readings do register the tale's own ambivalence toward the value of romance, they fairly pick up on the tale's profound and pervasive self-scrutiny, which indeed also begins with this very generic self-designation. For, at least to those who know the actual source of the story, the obvious irony of this self-designation is that it is a lie: the tale, in the form that Chaucer found it, is not a Breton *lai*, or even really a romance. The self-designation is consequently itself a fiction, an untrue story about the ensuing untrue story, a device that, in reflexively doubling its own meta-literary gesture, casts into relief, and offers the tale itself up to, the opposing answers to the question about value that that gesture raises. On the one hand, if the *Franklin's Tale* as a romance is found to possess distinctive value, then the opening fiction about the fiction is itself valuable: the naming of Boccaccio's story as a Breton *lai* becomes not mere deception but an instance of what the story itself seems to represent – a beneficial, quasi-magical transformation. But on the other hand, if the generic self-labeling is identified as a magician's trick of misdirection, it may serve to disclose the more cynical truth not just of the actual nature of the story at hand but also of the putative value of secular fiction that the pretended romance would have supposedly made manifest.

Moreover, the manner in which the details of the prologue develop this ironic, ambivalently open-ended, axiological self-querying gesture has at least two further crucial implications for our reading of the tale that follows: that generically the tale may covertly be something other than the romance that the narrator declares it to be, and that the narrator himself is something of a trickster, always potentially, but rarely definitely, meaning something other than – even the opposite of – what he says.[18] Here is the prologue in full:

> Thise olde gentil Britouns in hir dayes
> Of diverse aventures maden layes,
> Rymeyed in hir firste Briton tonge,
> Whiche layes with hir instrumentz songe
> Or elles redden hem for hir plesaunce;
> And oon of hem have I in remembraunce,
> Which I shal seyn with good wyl as I kan.
> But, sires, by cause I am a burel man,
> At my bigynnyng first I yow biseche,
> Have me excused of my rude speche.
> I lerned nevere rethorik, certeyn;

Thyng that I speke, it moot be bare and pleyn.
I sleep nevere on the Mount of Pernaso,
Ne lerned Marcus Tullius Scithero.
Colours ne knowe I none, withouten drede,
But swiche colours as growen in the mede,
Or elles swiche as men dye or peynte.
Colours of rethoryk been to me queynte;
My spririt feeleth noght of swich mateere.
But if yow list, my tale shul ye heere. (V.709–28)

The first five lines, as Loomis and others have shown, comprise the adaptation of the Middle English lay prologue. The immediately following two lines then comprise the narrator's story about his story: his pretense that he has "oon" of the just described Breton *lais* "in remembraunce," which he will "seyn with good wyl" to the extent that he "kan." The latter remark, which seems at first almost a throwaway line, in fact holds fraught significance. Although here the primary, surface sense of the phrase "with good wyl" is, as the *MED* indicates, "readily" (*god wil* phr. 2c), in its function as part of the narrator's lie it also, possibly ironically, secondarily connotes "benevolence" (*god wil* phr. 1b) or good intentions. It conveys that the narrator's pretense is beneficent, but by that same token, it also insinuates the possibility of the opposite: that he simply continues to lie, deceiving us about the good intentions of his deception. As we saw in the previous chapter, the Squire's comparatively more unequivocal assertion of his good will, and hence of the earnestness of the romance that he will tell, emerges in contradistinction to the insincere, romance-undercutting fabliau of the Merchant's performance.[19] Here in the introduction to a Breton *lai* that is not actually a Breton *lai*, both possibilities reside within the same narrator's remark.

The narrator's story about his story, therefore, both declares his sincerity and puts it into doubt. His "good wyl" defines the tale that follows as a species of earnest romance but hints that it may be something more like fabliau parody, a more subtle version of the tale of January, May, and Damian that Chaucer at some point would assign to the Merchant, and which he may or may not have already written. The first implication of the prologue as whole, then, is that we may expect the romance that follows to be haunted by its fabliau evil twin and, accordingly, the axiology of the fabliau real to lurk behind the axiology of romance renewal and transformation, with the former constantly threatening to pull the latter down to its level. This expectation, indeed, has been borne out in the history of the tale's critical response, as numerous readers have detected some sort of tension and even contradiction between the romance the narrator proposes and the story that he actually tells. Most typically, readings of this sort argue that Chaucer or the narrator intentionally or unwittingly subverts romance conventions, although critics do not usually explore the nature of the countervailing generic force that effects this subversion; frequently, instead, they have ascribed a dramatic function to the subversion – as indicative of, for example, the narrator's bourgeois bungling of, or hostility toward, an aristocratic genre.[20] A few critics, however, do identify the underlying opposing generic tendency as fabliau potential, and I will adopt some of their insights in the discussion that follows.[21] These readings, though, along with those that do not specify the generic character of the subverting force, generally lack a convincing account of Chaucer's motivation, a persuasive explanation of the aims of such a self-subverting romance. Accordingly, what I add to them is the explanation that in the *Franklin's Tale* Chaucer seeks, as he does in various works throughout his career, to articulate and defend a distinctive value for fiction, and that, as elsewhere, his unflinching pursuit of this project entails a degree of axiological self-interrogation, which in this instance takes the form of a pseudo-Breton *lai* haunted by a fabliau.

The second implication of the complete prologue arises in relation to the lines that follow the narrator's story about his story, in which he shifts his focus to his own narration but continues to lie. As critics have often pointed out, the narrator's twelve-line apology for his "rude speche" and ignorance of "rethorik" actually itself stands as rather unambiguous testimony to his knowledge of the arts of speech.[22] As a strategically placed instance of *diminutio*, it ascribes to the narrator, at the very threshold of his narration proper, an unmistakable capacity for winking irony. Those critics who pursue a negative dramatic reading of the tale, in which the narrator is a fumbling aristocratic wannabe, have found various ingenious ways to account for this evident moment of narratorial wit. But we may much more straightforwardly account for it, especially in light of the first part of the prologue, as another reappearance of the clever, playful, pointed irony that characterizes the narration of, say, the *Nun's Priest's Tale* or, more germanely, the *Merchant's Tale* and the envoy of the *Clerk's Tale*.[23] In other words, one of the primary functions of this preliminary narratorial aside is to cue readers to the *tone* of the narration (rather than the character of the narrator) and especially the tone in which we are to hear its several later asides. Too often, critics, even those who fully appreciate the irony of this opening aside, take the narrator's later comments – such as his Christian denigrations of pagan astrology despite his apparent elaborate knowledge thereof – straight up, a reading of tone that then creates interpretive puzzles that they typically resolve with reference to the personality or class status of the Franklin.[24] But if we put aside those latter interpretive keys, we see that, as with most of the *Canterbury Tales*, Chaucer establishes a narratorial tone at the outset, that, while capable of broad emotive range, remains nonetheless consistent in its wry rhetorical self-consciousness.

"In pley"

A similar disregard for the self-consciousness in respect to genre, rhetoric, and language established by the tale's prologue has characterized a prominent strain of the critical discussion of Dorigen's rash promise. Canvassing medieval sources to determine that the promise, in the narrative context in which Chaucer renders it, is invalid on moral, doctrinal, and legal grounds, critics have explained the fact that Dorigen, Aurelius, and Arveragus nonetheless take it to be binding as reflecting their flaws, those of the tale's teller, or both.[25] Yet, by rechristening his source material a Breton *lai*, Chaucer has created the generic space in which the absolute binding power of promises, no matter how rash or irrational, is a given; and by then complicating the circumstances of the promise in the manner in which he has developed its narrative context, he has signaled, not that we should simply find the promise a "moral absurdity," but that we should scrutinize the nature and values of the kind of secular fiction in which it possesses this binding power.[26] And by "scrutinize," as I suggested above, I do not mean that Chaucer pursues only a critique or rejection of romance conventions. Those conventions are too easy a target – their critique too simple a project – to account for the complexities of the *Franklin's Tale*. Rather, what is at stake in the tale, and encapsulated by the manner in which Chaucer renders the rash promise, is the question of whether the category of secular fiction, as epitomized by romance, has any worthwhile purpose at all.

The complicating circumstances with which Chaucer, in comparison with Boccaccio, surrounds the promise are myriad and readily identifiable, including such narrative innovations as the relatively close proximity and verbal echoes between Dorigen's marriage vow to Arveragus and her consequently adulterous pledge to Aurelius. Most baldly signaling the *metafictional* function of the promise is that in the diegetic world of the tale Chaucer precisely and explicitly represents it as a fiction, uttered by Dorigen "in pley" between her declaration that she will "nevere been untrewe wyf / In word ne werk" and her assertion that the conditions in which she would be otherwise "shal never bityde" (V.984–1001). Simply an ingenious trick in Boccaccio, in the *Franklin's Tale* Chaucer marks the promise as a species of discursive "as if," a fiction within a fiction. And in its context, at least from Dorigen's perspective, we are plainly to take it as *merely* a fiction, that is, as having no bearing on the real world. But this very contrasting between the real and fictional betrays how the real – in this case, Dorigen's love of and loyalty to Arveragus – depends on, via distinction from, the fictional: we know that Dorigen's promise to Arveragus was a real one because, although it shares the same verbal form as her promise to Aurelius ("Have heer my trouthe" [V.759, V.998]), it was, unlike the latter, not uttered "in pley."

Or was it? While I do not believe that Chaucer means us to question the sincerity of Dorigen's marriage vow,[27] the verbal identity of the two promises nonetheless has the effect of underscoring the epistemological uncertainty in the relations among verbal form, human intention, and human action, and the peculiar vulnerability of promises to this uncertainty. As a species of a performative, promises, as Leslie Arnovick writes, "do more than express intention … through them a speaker exercises agency. The utterance of a performative actually initiates a change in reality: if successful, it will cause the world to be changed to reflect the speaker's words."[28] As illustrated in the case of Dorigen's marriage vow, however, this "change in reality" is not immediately a physical change but rather first involves a shared reinterpretation of the world through the lens of the promise, and only second occasions the actions, such as sexual fidelity, which appear as both consequences of the promise and evidence of the interpretive correctness of its lens upon the real. In effect, a promise is a pledge by both parties, as well as their surrounding community, to behave "as if" the terms of the promise in fact compelled them to do so. It possesses, that is, a discursive structure identical to fiction, differing from the latter not in form but, initially, in the framework of an implied or explicit declaration of sincerity, instead of a qualification such as "in pley"; and, subsequently and more crucially, in actions that appear compelled by that declared sincerity but are rather what constitute it in fact. Moreover, because Dorigen's marriage vow has no temporal terminus, its status as a nonfiction may only be verified by a lifetime of active conformance to its terms, and so, while she lives, the vow is always to some degree a story about her past, current, and future life that may or may not be a true one – that may or may not turn out to have been made, like the vow to Aurelius, in play.[29]

In the situation of the *Franklin's Tale*, this discursive uncertainty is compounded, and its significance heightened, by the tale's widely recognized staging of its characters' generic roleplaying – how Chaucer seems, not just to depict romance stereotypes, but to dramatize the characters' active conforming to sometimes conflicting generic expectations. Thus, the by-the-numbers courtly romance opening – in which Arveragus, in "wo," "pyne," and "distresse," performs "many a greet emprise" to prove "his worthynesse" and move "his lady" to "pitee" – serves as the preamble to the famous marriage agreement, in which Arveragus, having earned the privilege to take on the role of "housbonde" and "lord," asserts that he will nonetheless continue to play the role of "lovere to his lady," even while she pledges to be his "humble trewe wyf" (V.730–58). Predictably, critics have been divided about whether Chaucer/the Franklin proposes this arrangement as an ideal or as a self-consuming contradiction in terms (or just a travesty), and they have spilled much ink over such details as Arveragus's reserving, despite his pledge to continue as Dorigen's subject, "the name of soveraynetee" (IV.751). But they have agreed that the possibility of simultaneously playing the roles of knightly suiter and husband, and of courtly lady and wife, is one of the tale's primary concerns.

The denominational overlap between "playing a role" and performing a speech act "in play" is of course no lexical accident. The former, as the performance of a predefined social identity, shares the narrative "as if" structure of the latter, and ranges in social valence from manifest fictionality (like the promise made in play) to an apparently real social condition that, like the vow made in earnest, is always haunted by the possibility of being merely a pose. Crucially, in the *Franklin's Tale* Chaucer links these two kinds of social fictions in a relation of mutually confirming interdependence. On the one hand, the performance of roles (knight and husband, lady and wife) serves as the action that demonstrates, and hence constitutes, the sincerity of performative speech acts (the marriage vow): inasmuch as Dorigen and Arveragus perceive their actions in alignment with these roles – and their actions are so perceived by others – those actions confirm the continued *trouthe* of the promise. Conversely, on the other hand, Chaucer characterizes the promise as that which demonstrates the alignment of notional roles with real actions, as it is the promise that, as both outcome of past roleplaying (the result of the by-the-numbers courtship) and framework for future roleplaying, defines the bearing of that roleplaying on real life. The authenticity of one social fiction, in other words, confirms that of the other, and vice versa, and hence social, interpersonal authenticity has the structure of a tautology.

It is this tautology that makes the relation among intention, verbal form, and human action so doubtful, because intention – although seemingly essential to a promise's authenticity – turns out not to matter, at least in a pragmatic, social sense. One may make a promise insincerely, but nonetheless play the roles that the promise demands accurately and consistently; and so even if one plays those roles as self-conscious poses, the two social fictions will still confirm each other, making both promise and roleplaying, for all *practical* purposes, authentic. Conversely, no matter how sincere the promise, or how earnest the roleplaying, if actions do not align with verbal form, the promise – again, for all *practical* purposes – becomes false and the actions feigned.

This situation is, of course, familiar to anyone who has ever made promises and played roles, which is to say most if not all human beings as social creatures, in Chaucer's day as well as ours. Indeed, given the social valence of the Middle English concept of *trouthe*, which encompassed in one word both authentic performance of social identities and verbal veracity, the tautology of roleplaying and promises, and the consequent marginalization of intent, was likely even more salient then than now. And in fact, early on in the *Franklin's Tale*, Chaucer seems to go out of his way to signal this always uncertain alignment of intent, promising, and roleplaying by including the uncharacteristically snide narratorial comment that leads into the section containing Dorigen's complaint against the "grisly feendly rokkes blake" (V.868): "For his [Arveragus's] absence wepeth she and siketh, / As doon thise noble wyves whan hem liketh" (V.817–18). With this remark in mind (perhaps the narrator's most Merchant-like moment in the tale),[30] it is difficult not to recognize the subsequent complaint as an extended instance of conscious roleplaying, one which "liketh" her to perform, and which thus leaves its sincerity, if not in doubt, at least provisional.

It is this provisionally authentic instance of roleplaying, then, that serves as the foil for the subsequent rash promise passage, the garden scene with Aurelius in which, as virtually all its critics have noted, Dorigen and the squire take up the stereotypical feminine and masculine poses of *fin'amor*, with Dorigen doing so manifestly inauthentically but wholly appropriately in the scene's generic/social context. Indeed, not only do the roles of abject suitor and *daungerous* lady played here mimic those played by Arveragus and Dorigen at the tale's outset, but also the paradoxical terms of the latter couple's marriage vow in effect require Dorigen to continue to play the role of *daungerous* lady, as well as "humble trewe wyf."[31] Hence, in a reflection of that paradox, Dorigen's promise to Aurelius to love him "best of any man" if he manages to "remoeve alle the rokkes" from the shore – as a demand for a "greet emprise" from one who feels "wo" and "peyne" and would move her to "pitee" – constitutes an action that serves as evidence for the authenticity of her promise to Arveragus. Far from rash, from this perspective Dorigen's promise to Aurelius is quite shrewd: by giving an unwanted suitor an apparently impossible task, she manages to be both courtly lady and faithful wife. Moreover, as Crane has pointed out, this shrewdness extends to the discursive trap of courtly language more generally, in which the lady's "no," taken as *daungerous* speech, communicates to the suitor "keep asking."[32] Dorigen's "yes, but only if" is hence the only response that will send the suitor away, and she has proposed a task calibrated to keep him away permanently.

Crucially, however, for the rash promise to serve these functions, it must be understood to be binding. If she were to make the promise with no manifest obligation to keep it, she would both falsify her courtly lady roleplaying and transform the suitor's proposed task into a rather transparent figure for saying "no" (which would then again take on the meaning of "keep asking"). At the same time, of course, she cannot utter the promise wholly earnestly without committing adultery in intent. Hence, although Dorigen makes the promise "in pley," her roleplaying in this moment, *despite* being explicitly flagged as merely roleplaying, has the same pragmatic status as her roleplaying as faithful wife. What Chaucer has in this way accomplished in his adaption of Boccaccio's story to this new generic context is to foreground that which is latent in all social fictions: that we do not need to believe the stories that we tell ourselves about our commitments and identities in order for them to be, for all practical purposes, real.

Moreover, in this generic context, the conflict that emerges in this scene between the two contrasting stories that Dorigen is telling herself about her commitments and identities – between, that is, *daungerous* lady and "trewe wyf" – appears, precisely, as a generic conflict. As many readers have noticed, Dorigen's explanatory remark, following her acknowledgment of the absurdity of the task that she has proposed for Aurelius, is unusually blunt and coarse, far from the language and sensibility of *fin'amor*:

> What deyntee sholde a man han in his lyf
> For to go love another mannes wyf,
> That hath hir body whan so that hym liketh? (V.1003–5)

Almost tauntingly titillating in its tacit demand that Aurelius imagine Arveragus's repeated sexual access to Dorigen's body, the rhetorical question strips the stereotypical *fin'amor* love triangle of its sheen of noble sensibility, recasting it in basic terms of sexual possession and appetite.[33] From the generic point of view of romance, the question cannot be answered affirmatively or negatively without the whole generic edifice collapsing. From the perspective of, say, Nicholas in the *Miller's Tale* – or, more aptly, Damian in the *Merchant's Tale* – however, the question is unanswerable for a wholly different reason: in a fabliau point of view, it simply goes without saying that any corporeal *deinte* is worth having, and indeed such pleasures are all the more desirable if they come at the expense of those who would seem to possess exclusive possession of them. What Dorigen's question makes manifest, therefore, is a fundamental conflict between romance values, in which love figures as a noble ideal that transcends the ordinary requirements of society, and fabliau values, in which appetite and material competition are conceived as the real in respect to which mystifications like noble love serve either as delusions or instruments of deception.[34] Dorigen's question in this way insinuates an understanding of the entire *Franklin's Tale* as a fabliau parody of romance (one about a squire who, with the assistance of a greedy, wily clerk, tricks a knight into forcing his own wife to cuckold him), a parody that is merely more fully disguised than that of the *Merchant's Tale* – which is to say that the question serves as the tale's tacit acknowledgment that the fabliau real may well be an accurate assessment of human social life.

Once so brought to the surface, this acknowledgment infects (to some indeterminate degree that will forever divide critics) the plot and themes of the entire tale. Yet it is too simple then to conclude that Chaucer seeks in this way to subvert the romance genre, because, unlike in the *Merchant's Tale*, the fabliau real never fully emerges as the story's *sentence*; rather, the romance throughout stubbornly clings to ingenuousness, despite its odd, persistent undertone of generic self-doubt. Indeed, Aurelius's response to Dorigen's question stages precisely this maneuver:

> Aurelius ful ofte soore siketh;
> Wo was Aurelie whan that he this herde,
> And with a sorweful herte he thus answerde:
> "Madame," quod he, "this were an inpossible!"
> Thanne moot I dye of sodeyn deth horrible."
> And with that word he turned hym anon. (V.1006–11)

Rather than answer the question that Dorigen has just voiced – which, as we have seen, cannot be answered without stopping the romance in its tracks or turning it into a fabliau – Aurelius simply ignores it.[35] He responds instead to the pledge that she made "in pley," and he is overcome with despair not because he understands that promise as facetious, but because he understands it as binding but its terms unachievable. That is, he believes in the story of the relationship between himself and Dorigen that the promise enacts, which in turn enables him to continue to play the role of lovesick squire – sighing, sorrowing, and falling into an erotic melancholy that he claims will kill him. The romance thus hurdles over the disclosure of the fabliau real by a kind of willing suspension of disbelief, or, rather, a willful maintenance of belief in a social fiction in the face of an ugly underlying truth of human relations. And it is this maneuver that, writ large, the tale performs as a whole, in which ugly truths repeatedly yield to such social fictions as *gentilesse, fredom*, and the master signifier of *trouthe* itself, that which Arveragus eventually declares to be the "hyeste thing that man may kepe" (V.1479). In this light, Arveragus's insistence on keeping *trouthe* does not only derive, as several critics have argued, from a kind of slippery-slope reasoning, in which a failure to keep a specific promise, no matter what the circumstances, casts doubt on one's personal integrity, thereby putting into question all of one's promises, past, present, and future.[36] *Trouthe*, in addition, becomes the general principle of belief that enables the very things in which we wish to believe to possess any practical existence whatsoever.[37]

"Magyk natureel"

One might rephrase the above formulations as the claim that a belief in social fictions *transforms* ugly truths into *trouthe*, a notion that in both Boccaccio's versions of the story and Chaucer's *Franklin's Tale* thematically links the social metamorphoses of the erotic triangle and its resolution with the figure of the magician and his activities at the narrative's center. Indeed, if Chaucer knew the version of the story in *Il Filocolo*, we may fairly suppose that he found especially inspiring the latter's lengthy, spectacular account of Tebano's pagan-god-assisted transformation of a barren January garden into its flourishing May opposite. There Chaucer would have spotted the thematic potential of a magic that turns winter into spring, the literarily reflexive potential of the figure of the magician, and the bearing of both of these on the transformations that mark the resolution of the story's erotic triangle.[38] Regardless of the actual source of Chaucer's inspiration, however, with the clerk and his role in the story, as many readers have recognized (especially V. A. Kolve in an influential 1991 study), Chaucer unmistakably telescopes the tale's more abstract self-reflexive concerns about fiction and genre into a concrete figure for a maker of romance fictions.[39] In this manner, he focuses the tale's axiological self-questioning and brings it to the surface, thereby ultimately building a case for the value of secular fiction as a discourse that possesses a uniquely transformative agency precisely because of its acknowledgment of its murky foundations.

The tale's initial consideration of "magyk natureel" (V.1125) associates it ambiguously and ambivalently with, on the one hand, esoteric "curious" pre-Christian lore that may or may not actually enable one to manipulate nature, and, on the other hand, with contemporary court spectacle. Aurelius's brother, desperate to help his melancholic sibling, remembers seeing a book left by a "bachelor of lawe" at university in Orléans ("Al were he ther to lerne another craft"),

> Which book spak muchel of the operaciouns
> Touchynge the eighte and twenty mansiouns
> That longen to the moone, and swich folye
> As in oure dayes is nat worth a flye, –
> For hooly chirches feith in our bileve
> Ne suffreth noon illusioun us to greve. (V.1129–34)

The context of Aurelius's preceding prayer to Apollo – in which he asks the god to have his "blissful suster, Lucina the sheene" cause "so greet a flood . . . / That fyve fadme at the leeste it oversprynge / The hyeste rokke in Amorik Briteyne" (V.1045, 1059–61) – would seem to suggest that, in the supposedly pagan diegetic world of the story, the astronomical lore of this "book" that speaks "muchel of the operaciouns / . . . / That longen to the moone" possesses real transformative agency, albeit of uncertain source and extent. The narrator's rather abrupt and intrusive castigation of the idea of this agency oddly then appears to confirm that agency in the very declaration of its fundamentally delusive nature. Keeping in mind the winking wiliness of this narrator, we are not, as I suggested above, to read this castigation as an anxious, straightforward distancing of the supposedly pagan past of the story from the Christian present of the telling, as it has been frequently read.[40] In addition to its possible function as an insider's joke on Boccaccio, a close look at its rather tricky syntax discloses a more complicated, ambiguous sentiment. I take the genitive construction of line 1133 to mean "For faith in the belief of [i.e., mandated by] our holy church," and thus understand the whole clause to declare that our belief in prescribed Christian doctrine does not allow any "illusioun" achieved by "magyk natureel" to harm us (see *MED faith* n. 1a, citing this line, and *sufferen* v. 8b). Notably, it does not then question the illusion-generating fecundity of "magyk natureel" but rather suggests that the latter is in fact potent, requiring the talisman-like protection of Christian faith, which in "oure dayes" disables the threat of this magic that by implication was a force to be reckoned with in the pre-Christian past, or indeed to those without the talisman in the present.[41] In this way, it oddly puts "our bileve" and "magyk natureel" in parallel, the two differing in this momentary aside more by their relative strength than by anything specific about their nature. The statement is therefore scarcely the nervous or dogmatic affirmation of Christian piety it has often been taken to be, but instead more of a wry commentary on the sort of piety that makes "our bileve" simply a more potent form of magic. Remaining undisturbed by the aside is the ambivalent illusion-making power of "magyk natureel" itself.

In the lines that follow, Aurelius's brother describes what is in fact a rather different kind of illusion-making. Despite the continuity that the narrator indicates by his depiction of the "book" of "magyk natureel" as the trigger of Aurelius's brother's next recollection, the "diverse apparences" of "subtile tregetoures" (V.1140–41) that the brother goes on to describe are not the effects of pagan astronomical lore but rather of mechanized court spectacle, produced not by powerful pre-Christian magicians but by contemporary medieval "craftsmen, *artisans mécaniques.*"[42] Indeed, Chaucer's inspiration for this passage, as Loomis long ago proposed, may well have been the actual entertainments that King Charles V included in the extravaganza arranged for the 1378 visit of Emperor Charles IV to Palais de la Cité. But regardless of its source, as Loomis shows and Scott Lightsey has recently explored at length, Chaucer's and his immediate audience's knowledge of such spectacle is not in doubt.[43] The abrupt transition from arcane, presumably pre-Christian "folye" to the more familiar and spiritually neutral illusions created by "tregetours withinne an halle large" (V.1143) thus seems odd, prompting one critic to argue that the conflation of the two reflects the narrator's fallibility.[44]

Yet not only, as I have suggested, do we have little warrant for detecting such fallibility (and rather more for assuming an assured narratorial irony), but also the passage does not in fact conflate the two kinds of illusion; instead, and more significantly, it juxtaposes them toward uncertain implication. Aurelius's brother says that he is "siker that ther be sciences / By whiche men make diverse apparences, / *Swiche* as thise subtile tregetoures pleye" (V.1139–41): he does not say that "magyk natureel" is the *same* as the obscure but wholly human-engineered craft underlying court spectacle, but rather that it is capable of creating illusions of a *similarly* grandiose, veracious quality and aristocrat-pleasing effect. The spectacles of the *tregetoures*, however inscrutably ingenious, were, of course, understood by their aristocratic audiences to be more emblems of the mystification of noble aura than actual mysteries, part of the lavish entertainment that both in its contents (lions and castles) and extravagance reflects and confirms the nobility of the lord who pays for it and the audience members privileged with invitations. They are in this way – just like the steed of brass in the *Squire's Tale* – theatrical equivalents of that other form of noble entertainment, courtly romance, and specifically romance in its function as a technology of social distinction.[45]

When Aurelius's brother returns, then, from his recollection of the illusions of *tregetoures* back to his hope to find "som oold felawe . . . / That hadde thise moones mansions in mynde, / Or other magyk natureel above," who is able thereby to make "alle the rokkes blake" appear "yvoyded everichon" for "a wowke or two" (V.1153–61), we must now ponder the relation between such an "oold felawe" and these *tregetoures*. If the insinuation is that they are functionally equivalent, then – since the *felawe* and his illusion-making will serve as icons for the poet and his fiction-making – we may detect, with Lightsey and others, a disenchanting effect. We may perceive a disclosure of the man-behind-the-curtain, which reflexively exposes the delusory nature of the romance at whose center we encounter such a *felawe*, whose knowing deception makes him more capable, but also more ethically culpable, than the self-deceived romance posers Arveragus, Dorigen, and Aurelius. Yet this insinuation, if it is even present, is only that. The juxtaposition may convey as much distinction as similarity, expressing the belief that if mere *tregetoures* are able to create the illusion of a barge floating on water "withinne an halle large" (V.1143), then, surely, a wielder of the much more potent (and, though not supernatural, also not merely human-engineered) "magyk natureel" would be able to perform the much grander feat of making a coastline of rocks appear to vanish, "To mannes sighte" (V.1158), for a week or two. That this is indeed what the clerk of Orléans subsequently accomplishes ("But thurgh his magik, for a wyke or tweye, / It semed that alle the rokkes were aweye" [V.1295–96]) sustains the possibility that this "magik," in the very scope of its illusion-making power, is something other, and something greater, than mere stagecraft.[46] (And it appears also to be something greater than a canny prognostication of an unusually high tide, as critics frequently assume; for, as I have quoted, Chaucer is careful to indicate that the clerk manages to sustain the illusion for the full "wyke or tweye" that Aurelius's brother originally imagines, a duration for which even the most ingenious meteorological explanations cannot account.)[47]

It is in this context of competing possibilities for "magyk natureel," and of the uncertainties that these possibilities engender, that we are to read the subsequent passage recounting the experience of Aurelius and his brother at the home of the clerk of Orléans. Here, as many have noted, the association between the creation of magical illusion and the composition of courtly romance, already suggested by the digression on court spectacle, becomes unmistakable, as the "diverse apparences" that the clerk manufactures consist pointedly of a series of conventional romance topoi, culminating in an image of Aurelius's own self-mystified construal of his and Dorigen's relationship: "his lady on a daunce, / On which hymself he daunced" (V.1200–1). Yet, at the same time that this passage brings into clear focus the self-referential significance of "magyk natureel," it also brings the ambivalence toward magic – which is to say an ambivalence toward the value of secular fiction – to a kind of thematic boiling point. On the one hand, as several critics have argued, the clerk's illusion-making power, "al this sighte merveillous" (V.1206), seems remarkably potent, quite beyond that of late medieval stagecraft, occurring impromptu "in his studie, ther as his bookes be" (V.1207) and attaining a level of detail and (with the final image) unpremeditated customization on a different scale than that of the barges, castles, and lions of court spectacle. "Behind the figure of a magician in his study," Kolve writes, "one sees the figure of a poet among his books";[48] and the former figure, not only in his demonstrable powers but also in his evident wealth and social status (possessing a house "So wel arrayed" that "Aurelius in his lyf saugh nevere noon" [V.1187–88] and having a "squier" [V.1209] as a gentleman servant), is scarcely equivalent to a *tregetour*. On the other hand, as Kolve continues, the magician/poet comparison "is for poetry as troubling as it is exalting."[49] Indeed, even before we reach the culminating financial negotiation, which for Kolve and others is the most troubling aspect of the passage, we may observe that the spectacle that the clerk manufactures consists wholly of masculine predatory images – and, more subtly and much less frequently commented upon, but perhaps just as significantly – that the account of the clerk's illusion-making potency is bookended by reminders of human physical existence: small, usually overlooked details that, superfluous in respect to plot, for that reason serve pointedly to belie a magical power that seems to transcend the limits of nature.

Initially, following the inexplicable prescience ("a wonder thyng") of the "yong clerk" whom Aurelius and his brother meet outside Orléans, Aurelius's brother asks this youth about the "felawes / The whiche that he knowe in olde dawes" and hears that "they dede were" (V.1179–81).

Later, following the spectacular display of the magician's powers, after the latter claps his hands to dispel the illusions, he enquires from his squire whether supper is ready. He points out that "Almoost an houre" has passed since he requested his attendant "soper for to make" (V.1211–12), thereby terminating their immersion in the world of romance with a blunt acknowledgment of the corporeal fact of hunger. The clerk's tone in this exchange with the squire has been read as irritable and for this reason has been connected to the ire that the *General Prologue* suggests that the Franklin directs toward his cook when the latter's sauce is not satisfactorily "Poynaunt and sharp" (I.351–52).[50] But given the clerk's subsequent remark upon hearing that supper is ready – "Thise amorous folk somtyme moote han hir reste" (V.1218) – his mention of the nearly elapsed hour seems more likely to express concern for his guests, specifically, concern for their hunger and need of sleep. The display of the magician's apparent powers over nature, therefore, is sandwiched between signals of the limits that nature imposes on human existence. Hoping to find an "oold felawe" whose knowledge of the "moones mansions" gives him the power to make coastal rocks disappear, Aurelius's brother hears that all those old fellows have succumbed to the natural limits of the physical body; later, seeming to summon effortlessly whole "parkes ful of wilde deer" (V.1190) into his study, the clerk of Orléans nonetheless tacitly acknowledges the greater power of simple human corporeal need: he has no power over time and no power over the fundamental human requirements to eat and rest.

Indeed, the clerk's illusion-making, in one sense, merely serves as a diversion to pass the time needed for the preparation of supper, with the suggestion that the "amorous folk" – that is, those who wish to live in the world of romance – more importantly require sustenance and "reste." With the clerk's display of his powers figuring those of the romance poet, Chaucer here thus contrastively conjoins the demands of physical corporeality, as the real, with the unreality of the idealizing of desire that romance as a genre enacts. In the crucial, central episode of the magician's study (one wholly original to Chaucer), this corporeal, material real, which in essence is the same as the fabliau real, both defines the limits of poetic power and, as the ensuing financial negotiation insinuates, is the imperative that motivates the poetic maker in the first place.

With the financial negotiation, we seem to be firmly catapulted into the world of the *Merchant's Tale*. In effect, as many have characterized it, when the clerk "made it straunge, and swoor, so God hym save, / Lasse than a thousand pound he wolde nat have" (V.1222–23), he offers to serve as pimp – or, more precisely, he offers to facilitate a rape for money, and for a fee so exorbitant that he ensures the victimization of the rapist, as well as of the raped.[51] The clerk's illusion-making – the figure for poetry making – becomes wholly an instrument for realizing the aims of his own and Aurelius's corporeal desire, with the illusory removal of the rocks (itself a succinct image for the superficial covering-over of the real) corresponding to, and facilitating, Aurelius's illusory self-understanding as a lovesick squire seeking to complete the task set for him by his courtly lady. Underneath the sea, the rocks are still there; underneath the pose of *fin'amor* and a third troth-plighting, lie greed, deception, conspiracy, and attempted rape.

Kolve acknowledges that "[t]hings swiftly take a sinister turn as the magician-clerk transforms himself into a shrewd business man, demanding a ruinous price for making the rocks (seem to) disappear." But he claims that with this turn Chaucer uses the self-reflexive passage to articulate by contrast his own poetic vision and ethos (i.e., his axiology): "Chaucer defines his own art by its difference, proving himself no trafficker in appearances-for-their-own-sake, no vendor of easy fantasies, no lousy juggler, no clerk of Orléans."[52] In this way, Kolve reads the tale as a whole as providing (in a complex manner that integrates clerical and courtly perspectives on human life) the kind of romance renovation and renewal that, as we have seen, is under interrogation in the IV-V sequence, with "the *real* magic in *The Franklin's Tale* . . . [being] that which (at the end of the tale) transforms selfishness into generosity, debt into forgiveness, and courtly loving into courteous living."[53] For those who, like Kolve, offer such affirmative readings, the *Franklin's Tale* succeeds in the end – despite the "sinister turn" that seems to disclose the fabliau plot and axiology that have been lurking in the shadows – at becoming exactly what the *Squire's Tale* attempts but ultimately fails to be: a romance that transcends its instrumental function and fashions an imaginary world that may help readers in the real world achieve the ideals that it depicts.[54] In this understanding, the fabliau axiology signaled by the financial negotiation is ultimately transformed into a romance axiology, with the proposed exchange of money replaced by an actual exchange of acts of *gentilesse* and *fredom*.

To be sure, Aurelius abandons his rape attempt and the clerk never collects his thousand pounds; nonetheless, it is difficult to see exactly where the line falls between the sordid instrumental illusion signaled by the clerk's financial negotiation and the "real magic" of the tale's conclusion. Kolve suggests that the contempt that the narrator later directs toward astrology (V.1271–72, 1292–93) marks this line,[55] but, as we have seen, there is good reason to suspect that the witty and shrewd narrator has his tongue firmly planted in his cheek here, as in other, similar moments in the narration (and, as several critics have pointed out, the narrator's apparent negative attitude toward astrology is belied by his rather intricate knowledge thereof).[56] Moreover – and more damningly – there are compelling reasons to understand the supposedly magical transformations of the tale's conclusion as entirely continuous, in their actual sordidness and instrumentality, with the financial transaction at the tale's center. Critics divide rather severely over the significance of the tale's ending in this regard (and thus about the tale as a whole), with views akin to Kolve's countered by those who understand the thousand-pound exchange to infect all that is to come, within a tale that has been tainted from the start. From this perspective, the tale's conclusion, far from a magical transformation, is merely another false illusion, consisting of the actions of a series of deceiving, deceived, and self-deluded men: their passing the body of a woman back and forth and their engaging, in actuality, in homosocial, material exchange through the means of symbolic capital (consolidating, in this way, their gender and class dominance), while on the surface proclaiming their shared beliefs in the illusions of *gentilesse* and *fredom*.[57] The tale's denouement, in this view, simply repeats in a more subtle register that of the *Merchant's Tale*. Each of the three men play the roles of both January and May, as individuals who both practice deception and who are willing to be deceived so that the fabliau real that governs human existence may be comfortably blanketed over by the instrumental fictions that keep everyone happy. Indeed, the (notably wealthy) clerk and poet figure, in this light, becomes a neat double of the stereotype of the wealthy and socially grasping London merchant, as one who has purchased his acceptance into the aristocratic circle by in effect loaning an aristocrat one thousand pounds and then forgiving that debt.[58]

In fact, the tale provides ample yet inconclusive evidence for both affirmative and disenchanted readings, but it does not itself choose between them, as signaled dramatically (in both senses of that adverb) by its famous termination in a *demande*. In one sense, in asking "Which was the mooste fre" (V.1622), the narrator indicates that the choice lies with the reader, who may of course answer "none of the above" or "all of the above" as assuredly as identifying any single character. But in another sense the *demande* signals the indeterminacy of the tale itself in this respect and its encouragement for readers, conceived collectively, to consider the claims of *all* positions, however mutually exclusive. In this manner, it offers a vision of the social value of secular fiction that recognizes simultaneously its deceptiveness, utility, and transformative power. It suggests that while indeed the world operates according to the fabliau real – by the ethos of the *Merchant's Tale*, in which virtue consists of using all discursive means, however deceptive, to put oneself in advantageous positions that serve one's desire – this world ultimately also requires trust, or, more specifically, the shared belief that the speech acts that we call promises do have bearing on our lives, that the fictions that they enact are true.

As we might expect, this indeterminate axiological ambivalence, while most manifest in its ethical and social dimensions with the sequence of actions that form the tale's conclusion, appears most powerfully in its meta-literary significance in the clerk's book-lined study. From the point of view of the conclusion, the clerk's earlier financial transaction emerges as a *via negativa* toward what may or may not be the beneficent, rejuvenating transformations at the tale's end. The clerk's asking for money initiates the chain of demands that leads to Arveragus's insistence on what may or may not be, in this instance, the delusory principle of promise-keeping *trouthe*, which in turn provokes Aurelius's self-recognition of his actual fabliau motives – his intended act of "cherlyssh wrecchednesse / Agayns franchise and alle gentillesse" (V.1523–24) – which results in what may or may not be his reformation. The clerk's illusion-making is hence the instrument that seems ultimately to dispel, not facilitate, Aurelius's illusory *fin'amor* longing and the sordid corporeal desire for which that longing was a masquerade, like the sea covering the rocks. Its magic seems thereby to transform the fabliau real into what may be the notional but more truly 'real' virtues of "franchise and alle gentillesse." And yet, this magic may instead be the instrument that realizes the more profound deceptions of the virtues that enable men to dominate women, as well as each other, in a world of bodies and money.[59]

From the point of view of the tale's ending, the clerk's magic is all of these things at once: it is that which brings about the reintegration of the social world that was disrupted by Aurelius's misconception of romance desire, and it is that which most exposes the tale's underlying fabliau axiology to us and facilitates the misrecognition of that axiology by the men joined in an affinity of wealth and power. Dorigen, in her first complaint, calls on God (presumably a pagan supreme deity) to make the rocks disappear (V.891–92); Aurelius, in his first complaint, calls on Apollo and Lucina to do the same (V.1059–76). They both ultimately receive the "myracle" (V.1299) for which they ask, not from God or gods, but from a man's trick of illusion-making. What Chaucer in the *Franklin's*

Tale proposes is that secular fiction, as represented by the clerk's magic and as epitomized by the promise as speech act (by *trouthe*), is essentially this trick/miracle: an insubstantial, instrumental, wish-fulfilling lie, but one which belief/self-deception may render beneficently/corrosively efficacious in the social and material world of bodies, money, power, and competition. The tale suggests that fiction, like a promise, will shape the real (i.e., the fabliau) world as long as we continue to act as if that fiction were true, even if we do not actually believe that it is.[60] Chaucer leaves it up to us (an "us" signified by the characters, the pilgrims, and the implied readers) to determine the positive or negative valence of this trick/miracle, but as the phrasing of the concluding *demande* suggests, he seems most to want us to duplicate it: to invent *fredom* and *gentilesse* where there is none, while being conscious that we are doing so; and, by recognizing our own creativity in this regard, to acknowledge our axiological agency, our ability (with, say, each promise that we utter) to make the social and material world a better place by pretending that it is not as bad as it is.

This staging of the reader's axiological self-recognition and agency, in turn, supplies a *raison d'être* for the very mode of secular fiction that the *Franklin's Tale* has had under scrutiny. For, like any belief system, the belief in the transformative power of fiction (understood in its broadest sense) needs constant renewal, as it is always subject to doubt, especially when it involves recognition of its very insubstantiality. The poet, in this sense, becomes the illusionist whose aim is to disclose the fact of mere illusion – that the rocks are still under the sea, that romance ideals are instruments of deception and self-delusion – but who nonetheless pleases us with the trick, encouraging us to collude in pretending that the illusion is real, because such collusion is the trick's true value.

This then is the literary axiology of the *Franklin's Tale*: it asks us at once to believe in and not be fooled by fiction as a general discursive category, and it proposes that the value of the narrower discursive category of secular literature is to remind us of the illusory, instrumental nature of fiction while ultimately recommending a reaffirmation of belief. To be unwittingly fooled by fiction, the tale indicates, is to act like Aurelius, who wreaks havoc on the social world by misrecognizing his own desire as the ideals of *fin'amor*; but to disbelieve in fiction is to dwell in a world in which the clerk receives a thousand pounds to force Dorigen to have sex with Aurelius – in which, that is, money and appetite reign supreme, and virtues are mere tools of deception. The best path, as seems very characteristic of Chaucer, is the middle way, and it is this middle way that secular fiction may dramatize and, in the process of its reading, enact.

Hence, on the one hand, the *Franklin's Tale* is indeed not so different in the end from the *Merchant's*, in which January, confronted by an image of the fabliau real, is nonetheless deluded, and perhaps self-deluded, into a belief in May's virtue, and which condition of perhaps willed blindness ensures continued social harmony, the reproduction of patriarchy, and even some limited sort of satisfaction. But, on the other hand, because for the *Merchant's Tale* the dispelling of the illusion of fiction is the point of the literary fiction, it leaves little axiological justification, if any, for the activities of the literary maker. In contrast, because the point of the *Franklin's Tale* is not just to dispel the illusion but also encourage continued belief in it, the literary maker has the potential to serve as a kind of sustainer of civilization, helping to subjugate economic competition and corporeal desire to ethereal, evanescent notions of community and "higher" values. Like the clerk of Orléans, the literary maker is one who knows that the beliefs that we live by are illusions, but one who also knows that they are nonetheless a potent means with which to organize our world; and, for this reason, the value of secular fiction is to sustain these beliefs by making us conscious of our complicity in fabricating them. Why Chaucer assigns this literary axiology to the Franklin is the subject of the remainder of this chapter.

Axiological Person

Most critics, despite the wide divergence in their interpretations of the *Franklin's Tale*, have tacitly agreed that the pilgrim's portrait and link form a single, unified characterization, and that the tale is in some fashion eminently suited to this characterization. And, indeed, in comparison with the portraits, prologues, and epilogues of the other components of IV-V, the characterological field developed in the Squire-Franklin link does seem more continuous with that developed in the Franklin's portrait. Nonetheless, the habit of reading them as one composition – in addition to ignoring the evidence of their likely compositional independence – has obscured their distinctive functions (which are, in my terms, respectively those of fashioning an axiological person and of thematically soldering that axiological person to a literary axiology), substituting for them the single function of character development, which tends to misconceive Chaucer's purposes. Moreover, the unusual interpretive challenges of the link have encouraged critics to solve its problems by disambiguating aspects of the portrait that, as I will contend, are more aptly kept open. In this section, therefore, I consider the Franklin's portrait in isolation of both tale and link in order to establish the axiological person, drawn by that portrait, that later became one of the preexisting puzzle pieces that Chaucer used to construct the Franklin's performance and the axiological apologia of the termination IV-V.

The disambiguating foreclosure in the critical response to the portrait is evident in the stark division of opinion regarding the character of the Franklin, as it has been read in circularly reinforcing concert with affirmative or disenchanted readings of the tale. To be sure, such tale/portrait circularity and mixed opinions are the norm in *Canterbury Tales* criticism; yet the balance of disagreement and interpretive depth of its implications vary significantly from one teller/tale pair to another. As we have seen, opinions of the Clerk are on balance positive, while those of the Merchant are more often than not negative, and these views have shaped (and have been shaped by) critical accounts of their respective tales. Opinions of the Squire's portrait are more thoroughly divided, with some seeing a straightforward romance-idealization of an aristocratic youth, and others finding some element of ethical and spiritual emptiness; and perceptions of how "flawed" the *Squire's Tale* may be have been calibrated with these respective readings of the portrait. Opinions of the Franklin's portrait have divided similarly, but this division has been more complex and profound in its implications. For some, the Franklin's portrait paints a picture of a genial, generous man who, while not perfect, offers one of the few models of secular virtue among the pilgrims and, in comparison with the Knight and Plowman, perhaps the only practicable model. For others, the Franklin is a virtual personification of spiritually empty materialism, whose desire to emulate the gentles through conspicuous consumption discloses his misconception of virtue and his underlying cupidity.[61] Affirmative or disenchanted readings of the tale, respectively, follow from these views and are in fact the framework from which those views issue.

In this section I argue that the axiological person represented by the Franklin's portrait encompasses both poles of critical opinion. I claim that the ambiguous ambivalence that is an inherent part of the performance of this particular social identity is what attracted Chaucer to it, and that it led him further to signal the overlap between this social identity and his own. This signaling of biographical overlap ensures in turn that the axiological person of the Franklin, like those of the other pilgrims of IV-V, becomes a player in the metapoetic, meta-axiological economy of the *Tales*. To pursue this argument, this section focuses on two of the longstanding debates about the Franklin's portrait: the still-vexed question of the social meaning of the franklin status in

Chaucer's day, and the disagreement over the positive or negative valence of the Franklin's manifest materialism.

"A Frankeleyn"

Although investigations of the social meaning of the franklin status go back at least to the early nineteenth century, for present purposes we may depend on the important surveys of the historical evidence by Henrik Specht, Nigel Saul, and Peter Coss.[62] In a monograph devoted to the question, Specht concludes, against the then prevailing view, that the Franklin would have been understood as unambiguously gentle: "Chaucer's Franklin was thus ... a fairly unexceptional [i.e., typical] member of the country gentry. By position and authority, way of life, and common esteem he was indeed, in terms of social status, a true and worthy 'gentilman.'"[63] Saul, reviewing Specht's evidence and introducing his own, finds to the contrary that the portrait's collection of social attributes makes the Franklin quite "uncharacteristic of the class from which he is supposed to be drawn," a class that Saul determines to have been "inferior in quality to those of noble and gentle birth."[64] Coss's recent consideration of the question largely confirms Saul's view but calls somewhat more attention to the socially unsettled situation that Saul also recognizes, which is that in Chaucer's day – which was the period immediately preceding the one in which the formal status of gentleman emerged – the social meaning of the relatively infrequently used term *franklin* varied depending on context. In a rural, local context where no squire, knight, or higher nobleman immediately resided, the status of franklin likely did function to distinguish such men from the peasantry, positioning them in effect within the class of *gentils gentz*. But in direct comparison to men who bore arms, the term could (but did not have to) hold the opposite valence, signifying a landholder who fell on the other side of the line separating the gentles from the churls. "The late fourteenth-century franklin," Coss concludes, "was thus an ambivalent figure," and he remained so until new social gradations narrowed the semantic range of the term. In particular, with the 1413 Statute of Additions, which ushered into usage the status of gentleman, the franklins "were split in twain, with some moving above the dividing line between gentle and non-gentle, but most remaining below"; and, as the new title of gentleman took hold, "older and imprecise terms such as franklin fell away and the divide between gentleman and yeoman increasingly dominated contemporary thought."[65]

The impetus to plant Chaucer's Franklin firmly and unambiguously on one side or the other of the social divide may thus be more a modern historiographical habit than a late fourteenth-century imperative. On the one hand, the line between gentles and churls was, of course, the most salient social divide for late medieval English men and women; on the other hand, exactly how some specific social identities sorted across this divide could in some instances be more fluid than fixed, varying depending on context and relative standing in respect to the most proximate social others. In Chapter 2, I considered this fluidity in respect to merchants, who were functionally equivalent to nobility in some contexts but mere commoners in others. The franklin status, as contemporaries seemed to have perceived,[66] possessed a like fluidity, albeit in a rather different socially inflected manner.

Moreover, as Specht, Saul, and Coss all recognize, the ambiguity of the franklin status is severely compounded in the *General Prologue* portrait by the fact that Chaucer ascribes a set of offices to his pilgrim that in combination franklins simply did not possess (and rarely occupied individually), and which were much more characteristic, in Chaucer's day, of knights and the better-off esquires. As the *General Prologue* narrator asserts, "At sessiouns ther was he lord and sire; / Ful ofte tyme he was knyght of the shire. / . . . / A shirreve hadde he been, and a contour" (I.355–59). The Franklin, that is, has served as a justice of the peace, frequently as an MP, as a sheriff, and as whatever a *contour* denotes.[67] Notwithstanding the uncertainty surrounding the latter office, the historical record attests that the former three roles were all well beyond the sphere of the typical fourteenth-century franklin, and there is virtually no precedent for their combined occupation by a man of that stature. As Coss observes, "We thus seem to have a dichotomy between, on the one hand, the social position of franklins in real life and, on the other, the roles Chaucer has his Franklin perform. This in a nutshell is the fundamental problem in interpreting Chaucer's description of the Franklin."[68] Saul, Coss, and many others have sought to crack this nut by interpreting the offices as exaggerations – as indications of the Franklin's pretense toward a social stature for which those offices would be appropriate, and hence as a signal that we are to understand the portrait as a whole as a species of satire. As Saul succinctly asserts, Chaucer "was writing a parody of a *parvenu*."[69] Others, not surprisingly, have read the offices in precisely the opposite fashion: as signifying the unusual social respectability and responsibility of this particular franklin, and hence as a signal of the sympathetic and perhaps even idealizing nature of the portrait.[70]

This sympathetic reading – if, following the historical record, we may assume that the discrepancy between the Franklin's status and his office holding would have been readily recognized by Chaucer's contemporaries – attributes too little to the discrepancy, glossing over what, at the very least, would have raised eyebrows. Yet the satirical reading, conversely, attributes too much to it, perceiving insinuations of a grasping, socially ambitious personality in what is actually a straightforward notice of offices that the Franklin actually held, not ones he only aspired to possess. Indeed, the neutral facticity of this notice becomes underscored in contrast with the explicit insinuations of social ambition in the immediately following portrait of the guildsmen, who have not in fact held the office of alderman but merely "*semed* ech of hem a fair burgeys / To sitten in a yeldehalle on a deys" and who each "Was shaply for *to been* an alderman" (I.369–72).[71] Both the sympathetic and satirical readings, in other words, simplify the thematic import of the portrait by attempting to resolve the ambiguity created by the office/status discrepancy in one direction or another, when it is more likely that Chaucer sought to complicate this import by compounding the ambiguity of an already liminal social status.[72]

The attestation of the historical record to both this liminality and the relatively infrequent occurrence of the *franklin* label make probable that this liminality is one of the reasons why Chaucer chose to include a pilgrim with this social identity. As Michael Johnston has observed about Middle English literature generally, "franklins were useful figures for literary thought experiments exploring the boundaries of gentility."[73] But much more pointedly indicating the importance of this liminality (especially to Chaucer's contemporary readers) is the fact that, as is well known, two of these offices (justice of the peace and MP) are ones that Chaucer himself held, and that Chaucer's own social status – as I have had several occasions in this book to remark, and as has been thoroughly examined by Paul Strohm, Patterson, and others – was itself fluid, liminal, and ambiguous.[74] Indeed, if we put aside the ever-tempting biographical speculations about their similarities of personality, joviality, and taste for fine living, we see that what the Franklin and Chaucer most share (again, as Chaucer's immediate circle of readers could not fail to notice) is precisely the fact that they were, in terms of social status, manifestly under-qualified for those offices. About Chaucer's election as MP, for example, Strohm observes, "His qualifications were so dubious when compared with those of others in his category of representation that only a special interest in his election by supporters of the king can explain what he was doing there."[75] Although Chaucer's rank as esquire in one way provides him with more minimal qualifications for these offices than the Franklin, Chaucer was, as I reviewed in the previous chapter, merely an esquire *de meindre degree*, who held title through royal service and not, as was much more typical of those esquires in Parliament and serving as justices of the peace, through ownership of land. In fact, as Coss reports, the graduated poll tax of 1379 in effect equated franklins and lesser squires, with franklins "required to pay either at the rate of 6s. 8d. or of 3s. 4d.," depending on their amount of property, thereby "making them equivalent to the esquires of lesser estate who paid 6s. 8d. and to the esquires 'not in possession of land or rents' who paid 3s. 4d."; and most franklins, Coss further notes, paid 3s. 4d., giving the typical franklin the same status, at least for purposes of taxation, as Chaucer the esquire "not in possession of land or rents."[76]

I do not, however, follow the critical tradition that sees in this biographical overlap a warrant to identify the Franklin in more general ways with Chaucer, with that pilgrim reflecting, for example, "the sunny side of Chaucer's personality" and "the genial narrator of Chaucer's earlier poetry."[77] Instead, no more – and no less – than with the biographical overlaps with the Clerk, Merchant, and Squire, we may more confidently conclude that this biographical connection signals Chaucer's interest in exploring one particular aspect of his own multifaceted social identity, ultimately vis-à-vis his avocation as a writer of fiction. With all the IV-V pilgrims, that is, Chaucer signals his interest in scrutinizing the normative axiology that is encouraged and to some degree required by a particular facet of one of the social identities with which he has experience (the facet that constitutes the biographical overlap). With the Franklin, Chaucer explores the axiology of the peculiar liminality of a man on the cusp of the gentle class, one who, in contrast with the Clerk and Squire – who are liminal in their own, different ways – has no sure footing in the traditional estate to which he aspires; and one who also, in contrast with the Merchant, has no alternative axiological tradition.

Chaucer, although not a franklin, found himself in several respects in an analogous social position at the time in which he was actively compiling the *Canterbury Tales*. On the one hand, with the termination of his controllership and the rather extended semi-return to his mercantile heritage that position represented, along with his accompanying departure from London, the residual mercantile element of his social identity would have been at a low point. On the other hand, in that very departure from London, Chaucer was also at some distance from both the center of the royal civil service that underwrote his claim to gentility and the coterie of readers and fellow writers that in lieu of any institutional basis was the ground of his clerkly identity.[78] With the Franklin, therefore, Chaucer examines the axiological contours of the social liminality that most resembled his own at the time he was putting together the *Tales*. Although no more of a general stand-in for Chaucer than any of the other pilgrims of IV-V, the Franklin does represent the axiological person that most corresponded to Chaucer's actual social position at the (likely) time of the composition of the *General Prologue*.

"Epicurus owene sone"

While the civic offices that the *General Prologue* narrator assigns to the Franklin have constituted the most historically puzzling element of the portrait, the Franklin's voracious gourmandizing materialism has been its most critically controversial. This latter aspect is, obviously, the portrait's most striking and ubiquitous subject matter. From the Franklin's delight in his morning "sop in wyn" (I.334), to his apparent devotion to Epicureanism, the quality of his bread and ale, and the "fissh and flesh" that was "so plentevous / It snewed in his hous of mete and drynke" (I.344–45), almost the whole portrait develops various aspects of this characteristic; out of thirty lines, only the first two or three and the last five or six (which include the ones mentioning his offices) describe anything else about the Franklin. For some critics, this materialism stands unequivocally as a negative, if only implied, moral and spiritual judgment against the pilgrim. The allusion to Epicureanism, for example – given its echo in the *Merchant's Tale* in respect to January (IV.2021–22; and January also enjoys "a sop in fyn clarree," V.1843) and Boethius's account of the philosophy's inadequacies in the *Consolation* – would seem to establish firmly by the portrait's sixth line the dubious nature of the pilgrim's axiology.[79] After this cue, most of the remainder of the portrait may be read as an unambiguous portrait of a glutton, who organizes the "deyntees" on his menu "After the sondry sesons of the yeer" (I.346–47) and berates his cook "but if his sauce were / Poynaunt and sharp" (I.351–52).

Other critics, however, take as more important cues the narrator's mention of the Franklin's "sangwyn" "complexioun" (I.333) and his comparison of the pilgrim to "Seint Julian" (I.340). Jill Mann, for example, argues that Chaucer chooses to identify explicitly the Franklin's complexion not to hint at a connection between sanguinity and gluttony but rather because, "of all humours, the sanguine is the most attractive. Chaucer uses it, that is, to persuade us of the healthy and generous nature of the Franklin's gourmandise; he associates the mountains of food, not with a diseased and queasy glutton, but with a fresh-complexioned man with an excellent stomach." And, she claims, "Any inclination on our part to read the Franklin's admiration for Epicurus as a sign of his selfish materialism is swiftly counteracted by the second comparison, with St Julian."[80] From this point of view, the Franklin illustrates not the sin of gluttony but the virtues of liberality and hospitality, with his concern over his "deyntees" and his chiding of his cook indications of his good taste and prudence, and the allusion to Epicureanism merely "a hyperbolical little jest."[81]

This critical gridlock, as I have suggested, derives in large part from the requirements of fitting the portrait to affirmative or disenchanted readings of the *Franklin's Tale* and the Squire-Franklin link, as well as from the general tendency to divide the portraits between sheep and goats. If instead we consider the portrait only in the immediate literary context of the *General Prologue* (as arguably Chaucer did when composing it), and specifically in comparison with the axiological persons established by the portraits of the other IV-V pilgrims, we may see how the Franklin may simultaneously be hyperbolically materialist and represent a reasoned, and realistic, axiological orientation for a man of his status in fourteenth-century England.

Most obviously, in the portrait's single-minded attention to the Franklin's delight in his own and others' consumption of food and drink, the portrait stands as a kind of photographic negative of the Clerk's, given the latter portrait's thoroughgoing emphasis on that pilgrim's asceticism. In this respect, the Franklin's portrait doubles the function of the Merchant's, which, as we saw in Chapter 2, offers a mercantile materialism that counters the Clerk's rejection of a world of things and his embrace of a world of thought within the idealized intellectual institutional oasis of the university. The Merchant's portrait proposes instead the accumulation of material profit as a practical and even virtuous response to the imperatives and uncertainties of human economic existence that the Clerk's portrait signals but suppresses. In the further context of the IV-V sequence, as we saw, this contrast becomes one of maturity versus extended adolescence, of sober recognition of the demands of the "real" world versus the impractical, naive escapism of the eternal student. The Franklin, with a beard as white "as is the dayesye" (I.332), would appear to reinforce this contrast, with his civic duties tacitly recommending his brand of worldly materialism as more useful, and more practical, than a life of taking handouts from friends and relatives to spend on books. And yet, the Franklin's materialism is in a wholly different key than the Merchant's, so much so that the photographic negative metaphor oddly also applies to the contrast between these two: as a precise inverse of the Merchant's axiology of accumulation, the Franklin's portrait recommends instead an axiology of consumption. Rejecting the ascetic renunciation of the eternal student and recognizing, like the Merchant, the ineluctable human immersion in the world of things, the Franklin nonetheless represents a response to this immersion that is the polar opposite of that represented by the latter.

The significance of this response – the significance, that is, of the Franklin's ethos of consumption and sociability, in contrast with the Merchant's ethos of accumulation and social reticence – emerges in comparison with the Squire's portrait. Not coincidentally, like the Franklin's portrait most of the Squire's is tightly focused on a single characteristic, which as we saw in the previous chapter is the young man's performance of chivalric ostentation, or aristocratic sociocultural display, especially along the vector of romance idealizations of behavior. In this respect, the description of the Squire complements the crusading militarism of the Knight, with their combination forming, as Craig Taylor puts it, "a complete portrait of aristocratic masculinity."[82] Yet this composite portrait is not in fact entirely complete, as it lacks a representation of the male aristocrat in his crucial and defining social, economic, political, and cultural role as manor lord and local government agent. As Coss observes, "Chaucer's Knight and Squire seem to occupy a different social space from the country gentry, even though in reality they and the office-holding Franklin represent two sides of the same gentry coin: the chivalric and military life on the one hand, employment as royal agents in the counties and representatives of their communities on the other."[83] The Franklin, therefore, despite the murkiness of his social status, embodies a particular facet of aristocratic axiology, the entire constellation of which Chaucer has divided among three pilgrims, enabling scrutiny of its different and competing parts.

Both Coss and Saul understand Chaucer's assignment of this role to the socially dubious status of franklin as dictated by the fact that he had already used the Knight and Squire to represent other facets of nobility, and thus, "[t]o fill the role of the office-holder, to which we would expect to find the knight or the esquire assigned, we are therefore left with a franklin not representative of the actual franklins of the day," and the effect is to produce a satire on class pretension.[84] Coss and Saul, however, seem to assume that Chaucer had no control over which pilgrims to include in the *General Prologue*. That is, basing their detection of satire on the mismatch between the Franklin's status and his offices, they make the rather unpersuasive assumption that Chaucer was somehow constrained in his assignment of social roles by his own artistic choices about which pilgrims to include. Instead, as with my contention about the mismatch between offices and status, the better explanation of this role assignment lies in Chaucer's interest in the liminality of the franklin status and the nature of its biographical overlap.

If the Squire's highly stereotypical portrait is best understood as the representation of a normative social performance of masculine gentility within the dimension of chivalric ostentation, the Franklin's materialism is best understood as a like normative performance of gentility, but instead within the complementary dimension of the country householder or, as the narrator sums it up in the portrait's final words, in the role of "worthy vavasour" (I.360). The latter title, as Coss has shown, was not in fact used in England outside of romance literature, and hence for Chaucer it was not a social synonym for *franklin* but rather the label for a stereotypical model of gentility that forms a symbiotic axiological complement to that of the chivalric model.[85] As Roy Pearcy argues, in the romance schema the domesticity, worldly wisdom, sociability, and hospitality of the vavasour represent the real social goods – actual aristocratic society – that the idealized virtues of courage and military prowess professed by the knights errant aim to protect and preserve. At base, the vavasour represents the material existence of the aristocracy, while the knight errant represents the ideals that legitimate and guard this material existence, so that "when a romance writer brings knights and vavassors into confrontation he creates an opportunity to explore relationships between a life style characteristically devoted at its highest level to the definition and support of cultural ideals, and one characteristically devoted at its lowest level to physical survival."[86] As Pearcy's latter description insinuates, moreover, the materialist axiology of the vavasour may ethically degenerate; he may become a figure of greedy self-interest, whose material attachments become obstacles to knightly ideals, or, within a fabliau, the figure of noble pretension hiding base desire that makes him the target of generic scorn. Pearcy turns to the *Franklin's Tale* and Squire-Franklin link to argue that Chaucer's Franklin lies somewhere between the romance and fabliau figures – that he represents a man who nostalgically strives to conform to the former but whose proto-bourgeois materialism, as especially evident in tale and link, inevitably pulls him some degree toward the latter.

Such a socially, generically, and historically liminal figure who signifies a materialist ideal, as well as its possible degeneration, is in a general way indeed what I believe that the portrait represents. If we limit ourselves to the portrait, however – and put aside the always-tempting supposition that Chaucer possessed a historically prescient perspective on the large-scale social changes in which the bourgeoisie would eventually play a dominant role – the more precise significance of this liminality emerges. In particular, we must return to the implications of Chaucer's assignment of the actual social status of franklin to the literary role of vavasour. In this regard, the Squire's portrait again provides a revealing comparison. In the previous chapter, I placed that portrait in the context of the late fourteenth-century growth of the squirearchy as encompassing a socially diverse set of men, some of whom fit the traditional model as members of old, titled, landed families who will eventually attain knighthood and even higher rank, and others of whom, like Chaucer, represented social innovations, as they were landless commoners whose royal service and connections bestowed upon them the greatest title that they will ever have. The Squire's form of aristocratic display, his embodiment of the old-fashioned romance stereotype, is thus, on the one hand, well suited to his status as a knight's son, and, on the other, in this very suitability calls attention – especially by its inclusion of verse composition – to the distance between the Squire's normative, traditional performance of his social status and, in his very writing of the *Canterbury Tales*, Chaucer the squire's performance of his own much murkier status. Like the Squire's portrait, that of the Franklin represents a stereotypical form of aristocratic display (the vavasour), but, unlike the Squire, the Franklin as we have seen occupies a homologous social position to Chaucer's, as he is situated at the very bottom of the social range for which a performance of gentle status is even possible – that is, for which a performance may (possibly) be socially recognized as authentic rather than as imposture. Indeed, as the Franklin lacks a recognized aristocratic title, the basis of his claim to gentility is even less tangible than Chaucer's, and hence consists in large part in how convincing his performance thereof is.

As historians have emphasized, in late medieval England a compelling performance of gentility in fact served as the most essential criterion for defining the bottom strata of the provincial gentle class. Although copious land ownership and prestigious office holding helped to secure one's class status, for those in the bottom strata, possession of land and office did not guarantee that status, and the lack of their possession did not prohibit attaining that status. As Philippa Maddern explains, "Not all claimants to gentility could muster a credible bloodline, evidence of long-standing royal service, or sufficient landed income. But almost all could lay claim to some aspect of the broad range of gentle qualities and behaviours." Therefore, she continues,

> To be a member of the gentry was to be constantly undertaking a performance: behaving like a gentleman/woman in the eyes of the world, and particularly for the benefit of the "gentry" society whose recognition alone could establish who was gentle and who was not . . . claimants to gentility were involved in a world of fluid social meanings, where their social status was continually being tested and negotiated by peers and neighbors in their community of honour. Within this community, to be a gentleman/woman was to be forever acting out a role . . . Before a perpetual audience of superiors, peers and inferiors, they acted their parts in a world which, to them was truly always a stage.[87]

Moreover, as we would expect, the less secure one's foothold in the gentry, the more urgent it was that one put on a convincing performance thereof; as Raluca Radulescu and Alison Truelove observe, "While the established gentry flaunted their perceived right to gentility in order to maintain their privileged position, the newly risen or aspiring members of the group sought in any way that they could to justify their claim to their elevated status."[88]

The hyperbole of the Franklin's materialism, therefore, is explicable in this light: because he was so much on the fringes of gentility – or even just outside the pale – to play the role of vavasour convincingly, he cannot, so to speak, hold back. His food and drink must be of the utmost quality, he must present himself convincingly as a man of fine living, and, most important, he must be an exceptionally generous host. "His hospitality, however liberal," Janet Thormann writes, "is not an exchange, nor is it an offer of charity towards others, but a display imitating aristocratic magnanimity, the generosity that is one of the identifying traits of the nobility he endeavors to claim through the imitation."[89]

In following Thormann regarding the Franklin's imitative practice, however, I do not also follow her historicist version of the parvenu reading, which damns the Franklin with an unwarranted retrospective economic teleology.[90] Because *all* social identities are produced and maintained by performances that consist of imitations of sociocultural norms, and because the gentry as a group were especially conscious of the imperative of compelling performances to produce and maintain their status, the Franklin, like any country householder who quite reasonably wished to be recognized as gentle, simply behaves according to social expectations. Inasmuch as we can take the narrator's word for both the extremes and authenticity of his performance – that he really was as generous as "Seint Julian" who served the finest "mete and drynke" – we may understand the Franklin's hyperbolic materialism as functionally equivalent to his office holding: it stands as conventional, socially recognizable evidence for his achievement of the very gentle status that his explicitly and initially named identity as a franklin makes uncertain. Or, to put this another way, because the stereotype of vavasour hospitality and materialism was the most accessible sociocultural norm for this socially borderline individual to imitate, a materialism focused on consumption and pleasure – an Epicurean axiology – becomes an ideal, not a vice. It represents a successful performance of the social status that a franklin could reasonably seek to attain, not a morally empty, proto-bourgeois aping of one's social betters.

The axiological person represented by the Franklin, therefore, is one in which desire for the things of the world sits at the center. On the one hand, this desire is much like the Merchant's, in that it is encouraged and even required by his social identity, and so in a franklin's axiological environment becomes a virtue, despite being, in a spiritual environment (or in the Clerk's intellectualized version of this), a rather unequivocal sin. Like merchants, the social identity of franklins, especially those aspiring to gentility, depended upon prosperity. But on the other hand, unlike the Merchant, the Franklin's mode of materialism places sociability, the sharing of the consumption of things, over the maximization of profit: a sociability that – even while demonstrating the Franklin's prosperity and hence, like the Merchant's profit, serving as an instrument of socioeconomic advantage – binds the Franklin to his neighbors.[91]

Chaucer, by giving to the Franklin offices equally inappropriate to him as they were to himself, signals his structurally similar social circumstances and hence his vested interest in exploring the viability of an axiology that in a sense straddles that of Squire and Merchant: like the former, the axiology prefers the route of misrecognized cultural capital over the flouting of capital per se (or the concealment of the lack thereof), but like the latter it unabashedly elevates material desire to its central principle of virtuous living. It offers, as a real-world axiology for an untitled but prosperous middle-aged man, the rule that good living makes a good life. That this materialism may be merely a rationalization of *cupiditas* is, of course, evident in the portrait's thoroughgoing moral ambiguity and the critical polarity that it has engendered. Like the tale of Dorigen, Arveragus, and Aurelius, the axiological person represented by the Franklin at once conveys an ideal both attractive and practical and one that insinuates that it may be merely a species of self-deceiving self-interest. Whether or not

Chaucer wrote the tale with the Franklin in mind – and, as I have argued, the evidence that he did so is no more certain than the evidence that he did not – the nature of this shared ambivalence, as the Squire-Franklin link attests, played a decisive role in the assignment.

Squire-Franklin

As I have mentioned, readings of the Franklin's portrait have irresistibly also drawn upon the Squire-Franklin link, as that link's depiction of the Franklin's interactions with the Squire and Host, and its record of the Franklin's comments about his son, significantly (and in a remarkably small space) develop the Franklin's character along dimensions that are only suggested in the portrait. And, certainly, this deepening of the characterological field greatly intensifies the ambivalence and ambiguity of the axiological person established by the portrait. In keeping with my assumptions, however, I see this intensification not as part of the original establishment of the axiological person but instead as Chaucer's means of creating a composite work out of the independently written portrait and tale. Specifically, with this link Chaucer seizes upon the ambivalence shared by the latter in order to forge a tale-telling performance that may serve as the terminus to the IV-V dialectical drama, a performance that recognizes the axiological apologia of each of the preceding components of the sequence, finds them inadequate, and offers an alternative that incorporates aspects of each. Most particularly, as the link was almost certainly written, as I have argued, at the same time as the Merchant-Squire link (and probably also the Clerk-Merchant link), it revisits and reworks the issues raised there, especially the relationship between verbal cultural performance and class, and, more generally, between mystification and disenchantment.

Notoriously, however, this brief passage presents some severe interpretive conundrums, and the divergent manners in which critics have resolved these have tended to shape their understanding not just of the passage, but also of the character of the Franklin, of the significance of the tale that he tells, of whether the *Squire's Tale* is or is not to be understood as parody, and of the relationship between the Squire's and Franklin's performances.[92] This section will proceed, therefore, by revisiting some of the most prominent of these conundrums as a means of clarifying my reading of the link – my argument about how Chaucer uses the Franklin's peculiarly liminal social position, and its attendant ambivalence toward the relation between discourse and desire for things of this world, as a framework for the tale of Dorigen, Arveragus, and Aurelius.

Among the most severe of these conundrums is the question of the discursive status of the passage as a whole: whether it represents the Franklin's conscious interruption of the *Squire's Tale*, an unintended interruption of a tale that the Franklin thought complete, a response to a complete tale that either Chaucer never got around to finishing or that was lost before the initial manuscripts of the *Tales* were assembled, or something else. The majority of critics adopt the first view and thus read as ironic the first line of the link where the Franklin seems to acknowledge, if somewhat vaguely, a completed performance, with "In faith, Squier, thow has thee wel yquit" (V.673) meaning literally "In faith, Squire, you have fulfilled your tale-telling obligation well."[93] These critics take this statement to be a polite but definitive interruption that diplomatically masquerades (either obsequiously or condescendingly) as a compliment for a tale well told. Supporting this position is, obviously, the fact that the *Squire's Tale* as we have it ends in mid-sentence, as well as the precedent of the other interrupted tales. For many readers these features are enough to make the passage's status as an interruption a self-evident given, and so they simply assume it and move on to the conundrum of what the interruption, in this ironic form, may mean.[94]

A minority critical tradition, however, has pointed out that the evidence for an interruption is not so certain and that other possibilities are at least as likely and perhaps more so. Seaman, for example, argues that the manifest differences between the explicit tale interruptions (of the *Monk's Tale* and *Sir Thopas*) and these "wordes of the Frankelyn to the Squier" (as Ellesmere's rubric describes the passage) make those explicit interruptions evidence against, rather than precedents for, the latter as a tacit interruption.[95] John Burrow, also finding the explicit interruptions unpersuasive as precedents, suggests that the interpretation of the *Squire's Tale* as intentionally (i.e., meaningfully) unfinished (rather than just merely unfinished or accidentally fragmentary), and hence interruptible at all, is anachronistic.[96] And Stephen Partridge argues that the preservation of a blank space following the *Squire's Tale* across manuscript traditions suggests that Chaucer's earliest scribes "understood it differently from the complete tales, on the one hand, and the two clearly interrupted tales, on the other."[97] He then suggests that the blank space itself may go back to Chaucer and reflect the author's uncertainty about whether and how to complete the tale, and thus his signaling of its provisionally incomplete status.

Whether or not one accepts Partridge's interpretation of this pattern of blank space in the manuscripts, his argument does salutarily remind us that especially in respect to the question of the Franklin's interruption, the manuscripts cannot be ignored. Given in particular the manuscript evidence that indicates the likelihood that the Squire-Franklin link represents one of Chaucer's final additions to the *Tales*, a scenario in which he originally wrote the *Squire's Tale* as a meaningfully interrupted tale, but then waited until later to write the interruption itself, seems improbable. Of course, he may have originally produced a provisionally incomplete *Squire's Tale* and then, when later writing the Squire-Franklin link, retroactively took advantage of its fragmentary form to stage an interruption.[98] But if he did so, he apparently did not leave clear indications of this intention. The link itself, as I have mentioned, almost certainly survived originally as a single leaf; and, as Partridge suggests, the blank space at the end of the *Squire's Tale* most likely represented the end of the gathering that held Chaucer's copy. If Chaucer wished, therefore, to make clear that the Squire-Franklin link is an interruption, he would have needed to include some unambiguous indication of that on the single leaf, since otherwise, given the blank space in the exemplar, the scribes would naturally assume the tale to be merely incomplete, whether or not they also believed that Chaucer intended to finish it. But the one thing that we do know is that Chaucer did not leave such an unambiguous indication: the best that we have in this regard is the Franklin's possibly ironic acknowledgement of a completed tale, and, if he did mean this to signal an interruption, the scribes, at least, did not appear to get the message.[99]

I do not find, therefore – if we do not already assume that the *Squire's Tale* stages such a poor tale-telling performance that it manifestly demanded some intervention – that the Squire-Franklin link is self-evidently an interruption. Perhaps, instead, the odd prospectus that the Squire supplies for the remainder of his tale in V.651–70 signals a complete tale told offstage, as it were, or as William Kamowski has happily phrased it, "an authorial ellipsis in place of the rest of the Squire's performance."[100] Such an "ellipsis" itself may have a variety of rather different meanings, one of which is simply that Chaucer did not know how (or at the moment was just not able) to complete the tale, and thus, at least for the time being, was content to leave the ending in the imagination of the reader, signaling this status not only by the prospectus but also by the tale's mid-sentence terminus, followed by a blank space. In this scenario, the later-written Squire-Franklin link represents not an interruption but rather the Franklin's response to a completed performance that we do not hear but which we may fairly imagine as being rather long. This scenario – as it explains both the textual and manuscript evidence and has some precedence in the habit of Chaucer's elsewhere leaving works unfinished – seems to me more likely than the others, although, like all the explanations, it is admittedly a house of cards, if a somewhat more stable one.

Even if one merely grants this scenario probability, however, it serves to put pressure on readings of the Squire's performance as intentionally bad (since those readings, pointing to the precedent of the Host's interruption of *Sir Thopas*, often take the Franklin's putative interruption as a definitive indicator of this badness). More germane to this chapter, this scenario compounds another crucial interpretive conundrum of the Squire-Franklin link: the degree of sincerity or insincerity we are to perceive in the Franklin's words to the Squire. If the Franklin interrupts the Squire but pretends not to, then he is more-or-less disingenuous from the start, and hence we seem licensed to presume that this insincerity continues unabated through the following lines of elaborate, if tellingly qualified, praise of the Squire's "eloquence":

> "In feith, Squier, thow hast thee wel yquit
> And gentilly. I preise wel thy wit,"
> Quod the Frankeleyn, "considerynge thy yowthe,
> So feelyngly thou spekest, sire, I allow the!
> As to my doom, ther is noon that is heere
> Of eloquence that shal be thy peere,
> If that thou lyve; God yeve thee good chaunce,
> And in vertu sende thee continuance,
> For of thy speche I have greet deyntee." (V.673–81)

In light of the Franklin's supposed interruption-masking-as-a-compliment, it is easy to perceive irony in his pointed qualification of "considerynge thy yowthe" and his fulsome but future-tense declaration that no one "*shal* be" the Squire's "peere" in "eloquence" if the Squire lives long enough to fulfill his putative oratorical promise. As the Squire is perhaps the youngest member of the group, one may understand the Franklin to be insinuating that, in fact, the Squire has a long way to go before becoming anyone's "peere" in "eloquence," and that we must hope that God indeed provides him "good chaunce" so that he may improve.

Such apparently unequivocally ironic praise has encouraged rather definite readings of the Franklin's character, yet ones that (exhibiting another of the link's interpretive conundrums) divide antithetically according to the tone in which critics hear this irony voiced. For many, the irony is obsequious, and in this way Chaucer discloses the Franklin to be an aristocratic wannabe flattering his social better in the hope of obtaining inclusion in his ranks.[101] The Franklin becomes, that is, an obvious parvenu, and this characterization then retroactively colors our understanding of his portrait and predetermines our reading of the subsequent tale. Others, however, hear the Franklin's tone as condescending (whether gently patronizing or more severely judgmental), which typically leads them to precisely the opposite judgment of the pilgrim. In this reading, the Franklin's disingenuous praise represents a mature, tactful defusing of the awkward situation of one of the *gentils* embarrassing himself in front his social inferiors, and it also signals the Franklin's intention to offer, with his own tale, a polite, paternal, corrective lesson for a youth of dubious rhetorical abilities and questionable understanding of the nature of nobility.[102]

If, however, we leave open the possibility that the Franklin's words to the Squire do not constitute an interruption but rather a response to a tale completed offstage, then those words are not *prima facie* insincere, and so do not necessarily ironize what follows. Rather than either obsequiousness or condescension, therefore, we may hear instead, in such remarks as "considerynge thy yowthe," the earnestness of appropriate compliment spoken by an old man to a much younger one of (ambiguously) higher social status. Yet even in this reading we still have grounds to be suspicious of the Franklin's motives, given the unique status of this link as the longest apparently positive tale-response spoken by anyone other than the Host; as a response spoken by a man of liminal class status to a tale told by his social superior; and as one that uses what seems to be an expression of intra-class solidarity, in contrast with the more typical inter- or intra-class rivalry, as a means of tale transition (other than, perhaps, the Reeve-Cook link – a notable exception).[103] Perhaps we *are* to hear some uncertain note of obsequiousness or condescension, but *still* understand the remarks as earnest. We may understand them as the Franklin's seizure of the opportunity to chat with one of the *gentils* by being the first pilgrim to voice the socially appropriate compliment, which, although the expected protocol, is not for that reason insincere, even if it may be manipulative. Rather than determining the compliment to reflect the Franklin's capability for deception or simply his poor judgment,[104] we may subscribe to his opinion (or at least understand that Chaucer wishes us to), even while questioning the intent of his voicing it. In other words, when we do not assume that the Franklin interrupts the Squire, the possibility arises that heartfelt speech and socially instrumental discourse become indistinguishable, and that it is the very ambivalent ambiguity in this regard that Chaucer seeks to convey.

Such an uncertain intermingling of sincerity and instrumentality in fact begins in the first words of the Franklin to the Squire, when the former addresses the latter using the second-person singular and then continues to do so throughout the link.[105] In this respect, the Host's address to the Squire in the Merchant-Squire link in the polite second-person plural offers a telling contrast. For the Franklin, apparently, the proximity of his class status to that of the Squire's enables the age difference between the two to be the determining factor in the choice of pronoun, whereas for the Host the difference in class status determines the use of the plural, regardless of the age difference. And lest we think that Chaucer in this regard is merely neutrally representing social convention, he has not only given the words of the Franklin an unusual density of second-person pronouns – a remarkable eleven instances in the nine lines quoted above – but he has also cast the Franklin's use of the singular into relief with the famously annoyed "wordes of the Host to the Frankeleyn" (to quote the second half of Ellesmere's rubric). For, other than in the Host's initial contemptuous interjection – "Straw for youre gentillesse!" (V.695), in which, as we will see, the antecedent of the pronoun is ambiguous – the Host addresses the Franklin in the second-person singular (lines V.696 and V.702). For the Host, apparently, the Franklin's class status is proximate enough to his own that his position as leader of the group determines his choice of pronoun, a choice that elsewhere throughout the links Chaucer has been careful to adjust according to the specific social situation represented.[106]

While it is obvious that the Host in this manner tacitly rejects the Franklin's tacit self-inclusion among the *gentils*, what is less evident to us, but which would likely have been clear enough to Chaucer's readers, is how the Host's treatment of the Franklin actually underscores the ambiguity and fluidity of rank in late fourteenth-century London. For, as Martha Carlin has shown, the Host as innkeeper – and specifically as one modeled upon the historical Harry Bailly – was not at all the mere publican that he has often been taken to be. Rather, Bailly, not unlike other innkeepers, was a wealthy businessman who "twice represented Southwark in Parliament, and was appointed six times to serve as a tax collector or controller there, and twice as coroner." "He must," Carlin concludes, "have been a man of considerable local authority" – rather like the Franklin, as Chaucer represents him.[107] Such urban prosperity and civil service, as several commentators have noticed, also bring the Host vaguely into the same sphere as Chaucer, whom he likewise addresses in second-person singular, with something of the same coarseness that he directs toward the Franklin.[108] However, in the Host's jocular exchange with another urban commoner, the Merchant, he uses the plural, as he does with the Man of Law, in whose company the Franklin rides (and as the Host does with the Clerk, despite his cutting feminization of that pilgrim). Apparently, for the Host the Merchant's sheer wealth and the Man of Law's high office entail enough social stature to require the polite designation that is automatic for the established *gentils* of the Knight and his son, whereas lesser prosperity and office holding do not.

Yet, given the fact that franklins paid in poll tax more or less the same as squires – at the most typical rate of 3s. 4d., some 1s. 4d. more than Bailly and his wife together paid in 1381 – we cannot simply assume that the Host's pronominal social determinations reflect stable, fixed rules current in the late fourteenth century.[109] In fourteenth-century London and its environs, in particular, there was a great deal of fluidity between wealthy merchants and wealthy country freeholders, as the former often purchased manors and sometimes resided outside town, and the latter often invested some of their capital in mercantile activities; and lawyers, moreover, were prone to do both of these.[110] Indeed, since the Host's rough treatment of Chaucer is no doubt intended, for Chaucer's immediate circle of readers, as an inside joke, the Host's tacit claim to equivalent or greater social status than Chaucer (despite, from his initial question of "What man artow" [VII.695], being seemingly ignorant of the latter's status), may well be part of the humor. The Host's perceptions of relative social degree are hence not to be straightforwardly equated with Chaucer's; while they may represent one fourteenth-century norm, they do not preclude alternatives.

What Chaucer stages in this link, therefore, is the very uncertainty about who in this instance is following the correct social protocol, which in turn reflects the uncertain social status of such a liminal figure as the Franklin, made even more liminal by Chaucer's description of him in the *General Prologue*. As discussed in the preceding section, for all individuals who claimed gentle status, but especially for the borderline claimants, the production and maintenance of this status depended above all other factors on a socially convincing performance of gentility, which is to say a performance that receives social recognition as authentic. The Franklin, in complimenting the Squire's eloquence, is performing precisely this act of social recognition for the Squire, and by using the second-person singular, he performs that recognition from an inclusive vantage point, as implying "you're one of us": and in this way he simultaneously performs his own gentility. In this kind of self-reflexive status performance, as

Maddern puts it, "both to recognise [gentility] and to be recognised enhanced one's status."[111]

Nonetheless – as Harry's later reaction makes clear – the Franklin cannot rely on this self-reflexive stratagem as straightforwardly as could a man equal to or higher than the Squire's status. For to be perceived as authentic to the higher born, the Franklin's performance of his gentle status must acknowledge in some fashion the clear class difference between them, even while emphasizing their proximity. He must not threaten the Squire's perception of his class status by insinuating that it is as low as his own, even while suggesting that his own is in the same general category as the Squire's. And thus it is precisely the Franklin's flattery of the Squire *manifestly understood as such*, and the presumption of the inclusive language in which he voices it, that together serve this function. For it is appropriate and even expected both for the lower-born to flatter the higher-born and for an elder man to address a youth of similar rank in the second-person singular. The Franklin's flattery, recognized by the entire group as such, reassures the Squire of his social superiority, even while the Franklin's pronominal use marks out the difference between himself and the gentles on the one hand and the rest of the pilgrims on the other.

As manipulative as this stratagem may seem, it is entirely authentic to the liminality of the Franklin's actual social status. Indeed, if the Squire were to perceive it otherwise – that is, not as flattery but as wholly ingenuous evaluation of his storytelling that thereby presumes the Franklin to hold a social status in which it is appropriate to cast judgment on someone of the Squire's rank – that stratagem would fail. What the Franklin does in the first nine lines of the link is hence simply what is genuinely appropriate to his liminal social station, the very indefiniteness of which requires some manifest calculation among different alternatives of how to construct that social station in any particular social context. That calculation in itself does not betray inauthenticity, but at least in this instance is rather an essential part of an authentic performance of his liminal status. His advertisement of the instrumentality of his discourse – his manifest flattery and the density of his use of the second-person singular – serves to make that discourse appear genuine, even heartfelt.

With characteristic coyness, Chaucer does not supply us with a response from the Squire, leaving it to the reader to determine whether or not this silence holds any significance for the mutual recognition between *gentils* that the Franklin's gambit requires. Instead, the Franklin keeps speaking,[112] extending his compliment in an appropriately self-derogating fashion by comparing his own son negatively with the Squire:

> I have a sone, and by the Trinitee,
> I hadde levere than twenty pound worth lond,
> Though it right now were fallen in myn hond,
> He were a man of swich discrecioun
> As that ye been! Fy on possessioun,
> But if a man be vertuous withal!
> I have my sone snybbed, and yet shal,
> For he to vertu listeth nat entende;
> But for to pleye at dees, and to despende
> And lese al that he hath is his usage.
> And he hath levere talken with a page
> Than to comune with any gentil wight
> Where he myghte lerne gentillesse aright. (V.682–94)

Ostensibly, this digression serves as a further means for the Franklin to perform his gentle status by demonstrating his grasp of what constitutes it: not mere "possessioun" but rather "discrecioun," "vertu," and, most important, "gentillesse." Such an understanding accords with the medieval commonplace (voiced by the "olde wyf" in the *Wife of Bath's Tale* and by Chaucer in the short poem *Gentilesse*) that nobility consists of active demonstration of virtue rather than passive inheritance of blood.

In theory, this commonplace puts *gentilesse* within reach of anyone. As Saul has explained, the ideology of gentility as virtue was especially encouraged by twelfth-century clerical writers, serving their interest by freeing gentility from the requirement of lineage.[113] In this form it was, as Saul and many others have pointed out (especially those who favor the parvenu or proto-bourgeois reading of the Franklin) useful to up-and-coming commoners like Chaucer and his fictive doppelgänger.[114] Nonetheless, in the predictable dynamic of containment, the dominant landed class did not have difficulty reinterpreting this ideology so that in practice it reinforced the status quo. As Saul remarks, the "object" of "[g]entility as a value system . . . was to affirm and sustain the preeminence of the landed elite, and this it did by enveloping them in an aura of glamour and mystique."[115] Hence, while the ostentation epitomized by the Squire's portrait constituted one rather obvious aura-generating instrument, the notion of gentility as virtue – understood as the natural inclination toward virtue of the higher born – became another, more subtle one. The gentility-as-virtue ideology in this way contributed to the mystification of social dominance – dominance that was in fact obtained and perpetuated via "possessioun" (whether inherited or otherwise acquired) but justified on the basis of less tangible and quantifiable qualities of the individuals who dominate.

The Franklin's concern with gentility here thus does not merely represent an adoption of an ideology convenient to a parvenu, but more precisely, and more importantly, it serves as his tacit claim that the status quo that this ideology reinforces also pertains to him. He espouses gentility as virtue, in other words, not principally because it provided an avenue toward elite status for those without elite heritage, but because espousing gentility as virtue is what those who would be recognized as possessing elite heritage actually do in order to constitute and perpetuate their status.[116] Many readers, however, have understood these remarks by the Franklin as attempting but failing (wittingly or not) to serve this purpose. In this view, the Franklin, seeking to espouse aristocratic ideology, instead betrays – especially with his mention of "twenty pound worth of lond" as in effect the price he is willing to pay for "discrecioun" for his son – a materialism that demystifies gentility and calls attention to his proto-bourgeois attachment to "possessioun."[117] Critics have noted in this regard that the Franklin seems just as anxious about his son's eagerness to "despende / And lese al that he hath" as he is about his son's failure to "lerne gentillesse," or indeed that, for the Franklin, his son's pecuniary extravagance appears to constitute the latter failure.[118]

Yet, if we understand the preceding passage as the Franklin's ingenuous performance of gentility, a performance that to be sincere must also, given his liminal status, betray to some degree the social instrumentality of his discourse, then we see that this digression serves as an elaboration of that performance. In seeming to mention offhand "twenty pound worth lond," the Franklin indirectly asserts the basis for his inclusion among the *gentils*, insinuating the extensive land ownership that everyone knew underwrote social dominance (at least traditionally) and thereby calling the Squire's attention to their similarity in this regard. But in the same gesture he signals his recognition of the value of cultural and social capital, his understanding that non-tangibles like "discrecioun" are crucial to the mystique of class difference; and then, by berating his son for wastage, he conveys that the latter is no mere farmer's son but rather has the leisure time and resources "to pleye at dees, and to despende," apparently within an aristocratic household where he is able to "talken with a page."[119] Oddly – or cleverly – that is, the Franklin, in castigating his son for not being like the Squire, characterizes him as already squire-like in his habits.[120] The problem with the son, in this sense, is not that he is failing to behave like a squire, but that he is not consciously (i.e., calculatedly) learning how to be noble –

learning, for example, how the discourse of "vertu" is a means of class advancement. The point of all this, for the Franklin, is that he, as a franklin, has something to prove: again, as a liminal figure, he cannot perform gentility in the same manner as, say, a knight would, for then he would appear as an obvious poser. Instead – very much like his performance of Epicurean materialism in the *General Prologue* portrait – if his performance is to be recognized as authentic, he must sincerely represent his liminal social condition, and do so in a way that establishes his gentle qualifications, which in turn inevitably betrays the necessity for his doing so and hence the instrumentality of his discourse.

As in the *General Prologue* portrait of the Franklin, Chaucer signals in this passage his personal interest in these complexities of social liminality (and hence their bearing on the personal axiological agon staged by IV-V) through winking tidbits of autobiographical allusion, albeit rather more cryptic ones in this instance. The first of these is the strikingly specific amount of "twenty pound." Some scholars have associated this amount with that which made a landowner liable for distraint for knighthood and hence understand this figure of speech to function as another of the Franklin's indirect claims to possess the basis for gentle status. By Chaucer's day, however, the traditional twenty-pound income threshold for distraint had been raised to forty pounds.[121] Instead (or in addition), then, if we assume that the Squire-Franklin link was written very late (after February 1394), then we may recognize the amount as exactly that of Chaucer's exchequer annuity – a specific sum that no doubt was especially salient to him.[122] A second signal of personal investment is the strangely derogatory remark about conversing with "a page." Since the position of page, albeit very low in the noble household hierarchy, was nonetheless within that hierarchy, it was not an unusual initial post for an aristocratic youth; there would thus seem to be nothing untoward about a franklin's son conversing with a page, perhaps even as a means to "lerne gentillesse aright." But when we recall that Chaucer himself began his career as courtier as a page – one who later became a squire who, among other things, wrote poems about the nature of *gentilesse* – we may recognize this remark as an obscure instance of Chaucer's characteristic simultaneously self-congratulating and self-derogating humor, as in the more obvious and extensive instance in the *Man of Law's Introduction*.[123] Calling attention to the liminal status that Chaucer shares with the Franklin, these signals jocularly raise the questions of whether "discrecioun" is worth the entire amount of Chaucer's annuity, and whether one might learn about "gentillesse" from the poetry of someone marginally gentle like Chaucer. In this way, in their very humor, they make more urgent the exploration of the relations among economic, ethical, social, and literary value that the Franklin's performance, and IV-V as a whole, have pursued.

To return to where we left off in the link, how we are to understand – or, how we are to judge – the Host's sudden impatience with this sincerely self-promoting monologue presents, as I have already suggested, yet another conundrum:

> "Straw for youre gentillesse!" quod oure Hoost.
> "What, Frankeleyn! Pardee, sire, wel thou woost
> That ech of yow moot tellen atte leste
> A tale or two, or breken his biheste."
> "That knowe I wel, sire," quod the Frankeleyn.
> "I prey yow, haveth me nat in desdeyn,
> Though to this man I speke a word or two."
> "Telle on thy tale withouten wordes mo." (V.695–702)

On the one hand, the Host's second-person singular pronouns appear to deny the Franklin the recognition as gentle that he seeks. On the other hand, the Franklin was not so much seeking this recognition from the Host as from the Squire, a point that the Franklin seems to make by politely stating his wish to speak a "word or two" more with the latter, thereby implying the appropriateness of his having an intimate conversation with a knight's son. This stratagem underscores the fact that the Host, however he may perceive the situation, does not have the power to declare whether or not the Franklin merits such an intimate conversation with a young aristocrat, since recognition from the Squire of the Franklin's gentle status would override any such judgment from an innkeeper. And in this regard, it is significant that despite his apparently irate tone, the Host does not straightforwardly declare that someone of the Franklin's status has no basis to speak of *gentilesse*, as when the Host impugns the Reeve's social presumption by mocking the latter for his clergy-like lecture ("What shul we speke alday of hooly writ? / The devel made a reve for to preche" [I.3902–3]). Neither does the Host, as he does with the Miller, explicitly contest the appropriateness of the Franklin's self-insertion into the tale-telling order. Rather, notwithstanding his "Straw" remark, he seems to understand the Franklin's interjection like he understands the Merchant's, as an indication that the pilgrim has a tale to tell, and he simply uses his authority as manager of the contest to insist, brusquely, that the Franklin move on to that tale.[124]

Indeed, while the initial "Straw" remark does convey how little value the Host sees in the Franklin's concern with *gentilesse*, the ambiguity of "youre" leaves us unsure of how to judge the Host's judgment. If "youre" refers specifically to the Franklin, then the Host would seem to be confirming the Franklin's claims to *gentilesse*, by using the polite second-person plural, in the very act of rejecting it. And even if we suppose that he is using this form of the pronoun sarcastically, he thereby invokes the possibility that it is appropriate, especially if, again, we are not to trust the pronominal social determinations of an innkeeper. If "youre" is instead the actual plural, it must refer to the *gentilesse* shared by the Franklin with the Squire and, by implication, other *gentils*, which would seem to concede that the Franklin does have a claim on gentle status, even if the Host resents this.[125] And if "youre" serves rather as an impersonal, generalizing designation,[126] it indicates that the Host finds the very topic of *gentilesse* tedious, which instead of reflecting poorly on the Franklin may contribute to the *Tales*' pervasive characterization of the Host as boorish.

Rather than decisively pronouncing judgment on the Franklin's gentle status, then, the Host's interjection calls further attention to that status's continued indeterminacy in the absence of a response from the Squire. In this light, the wording of the link's final lines is especially revealing:

> "Gladly, sire Hoost," quod he, "I wole obeye
> Unto your wyl; now herkneth what I seye.
> I wol yow nat contrarien in no wyse
> As fer as that my wittes wol suffyse.
> I prey to God that it may plesen yow;
> Thanne woot I wel that it is good ynow." (V.703–8)

In this oft-noticed, excessively polite rejoinder to the Host's terse refusal of the Franklin's request to continue speaking with the Squire, the Franklin addresses the Host with the second-person plural. Given, however, the Franklin's tacit resistance (in his seeking to continue his pursuit of conversation with the Squire) to the Host's tacit judgment of his class status, and given the Franklin's use of second-person singular with the Squire, we may understand his politeness here not as an acknowledgment of a class status akin to the Host's but rather as an attempt to signify a *superior* class status in the same manner as the Squire does in the Merchant-Squire link (which, to recall, was likely written in tandem with this passage).[127] Indeed, these lines' echoes of the earlier passage are striking, as both use the same lexis to emphasize the speaker's agency in his submission to the Host's authority – his willingness to conform his will to the Host's. While the Squire declares, in response to the Host's request, "I wol seye as I kan / With hertly wyl, for I wol nat rebelle / Aganyn youre lust" (V.4–6), the Franklin states, in virtual paraphrase, "I wole obeye / Unto your wyl . . . / I wol yow nat contrarien in no wyse . . . " In the former case, the Squire's use of the second-person plural is clearly a form of *noblesse oblige*, his willing granting to the Host of an artificially inflated status as part of the tale-telling game; and, lest we mistake this, his explicit declaration that he "wol nat rebelle" conveys the point that he would have the right to do so. The Franklin apes this tactic in his declaration that he will "nat contrarien" the Host's authority and in this way reinterprets the Host's terse command as the kind of polite request that the latter makes of the Squire – an exceptionally clever tactic in that it leaves the Host with nothing to say.[128] The Host has sought to use his authority as leader of the group to put the Franklin's claim to gentle status in question, but the Franklin finesses the Host's social determinations with refined politeness, agreeing to the dramatic fiction of the Host's authority in a manner that, as itself an example of *gentilesse*, serves also as a counter-reassertion of his gentle status.

With the Franklin having the final word, Chaucer in effect leaves it to us to judge the result of his concluding submission to the Host – whether it comes across as a pose, as groveling, or as a demonstration of the very gentility that he claims the Squire exemplifies and that he wishes for his son. Here and in the rest of the link, Chaucer has laid bare the mechanisms of the discursive construction of class status and has raised the question of whether, so disclosed, this discourse, this means of class domination, cannot also be a sincere and even authentic instance of the secular virtues of civility and generosity – of *gentilesse*. In this way this link, as the framework in which we are to understand the ensuing tale, revisits and revises the Merchant-Squire transition. As we saw in the last chapter, the latter link places the *Squire's Tale* within the framework of the question of whether secular fiction, delivered with earnest good will, may have a distinctive, restorative value despite its also being a vehicle for the Squire's necessarily blinkered (because in that way sincere) assertion of class superiority. The framework established by the Squire-Franklin link is similar, except – by its self-conscious display of the discursive mechanisms of the constitution of class status – it offers an unblinkered acknowledgement of the instrumentality of discourse, and therefore asks the further question of whether good will may coexist with knowing manipulation and a desire to dominate. It asks, that is, the very question that the ensuing *Franklin's Tale* explores in a manner that, as we have seen, also puts at stake the value of literature and of the occupation of the literary maker.

The Axiological Apologia of the Conclusion of IV-V

That the Squire-Franklin link formulates this particular question is of course no accident, since, as I have proposed, the passage represents Chaucer's rereading of his own tale of Dorigen, Aurelius, and Arveragus in light of the *Squire's, Merchant's,* and *Clerk's Tales*, and his ultimate decision to place what came to be the *Franklin's Tale* last in this sequence. So constructed and positioned, the Franklin's performance responds most immediately to the ultimate collapse of the Squires's. One the one hand, as I argued in the previous chapter, we may not merely assume that with the *Squire's Tale* Chaucer intends to stage a poor tale-telling performance. But on the other hand, as I also claimed, by incorporating that tale into IV-V by means of the Merchant-Squire link, Chaucer does mean to represent the axiological apologia of the Squire's performance – at this point in his own life – as an insufficient defense of the value of literature and of the maker of fictions. As I concluded, this axiological apologia founders not so much because the imaginative, renovating power that it claims for romance fiction coincides with the instrumental function of aristocratic display, but because, to be efficacious, this axiological apologia requires self-mystification in respect to the latter: to put this point over-simply, it requires that to believe in the rejuvenating power of fiction, one must also be an elitist. And however much Chaucer may have desired to be a simple elitist, his own circumstances late in life, following his long career in the customs house and his departure from London, prevented him from being so in a manner that did not involve some amount of self-deception, bad faith, or – perhaps most problematic – potential exposure as social imposter.[129] In this light, we may understand the axiological person of the Franklin – whose liminality, as we have seen, embodies precisely the borderline-elite aspect of Chaucer's biographical circumstances – as a vehicle for revisiting the possibilities of the Squire's performance from a perspective that takes into account elitism without also laying claim to it, with the mystification that would entail.

As developed in the Squire-Franklin link, this perspective expresses an axiology that Chaucer has tuned to echo that of the tale of Dorigen, Arveragus, and Aurelius. In that tale's conclusion, the implicit equation of Aurelius's supposed newfound *gentilesse* with the £1,000 it could have cost him solders together the categories of the ethical and economic without thereby necessarily reducing the former to the latter. Analogously, in the link the Franklin's insinuation of £20 as the value of aristocratic "discrecioun" underscores the instrumental function of the latter and the ultimately economic basis of class domination, without thereby necessarily discrediting "discrecioun."[130] For the tale, the potential transformation of a fabliau ethos of competition, appetite, and greed into the romance magic of cascading generosity depends upon a willingness to believe in the latter magic, which in turn rests upon a sober grasp, rather than ignorance or repression, of the former ethos.[131] Likewise, at the end of the link, the Franklin acquiesces submissively to the Host's authority (or pretends to do so; as with promises, there is no pragmatic difference), even while using that acquiescence to insinuate his own superior class status, and the result is a seemingly peaceful, civil termination to a somewhat fraught interchange, one that honors the initial social contract and thus enables the tale-telling contest to continue. If the tale ultimately argues that a sincere commitment to the distinctive value of secular fiction can only be achieved by acknowledging the intractable fusion of the economic and ethical, the real and ideal, and the instrumental and authentic, the portrait and link together reaffirm this argument but also render it as the peculiar and necessary axiology of the liminal Franklin, whose social position entails a simultaneous belief in the ideology of *gentilesse* and the recognition that it serves as means of class domination.

The specific sort of liminality that Chaucer shares with the Franklin serves, therefore, to crystalize the axiological apologia of the Franklin's performance: the argument that the value of *his* (i.e., Chaucer's, by way of the Franklin's) literary fiction, if not necessarily the value of fiction per se, is that it may possess, with the reader's cooperation, the restorative, civilizing function to which the genre of romance lays claim, but without being self-deceived about the materialist, self-interested instrumentality to which all discourse tends; that this fiction may strive for the ideal without mystifying the real; that it may be manipulative without being deceptive; and that it may interrogate the social fictions that organize society even while it serves itself as such an instrument of social organization. This sort of fiction, the Franklin's performance contends, is that which its middle-aged, literarily self-conscious, socially liminal author is unusually (if not uniquely) well-positioned to produce. The hope that it both thematizes and stands as evidence for is that it makes the activities of this particular literary maker honest and valuable – that is, not detrimental to the soul and useful for the common good – and therefore justifies the time and energy that its author and his readers put into producing and consuming it.

IV-V Unfolded

To consider this axiological apologia in comparison with that of the Squire's performance, and from there back through the rest of the IV-V sequence, we may return to the Squire-Franklin link and take into account a feature that legions of its readers have commented upon and that becomes unmistakable when the Franklin's careful remarks about the Squire's "yowthe" evolve into a concern about the habits of his own "sone": the implied parallel between the Franklin's son and the Squire, and hence the fatherly role that the Franklin seeks to play toward the latter, despite (or because of) the presumed presence of the Squire's actual father.[132] Although within the fiction of the *Canterbury Tales* frame the Squire is poised to grow into knighthood, in Chaucer's day (as Chaucer the squire certainly knew) squires more typically grew into a social position rather more like the Franklin's: into wealthy rural landowners who served in local and national offices, whose military experience would have been limited and nothing like that of Chaucer's Knight.[133] More specifically, if, as I argued in the previous chapter, the axiological person of the Squire corresponds to the artist as the young man whom he resembled but could not (given his actual social circumstances) become, the axiological person of the Franklin corresponds to the artist as he now is, recalibrated so as to make the pilgrim's socioeconomic circumstances more congruent with that of the Squire's.

With the Franklin's performance, therefore, we have the final movement of the IV-V sequence's quasi-biographical son/father dynamic, in which Chaucer draws upon various elements of his own personal social history in order to stage and interrogate different phases of his evolving literary axiologies. For the Clerk – who represents Chaucer's bookish persona and hence, axiologically, the time, energy, and expense that Chaucer as a kind of lay clerk devoted to intellectual pursuits – Chaucer develops a version of the meta-axiology of such earlier efforts as the *House of Fame*. Embodied by the book-loving Clerk and illustrated by the ultimately playful mulitvalency of that pilgrim's rendering of Petrarch's tale of Griselda, this version of Chaucerian meta-axiology, as we saw in Chapter 1, is distinguished by its specific institutional location, the university. This location provides an axiological environment that enables Chaucer to imagine this meta-axiology as a defining characteristic of an actual masculine occupation rather than as just a notional mode of authorship that is legible within such axiological environments as the customs house but functional only in a vague, analogous fashion.

The Merchant's performance emerges, then, as a stern paternal critique of the naïve escapism of this occupation as the Clerk's performance imagines it, a critique that argues that actual eternal students like the Clerk, if there were any, would ceaselessly be on the verge of poverty and (from the perspective of the normative function of the late fourteenth-century English university) of little use to society. In this view, the Clerk's meta-axiology is merely an attempt to avoid confronting the true nature of value in the sublunary realm, which is finally nothing else but the material desires of flesh-and-blood individuals. In arguing, as we saw in Chapter 2, that all discourse is a self-interested instrument of these desires, the Merchant's axiological apologia, delivered with the force of Chaucer's own paternal heritage and his long experience on the Wool Wharf, condemns the Clerk's axiological apologia as the overly clever wishful thinking of an adolescent (a figurative adolescent, if not necessarily a literal one) who refuses to take on normative masculine adult responsibility.

In reducing all discourse, literary or otherwise, to an instrument of desire, however, the Merchant leaves no function for secular fiction other than to make this single self-deconstructing point – a point that if efficacious only needs (and in fact only ought) to be made once. The Squire's performance then responds to this ground-clearing in the general fashion of youthful idealism countering wizened cynicism. Denying the Merchant's negative literary axiology, the Squire's performance reinstates literary value as the power of the distinctive discourse of romance fiction: the power to provide a restorative vision of a world governed by exactly the kind of ideals that the Merchant's world of the fabliau real understands as mere smokescreens for material desire. Moreover, by associating this literary axiology with the normative sociocultural practice of a young aristocrat, the Squire's performance understands literary discourse as also possessing the concrete value of the cultural capital that helps distinguish the elite from the common. In this way, the Squire's axiological apologia at once presents a positive literary value; solves the problem of the naïvely insular, or even nonce, social value of the Clerk's eternal studenthood; and trumps the Merchant's claim on the real by countering the fabliau world with the equally real but socially more dominant world of aristocratic display. Replicating Chaucer's own move away from his mercantile paternal background, the Squire in IV-V figuratively becomes the son who outdoes his father, who may justify his writing of secular fiction as precisely part of the practices that have propelled him up the socioeconomic ladder.

Yet because the combination of idealizing renewal and instrumental cultural capital in this axiological apologia seems to require that the former serve to mystify the latter, this axiological apologia ultimately appears to confirm the Merchant's understanding of the underlying materially instrumental nature of discourse, thereby turning the Squire's belief in a distinctive value for fiction into a species self-delusion. The Franklin's performance then responds to this collapse by replaying the Squire's performance in a manner that incorporates and transcends all prior positions in the dialectic. The Franklin's performance claims, like the Squire's, that romance fiction possesses a distinctive rejuvenating value. But the Franklin adds that it only authentically attains this value by staging a paradoxical, reflexive act of doubting belief in its own discourse: by dramatizing, and encouraging in the reader, a self-conscious act of belief in the possibility that the materially instrumental discourse of the Merchant's axiology, while inescapable as such, may simultaneously be the bearer of ethical and civilizing ideals that restore and perpetuate social harmony. And by proposing that the value of fiction arises precisely by *staging* the process by which it comes to have value, the Franklin's axiological apologia is ultimately just as meta-axiological as the Clerk's.

Indeed, within the Franklin's performance this meta-axiology is itself staged, like a series of nested boxes, when the Host in the Squire-Franklin link demands that the Franklin keep "his biheste." Because the Franklin proceeds to do so, the performance turns the entire ensuing romance fiction – a fiction about the belief required for the fictional entailment of a fictional promise to have real effect on the world – into an example of what it preaches. Yet, as this instance of self-reflexivity suggests, in contrast with the social insularity of the Clerk's meta-axiology, the Franklin's is imagined as the very basis of social integration: it is that which makes the Franklin polite in the face of class resentment, it is that which helps hold the group together under the fiction of the Host's authority, it is the principle of belief that makes him *fre* – or at least behave as if he is so. And, of course, because this self-reflexivity serves also – in the politeness of his response to the Host's demand, and in the message of the tale that fulfills his promise – as a demonstration of the Franklin's *gentilesse*, it is simultaneously an assertion of social superiority, and hence an instrument for realizing his material desire.

In effect, the Franklin, as a father-figure speaking to a son-figure, provides the same dose of 'reality' as the Merchant does to the Clerk. But he does so not by rejecting the son's axiological apologia as hopelessly naïve and immature, but rather by preserving the idealism of youth in *a* manner that also recognizes the demands of sublunary life emphasized by the Merchant. In this way the Franklin models for the Squire, and responds to the Merchant with, the "new masculine modality" that Isabel Davis has identified as emerging among middle-strata men of late medieval England: "a kind of *urbanitas*, a pragmatic, non-heroic identity that is an unsteady accommodation between the 'common good' and the interior, appetitive self."[134] Inasmuch as Chaucer, the merchant's son, became a youthful squire with bookish tendencies who eventually grew up to become something like the Franklin, the terminal position of the Franklin's performance in IV-V expresses Chaucer's provisional acceptance of this mode of masculinity and its axiology. And this acceptance necessarily issues a corrective to Chaucer's earlier literary axiologies, supplanting them with a still optimistic but warier grasp of the value of secular literature in a fallen world. With the Franklin's performance, Chaucer constructed for the *Canterbury Tales*, his final work of fiction, the strongest case that he in good faith was able to muster for the value of secular literature, a case equal to that of the axiologically quite similar, if generically quite different, *Nun's Priest's Tale*. Alas, however, if we are to believe the *Retraction* – and this is no small if – it was not to be strong enough.

Notes

Introduction: *Canterbury Tales* IV-V and Literary Value

1. Meyer-Lee, "Fragments IV and V." For confirmation of this argument and further elaboration, see Horobin, "Compiling."
2. In the case of the Merchant-Franklin transition, the Hg scribe appears to have made provision for a link by leaving the bottom half of folio 152v blank and then beginning the *Franklin's Tale* on what is now folio 154r with the tale's thirteenth line. In this fashion, he probably thought himself shrewdly prepared for any eventuality: if the link never materialized, he could copy the first twelve lines of the *Franklin's Tale* on folio 152v; if it did appear, he could either squeeze everything onto the latter folio or add a new leaf. Undoubtedly much to his dismay, the link that he ultimately received not only connected the *Merchant's Tale* to the earlier copied *Squire's Tale*, but it was also too long to squeeze onto folio 152v and too short to fill completely the new leaf, leaving expanses of blank space that betray his patchwork effort. See Doyle and Parkes, "A Paleographical Introduction," pp. xxx–xxxi.
3. For the purposes of this book, I need not enter into the debate about the identity of Hengwrt's main scribe, a.k.a. Scribe B. But I do follow the majority view that this scribe also copied Ellesmere. See Mooney and Stubbs, *Scribes and the City*, for the Adam Pinkhurst identification; and Warner, *Chaucer's Scribes*, for a refutation.
4. Horobin, "Compiling," esp. p. 338. Stephen Partridge, in personal communication, has expressed skepticism about this explanation, observing that scenarios that involve unbound leaves are a traditional crutch used to explain otherwise inexplicable manuscript features. As I address briefly in a further note below, other scenarios are certainly possible, and, in lieu of new evidence, all are intractably speculative.
5. Meyer-Lee, "Fragments IV and V," p. 11.
6. For the fullest articulation of Blake's argument for the links' inauthenticity, see *The Textual Tradition*, a position that he later appeared willing to put aside –

see, e.g., "The Links." For Manly and Rickert's tale order groups, see *MR* 2.475–94 and the following three tables compiled by Robert Campbell.

7. I am aware that I am assuming that the condition of the Hengwrt exemplars has special bearing on our knowledge of the state of Chaucer's own copies and hence of the likely sequence of his composition, and that there is no firm support for this assumption other than the fact that Hengwrt appears to be the earliest copy of the *Canterbury Tales* and that some of those involved in the production team likely had some direct relationship with Chaucer. Without this assumption, however, we have far less basis for any contentions about the state of Chaucer's own copies, and so my scenario remains just as likely as others, if not more so. Such other scenarios, with quite different interpretive implications, include, for example, that Chaucer may have written the links at the same time as the IV-V tales, but composed them on single leaves because he initially wanted to circulate those tales independently; or that the Hengwrt production team may have taken the links from a full copy of the *Tales*, different from the Hengwrt exemplars, that only became available after they had copied most of the manuscript. Not surprisingly, I find my scenario to be the most plausible explanation of the manuscript and textual evidence. Nonetheless, as I discuss in what follows, I am not so much asking readers to agree with this judgment of "most" as I am arguing that they must recognize the necessity of positing the plausible. For a recent consideration of the bearing of the composite structure of Hengwrt on Chaucer's own copies – and an exhortation to consider such codicological or "stratigraphical" evidence in efforts to characterize Chaucer's intentions – see Da Rold, "New Challenges."
8. Howard, *The Idea*, p. 6.
9. Some important recent studies, however, do voice their enabling assumptions, and those assumptions' limits, in this regard. See, for example, Ginsberg, *Tellers, Tales, and Translation*; Bahr, *Fragments and Assemblages*; and Scala, *Desire in the* Canterbury Tales, "The Deconstructure," and *Absent Narratives.*
10. Paratextually, of course, the pilgrims are also identified via the system of rubrics in Hengwrt (e.g., "Here bigynneth the Squiers tale," f. 129r, in the main scribal hand), as well as by the running heads (although those are predominantly in a different hand and added after the copying of the text). In some fashion, therefore – perhaps by the rubrics themselves – Chaucer transmitted the IV-V pilgrim assignments in the Hengwrt exemplars despite the missing links, and so he certainly had determined those assignments by the time that those exemplars were copied. My doubt pertains rather to the moment of his original composition of the portraits and tales, as nothing in those tales unambiguously indicates a specific assignment, and the links that do perform the identifications, as I have said, appear to be separate and later compositions.

11. Cf. Christopher Cannon's contentions about the "patchwork" nature of the *Tales*: *From Literacy to Literature,* esp. pp. 183–96.
12. More precisely, if admittedly absurdly, the assemblage of IV-V is like a parfait in which some of the layers consist of leftovers from another dessert.
13. Jordan, *Chaucer and the Shape of Creation*, p. 118.
14. For example, Jordan, *Chaucer and the Shape of Creation*, esp. pp. 111–13; Benson, *Chaucer's Drama of Style*, esp. pp. 3–25; Pearsall, *The Canterbury Tales*, esp. pp. 39–45; Lawton, *Chaucer's Narrators*, esp. pp. 90–105, and, more recently, *Voice,* pp. 151–80; Leicester, Jr., *The Disenchanted Self*, esp. pp. 1–13.
15. See Spearing, *Textual Subjectivity* and *Medieval Autographies*; and, for the poster child of dramatic criticism, Lumiansky, *Of Sondry Folk.*
16. Lawton, *Chaucer's Narrators,* p. 97.
17. Especially helpful on this point is Zieman, "Escaping the Whirling Wicker."
18. See, e.g., Bourdieu, *The Field of Cultural Production* and *Distinction.*
19. For brief remarks on this topic, see Catherine Sanok's and my introduction to *The Medieval Literary,* pp. 1–12. To be clear, however, in mentioning these (very loosely defined and overlapping) critical movements in this context, I am by no means impugning them. On the contrary, in a general sense I would affiliate my efforts in this book with them – although, like many of these movements' practitioners in the field of Middle English literature, and as I hope will be readily evident, I do so while standing on the shoulders of the historicist approach exemplified, in different ways, by Middleton, David Wallace, Lee Patterson, Paul Strohm, and others.
20. See Meyer-Lee, "Toward a Theory"; Latour, *Reassembling the Social, Pandora's Hope*, and "An Attempt," among the many of Latour's relevant studies; and Simmel, *The Philosophy of Money.*
21. This example came to me after meeting exactly such a poet, although I do not intend definite reference to anyone.
22. *The Strumpet Muse*, p. 58.
23. Mann, *Chaucer and Medieval Estates Satire*, p. 202.
24. Fowler, *Literary Character*, p. 16; see more generally pp. 1–31, which includes analyses of *General Prologue* portraits.
25. Mann, *Chaucer and Medieval Estates Satire*, p. 85, emphasis hers.
26. I refer, of course, to "Chaucer the Pilgrim" in Donaldson, *Speaking of Chaucer*, pp. 1–12.
27. See Farrell, "Hybrid Discourse"; and Bakhtin, *The Dialogic Imagination*, esp. p. 316. See also Farrell's "The Chronotopes of Monology in Chaucer's *Clerk's Tale*" and Lawton, *Chaucer's Narrators*, esp. pp. 1–16.
28. Cf. Lawton, *Chaucer's Narrators*, esp. p. 104. Lawton's later analytical category of *voice* (in *Voice*) usefully combines elements such as style and tone.

29. For a cogent complaint about static conceptions of context and a recommendation for an alternative approach informed by Latour, see Felski, "'Context Stinks!'"
30. Of course, whatever insight these rules and principles yield must necessarily come at the expense of obscuring aspects of IV-V that other approaches more successfully highlight, especially gender studies and psychoanalytical approaches, such as those exemplified by Crocker, *Chaucer's Visions of Manhood*; and Scala, *Desire in the* Canterbury Tales. Value and desire are, obviously, closely coupled phenomena, and hence by focusing so much on the former I have inevitably diminished the complexities of the latter.
31. For a helpful overview of normative models of masculine adolescence and adulthood, see Karras, *From Boys to Men*.
32. *Magisters* such as A. J. Minnis and Peter Travis, for example, have written celebrated monographs that branch out from focuses on, respectively, the Wife of Bath and the Pardoner (*Fallible Authors*) and the *Nun's Priest's Tale* (*Disseminal Chaucer*).
33. Meyer-Lee, "Manuscript Studies."
34. In some equally crude but trenchant ways, this position selectively incorporates some of Michel Foucault's understanding of the relations among discourse, power, and desire – as in, for example, *Discipline and Punish* – notwithstanding Foucault's and Bourdieu's myriad differences.
35. Prendergast, "Canon Formation," conceives of this sort of literary value as the basis for canonicity.

1. Clerk

1. Brief connections are made by Rossiter, "Chaucer Joins"; and Bodden, *Language as the Site*.
2. Minnis, *The Shorter Poems*, pp. 161–251, offers helpful commentary on the critical tradition on the *House of Fame*. A paradigmatic discussion of the *trecento* influence is Wallace, "Chaucer's Italian Inheritance."
3. For a similar, but differently emphasized, exploration of the multidimensional fashion in which Chaucer's controllership inflects the *House of Fame*, see Hsy, *Trading Tongues*, pp. 27–41, whose admirable study appeared, regrettably, after the completion of the present section.
4. Green, *Poets and Princepleasers*, esp. pp. 101–34.
5. See, in general, *CLR*, pp. 148–270, and, for the calculation of the number of documents for which Chaucer was responsible, p. 179.
6. Patterson, *Chaucer and the Subject of History*, p. 37; see also *CLR*, p. 152.
7. Coleman, "The Collectors of Customs," p. 192; Carlson, *Chaucer's Jobs*, p. 6; Strohm, *Chaucer's Tale*, p. 91. My consideration of the controllership, which

I developed before having the benefit of Strohm's biography, is largely congruent with the latter.

8. Baker, "The English Customs Service," although the quotation is from Coleman, "The Collectors of Customs," p. 185.
9. Baker, "The English Customs Service," p. 10.
10. Baker, "The English Customs Service," p. 10.
11. For Hermesthorpe, see *CLR*, p. 170; and Coleman, "The Collectors of Customs," p. 192.
12. Strohm, *Chaucer's Tale*, pp. 90–136.
13. See Baswell, *Virgil in Medieval England*, p. 233, and, more generally, pp. 223–48.
14. See, e.g., Simpson, *Reform and Cultural Revolution*, p. 167.
15. On this point, see Baswell, *Virgil in Medieval England*, p. 237.
16. See *Aeneid*, IV.189–94.
17. For these intertextual nods, see, *inter alia*, Kiser, *Truth and Textuality*, pp. 25–41.
18. David, "Literary Satire," p. 339.
19. For the functional architecture of the customs house in Chaucer's day, see Mills, "The Collectors of Customs," pp. 180–81, and, for more detail, her earlier study, "The London Customs House."
20. This positional detail, however, comes from the *Metamorphoses*, unlike the architecture of the tidings/fame complex, which is original to Chaucer.
21. For the "name in honde" contradiction, see, e.g., Boitani, *Chaucer and the Imaginary World of Fame*, p. 170.
22. Carlson, *Chaucer's Jobs*, p. 11.
23. For an incisive account of the critical tradition through the 1980s, see Morse, "Critical Approaches."
24. Green, "Griselda in Siena," and "Why Marquis Walter"; Clarke, *Chaucer and Italian Textuality*; Rossiter, *Chaucer and Petrarch*; Morse, "Critical Approaches." For a recent dissenting view regarding the tale's difficulties, see Ashe, "Reading like a Clerk."
25. For the sources of the *Physician's Tale* and the *Clerk's Tale*, see, respectively, Bleeth, "The Physician's Tale," and Farrell and Goodwin, "The Clerk's Tale," in *Sources and Analogues*, Vols. 2 and 1. See also for the *Clerk's Tale* the still very useful Severs, *The Literary Relationships*. All quotations of Chaucer's principal sources for the *Clerk's Tale* and translations thereof will be from Farrell and Goodwin and cited by line number in the text. For the distinctiveness of Chaucer's naming of Petrarch here, see Farrell, "The 'Envoy,'" p. 332.
26. Wallace, *Chaucerian Polity*, esp. pp. 261–98; and Middleton, "The Clerk and his Tale," rpt. in *Chaucer, Langland*.
27. Middleton, "The Clerk and his Tale," pp. 106–7.

28. See *Riverside*'s note to IV.41 (p. 880) and Farrell's comments about the variants in Petrarch's moralization in *Sources and Analogues*, 1.129 n. 26.
29. Middleton, "Chaucer's 'New Men,'" p. 45.
30. Wallace, *Chaucerian Polity*, p. 287; Schwebel, "Redressing Griselda," p. 294.
31. See the note to lines IV.43–51 in *Riverside*, p. 880; and *Sources and Analogues*, p. 2.140.
32. Both Galloway, "Petrarch's Pleasures," and Ginsberg, *Chaucer's Italian Tradition*, albeit in different manners, call attention to the importance of the prohemium in the *Historia*, as well as in the *Clerk's Tale*, if in the latter to a distinctive effect.
33. Severs, *The Literary Relationships*, p. 229; Salter, *Chaucer*.
34. Latin from *Biblia Sacra iuxta Vulgatam versionem*, ed. Gryson et al. Douay-Rheims translation from*The Clementine Vulgate Project.*
35. Citations of the Wycliffite bible are from *The Holy Bible*, ed. Forshall and Madden; here from the later version. Jerome modeled *intemptator* on the negated Greek ἀπείραστός, or *a-peirastos*, with both the Latin and Greek word uniquely present in scripture here. Reference works such as Harden, *Dictionary of the Vulgate*, and Stelten, *Dictionary of Ecclesiastical Latin*, gloss Jerome's *intemptator* as "one who does not tempt," although today the Greek is glossed as an adjective, "incapable of being tempted"; see, e.g., *Interlinear Greek-English New Testament*, ed. Berry. Accordingly, modern translations render the clause passively, as in the NIV translation's "for God cannot be tempted by evil" or the "Deus enim non tentatur malis" of the *Nova Vulgata.*
36. Citations from *Glossa Ordinaria* (Migne edition) are from *The Clementine Vulgate Project*; translations mine.
37. For an attempt to use this neat division between external and internal temptation to solve the puzzles of the *Clerk's Tale*, see McNamara, "Chaucer's Use," a study that illustrates both the clear applicability of the doctrinal point but also the difficulty of its application.
38. Farrell corrects his faulty translation of this clause in the first volume of *Sources and Analogues* ("God is the appropriate tester of evils") in the corrigenda included in the second volume, where he follows the Rheims and Wycliffite rendering: "God is not a tempter of evils" (p. 2.822). In contrast, the most widely available translations of this passage – those of Robert Dudley French included in *The Canterbury Tales*, ed. Olson and Kolve; and of Warren Ginsberg in *Riverside* – render the clause as "He/God cannot be tempted by evil." As indicated above, this translation reflects the modern reading of the original Greek, rather than how Petrarch likely understood the Vulgate. (French and Ginsberg translate from Severs, but the latter's text, in this clause, is the same as Farrell's.) Ginsberg, however, in his note to Chaucer's allusion to James 1:13 in IV.1153–55, supplies "God is not

a tempter of evils," and – given that Hengwrt's and Ellesmere's glosses do indeed read *intemptator* and not *intemptatur* – this was likely Chaucer's understanding. I owe thanks to Professor Farrell for helping me work through this complication, and for confirming, in personal communication, Petrarch's reading of James 1:13.

39. See the entries for *tempt, temptation, temptations, tempted, tempter,* and *tempteth* in Tatlock and Kennedy, *A Concordance.*
40. See, e.g., Kirk, "Nominalism."
41. Although in this instance "heigh stile" is a translation of what Chaucer took to be Petrarch's own description of his style at this point.
42. While the equivocation in *Le Livre Griseldis* is itself unequivocal, Chaucer's text of the *Historia* may have rendered Petrarch's subtler phrasing more absolutely: in Hengwrt, Ellesmere, and other manuscripts, the gloss supplying the Latin moralization appears to read "non tamen" (not however) rather than "non tam." *The Hengwrt Chaucer Digital Facsimile* transcribes "tum," but Farrell (from personal communication) believes that Manly and Rickert's reading of "tamen" instead correctly recognizes the minims and abbreviation mark; see *MR* 3.507. For the same reason, later in the gloss, the facsimile's "probat tum" should be "probat tamen" although in this case Manly and Rickert's reading restores the Petrarchan text. In general, as Farrell observes (*Sources and Analogues* 1.129 n. 26), there is a much higher rate of textual variation in the moralization of the *Historia* than in the narrative, suggesting that modern readers are not the only ones who have found it puzzling.
43. For a particularly sophisticated and influential version of this kind of argument, see Dinshaw, *Chaucer's Sexual Poetics*, pp. 132–55.
44. Morse, "The Exemplary Griselda," p. 54. One of Chaucer's early readers, the poet of the *Canterbury Interlude*, appears to confirm the meta-axiological tendencies of the Clerk when he has the latter hold forth upon the value of the *Friar's* and *Summoner's Tales*. See the edition in *Continuations and Additions*, ed. Bowers, ll. 251–62.
45. Chickering, "Form and Interpretation," p. 352.
46. See, e.g., Skeat's note to IV.1162 in *The Complete Works.*
47. Severs, "Did Chaucer Rearrange," offers an especially compelling argument in this regard. The variation consists of the absence of the "Wyves love of Bathe" stanza (IV.1170–76) and the placement of the "Ye archewyves" stanza (IV.1195–1200) at the end of the envoy.
48. See, e.g., Farrell, "The 'Envoy,'" who thoroughly reviews the debate and evidence.
49. For a similar position on the envoy, see Chickering, "Form and Interpretation," which responds to Farrell, "The 'Envoy.'" Offering some further support for this view is the fact that, as Farrell reports, there is a "very

high" correlation between *Clerk's Tale* manuscripts with envoy rubrics and those with glosses from Petrarch's *Historia*, and "there is an excellent possibility" that the latter go back to Chaucer; see "'The Envoy,'" p. 336 n. 11.

50. For the *locus classicus* of this view, see Kittredge, *Chaucer and His Poetry*. Two recent studies that understand the epilogue as staging a complex interaction with the Wife of Bath's performance, but which also incorporate into their readings particularly thoughtful accounts of the uncertainties introduced by the rubric, are Scala, *Desire in the* Canterbury Tales; and Carney, "How to Say 'I.'"
51. Chickering's happy description of the "mad sort of logic" of this self-canceling, self-reflexive moment in the song ("Form and Interpretation," p. 365) aptly also describes much of the *House of Fame*.
52. Across the manuscripts, the pairing of the prologue and tale is a tight, unambiguous one. Hengwrt betrays no signs of discontinuity or scribal hesitation, and all more-or-less complete manuscripts of the *Canterbury Tales* reproduce the pairing, except two that are missing leaves at the point of the prologue: see *MR* 1.109, 1.171, and 2.261. Even Si, which contains just the Clerk's performance and Fragment III, contains the prologue.
53. Kittredge, *Chaucer and His Poetry*, pp. 193–201. As Scala, "The Women in Chaucer's 'Marriage Group,'" has observed, the idea of the marriage group was first mooted not by Kittredge but by E. P. Hammond in *Chaucer: A Bibliographical Manual.*
54. Ashe, "Reading like a Clerk," p. 942.
55. Knapp, *Chaucer and the Social Contest*, pp. 129–40; Patterson, *Temporal Circumstances*, pp. 51–65; Dinshaw, *Chaucer's Sexual Poetics*, pp. 132–55; Ginsberg, *The Cast of Character*, pp. 134–65, *Chaucer's Italian Tradition*, pp. 240–68, and *Tellers, Tales, and Translation*, pp. 145–61.
56. Briggs, "The Clerk," pp. 202–3.
57. Middleton, "The Clerk and His Tale," p. 110.
58. Middleton, "The Clerk and His Tale," p. 111.
59. Middleton, "The Clerk and His Tale," p. 112.
60. See, e.g., Ginsberg, *Tellers, Tales, and Translation*, pp. 174–75.
61. For this critical tradition, see *Variorum GP*, 2.268.
62. Clanchy, *From Memory to Written Record*, esp. pp. 228–32.
63. See *CLR*, p. 148, for this requirement. Chaucer served also, of course, as "clerc de noz [the king's] oevereignes"; see *CLR*, p. 402.
64. Zieman, *Singing the New Song*, pp. 49–56.
65. Gower's epithet appears in the first recension of the *Confessio Amantis*, l. 8.2954*. See *The Complete Works*, ed. Macaulay, Vol. 3.
66. See Briggs, "The Clerk," pp. 190–91, for how the university's institutional fantasy of autonomy from church and state was, in practice, a compromise of dual and sometimes conflicting dependencies.

67. Cobban, *English University Life*, p. x.
68. Because the academics who study Chaucer tend to share this vision – i.e., because they aspire to work within essentially this same axiological environment – the Clerk's portrait has most often been grouped with those of the Parson, Plowman, and (usually) the Knight as among the few depictions of estates ideals. There have, certainly, always also been doubters in this regard, who, for example, have worried over the perhaps unreasonable cost of the "[t]wenty bookes" the *General Prologue* narrator says that the Clerk would like to have at his "beddes heed" (I.293–94). For this latter critical tradition, see *Variorum GP*, pp. 2.268–69 and 2.276–77; and more recently, Johnston, *Clerks and Courtiers*, pp. 146–63; and Hodges, *Chaucer and Clothing*, pp. 160–98.
69. Mann, *Chaucer and Medieval Estates Satire*, pp. 74–76.
70. Lytle, "The Careers," p. 217. This attitude toward the university is evident in the calculated complaint of Rame, Beryn's stepmother in the *Tale of Beryn*, to her husband Faunus: "Sith Beryn is [Faunus's] first sone and heir," she worries about her own potential son's livelihood, "But yf that he had grace to scole for to goo / To have som maner connyng that he myghte trust to." Cited from *Continuations and Additions*, ed. Bowers, ll. 1204–6.
71. Lytle, "The Social Origins," p. 447.
72. Cobban, *English University Life*, p. 19.
73. See Cobban, *English University Life*, p. 24; cf. Evans, "The Number," pp. 497–98.
74. Swanson, "Learnings and Livings," p. 83.
75. For discussion of the regency system, its economics, and its career status and prospects, see, Cobban, *English University Life*, pp. 55–93.
76. Cobban intends his remark about "crude market forces" (*English University Life*, p. 64) as a pejorative one with respect to the late twentieth-century British university. For Wyclif, see, *inter alia*, Courtenay, *Schools and Scholars*, p. 355.
77. Cobban, *English University Life*, p. 24.
78. Courtenay, *Schools and Scholars*, p. 27.
79. See *Variorum GP*, pp. 2.272–73.
80. Cobban, *English University Life*, p. 152.
81. Karras, *From Boys to Men*, p. 93.
82. For contrasting views on this utility, see Swanson, "Learnings and Livings," p. 84; and Cobban, *English University Life*, p. 151.
83. Courtenay, *Schools and Scholars*, p. 33.
84. See Dillon, "A Clerk," p. 113.
85. For *pauperes*, see Karras, *From Boys to Men*, pp. 71–72; and, for general discussion of the financing of a university education, Cobban, *English University Life*, pp. 25–42.

86. See Lytle, "Patronage Patterns," and the responses to his thesis in Courtenay, *Schools and Scholars*, pp. 118–46; Evans, "The Number," esp. pp. 533–38; and Swanson, "Learnings and Livings," esp. pp. 86–96.
87. See Lytle, "The Careers," p. 244; and Mann, *Chaucer and Medieval Estates Satire*, pp. 79–80.
88. Briggs, "The Clerk," pp. 194–99 and Appendix A, pp. 203–4.
89. This habit of usage makes the conclusion of the *Wife of Bath's Tale*, when the knight "hente hire [his transformed wife] in his armes two" (III.1252), that much more problematic. Perhaps feeling the strangeness of the word in the Clerk's portrait, the scribe of Ha^4 wrote "sende"; see *MR* 5.26.
90. Even undergraduates had many opportunities to teach at Oxford, and bachelors studying for a higher degree were depended on, for example, for cursory lectures; see Cobban, *English University Life*, pp. 173, 178. Fleming, "Chaucer's Clerk and John of Salisbury," proposes that this line echoes a comment from John of Salisbury's *Policraticus* 7.15. Although Chaucer may have picked up the phrase from any number of places, or just come up with it independently, the defense that John of Salisbury pursues here of the life of the true philosopher against the views of the Epicureans is indeed resonant with the Clerk's portrait. See *Ioannis Saresberiensis episcopi Carnotensis Policratici,* ed. Webb, pp. 2.156–57.
91. Donaldson, *Speaking of Chaucer*, p. 6; emphasis in original. For recent developments of Donaldson's view, see Denny-Brown, *Fashioning Change*, esp. p. 118; and Farrell, "Hybrid Discourse," pp. 68–72.
92. See, e.g., Severs, "Chaucer's Clerks," who claims that the Clerk "was in his early thirties" (p. 148). Both Briggs, "The Clerk," and Dillon, "A Clerk," among others, emphasize the portrait's ambiguity in this respect.
93. Cobban, *English University Life*, p. 21.
94. Cobban, *English University Life*, p. 59.
95. Astell, *Chaucer and the Universe*, p. 59.
96. Karras, *From Boys to Men*; quotations from pp. 16–17.
97. See Karras, *From Boys to Men*, pp. 67–108.
98. Mann, *Chaucer and Medieval Estates Satire*, p. 76. The phrase "under youre yerde," as Patterson has observed in respect to the *Shipman's Tale*, is doubly gendered, with "yerde" in medieval etymology deriving from *virgo* and "peculiarly appropriate to a maid child," but more directly, of course, denoting the phallic "rod" of authority (*Chaucer and the Subject of History*, p. 364).
99. Salter, *Chaucer*, pp. 37–65.

2. Merchant

1. Cooper, *The Structure*, pp. 143–44.
2. The quotations are from Ladd, *Antimercantilism*, p. 89.

3. Edwards, "Narration and Doctrine," p. 342.
4. Schleusener, "The Conduct," p. 237.
5. Brown, Jr., "Chaucer, the Merchant . . . Part 1," pp. 150–51.
6. Hansen, *Chaucer and the Fictions of Gender*, pp. 245–66; R. Jacob McDonie, "'Ye gete namoore.'"
7. Benson, *Chaucer's Drama of Style*, p. 117.
8. R. A. Shoaf, *Dante, Chaucer*, pp. 185–209; Lee Patterson, *Chaucer and the Subject of History*, pp. 333–44; Glenn Burger, *Chaucer's Queer Nation*, pp. 101–13; Ladd, *Antimercantilism*, pp. 79–91.
9. For detailed consideration of this point, see Epstein, *Chaucer's Gifts*, esp. 1–13.
10. Eberle, "Commercial Language."
11. See Blake, *The Textual Tradition*.
12. See, e.g., David, *The Strumpet Muse*, pp. 170–81.
13. Quotations from Bronson, "Afterthoughts," p. 596; and Kolve, *Telling Images*, p. 170.
14. Bronson, "Afterthoughts"; Donaldson, *Speaking of Chaucer*, pp. 30–45.
15. Donaldson, *Speaking of Chaucer*, pp. 32–33.
16. Bronson, "Afterthoughts," p. 596; Donaldson, *Speaking of Chaucer*, p. 33.
17. Finlayson, "The *Merchant's Tale*," p. 560, emphasis added.
18. See Wurtele, "The Blasphemy," p. 93.
19. Dempster, "The Original Teller of the *Merchant's Tale*."
20. Patterson, *Chaucer and the Subject of History*, p. 339.
21. Mandel, *Geoffrey Chaucer*, pp. 23–49.
22. Wallace, *Chaucerian Polity*, p. 293.
23. Wallace, *Chaucerian Polity*, p. 294.
24. In fact, in Chapter 4 I consider the possibility that Chaucer wrote the *Franklin's Tale* before the tale of January and May, making the latter a rewriting of the former instead of vice versa, and giving the tale of January and May two primary interlocutors.
25. See the theory argued by *MR*, 2.243–44, and the rebuttal by Severs, "Did Chaucer Rearrange."
26. Benson, *Chaucer's Drama of Style*, p. 117. Interestingly, as Edwards, "*The Merchant's Tale*," reports, the scanty evidence that we have of the *Merchant's Tale*'s earliest readers, such as Lydgate's allusion in the *Temple of Glas*, suggests that they heard the tone otherwise.
27. Taylor, "Chaucer's Reticent Merchant," p. 201; the implied allusion to Dante, she suggests, is to *Inferno* 25.94–99.
28. Howard, *The Idea*, p. 263.
29. Phillips, *An Introduction*, p. 130.
30. Patterson, *Chaucer and the Subject of History*, p. 334.
31. Hines, *The Fabliau*, pp. 176–96.

32. Hines, *The Fabliau*, p. 194.
33. For an intriguing analysis of the tale's narratorial style as precisely that of a stand-up comedian, see Hagen, "Chaucer's May," who similarly sees the narrator's superficial bitterness as a pose.
34. The quotation is from Jordan, *Chaucer and the Shape of Creation*, p. 136.
35. See, e.g., Crocker, "Performative Passivity," pp. 180–81.
36. E.g. Ladd, *Antimercantilism*, esp. pp. 89–90.
37. *The Canterbury Tales*, ed. Tyrwhitt, p. 4.262.
38. Lacking the Host's stanza are Ad^3 and Ha^4; Ha^5 has the missing leaf, and Manly and Rickert guess that it did not have the stanza (p. 1.232). Containing the stanza are Ad^1, Bo^2, Cn, Dd, Ds, El, En^1, En^3, Gg, and Ma.
39. See Morse, "The Value of Editing," p. 129.
40. Middleton, "The Clerk and his Tale," rpt. in *Chaucer, Langland*, p. 101.
41. For detail on the historical Harry Bailly, see Martha Carlin, "The Host," who asserts that "there can be no question that members of Chaucer's immediate audience would have been able to identify his Host, 'Herry Bailly', with the Southwark MP and innkeeper of the same name" (p. 472). The correspondence of Harry's fictional wife Goodelief with the historical Harry's wife of record, who was named Christian, is, as Carlin notes (p. 474), not as secure, but (especially in a patriarchal society in which wives' social identities were subsumed within their husbands') this likely did little to diminish what Carlin names the "reality effect" (p. 480) of the identification of the Host and his wife. That effect, as anyone who has read historical fiction knows, is itself part of the fiction; it is a literary device that evokes the category of the real, and thus not only does this evocation not require exact correspondence, its most powerful creative function lies in the failure of exact correspondence.
42. Middleton, "The Clerk and His Tale," p. 101.
43. Williams, "The Host," makes a similar point about this passage and also emphasizes the homosocial relationship it establishes with the Host; see esp. pp. 396–97.
44. Patterson, *Chaucer and the Subject of History*, p. 333.
45. Cooper, *The Structure*, p. 142. See also Brown and Butcher, *The Age of Saturn*, pp. 182–83, for a concise account of the tale's combination of romance and fabliau elements.
46. Cooper, *The Structure*, p. 82.
47. Pearsall, *The Canterbury Tales*, p. 167.
48. By "law of desire," I do not mean to invoke the psychoanalytical sense of the phrase, as that includes conceptual distinctions and elaboration that are beyond the scope of this book. Instead, by "desire" I mean, following Georg Simmel in *The Philosophy of Money*, simply the subjective complement of value. By "law of desire" I mean the supposition that the acquisition of desired objects underlies

all human motivation, which in a fabliau context entails that desires for objects pertaining to the individual body, whether for "survival" or "the satisfaction of appetite" (as Pearsall puts it), are primary.

49. See, e.g., Donaldson, *Speaking of Chaucer*, esp. p. 34.
50. See, e.g., Patterson, *Chaucer and the Subject of History*, esp. p. 337.
51. Benson, *Chaucer's Drama of Style*, p. 127.
52. Kolve, *Telling Images*, pp. 165–66. Hines, *The Fabliau*, pushes this argument even further; see esp. p. 196.
53. Here I allude to, of course, the influential thesis of Trigg, *Congenial Souls*.
54. See, for example, the studies of Benson, "The Marriage 'Encomium'"; and Edwards, "Narration and Doctrine" and "Some Pious Talk."
55. The setting may also evoke, as critics have argued, the usurious practices of Lombard bankers, as well as the tyranny of Lombard despots. Because of the likelihood, however, of the belated determination of the Merchant as narrator, I do not find that the setting thereby licenses us to read the entire tale as an expression of the supposedly usurious consciousness of the Merchant, as does, e.g., Shoaf, *Dante, Chaucer*.
56. Also, as many readers have noticed, January's remark that no "oother lyf . . . is worth a bene" is ironically later echoed in the narrator's account of May's devastating assessment of January's wedding night sexual performance as "nat . . . worth a bene" (IV.1854).
57. Edwards, "Narration and Doctrine," pp. 354–55. Cf. Jones, "January's Genesis," esp. pp. 59–60.
58. Pearsall, *The Canterbury Tales*, p. 204.
59. Cooper, *The Structure*, p. 143.
60. Quotation and translation from *Glossa Ordinaria. Pars 22, In Canticum Canticorum*, ed. Mary Dove, preface, l. 53, p. 77 (English ll. 68–69, p. 76). Subsequent citations of *Glossa's Canticum* preface are to this edition and given in the text by line numbers to the Latin. The implications of the male reader's cross-gender identification have been well explored by Astell, *The Song of Songs*.
61. *Legend of Good Women*, G 86.
62. For Astell's overview of the exegetical tradition, see especially the introduction and first chapter of *The Song of Songs*, pp. 1–41. In specific application of this tradition to the *Merchant's Tale*, Richard Neuse, "Marriage and the Question," traces it back to Augustine and in particular to comments in *De spiritu et littera*, where Augustine worries that "multa quae scripta sunt in Cantico canticorum carnaliter accipiat" (much may be taken in the Song of Songs carnally), so that it may lead "non ad luminosae caritatis fructum, sed ad libidinosae cupiditatis affectum" (not to the fruit of luminous charity but to a disposition of libidinous cupidity) (pp. 119, 129–30 n. 7; translation adapted from Neuse).

63. Astell, *The Song of Songs*, p. 19, drawing from Hugh's *Soliloquium de Arrha Animae.*
64. Astell, *The Song of Songs*, p. 28, adapting Hugh's remarks in *De Scripturis et Scriptoribus Sacris.*
65. Astell remarks on this passage in *The Song of Songs*, pp. 20, 27.
66. Astell, *The Song of Songs*, p. 27.
67. See, respectively, Howard, *The Idea*, pp. 262–63; Pearsall, *The Canterbury Tales*, p. 204; Neuse, "Marriage and the Question," p. 124.
68. Shoaf, among others, argues for the double meaning of "unlearned" and "lascivious" (*Dante, Chaucer*, p. 207).
69. For Augustine's remark, see note 62 above.
70. The narrator's *coup de grâce* in this regard may be Damian's subsequent lifting of May's "smok" (IV.2353), which, according to Taylor, provides a materialized, visual parody of "the traditional metaphor of allegory as a veil for truth" ("Chaucer's Reticent Merchant," p. 200) and hence effects a total reduction of allegoresis to the fabliau real. This point in turn suggests how the tale's well-known, quite extensive, and intricate burlesque of the Fall operates according to the expansion/contraction dynamic.
71. The skepticism might also be identified as Epicurean, in the sophisticated, materialist, rationalist strain that Alexander Murray, "The Epicureans," has identified in some late medieval circles. But the tale's allusion to Epicureanism by way of Boethius (in IV.2021–22, lines which echo ones in the Franklin's *General Prologue* portrait) actually makes this connection less likely, as it casts doubt on Chaucer's familiarity with the kind of Epicureanism that Murray describes.
72. David, *The Strumpet Muse*, pp. 178–79.
73. I allude of course to Middleton, "Chaucer's 'New Men,'" although Middleton's group of new men also includes the Squire and Monk, and does not include the Merchant.
74. Bronson, "Afterthoughts," pp. 585–86. Interestingly, the poet of the *Canterbury Interlude* depicts the Clerk heading into town in the company of the Merchant, Manciple, Miller, and Reeve, suggesting that at least one early reader of Chaucer did not perceive the two figures as antipathetic as we have come to think of them. See the edition in *Continuations and Additions*, ed. Bowers, ll. 295–96.
75. Reale, "A Marchant Was Ther," p. 97.
76. Goddard, "The Merchant," pp. 171, 186. For a thorough review of this critical debate, see Ladd, *Antimercantilism*, pp. 79–86; and see also the *Variorum GP*, pp. 2.250–51.
77. Mann, *Chaucer and Medieval Estates Satire*, p. 101.
78. Ladd, *Antimercantilism*, pp. 80–81, who makes this observation in the context of a general affirmation of Mann's analysis of the portrait. For historical

considerations of these and other elements of the portrait, see Cahn, "Chaucer's Merchants"; Goddard, "The Merchant"; Hodges, *Chaucer and Costume*, pp. 75–100; and Martindale, Jr., "Chaucer's Merchants." For the debate about the term *chevyssaunce* in particular, see the *Variorum GP*, pp. 2.265–66.

79. The listed senses are those for *MED sounen* v. 7. In strict usage, the senses "according with" (7b) and "encouraging" require a following preposition, as in, respectively, the line from the *Clerk's Tale* and the *Retraction*'s "the tales of Caunterbury, thilke that sownen into synne" (X.1086) (although the *MED* chooses "have to do with" for the latter). The *Riverside* glosses the Merchant's *sownynge* as "concerned with, or making known" and the Clerk's as "consonant with," and the *Retraction*'s "sownen" as "tend toward, conducive to." The *Variorum GP*, after reviewing the history of the line's interpretation, chooses "proclaiming" (p. 2.256).
80. Ardis Butterfield, *The Familiar Enemy*, p. 222, has neatly described how Chaucer's own game of hide-and-seek in this portrait mirrors mercantile strategies of concealment.
81. Quotation from Swanson, *Medieval Artisans*, p. 129.
82. See esp. the first chapter in Thrupp, *The Merchant Class*, pp. 1–52.
83. Kermode, *Medieval Merchants*, p. 4; Thrupp, *The Merchant Class*, p. 224. Nightingale, *A Medieval Mercantile Community*, p. 2, echoes this point.
84. For helpful comments on this passage in light of the fifteenth-century *Libelle of Englyshe Polyce*, see Hodges, *Chaucer and Costume*, p. 94. See also Bertolet, *Chaucer, Gower*, pp. 55–57, who neatly terms the Merchant "a person of anxiety" (p. 55).
85. For very detailed but differing accounts of the Merchant's activity of selling shields, see Cahn, "Chaucer's Merchants"; and Martindale, "Chaucer's Merchants." About the line "Ther wiste no wight that he was in dette," Johnson, "Was Chaucer's Merchant in Debt?," has argued that it means that the Merchant "was decidedly not in debt" (p. 51), and some have followed this reading, but Johnson's reasoning has been definitively refuted by Taylor's analysis of the line ("Chaucer's Reticent Merchant," pp. 193–95).
86. See Thrupp's fifth chapter in *The Merchant Class*, pp. 191–233, and esp. pp. 204–5.
87. Hodges's chapter on the Merchant (*Chaucer and Costume*, pp. 75–100) provides an extensive consideration of this point in respect to Chaucer's Merchant; see also the more compact discussion of Bertolet, *Chaucer, Gower*, pp. 55–57, and, more generally, Thrupp, *The Merchant Class*, pp. 143–54.
88. My quotation alludes to the magisterial study of Davis, *Medieval Market Morality*.
89. Ladd, *Antimercantilism*, p. 5.

90. Farber, *An Anatomy of Trade*, p. 62.
91. Farber, *An Anatomy of Trade*, p. 49.
92. Farber, *An Anatomy of Trade*, p. 63.
93. Davis, *Medieval Market Morality*, p. 93.
94. See Farber, *An Anatomy of Trade*, p. 14.
95. Davis, *Medieval Market Morality*, p. 91, and Goddard, "The Merchant," p. 174, both comment on this passage.
96. Cited from *Piers Plowman*, ed. Pearsall, ll. IX.22–29.
97. Langholm, *The Merchant in the Confessional*, esp. p. 235.
98. Thrupp, *The Merchant Class*, esp. pp. 180–88. See also Kermode, *Medieval Merchants*, pp. 116–55.
99. For this mixture of motives, see Kermode, *Medieval Merchants*, p. 153; Thrupp, *The Merchant Class*, pp. 24–25; and the still essential Wood-Legh, *Perpetual Chantries in Britain*.
100. Smith, *Arts of Possession*, p. 146. Ladd, *Antimercantilism*, offers a similar argument; see esp. p. 20.
101. Thrupp, *The Merchant Class*, p. 166.
102. Mandel, *Geoffrey Chaucer*, p. 4, captures this contrast well.
103. See *CLR*, pp. 2 and 8; and Pearsall, *The Life of Geoffrey Chaucer*, pp. 11–17. Chaucer's grandfather Robert Malin le Chaucer may have actually been a mercer who also dealt in wine: see Matheson, "Chaucer's Ancestry," p. 181.
104. Barron, "Chaucer the Poet," p. 29. See also Carlson, *Chaucer's Jobs*, p. 14.
105. See especially Thrupp's chapter on "Trade and Gentility," in *The Merchant Class*, pp. 234–87; and the recent confirmation of her research in Keen, *Origins of the English Gentleman*, pp. 125–31.
106. See Smith, *Arts of Possession*, pp. 21–37. The enthusiasm for trade shown by the landed class was apparently marked enough for Gower to complain about it in his *Mirour de l'Omme*; see, e.g., ll. 23749–60 in *The Complete Works*, ed. Macaulay, Vol. 1.
107. Kermode, *Medieval Merchants*, p. 313.
108. Goddard, "The Merchant," p. 177.
109. Thrupp, *The Merchant Class*, p. 318.
110. Goddard, "The Merchant," p. 179. For the detail of these suits, see *CLR*, pp. 384–401.
111. Reale, "A Marchant," p. 97. For the beard connection with Chaucer, see, e.g., Ladd, *Antimercantilism*, p. 79.
112. Brown, "Chaucer, the Merchant . . . Part II," pp. 255–56.
113. For a seminal account of Chaucer's social ambiguity, see *Strohm, Social Chaucer*, pp. 1–23 and esp. pp. 10–13.

114. See Thrupp, *The Merchant Class*, esp. p. 44; and, for the relationship between masters and apprentices, Hanawalt, *Growing Up in Medieval London*, pp. 129–71; and Karras, *From Boys to Men*, pp. 116–29.
115. See Matheson, "Chaucer's Ancestry," pp. 180–81.
116. *House of Fame*, ll. 652–53.
117. For merchants' sons in the university, see Lytle, "The Social Origins" and "The Careers"; and Thrupp, *The Merchant Class*, p. 161.
118. Indeed, apprentices were usually forbidden to marry until completing their term of service, which for some companies extended to age twenty-six; see Thrupp, *The Merchant Class*, pp. 192–93. For the achievement of manhood, see Karras, *From Boys to Men*, pp. 109–50.
119. Cf. Edwards, "*The Merchant's Tale*," p. 426.
120. Olson, *Literature as Recreation*; see esp. pp. 135–47.
121. See, e.g., Edwards, "*The Merchant's Tale*," p. 418; and Taylor, "Chaucer's Reticent Merchant," p. 197.
122. With this claim I do not mean to imply that actual merchants as a group were especially anti-literature. In fact, as far as book historians have been able to determine, merchants were at least as interested in what we now call literature as other segments of the secular middle strata, and perhaps more so; see, e.g., Scott, "Past Ownership." Instead, I am claiming only that Chaucer's own axiological self-doubt comes to take the form of a mercantile axiology.

3. Squire

1. Goodman, "Chaucer's *Squire's Tale*."
2. Cited from *Criticism*, ed. Bate, p. 85.
3. Peterson, "The Finished Fragment," p. 66.
4. Cooper, *The Structure*, p. 147.
5. R. A. Shoaf is among the few critics who have recognized how a mercantile lexis pervades the Host's remarks here, although I believe that he wrongly hears the tone as one of "vitriol and violence" (*Dante, Chaucer*, p. 201). See also Ginsberg, *Tellers, Tales, and Translation*, p. 167.
6. Carlin, "The Host," p. 472.
7. See Carlin's discussion of Goodelief, "The Host," pp. 473–75.
8. This possibility becomes even more likely, and rather more disturbing, if we accept Sebastian Sobecki's argument ("A Southwark Tale") that Chaucer first compiled the *Canterbury Tales* while resident in Southwark for an audience that included Harry.
9. For the homosocial community of husbands that this passage helps to evoke, and the complementary implied community of wives, see Williams, "The Host."

10. Mann, *Chaucer and Medieval Estates Satire*, p. 117.
11. See, e.g., Peterson "The Finished Fragment," p. 66.
12. Thomas Warton, *The History of English Poetry*, Vol. 1, p. 415. The anthropology of romance that I so briefly allude to in this and the preceding paragraph has many inspirations, the most proximate of which is Fradenburg, "Simply Marvelous," some of whose formulations I have adopted in a very general way and without reference to the psychoanalytic framework that undergirds them. This emphasis on the power of the marvelous and wondrous in the *Squire's Tale* seems to be gaining renewed traction: see, especially, Ingham, *The Medieval New*, pp. 112–40; and Karnes, "Wonders." For an expansive philosophical treatment of medieval romance along these lines, but which does not examine the *Squire's Tale*, see Knapp and Knapp, *Medieval Romance*.
13. Ganim, *Chaucerian Theatricality*, pp. 96–97.
14. Lawton, *Chaucer's Narrators*, p. 128.
15. Interestingly, Hengwrt and seventeen other manuscripts read "wyl" in place of "lust" in V.6, thereby incurring a fourth instance of the noun in eight lines; see *MR* 6.508. Although this reading may simply be the result of transposition, the apparently excessive repetition may instead be the *lectio difficilior*. If so, it would further reinforce the class implications of "hertly wyl": by using "wyl" in precisely the same sense as in V.1, but conversely in respect to the two speakers, the repetition underscores the Squire's social authority in his explicitly ceding that authority to the Host's "wyl."
16. In addition to the two instances already cited, Chaucer uses hertli as an adjective on only two other occasions, both of which appear to combine the senses of "loyal" and "genuine," albeit perhaps ironically: see *Canterbury Tales* IV.502 and *Legend of Good Women* F 2124.
17. This view and its critique are perhaps best epitomized by, respectively, Derek Pearsall's early study, "The Squire as Story Teller," and his later partial retraction (discussed below) in *The Canterbury Tales*, pp. 138–44.
18. The collections *Chaucer's Cultural Geography*, ed. Lynch; and *Rethinking Chaucerian Beasts*, ed. Van Dyke, each contain several essays on the *Squire's Tale* that address these topics.
19. Lynch, "East Meets West," p. 538. Cf. Lawton's comments on Lynch in *Voice*, pp. 156–58.
20. See, especially, David, "Recycling." From the tale's abundant astronomical references, North, *Chaucer's Universe*, dates the events of the tale to 1383, which – even if one accepts the array of presuppositions his method requires – does not preclude a pre-*Tales* origin.
21. See Furnivall, *A Temporary Preface*, esp. pp. 27–29.
22. On this point, see Larson, "*The Squires Tale*," p. 599.

23. See *The Squire's Tale*, ed. Baker, esp. pp. 59–73. More partisanly, Lawton surveys the critical history in *Chaucer's Narrators*, pp. 106–17, as does, much more briefly (and even more partisanly), Murrin, *Trade and Romance*, pp. 285–86.
24. Haller, "Chaucer's *Squire's Tale*," p. 290; Goodman, "Chaucer's *Squire's Tale*," p. 133.
25. Berry, "Flying Sources," esp. p. 288.
26. In addition to the discussion in *Chaucer's Narrators*, see Lawton's revisiting of the topic in *Voice*, esp. pp. 151–56.
27. Pearsall, *The Canterbury Tales*, p. 143.
28. Goodman, "Chaucer's *Squire's Tale*," p. 129.
29. For the tale's historically based setting, see especially Jordan, "Soviet Archeology"; DiMarco, "The Historical Basis"; and Murrin, *Trade and Romance*.
30. Fyler, "Domesticating the Exotic," p. 3. Fyler does go on to suggest, however, that the gifts also convey the disenchantment romance seeks to keep at bay.
31. See Crane, *Animal Encounters*; Kordecki, *Ecofeminist Subjectivities*; and Schotland, "Avian Hybridity."
32. With "fressh as May" we also encounter what appears to be an unmistakable nod to the description of the Squire in the *General Prologue*, which has inspired some rather ingenious explanations that perceive it in various ways as the Squire's knowing self-reference. Keeping to my interpretive limits, we can see this internal allusion more convincingly as Chaucer's shrewdly taking advantage, at some point in the compositional or even compilational process, of the repetition of what is otherwise a thoroughly conventional epithet, thereby bringing Lancelot as idealized courtly speaker into the characterological field of the Squire.
33. For this point about the analogues, see Lightsey, *Manmade Marvels*, p. 74; and Crane, *Gender and Romance*, pp. 138–39. For the pertinent text of one of these analogues, see DiMarco, "The Squire's Tale," pp. 176–80.
34. See Fyler, "Domesticating the Exotic," esp. p. 4. For a different view, see Karnes, "Wonders," esp. pp. 466–70.
35. Berry, "Flying Sources"; DiMarco, "The Dialogue"; Lightsey, *Manmade Marvels*.
36. See, e.g., Fyler, "Domesticating the Exotic," p. 5.
37. For this point, see Murrin, *Trade and Romance*, pp. 46–47.
38. See, e.g., Ingham, *The Medieval New*, p. 136.
39. Lawton in *Chaucer's Narrators* (p. 115) suggests that the tone of the narration is similar to that of the *Nun's Priest's Tale*, but he also puts aside the Merchant-Squire link as potentially inauthentic; in *Voice* he argues for similarity with the narration of the *Franklin's Tale* (and the latter with that of the *Merchant's Tale*).
40. For this point, see Karnes, "Wonders," p. 471.
41. That the horse, despite being a humanly constructed contrivance, nonetheless overflows the boundaries of the real is an important point to which Williams, "Magic," has called our attention.

42. For the horse's self-evident socially symbolic potency, see Crane, *Animal Encounters*, p. 137.
43. Berry makes a similar point: see "Flying Sources," p. 294.
44. Although the *pars secunda* of the tale is beyond the scope of this chapter, how such a consideration would proceed is evident. The homosocial bonding between men of wealth and power, by means of their sharing of the secret of the operation of the mysterious brass steed, has as its double the bonding between *gentil* females – Canacee and the Falcon – through the mediation of the magic ring, the social significance of which the Falcon's obsessive concern with *gentilesse* readily suggests. The masculine-coded, class-linked marvel of the tale's first part is matched by the feminine-coded class-linked marvel of the second.
45. Goodman, "Chaucer's *Squire's Tale*," p. 129.
46. Phillips, *An Introduction*, p. 37.
47. Taylor, "The Squire," p. 63; Hodges, *Chaucer and Costume*, p. 57.
48. Taylor, "The Squire," pp. 63, 76.
49. Given-Wilson, *The English Nobility*, p. 2.
50. Dyer, *Standards of Living*, p. 19.
51. I am thinking here, of course, of Pierre Bourdieu's concepts of symbolic and cultural capital, and the misrecognitions thereof, but the ideas are general enough not to require elaboration in terms of Bourdieu's theory. Coss, *The Origins*, among other studies, develops similar ideas in late medieval terms.
52. Karras, *From Boys to Men*, p. 24.
53. Karras, *From Boys to Men*, p. 27.
54. Orme, "Chaucer and Education," p. 43.
55. Gaylord, "A85–88," pp. 358–59.
56. Fyler, "Domesticating the Exotic," p. 5.
57. See Taylor, "The Squire," pp. 67–73; *The Canterbury Tales*, ed. Mann, p. 802; and Pratt, *Chaucer and War*, pp. 159–70.
58. Pratt, *Chaucer and War*, pp. 164–65.
59. See Keen, *Origins*, pp. 91–92.
60. As many have observed, Gower in his *Mirour de l'Omme* has particularly harsh words for the "chivaler" who seeks military combat for glory ("loos") or the love of his lady ("druerie"); see *The Complete Works*, ed. Macaulay, Vol. 1, ll. 23893–976. Froissart gives an account of a French squire challenging any of the knights and squires in Buckingham's host to individual combat for "love of his lady," to which challenge an English squire responds. See *Chronicles of England*, trans. Johnes, Vol. 1, Book II, Chapter 54 (pp. 613–15), and Pratt's summary of the account in *Chaucer and War*, p. 164.
61. See *Variorum GP*, pp. 2.86–87.
62. Coghill, *The Poet Chaucer*, p. 124.
63. Jones, "Chaucer's Anxiety," p. 315.

64. See *CLR*, pp. 123–24.
65. Strohm, *Social Chaucer*, p. 11.
66. Coss, *The Origins*, p. 219.
67. For the statute, see Coss, *The Origins*, p. 219. Farrell, among others, sees the Squire's carving as indicative of his humility; see "Austin, Joyce," p. 40.
68. Keen, *Origins*, p. 80. For discussion of the rise of the squirearchy, see esp. Keen, *Origins*, pp. 71–86; and Coss, *The Origins*, pp. 69–108 and 216–38.
69. Before *esquire* emerged as a title designating a social category, the term that most commonly designated the role of a man of non-menial background in service in a noble household, but not responsible for arms and horses, was *valet* (Latin *valettus*), although *esquire* also appears. As Coss describes, as *esquire* came to designate a social grade, it gradually replaced *valet* in this respect (see *The Origins*, pp. 226–38). Perhaps this explains an odd feature of the historical record of Chaucer's life: that in the very year in which he was first named a *valettus* (1367) he was also first named an *esquire*, and that these identifications appear respectively in two documents that refer to the very same grant (see *CLR*, pp. 123–24).
70. Keen, *Origins*, p. 73.
71. Strohm, *Chaucer's Tale*, p. 20.
72. Green, *Poets and Princepleasers*, p. 127.
73. Middleton, "The Idea of Public Poetry."
74. Strohm, *Chaucer's Tale*, p. 99.
75. See Karras, *From Boys to Men*, p. 23.
76. For the various practices constituting this norm, see, among many other studies, Mertes, *The English Noble Household*; and Orme, *From Childhood to Chivalry*.
77. Mertes, *The English Noble Household*, p. 54.

4. Franklin

1. Quotations from, respectively, Wheeler, "*Trouthe*"; and Seaman, "'As thynketh yow.'"
2. Seaman, "'As thynketh yow,'" p. 53.
3. Kittredge, *Chaucer and His Poetry*, p. 205.
4. For the debate about whether the *Retraction* originally accompanied the *Canterbury Tales* as a whole, see, e.g., Vaughan, "Creating Comfortable Boundaries," for one doubter. I find the reaffirmation of Partridge, "'The Makere of this Boke,'" persuasive.
5. For an attempt to identify unambiguous allusions, see Mandel, *Geoffrey Chaucer*, pp. 92–106.
6. Lee, "The Question of Closure," p. 190.

7. Quotations from Edwards, "Some Pious Talk," p. 113; and Cooper, *The Structure*, p. 149. For an old but thoroughly succinct account of these parallels, see Holman, "Courtly Love," pp. 242–43.
8. As Lee Patterson has so richly explored, the generic antagonism between this pair of tales powerfully resonates with the socioeconomic antagonism between their tellers (*Chaucer and the Subject of History*, pp. 244–79). If Chaucer originally had planned a similar sequence with what became the second and fourth components of IV-V, that would help to explain his eventual choice of tellers, since, as Michael Johnston, "Mercantile Gentility," has shown, in late medieval England franklins and merchants were perceived as social competitors.
9. For Boccaccio's versions of the story, see Edwards, "The Franklin's Tale." Whether Chaucer knew the version in *Il Filocolo*, the *Decameron*, or both; and whether he adapted it from manuscript or memory, I leave to others to debate.
10. See, *inter alia*, Beston, "How Much," pp. 329–30. Archibald, "The Breton Lay," makes the case for Chaucer's familiarity with the French tradition of *lais*.
11. For the first point about the Middle English lays, see, e.g., Finlayson, "The Form." For the second point, see, e.g., Riddy, "Engendering Pity," p. 54.
12. Crane, *Gender and Romance*, p. 237.
13. See Loomis, "Chaucer and the Breton Lays," esp. p. 24.
14. See, e.g., Finlayson, "The Form," p. 361; and Cooper, *The Structure*, p. 151.
15. Furrow, *Expectations of Romance*, p. 232.
16. Hume, "Why Chaucer Calls," p. 365.
17. Paradigmatic readings in this vein include Robertson, Jr., "Chaucer's Franklin"; and Miller, "Augustinian Wisdom" and "The Epicurean Homily." More recently, see, Lee, "Apollo's Chariot."
18. For a similar point, see Raybin, "'Wommen, of Kynde," p. 70.
19. Lawton, *Voice*, p. 159, also notes a possible connection in these uses of *wil.*
20. An early and still influential version of this dramatic reading is Lumiansky, *Of Sondry Folk*, pp. 180–93. An excellent example of the many readings that situate Chaucer more than the Franklin as the agent of subversion is Crane, *Gender and Romance*, pp. 102–13, as well as the more expansive version of this argument in Crane's earlier "The Franklin as Dorigen."
21. See, esp., Parsons, "No Laughing Matter."
22. See, *inter alia*, Miller, "Augustinian Wisdom," p. 248. Not everyone has been impressed by the narrator's rhetorical performance; see, e.g., Turner, "Speaking 'Amys.'" Yet even a rhetorically bungling admission of being a rhetorical bungler remains potentially witty and ironic.
23. Cf. Lawton, *Voice*, esp. 163–65.
24. See, e.g., Robertson, "Chaucer's Franklin," p. 21; and, more recently, Sweeney, *Magic in Medieval Romance*, pp. 157–58.

25. The still widely cited Gaylord, "The Promises," remains the classic articulation of this position. Others have defended the validity of the promise in light of medieval sources, e.g., Green, *A Crisis of Truth*, pp. 323–24.
26. The quip is from Gaylord, "The Promises," p. 364.
27. As does Wright, "Faith and Narrative."
28. Arnovick, "Dorigen's Promise," p. 127.
29. For a similar view, see Straus, "'Truth' and 'Woman,'" pp. 150–51.
30. See Lawton, *Chaucer's Narrators*, p. 4.
31. For this oft-noticed point, see, *inter alia*, Wheeler, "*Trouthe*," p. 100.
32. Crane, *Gender and Romance*, pp. 64–65.
33. For this point, see, *inter alia*, Hansen, *Chaucer and the Fictions of Gender*, pp. 275–76.
34. For this contrast between romance and fabliau, see Furrow, *Expectations of Romance*, p. 123.
35. Perhaps reflecting the oddness of Aurelius's complete disregard of Dorigen's remark, ten manuscripts make Dorigen's rash promise continuous with her rhetorical question, shifting down the couplet in which Aurelius receives confirmation of the conditions of the promise – "'Is ther noon oother grace in yow?' quod he. / 'No, by that Lord,' quod she, 'that maked me!'" (V.999–1000) – to precede his sigh in line 1006. (See the textual notes in *Riverside*, p. 1129.) Even in this rearrangement, however, Aurelius still ignores Dorigen's question and its implications.
36. See, e.g., Flake, "Love, *Trouthe*," p. 217.
37. Cf. Middleton's conclusion about the Franklin in "Chaucer's 'New Men,'" p. 55.
38. And perhaps it is Chaucer's wry reaction to such features of this passage as Tebano's prayer to Hecate that account for the hyperbole (and, as I suggest below, irony) of his narrator's disparaging comments about the "folye" of the "magyk natureel" of the clerk of Orléans (V.1125, 1131).
39. Kolve, "Rocky Shores," which also appears as Chapter 6 in his *Telling Images* (pp. 171–98).
40. See, e.g., Knopp, "Poetry as Conjuring Act," p. 343.
41. Among those who have noted this sense of the remark are Robertson, "Chaucer's Franklin," and Shoaf, "The *Franklin's Tale*," but both hear no irony, detect no wit, and understand it as illustrative of the Franklin's flaws.
42. Loomis, "Secular Dramatics," p. 244.
43. Loomis, "Secular Dramatics"; Lightsey, *Manmade Marvels*, pp. 55–80.
44. Luengo, "Magic and Illusion," p. 4.
45. On this point, see Lightsey, *Manmade Marvels*, esp. p. 67.
46. For this reason, I believe that it is inaccurate and potentially misleading to term the clerk of Orléans a *tregetour*, as many critics do.

47. For a recent example of the oft-repeated contention about tides, see Greene, "Moral Obligations," p. 99. Greene cites Olson, Laird, and Lytle, "High Tides," for support, but neither this study nor the thorough exploration of the problem by Wood in *Chaucer and the Country of Stars* provides an explanation of the "wyke or tweye" duration.
48. Kolve, *Telling Images*, p. 191. Similarly, see, *inter alia*, Knopp, "Poetry as Conjuring Act"; and Battles, "Magic and Metafiction," esp. p. 246.
49. Kolve, *Telling Images*, p. 191.
50. See, e.g., Battles, "Magic and Metafiction," pp. 254–55.
51. For a concise articulation of this view, see Fein, "Boethian Boundaries," p. 203.
52. Kolve, *Telling Images*, p. 192.
53. Kolve, *Telling Images*, p. 196, emphasis in the original.
54. Greene, "Moral Obligations"; and Nowlin, "Between Precedent and Possibility" are examples of recent affirmative readings in this vein.
55. Kolve, *Telling Images*, p. 192.
56. See, e.g., Battles, "Magic and Metafiction," p. 257.
57. See, *inter alia*, Straus, "'Truth' and 'Woman.'" For a contrary view, see Mann, *Feminizing Chaucer*, pp. 152–73.
58. See Johnston, *Clerks and Courtiers*, p. 102; and for an affirmative reading of this debt forgiveness, Epstein, *Chaucer's Gifts*, pp. 171–95.
59. For this view, see, e.g., Wheeler, "*Trouthe*," p. 113.
60. Cf. Ferster, "Interpretation and Imitation," esp. p 160.
61. For surveys of the critical disagreement about the portrait, see Sembler, "A Frankeleyn"; and *Variorum GP*, pp. 2.301–26, the latter of which records debates sustained now for over a century.
62. Specht, *Chaucer's Franklin*; Saul, "The Social Status" and "Chaucer and Gentility"; Coss, "Literature and Social Terminology" and "The Franklin."
63. Specht, *Chaucer's Franklin*, p. 141.
64. Saul, "The Social Status," pp. 21–22.
65. Coss, "The Franklin," pp. 234–35. See also Saul, "The Social Status," pp. 13–15.
66. For this point, see Johnston, "Mercantile Gentility."
67. For the difficulty of determining the meaning of *contour*, see, e.g., Coss, "The Franklin," pp. 237–38.
68. Coss, "The Franklin," p. 231.
69. Saul, "The Social Status," p. 22.
70. See, e.g., Greene, "Moral Obligations," pp. 96–97.
71. Cf. Epstein, *Chaucer's Gifts*, pp. 24–25.
72. For this emphasis on the Franklin's liminality, see, *inter alia*, Crane, *Gender and Romance* and "The Franklin as Dorigen."

73. Johnston, "Mercantile Gentility," p. 142.
74. See Strohm, *Social Chaucer*, pp. 1–23, and, much expanded if more speculative, his *Chaucer's Tale;* and Patterson, *Chaucer and the Subject of History*, pp. 32–39.
75. Strohm, *Chaucer's Tale*, p. 128. About Chaucer's appointment as justice of the peace, Strohm concludes that "he would have found himself by far the least qualified among the justices with respect to rank, influence, land ownership, or any other criteria of service" (*Chaucer's Tale*, p. 209).
76. Coss, "The Franklin," p. 230; see also p. 234.
77. David, *The Strumpet Muse*, p. 182.
78. Strohm, *Chaucer's Tale*, is acutely interested in these ramifications of Chaucer's departure from London; see esp. pp. 222–37.
79. For forceful deliveries of this view, see Miller's "Augustinian Wisdom" and "The Epicurean Homily"; more recently, see Watts, "*Verray Felicitee*"; and Ginsberg, *Tellers, Tales, and Translation*, pp. 94–96. As these and other critics observe, in addition to the *Consolation,* Chaucer would have encountered negative judgments of Epicureanism in John of Salisbury's *Policraticus*, Gower's *Mirour de l'Omme*, and Dante's *Inferno*.
80. Mann, *Chaucer and Medieval Estates Satire*, pp. 156, 157.
81. Quotation from Pearsall, *The Canterbury Tales*, p. 148. For other examples of this view, see, e.g., Blamires, *Chaucer, Ethics, and Gender*, esp. p. 132; Carruthers, "The Gentilesse," esp. pp. 284, 289–90; and Hersh, "'Knowledge of the Files,'" p. 438.
82. Taylor, "The Squire," p. 63.
83. Coss, "The Franklin," p. 244.
84. Saul, "The Social Status," p. 18.
85. See Coss, "Literature and Social Terminology."
86. Pearcy, "Chaucer's Franklin," p. 37.
87. Maddern, "Gentility" at pp. 26, 28, 31. See also Keen, *Origins of the English Gentleman*, esp. pp. 101–42.
88. Radulescu and Truelove, *Gentry Culture*, pp. 14–15.
89. Thormann, "Networks of Exchange," p. 219.
90. For example, Thormann argues that "the Franklin's courtly tale demonstrates that an economy of cash, a bourgeois exchange form, is penetrating the feudal, aristocratic economy founded in land ownership" ("Networks of Exchange," p. 222).
91. Cf. Crane, "The Franklin as Dorigen," p. 242.
92. For a reading of the link that offers an especially nuanced consideration of these conundrums, see Carney, "*The Franklin's Tale.*"
93. Although *Riverside*'s gloss is "conducted yourself well," the *MED* does not support this, preferring "do one's duty," which duty in this context is the obligation to tell a tale: see *quiten* v. 5a.

94. Among recent examples, see Stock, "Foiled by Fowl," p. 89.
95. Seaman, "'The Wordes'"; see also Larson, "*The Squires Tale*," pp. 604–5.
96. Burrow, "Poems without Endings"; see also Lawton, *Chaucer's Narrators*, pp. 116–17.
97. Partridge, "Minding the Gaps," p. 75.
98. Carney suggests this possibility; see "*The Franklin's Tale*," p. 90 n. 5.
99. In Hengwrt, the link does immediately follow the *Squire's Tale* without a blank space, but, as I explained in this book's introduction, this disposition almost certainly does not stand as the scribe's recognition of the link's status as an interruption. It is rather the result of his squeezing the link into the blank space that he had in fact left between the *Squire's Tale* and the *Merchant's Tale*, a post hoc maneuver that also necessitated adapting the words of the link to refer to the Merchant. Notably, when presumably the same scribe later copied the *Squire's Tale* into Ellesmere, he wrote the final two lines of the *secunda pars* and the first two lines of the *pars tertia* at the top of a leaf (f. 122v), but then left the rest of it blank, thereby restoring the blank space that he had retroactively obscured in Hengwrt; he then begins the link on the following leaf, copying it so that it correctly refers to the Franklin.
100. Kamowski, "Trading the 'Knotte,'" p. 408 n. 10.
101. Saul, "The Social Status," pp. 21–22, offers a précis of this kind of reading.
102. Still exemplary in this regard is Harry Berger, Jr.'s pair of 1960s articles on the "The F-Fragment," parts I and II, which develop this now common line of thinking in depth.
103. Cooper, *The Structure*, p. 147, notes the unusualness of two tales linked by compliment.
104. For the latter point, see, e.g., Haller, "Chaucer's *Squire's Tale*," pp. 293–95.
105. Chaucer's canny deployment of the second-person pronoun in this passage, perhaps because it appears more straightforward than it is, has attracted surprisingly little analysis. For brief notice, see Ginsberg, *Tellers, Tales, and Translation*, pp. 91–93; and Bertolet, *Chaucer, Gower*, p. 64.
106. Thus the Host refers to the Wife of Bath, Clerk, Knight, Man of Law, Friar, Merchant, Squire, and Prioress exclusively with the second-person plural; he refers to the Miller, Reeve, Cook, Summoner, Physician, Pardoner, Shipman, Canon's Yeoman, Manciple, and Chaucer exclusively in the singular. For rather pointed reasons, he switches between the two for the Parson, Monk, and Nun's Priest.
107. Carlin, "The Host", p. 461, although she does not make the comparison with the Franklin. See also Sobecki, "A Southwark Tale," esp. pp. 652–58.
108. See, e.g., Blenner-Hassett, "Autobiographical Aspects," p. 792.
109. As Cooper remarks more generally about the Host's view of the Franklin's pretense to gentility, "the host is a singularly unreliable commentator"

(*The Structure*, p. 149). For the Baillys' poll tax, see Carlin, "The Host," pp. 463–64, who does note that since Harry served as controller of the tax, he may well have secured an under-assessment for himself, making him by this measure actually perhaps somewhat closer to the social level of franklin and squire.

110. See Thrupp, *The Merchant Class*, pp. 234–87. As Johnston shows, even in a fifteenth-century poem that desperately wants to distinguish merchants from franklins, "[u]rban and rural economies . . . largely collapse together by the end of the poem" ("Mercantile Gentility," p. 148).
111. Maddern, "Gentility," p. 27.
112. Fancifully, we might imagine the Franklin pausing, ever so slightly, after "For of thy speche I have greet deyntee," waiting for either "I thank thee" or "I thank you" from the Squire, either of which would socially signify the Squire's recognition of the Franklin's recognition of the Squire's gentility. Hoping then that no one has noticed the Squire's enigmatic reticence (is he frowning at the Franklin? Smiling?), the Franklin shrewdly fills the uncomfortable gap by digressing upon his son. Some such theatrical rendering of this moment, however one would choose to stage it, would underscore that we must somehow account for the fact that Chaucer gives us a monologue that is attempting but failing to be a dialogue.
113. See Saul, "Chaucer and Gentility."
114. See Saul, "The Social Status," esp. pp. 21–23; and, for one of the more sophisticated such arguments, Lipton, *Affections of the Mind*, pp. 21–50.
115. Saul, "Chaucer and Gentility," p. 49.
116. On this point and its distinction from the parvenu argument, see especially Crane, "The Franklin as Dorigen," pp. 242–43.
117. See, e.g., Fein, "Boethian Boundaries," p. 202.
118. See, e.g., Bertolet, *Chaucer, Gower*, p. 65.
119. For the Franklin's two-pronged stratagem here, see Carney, "*The Franklin's Tale*," pp. 91–92.
120. Bertolet, *Chaucer, Gower*, p. 66; and Smith, *Arts of Possession*, pp. 40–41, are among those who make this point, although Smith, unlike Bertolet, is more willing to credit the Franklin for being aware of it.
121. Smith, *Arts of Possession*, pp. 40–41; and, more extensively, Storm, "Chaucer's Franklin," make the case for the reference to distraint. But both are aware that £40 was the norm in Chaucer's day.
122. See *CLR*, p. 514; and Storm, "Chaucer's Franklin," p. 168 n. 20.
123. Johnston recalls Chaucer's service as a page in this context, but does not see it as an inside joke (*Clerks and Courtiers*, p. 100). See also Carney's remarks about the oddness of the reference, "*The Franklin's Tale*," p. 91.

124. The Host's impatience in this regard is admittedly somewhat dramatically odd. Since the Host has not asked for a tale from the Franklin before issuing the reminder about his obligation to tell "A tale or two" (as he does with his reminders to the Man of Law and Clerk), the hot delivery of "wel thou woost" seems curiously unmotivated, unless we see it as inheriting the ire at social pretension evident in the "Straw" remark. Bertolet (*Chaucer, Gower*, pp. 146–48) proposes instead that the Host's anger derives from the Franklin's having usurped the Host's role as governor of the tale-telling contest, which the Franklin does by preventing the Squire from finishing his tale and making himself (the Franklin) that tale's judge. The Host, then, is reminding the Franklin that *everyone* ("ech of yow") is supposed to tell a tale, and so he should have allowed the Squire to finish. But this view requires the assumption that the Franklin has in fact interrupted the Squire. While one might argue, conversely, that the Host's reminder confirms that very assumption, the position of the reminder (deferred until after the Franklin's digression about his son) and its initiation (with the "Straw" comment), along with the Host's use of second-person singular, connect it more obviously to the Franklin's social pretense than to the Host's role as governor of the contest. Moreover, the rest of the interchange, in which the Franklin appears to ask for a slight delay before telling his tale, which the Host denies him, does not seem well-matched to the notion that the Host is angry at the Franklin's intrusion into the tale-telling game. Perhaps the solution to this minor crux is that the primary function of the Host's reminder is not so much dramatic as thematic, enabling as it does a happy placement of the notion of "biheste" just before the *Franklin's Tale*, about which I briefly comment in this chapter's conclusion.
125. See Specht, *Chaucer's Franklin*, p. 158.
126. Carruthers, "The Gentilesse," p. 293 n. 25, suggests this reading, citing the *OED*, although I do not find support for it in the since-published *MED*.
127. For this point, see Riddy, "Engendering Pity," p. 55, although she does not compare the Franklin's response to the Squire's.
128. The other pilgrims who explicitly call attention to their obedience to the Host are, notably, the Knight, the Man of Law, and the Clerk. The Parson, of course, refuses the Host's request and then modifies it to suit his purposes.
129. As Coss writes, Chaucer "was not really sufficiently elevated himself to be able to look down from above in a thoroughly disdainful fashion" ("The Franklin," p. 245).
130. The thematic relation between these two specifically stated amounts has been frequently commented upon; see, e.g., Carney, "*The Franklin's Tale*," p. 100.

131. And, as Riddy, "Engendering Pity," p. 63, and many others have pointed out, it also appears to rest on the silencing of women and their removal from the scene of masculine social exchange.
132. Berger, "The F-Fragment . . . Part I," remains one of the most elaborated readings of this kind.
133. On this point, see the previous chapter and, e.g., Coss, *The Origins*.
134. Davis, *Writing Masculinity*, p. 11.

Works Cited

Archibald, Elizabeth. "The Breton Lay in Middle English: Genre, Transmission and the *Franklin's Tale*." In *Medieval Insular Romance: Translation and Innovation*, ed. Judith Weiss, Jennifer Fellows, and Morgan Dickson. Cambridge: D.S. Brewer, 2000.

Arnovick, Leslie. "Dorigen's Promise and Scholars' Premise: The Orality of the Speech Act in the *Franklin's Tale*." In *Oral Poetics in Middle English Poetry*, ed. Mark C. Amodio. New York: Garland, 1994.

Ashe, Laura. "Reading like a Clerk in the *Clerk's Tale*." *The Modern Language Review* 101 (2006): 935–44.

Astell, Ann W. *The Song of Songs in the Middle Ages*. Ithaca: Cornell University Press, 1990.

Chaucer and the Universe of Learning. Ithaca: Cornell University Press, 1996.

Attridge, Derek. *The Singularity of Literature*. London: Routledge, 2004.

Bahr, Arthur. *Fragments and Assemblages: Forming Compilations of Medieval London*. Chicago: The University of Chicago Press, 2013.

Baker, Robert L. "The English Customs Service, 1307–1343: A Study of Medieval Administration." *Transactions of the American Philosophical Society* n.s. 51 (1961).

Bakhtin, M. M. *The Dialogic Imagination*. Trans. Caryl Emerson and Michael Holquist. Austin: University of Texas Press, 1981.

Barron, Caroline M. "Chaucer the Poet and Chaucer the Pilgrim." In *Historians on Chaucer*, ed. Rigby.

Baswell, Christopher. *Virgil in Medieval England*. Cambridge: Cambridge University Press, 1995.

Bate, Walter Jackson, ed. *Criticism: The Major Texts*. Enlarged ed. San Diego: Harcourt Brace Jovanovich, 1970.

Battles, Paul. "Magic and Metafiction in the *Franklin's Tale*: Chaucer's Clerk of Orléans as Double of the Franklin." In *Marvels, Monsters, and Miracles: Studies in the Medieval and Early Modern Imaginations*, ed. Timothy S. Jones and David A. Sprunger. Kalamazoo: Medieval Institute Publications, 2002.

Benson, C. David. *Chaucer's Drama of Style: Poetic Variety and Contrast in the* Canterbury Tales. Chapel Hill: The University of North Carolina Press, 1986.

Benson, Donald R. "The Marriage 'Encomium' in the *Merchant's Tale*: A Chaucerian Crux." *The Chaucer Review* 14 (1979): 48–60.

Berry, Craig A. "Flying Sources: Classical Authority in Chaucer's *Squire's Tale.*" *ELH* 68 (2001): 287–313.

Berry, George Ricker, ed. *Interlinear Greek-English New Testament.* Grand Rapids: Baker Book House, 1984.

Bertolet, Craig E. *Chaucer, Gower, Hoccleve and the Commercial Practices of Late Fourteenth-Century London.* Farnham, Surrey: Ashgate, 2013.

Beston, John B. "How Much Was Known of the Breton Lai in Fourteenth-Century England?" In *The Learned and the Lewed: Studies in Chaucer and Medieval Literature*, ed. Larry D. Benson. Cambridge: Harvard University Press, 1974.

Bible. *The Holy Bible, Containing the Old and New Testaments, with the Apocryphal Books, in the Earliest English Versions Made from the Latin Vulgate by John Wycliffe and His Followers.* Ed. Rev. Josiah Forshall and Sir Frederic Madden. 4 vols. Oxford: University Press, 1850.

Biblia Sacra iuxta Vulgatam versionem. Ed. Roger Gryson et al. Stuttgart: Deutsche Bibelgesellschaft, 2007.

The Clementine Vulgate Project. http://vulsearch.sourceforge.net/. 2005. (For Migne's Glossa and the Douay-Rheims.)

Blake, N. F. *The Textual Tradition of the* Canterbury Tales. London: Edward Arnold, 1985.

"The Links in the *Canterbury Tales.*" In *New Perspectives on Middle English Texts*, ed. Susan Powell and Jeremy J. Smith. Cambridge: D.S. Brewer, 2000.

Blamires, Alcuin. *Chaucer, Ethics, and Gender.* Oxford: Oxford University Press, 2006.

Bleeth, Kenneth. "The *Physician's Tale.*" In *Sources and Analogues*, ed. Correale and Hamel.

Blenner-Hassett, Roland. "Autobiographical Aspects of Chaucer's Franklin." *Speculum* 28 (1953): 791–800.

Bodden, M. C. *Language as the Site of Revolt in Medieval and Early Modern England: Speaking as a Woman.* New York: Palgrave Macmillan, 2011.

Boitani, Piero. *Chaucer and the Imaginary World of Fame.* Cambridge: D.S. Brewer, 1984.

Bourdieu, Pierre. *Distinction: A Social Critique of the Judgement of Taste.* Trans. Richard Nice. Cambridge: Harvard University Press, 1984.

The Field of Cultural Production. Trans. Randal Johnson. New York: Columbia University Press, 1993.

Bowers, John M., ed. *The* Canterbury Tales*: Fifteenth-Century Continuations and Additions.* Kalamazoo: Medieval Institute Publications, 1992.

Briggs, Charles F. "The Clerk." In *Historians on Chaucer*, ed. Rigby.

Bronson, Bertrand H. "Afterthoughts on the *Merchant's Tale.*" *Studies in Philology* 58 (1961): 583–96.

Brown, Jr., Emerson. "Chaucer, the Merchant, and Their Tale: Getting beyond Old Controversies: Part 1." *The Chaucer Review* 13 (1978): 141–56.

"Chaucer, the Merchant, and Their Tale: Getting beyond Old Controversies: Part II." *The Chaucer Review* 13 (1979): 247–62

Brown, Peter, and Andrew Butcher. *The Age of Saturn: Literature and History in the* Canterbury Tales. Oxford: Basil Blackwell, 1991.

Burger, Glenn. *Chaucer's Queer Nation.* Minneapolis: University of Minnesota Press, 2003.

Burrow, J. A. "Poems without Endings." *Studies in the Age of Chaucer* 13 (1991): 17–37.

Butterfield, Ardis. *The Familiar Enemy: Chaucer, Language, and Nation in the Hundred Years War.* Oxford: Oxford University Press, 2009.

Cahn, Kenneth S. "Chaucer's Merchants and the Foreign Exchange: An Introduction to Medieval Finance." *Studies in the Age of Chaucer* 2 (1980): 81–119.

Cannon, Christopher. *From Literacy to Literature: England, 1300–1400.* Oxford: Oxford University Press, 2016

Carlin, Martha. "The Host." In *Historians on Chaucer*, ed. Rigby.

Carlson, David R. *Chaucer's Jobs.* New York: Palgrave Macmillan, 2004.

Carney, Clíodhna. "*The Franklin's Tale*: The Generous Father and the Spendthrift Son." In *Transmission and Generation in Medieval and Renaissance Literature: Essays in Honour of John Scattergood*, ed. Karen Hodder and Brendan O'Connell. Dublin: Four Courts Press, 2012.

"How to Say 'I': The Clerk, the Wife and Petrarch." In *Chaucer's Poetry: Words, Authority and Ethics*, ed. Clíodhna Carney and Frances McCormack. Dublin: Four Courts Press, 2013.

Carruthers, Mary. "The Gentilesse of Chaucer's Franklin." *Criticism: A Quarterly for Literature and the Arts* 23 (1981): 283–300.

Chaucer, Geoffrey. *The Canterbury Tales of Chaucer.* Ed. Thomas Tyrwhitt. 5 vols. London: T. Payne, 1775–78.

The Complete Works of Geoffrey Chaucer. Ed. W. W. Skeat. 7 vols. Oxford: Clarendon Press, 1894–97.

The Squire's Tale. Ed. Donald C. Baker. The Variorum Chaucer. Vol. 2, part 12. Norman: University of Oklahoma Press, 1993.

The Canterbury Tales. Ed. Jill Mann. London: Penguin Books, 2005.

The Canterbury Tales*: Fifteen Tales and the General Prologue.* Ed. Glending Olson and V. A. Kolve. 2nd ed. New York: W.W. Norton and Company, 2005.

Chickering, Howell. "Form and Interpretation in the *Envoy* to the *Clerk's Tale.*" *The Chaucer Review* 29 (1995): 352–72.

Clanchy, M. T. *From Memory to Written Record: England 1066–1307.* 3rd ed. Chichester: Wiley-Blackwell, 2013.

Clarke, K. P. *Chaucer and Italian Textuality.* Oxford: Oxford University Press, 2011.

Cobban, Alan B. *English University Life in the Middle Ages.* Columbus: Ohio State University Press, 1999.

Coghill, Nevill. *The Poet Chaucer.* 2nd ed. London: Oxford University Press, 1967.

Coleman, Olive. "The Collectors of Customs in London under Richard II." In *Studies in London History Presented to Philip Edmund Jones*, ed. A. E. J. Hollaender and William Kellaway. London: Hodder and Stoughton, 1969.

Cooper, Helen. *The Structure of the* Canterbury Tales. Athens: University of Georgia Press, 1983.

Correale, Robert M. and Mary Hamel, eds. *Sources and Analogues of the* Canterbury Tales. 2 vols. Cambridge: D.S. Brewer, 2005.

Coss, Peter. "Literature and Social Terminology: The Vavasour in England." In *Social Relations and Ideas: Essays in Honour of R. H. Hilton*, ed. T. H. Aston et al. Cambridge: Cambridge University Press, 1983.

The Origins of the English Gentry. Cambridge: Cambridge University Press, 2003.

"The Franklin." In *Historians on Chaucer*, ed. Rigby.

Courtenay, William J. *Schools and Scholars in Fourteenth-Century England*. Princeton: Princeton University Press, 1987.

Crane, Susan. "The Franklin as Dorigen." *The Chaucer Review* 24 (1990): 236–52.

Gender and Romance in Chaucer's Canterbury Tales. Princeton: Princeton University Press, 1994.

Animal Encounters: Contacts and Concepts in Medieval Britain. Philadelphia: University of Pennsylvania Press, 2013.

Crocker, Holly A. *Chaucer's Visions of Manhood*. New York: Palgrave Macmillan, 2007.

"Performative Passivity and Fantasies of Masculinity in the *Merchant's Tale*." *The Chaucer Review* 38 (2003): 178–98.

Da Rold, Orietta. "New Challenges to the Editing of Chaucer." In *Probable Truth: Editing Medieval Texts from Britain in the Twenty-First Century*, ed. Vincent Gillespie and Anne Hudson. Turnhout: Brepols, 2013.

David, Alfred. "Literary Satire in the *House of Fame*." *PMLA* 75 (1960): 333–39.

The Strumpet Muse: Art and Morals in Chaucer's Poetry. Bloomington: Indiana University Press, 1976.

"Recycling *Anelida and Arcite:* Chaucer as a Source for Chaucer." *Studies in the Age of Chaucer. Proceedings*. 1 (1984): 105–15.

Davis, Isabel. *Writing Masculinity in the Later Middle Ages*. Cambridge: Cambridge University Press, 2007.

Davis, James. *Medieval Market Morality: Life, Law and Ethics in the English Marketplace, 1200–1500*. Cambridge: Cambridge University Press, 2012.

de Man, Paul. *Allegories of Reading: Figural Language in Rousseau, Nietzsche, Rilke, and Proust*. New Haven: Yale University Press, 1979.

Dempster, Germaine. "The Original Teller of the *Merchant's Tale*." *Modern Philology* 36 (1938): 1–8.

Denny-Brown, Andrea. *Fashioning Change: The Trope of Clothing in High- and Late-Medieval England*. Columbus: The Ohio State University Press, 2012.

Dillon, Bert. "A Clerk Ther Was of Oxenford Also." In *Chaucer's Pilgrims*, ed. Lambdin and Lambdin.

DiMarco, Vincent. "The Historical Basis of Chaucer's *Squire's Tale*." *Edebiyât: The Journal of Middle Eastern Literatures* 1 (1989): 1–22.

"The Dialogue of Science and Magic in Chaucer's *Squire's Tale*." In *Dialogische Strukturen/Dialogic Structures: Festschrift fur Willi Erzgraber zum 70*, ed. Thomas Kuhn and Ursula Schaefer. Tubingen: Gunter Narr, 1996.

"*The Squire's Tale*." In *Sources and Analogues*, ed. Correale and Hamel.

Dinshaw, Carolyn. *Chaucer's Sexual Poetics*. Madison: The University of Wisconsin Press, 1989.

Donaldson, E. Talbot. *Speaking of Chaucer*. London: The Athlone Press, 1970.

Doyle, A. I., and M. B. Parkes. "A Paleographical Introduction." In *The* Canterbury Tales*: A Facsimile and Transcription of the Hengwrt Manuscript*, ed. Paul G. Ruggiers. Norman: University of Oklahoma Press, 1979

Dyer, Christopher. *Standards of Living in the Later Middle Ages: Social Change in England c. 1200–1520*. Cambridge: Cambridge University Press, 1989.

Eberle, Patricia J. "Commercial Language and the Commercial Outlook in the *General Prologue*." *The Chaucer Review* 18 (1983): 161–74.

Edwards, A. S. G. "*The Merchant's Tale* and Moral Chaucer." *Modern Language Quarterly* 51 (1990): 409–26.

Edwards, Robert R. "Narration and Doctrine in the *Merchant's Tale*." *Speculum* 66 (1991): 342–67.

"Some Pious Talk about Marriage: Two Speeches from the *Canterbury Tales*." In *Matrons and Marginal Women in Medieval Society*, ed. Robert R. Edwards and Vickie Ziegler. Woodbridge, Suffollk: Boydell Press, 1995.

"*The Franklin's Tale*." In *Sources and Analogues*, ed. Correale and Hamel.

Epstein, Robert. *Chaucer's Gifts: The Logic of Exchange in the* Canterbury Tales, 2018.

Evans, T. A. R. "The Number, Origins, and Careers of Scholars." In *The History of the University of Oxford*, ed. J. I. Catto and T. A. R. Evans. 8 vols. 2: Late Medieval Oxford. Oxford: Clarendon Press, 1992.

Farber, Lianna. *An Anatomy of Trade in Medieval Writing: Value, Consent, and Community*. Ithaca: Cornell University Press, 2006.

Farrell, Thomas J. "The 'Envoy de Chaucer' and the *Clerk's Tale*." *The Chaucer Review* 24 (1990): 329–36.

"The Chronotopes of Monology in Chaucer's *Clerk's Tale*." In *Bakhtin and Medieval Voices*, ed. Thomas J. Farrell. Gainesville: University Press of Florida, 1995.

"Austin, Joyce, O'Brian, and Chaucer's Squire: Bakhtin and Medieval Narratology." *Medieval Perspectives* 23 (2008): 31–42.

"Hybrid Discourse in the *General Prologue* Portraits." *Studies in the Age of Chaucer* 30 (2008): 39–93.

Farrell, Thomas J., and Amy W. Goodwin. "*The Clerk's Tale*." In *Sources and Analogues*, ed. Correale and Hamel.

Fein, Susanna. "Boethian Boundaries: Compassion and Constraint in the *Franklin's Tale*." In *Drama, Narrative and Poetry in the* Canterbury Tales, ed. Wendy Harding. Toulouse: Presses Universitaires du Mirail, 2003.

Felski, Rita. "'Context Stinks!'" *New Literary History* 42 (2011): 573–91.

Ferster, Judith. "Interpretation and Imitation in Chaucer's *Franklin's Tale*." In *Medieval Literature: Criticism, Ideology, & History*, ed. David Aers. New York: St. Martin's, 1986.

Finlayson, John. "The Form of the Middle English *Lay*." *The Chaucer Review* 19 (1985): 352–68.

"The *Merchant's Tale*: Literary Contexts, the Play of Genres, and Institutionalized Sexual Relations." *Anglia: Zeitschrift für Englische Philologie* 121 (2003): 557–80.

Flake, Timothy H. "Love, *Trouthe*, and the Happy Ending of the *Franklin's Tale*." *English Studies* 77 (1996): 209–26.

Fleming, John. "Chaucer's Clerk and John of Salisbury." *English Language Notes* 2 (1964): 5–6.

Foucault, Michel. *Discipline and Punish: The Birth of the Prison*. Trans. Alan Sheridan. New York: Pantheon Books, 1977.

Fowler, Elizabeth. *Literary Character: The Human Figure in Early English Writing*. Ithaca: Cornell University Press, 2003.

Fradenburg, L. O. Aranye. "Simply Marvelous." *Studies in the Age of Chaucer* 26 (2004): 1–27.

Froissart, Sir John. *Chronicles of England, France, Spain and the Adjoining Countries, from the Latter Part of the Reign of Edward II. to the Coronation of Henry IV*. Trans. Thomas Johnes, Esq. 2 vols. London: William Smith, 1839.

Frow, John. *Cultural Studies and Cultural Value*. Oxford: Clarendon Press, 1995.

Furnivall, F. J. *A Temporary Preface to the Six-Text Edition of Chaucer's* Canterbury Tales *Part I*. London: N. Trübner for the Chaucer Society, 1868.

Furrow, Melissa. *Expectations of Romance: The Reception of a Genre in Medieval England*. Cambridge: D.S. Brewer, 2009.

Fyler, John M. "Domesticating the Exotic in the *Squire's Tale*." *ELH* 55 (1988): 1–26.

Galloway, Andrew. "Petrarch's Pleasures, Chaucer's Revulsions, and the Aesthetics of Renunciation in Late-Medieval Culture." In *Answerable Style*, ed. Grady and Galloway.

Ganim, John M. *Chaucerian Theatricality*. Princeton: Princeton University Press, 1990.

Gaylord, Alan. "A85-88: Chaucer's Squire and the Glorious Campaign." *Papers of the Michigan Academy of Science, Arts, and Letters* 45 (1960): 341–61.

"The Promises in *The Franklin's Tale*." *ELH* 31 (1964): 331–65.

Ginsberg, Warren. *The Cast of Character: The Representation of Personality in Ancient and Medieval Literature*. Toronto: University of Toronto Press, 1983.

Chaucer's Italian Tradition. Ann Arbor: The University of Michigan Press, 2002.

Tellers, Tales, and Translation in Chaucer's Canterbury Tales. Oxford: Oxford University Press, 2015.

Given-Wilson, Chris. *The English Nobility in the Late Middle Ages: The Fourteenth-Century Political Community*. London: Routledge & Kegan Paul, 1987.

Glossa Ordinaria. Pars 22, In Canticum Canticorum. Ed. Mary Dove. 170. Turnhout: Brepols, 1997.

Goddard, Richard. "The Merchant." In *Historians on Chaucer*, ed. Rigby.

Goodman, Jennifer R. "Chaucer's *Squire's Tale* and the Rise of Chivalry." *Studies in the Age of Chaucer* 5 (1983): 127–36.

Gower, John. *The Complete Works of John Gower*. Ed. G. C. Macaulay. 4 vols. Oxford: Clarendon Press, 1899–1902.

Grady, Frank and Andrew Galloway, eds. *Answerable Style: The Idea of the Literary in Medieval England.* Columbus: The Ohio State University Press, 2013.

Green, Richard Firth. *Poets and Princepleasers: Literature and the English Court in the Late Middle Ages*. Toronto: University of Toronto Press, 1980.

A Crisis of Truth: Literature and Law in Ricardian England. Philadelphia: University of Pennsylvania Press, 1999.

"Griselda in Siena." *Studies in the Age of Chaucer* 33 (2011): 3–38.

"Why Marquis Walter Treats His Wife So Badly." *The Chaucer Review* 47 (2012): 48–62.

Greene, Darragh. "Moral Obligations, Virtue Ethics, and *Gentil* Character in Chaucer's *Franklin's Tale*." *The Chaucer Review* 50 (2015): 88–107.

Hagen, Susan K. "Chaucer's May, Standup Comics, and Critics." In *Chaucer's Humor: Critical Essays*, ed. Jean E. Jost. New York: Garland, 1994.

Haller, Robert S. "Chaucer's *Squire's Tale* and the Uses of Rhetoric." *Modern Philology* 62 (1965): 285–95.

Hammond, E. P. *Chaucer: A Bibliographical Manual.* New York: Macmillan, 1908.

Hanawalt, Barbara A. *Growing Up in Medieval London: The Experience of Childhood in History*. New York: Oxford University Press, 1993.

Hansen, Elaine Tuttle. *Chaucer and the Fictions of Gender*. Berkeley: University of California Press, 1992.

Harden, J. M. *Dictionary of the Vulgate New Testament.* London: Society for Promoting Christian Knowledge, 1921.

Hersh, Cara. "'Knowledge of the Files': Subverting Bureaucratic Legibility in the *Franklin's Tale*." *The Chaucer Review* 43 (2009): 428–54.

Hines, John. *The Fabliau in English*. London: Longman, 1993.

Hodges, Laura F. *Chaucer and Costume: The Secular Pilgrims in the General Prologue*. Cambridge: D.S. Brewer, 2000.

Chaucer and Clothing: Clerical and Academic Costume in the General Prologue to The Canterbury Tales. Cambridge: D.S. Brewer, 2005.

Holman, C. Hugh. "Courtly Love in the *Merchant's* and the *Franklin's Tales*." *ELH* 18 (1951): 241–52.

Horobin, Simon. "Compiling the *Canterbury Tales* in Fifteenth-Century Manuscripts." *The Chaucer Review* 47 (2013): 372–89.

Howard, Donald R. *The Idea of the* Canterbury Tales. Berkeley: University of California Press, 1976.

Hsy, Jonathan. *Trading Tongues: Merchants, Multilingualism, and Medieval Literature*. Columbus: The Ohio State University Press, 2013.

Hume, Kathyrn. "Why Chaucer Calls the *Franklin's Tale* a Breton Lai." *Philological Quarterly* 51 (1972): 365–79.

Ingham, Patricia Clare. *The Medieval New: Ambivalence in an Age of Innovation*. Philadelphia: University of Pennsylvania Press, 2015.

Iser, Wolfgang. *The Fictive and the Imaginary: Charting Literary Anthropology*. Baltimore: The Johns Hopkins University Press, 1993.

Johnson, Oscar E. "Was Chaucer's Merchant in Debt? A Study in Chaucerian Syntax and Rhetoric." *Journal of English and Germanic Philology* 52 (1953): 50–57.

Johnston, Andrew James. *Clerks and Courtiers: Chaucer, Late Middle English Literature and the State Formation Process*. Heidelberg: C. Winter, 2001.

Johnston, Michael. "Mercantile Gentility in Cambridge, University Library MS Ff.2.38." In *Truth and Tales: Cultural Mobility and Medieval Media*, ed. Fiona Somerset and Nicholas Watson. Columbus: The Ohio State University Press, 2015.

Jones, Lindsey M. "Chaucer's Anxiety of Poetic Craft: The *Squire's Tale*." *Style* 41 (2007): 300–18.

Jones, Mike Rodman. "January's Genesis: Biblical Exegesis and Chaucer's *Merchant's Tale*." *Leeds Studies in English* n.s. 39 (2008): 53–87.

Jordan, Carmel. "Soviet Archeology and the Setting of the *Squire's Tale*." *The Chaucer Review* 22 (1987): 128–40.

Jordan, Robert M. *Chaucer and the Shape of Creation: The Aesthetic Possibilities of Inorganic Structure*. Cambridge: Harvard University Press, 1967.

Jusdanis, Gregory. *Fiction Agonistes: In Defense of Literature*. Stanford: Stanford University Press, 2010.

Kamowski, William. "Trading the 'Knotte' for Loose Ends: The *Squire's Tale* and the Poetics of Chaucerian Fragments." *Style* 31 (1997): 391–412.

Karnes, Michelle. "Wonders, Marvels, and Metaphor in the *Squire's Tale*." *ELH* 82 (2015): 461–90.

Karras, Ruth Mazo. *From Boys to Men: Formations of Masculinity in Late Medieval Europe*. Philadelphia: University of Pennsylvania Press, 2003.

Keen, Maurice. *Origins of the English Gentleman: Heraldry, Chivalry and Gentility in Medieval England, c. 1300–c. 1500*. Stroud: Tempus, 2002.

Kermode, Jenny. *Medieval Merchants: York, Beverley and Hull in the Later Middle Ages*. Cambridge: Cambridge University Press, 1998.

Kirk, Elizabeth D. "Nominalism and the Dynamics of the *Clerk's Tale: Homo Viator* as Woman." In *Chaucer's Religious Tales*, ed. C. David Benson and Elizabeth Robertson. Woodbridge: D.S. Brewer, 1990.

Kiser, Lisa J. *Truth and Textuality in Chaucer's Poetry*. Hanover: University Press of New England, 1991.

Kittredge, George Lyman. *Chaucer and His Poetry*. Cambridge: Harvard University Press, 1927.

Knapp, Peggy. *Chaucer and the Social Contest*. New York: Routledge, 1990.

Knapp, James F., and Peggy A. Knapp. *Medieval Romance: The Aesthetics of Possibility*. Toronto: University of Toronto Press, 2017.

Knopp, Sherron. "Poetry as Conjuring Act: The *Franklin's Tale* and *The Tempest*." *The Chaucer Review* 38 (2004): 337–54.

Kolve, V. A. "Rocky Shores and Pleasure Gardens: Poetry vs. Magic in Chaucer's *Franklin's Tale*." In *Poetics: Theory and Practice in Medieval English Literature*, ed. Piero Boitani and Anna Torti. Cambridge: D.S. Brewer, 1991.

Telling Images: Chaucer and the Imagery of Narrative II. Stanford: Stanford University Press, 2009.

Kordecki, Lesley. *Ecofeminist Subjectivities: Chaucer's Talking Birds*. New York: Palgrave Macmillan, 2011.

Ladd, Roger A. *Antimercantilism in Late Medieval English Literature*. New York: Palgrave Macmillan, 2010.

Lambdin, Laura C. and Robert T. Lambdin, eds. *Chaucer's Pilgrims: An Historical Guide to the Pilgrims in* The Canterbury Tales. Westport: Greenwood, 1996.

Langholm, Odd. *The Merchant in the Confessional: Trade and Price in the Pre-Reformation Penitential Handbooks*. Leiden: Brill, 2003.

Langland, William. *Piers Plowman: A New Annotated Edition of the C-text*, ed. Derek Pearsall. Exeter: University of Exeter Press, 2008.

Larson, Charles. "*The Squires Tale*: Chaucer's Evolution from the Dream Vision." *Revue des Langues Vivantes* 43 (1977): 598–607.

Latour, Bruno. *Pandora's Hope: Essays on the Reality of Science Studies*. Cambridge: Harvard University Press, 1999.

Reassembling the Social: An Introduction to Actor-Network-Theory. Oxford: Oxford University Press, 2005.

"An Attempt at a Compositionist Manifesto." *New Literary History* 41 (2010): 471–90.

Lawton, David. *Chaucer's Narrators*. Cambridge: D.S. Brewer, 1985.

Voice in Later Medieval English Literature: Public Interiorities. Oxford: Oxford University Press, 2017.

Lee, B. S. "Apollo's Chariot and the Christian Subtext of *The Franklin's Tale*." *Journal of Medieval Religious Cultures* 36 (2010): 47–67.

"The Question of Closure in Fragment V of *The Canterbury Tales*." *Yearbook of English Studies* 22 (1992): 190–200.

Leicester, Jr., H. Marshall. *The Disenchanted Self: Representing the Subject in the* Canterbury Tales. Berkeley: University of California Press, 1990.

Lightsey, Scott. *Manmade Marvels in Medieval Culture and Literature*. New York: Palgrave Macmillan, 2007.

Lipton, Emma. *Affections of the Mind: The Politics of Sacramental Marriage in Late Medieval English Literature*. Notre Dame: University of Notre Dame Press, 2007.

Loomis, Laura Hibbard. "Chaucer and the Breton Lays of the Auchinleck MS." *Studies in Philology* 38 (1941): 14–33.

"Secular Dramatics in the Royal Palace, Paris, 1378, 1389, and Chaucer's 'Tregetoures.'" *Speculum* 33 (1958): 242–55.

Luengo, Anthony E. "Magic and Illusion in *The Franklin's Tale*." *Journal of English and Germanic Philology* 77 (1978): 1–16.

Lumiansky, R. M. *Of Sondry Folk: The Dramatic Principle in the* Canterbury Tales. Austin: University of Texas Press, 1955.

Lynch, Kathryn L. "East Meets West in Chaucer's *Squire's* and *Franklin's Tales*." *Speculum* 70 (1995): 530–51.

ed. *Chaucer's Cultural Geography*. New York: Routledge, 2002.

Lytle, Guy Fitch. "Patronage Patterns and Oxford Colleges c. 1300-c. 1530." In *The University In Society*, ed. Lawrence Stone. 2 vols. Volume 1: Oxford and Cambridge from the 14th to the Early 19th Century. Princeton: Princeton University Press, 1974.

"The Social Origins of Oxford Students in the Late Middle Ages: New College, c. 1380–c. 1510." In *The Universities in the Late Middle Ages*, ed. Jozef Ijsewijn and Jacques Paquet. Leuven: Leuven University Press, 1978.

"The Careers of Oxford Students in the Later Middle Ages." In *Rebirth, Reform and Resilience: Universities in Transition 1300–1700*, ed. James M. Kittelson and Pamela J. Transue. Columbus: The Ohio State University Press, 1984.

Maddern, Philippa. "Gentility." In *Gentry Culture*, ed. Radulescu and Truelove.

Mandel, Jerome. *Geoffrey Chaucer: Building the Fragments of the* Canterbury Tales. Rutherford: Fairleigh Dickinson University Press, 1992.

Mann, Jill. *Chaucer and Medieval Estates Satire: The Literature of Social Classes and the "General Prologue" to the* Canterbury Tales. Cambridge: Cambridge University Press, 1973.

Feminizing Chaucer. Cambridge: D.S. Brewer, 2002.

Martindale, Wight, Jr. "Chaucer's Merchants: A Trade-Based Speculation on Their Activities." *The Chaucer Review* 26 (1992): 309–16.

Matheson, Lister M. "Chaucer's Ancestry: Historical and Philological Re-Assessments." *The Chaucer Review* 25 (1991): 171–89.

McDonie, R. Jacob. "'Ye gete namoore of me': Narrative, Textual, and Linguistic Desires in Chaucer's *Merchant's Tale*." *Exemplaria* 24 (2012): 313–41.

McNamara, John. "Chaucer's Use of the Epistle of St. James in the *Clerk's Tale*." *The Chaucer Review* 7 (1973): 184–93.

Mertes, Kate. *The English Noble Household 1250–1600: Good Governance and Politic Rule*. Oxford: Basil Blackwell, 1988.

Meyer-Lee, Robert J. "Manuscript Studies, Literary Value, and the Object of Chaucer Studies." *Studies in the Age of Chaucer* 30 (2008): 1–37.

"Fragments IV and V of the *Canterbury Tales* Do Not Exist." *The Chaucer Review* 45 (2010): 1–31.

"Toward a Theory and Practice of Literary Valuing." *New Literary History* 46 (2015): 335–55.

Meyer-Lee, Robert J., and Catherine Sanok, eds. *The Medieval Literary: Beyond Form*. Cambridge: D.S. Brewer, 2018.

Middleton, Anne. "The Idea of Public Poetry in the Reign of Richard II." *Speculum* 53 (1978): 94–114.

"Chaucer's 'New Men' and the Good of Literature in the *Canterbury Tales*." In *Literature and Society: Selected Papers from the English Institute, 1978*, ed. Edward W. Said. Baltimore: The Johns Hopkins University Press, 1980.

"The Clerk and His Tale: Some Literary Contexts." *Studies in the Age of Chaucer* 2 (1980): 121–50.

Chaucer, Langland, and Fourteenth-Century Literary History. Farnham, Surrey: Ashgate, 2013.

Miller, Robert P. "Augustinian Wisdom and Eloquence in the F-Fragment of the *Canterbury Tales*." *Mediaevalia* 4 (1978): 245–75.

"The Epicurean Homily on Marriage by Chaucer's Franklin." *Mediaevalia* 6 (1980): 151–86.

Mills, Mabel H., F.S.A. "The London Customs House during the Middle Ages." *Archaeologia* 83 (1933): 307–25.

"The Collectors of Customs." In *The English Government at Work, 1327–1336*, ed. William A. Morris and Joseph R. Strayer. 3 vols. 2: Fiscal Administration. Cambridge: The Mediaeval Academy of America, 1947.

Minnis, A. J. *Fallible Authors: Chaucer's Pardoner and Wife of Bath*. Philadelphia: University of Pennsylvania Press, 2008.

Minnis, A. J., with V. J. Scattergood and J. J. Smith. *Oxford Guides to Chaucer: The Shorter Poems*. Oxford: Clarendon Press, 1995.

Mooney, Linne R., and Estelle Stubbs. *Scribes and the City: London Guildhall Clerks and the Dissemination of Middle English Literature, 1375–1425*. Woodbridge: York Medieval Press, 2013.

Morse, Charlotte C. "The Exemplary Griselda." *Studies in the Age of Chaucer* 7 (1985): 51–86.

"The Value of Editing the *Clerk's Tale* for the *Variorum Chaucer*." In *Manuscripts and Texts: Editorial Problems in Later Middle English Literature*, ed. Derek Pearsall. Cambridge: D.S. Brewer, 1987.

"Critical Approaches to the *Clerk's Tale*." In *Chaucer's Religious Tales*, ed. C. David Benson and Elizabeth Robertson. Woodbridge: D.S. Brewer, 1990.

Murray, Alexander. "The Epicureans." In *Intellectuals and Writers in Fourteenth-Century Europe: The J. A. W. Bennett Memorial Lectures*, ed. Piero Boitani and Anna Torti. Tübingen: G. Narr, 1986.

Murrin, Michael. *Trade and Romance*. Chicago: The University of Chicago Press, 2014.

Neuse, Richard. "Marriage and the Question of Allegory in the *Merchant's Tale*." *The Chaucer Review* 24 (1989): 115–31.

Nightingale, Pamela. *A Medieval Mercantile Community: The Grocers' Company and the Politics and Trade of London 1000–1485*. New Haven: Yale University Press, 1995.

North, J. D. *Chaucer's Universe*. Oxford: Clarendon Press, 1988.

Nowlin, Steele. "Between Precedent and Possibility: Liminality, Historicity, and Narrative in Chaucer's *The Franklin's Tale*." *Studies in Philology* 103 (2006): 47–67.

Nussbaum, Martha C. *Poetic Justice: The Literary Imagination and Public Life*. Boston: Beacon Press, 1995.

Olson, Donald W., Edgard S. Laird, and Thomas E. Lytle. "High Tides and *The Canterbury Tales*." *Sky and Telescope* 99 (2000): 44–49.

Olson, Glending. *Literature as Recreation in the Later Middle Ages*. Ithaca: Cornell University Press, 1982.

Orme, Nicholas. "Chaucer and Education." *The Chaucer Review* 16 (1981): 38–59.

From Childhood to Chivalry: The Education of the English Kings and Aristocracy 1066–1530. London: Methuen, 1984.

Parsons, Ben. "No Laughing Matter: Fraud, the Fabliau and Chaucer's *Franklin's Tale*." *Neophilologus* 96 (2012): 121–36.

Partridge, Stephen. "Minding the Gaps: Intepreting the Manuscript Evidence of the *Cook's Tale* and the *Squire's Tale*." In *The English Medieval Book: Studies in Memory of Jeremy Griffiths*, ed. A. S. G. Edwards, Vincent Gillespie, and Ralph Hanna. London: The British Library, 2000.

"'The Makere of this Boke': Chaucer's 'Retraction' and the Author as Scribe and Compiler." In *Author, Reader, Book: Medieval Authorship in Theory and Practice*, ed. Stephen Partridge and Erik Kwakkel. Toronto: University of Toronto Press, 2012.

Patterson, Lee. *Chaucer and the Subject of History*. Madison: The University of Wisconsin Press, 1991.

Temporal Circumstances: Form and History in the Canterbury Tales. Basingstoke: Palgrave Macmillan, 2006.

Pearcy, Roy J. "Chaucer's Franklin and the Literary Vavasour." *The Chaucer Review* 8 (1973): 33–59.

Pearsall, Derek. "The Squire as Story Teller." *The University of Toronto Quarterly* 34 (1964): 82–92.

The Canterbury Tales. London: Routledge, 1985.

The Life of Geoffrey Chaucer. Oxford: Blackwell Publishers, 1992.

Peterson, Joyce E. "The Finished Fragment: A Reassessment of the *Squire's Tale*." *The Chaucer Review* 5 (1970): 62–74.

Phillips, Helen. *An Introduction to the* Canterbury Tales: *Reading, Fiction, Context*. New York: St. Martin's, 2000.

Pratt, John H. *Chaucer and War*. Lanham: University Press of America, 2000.

Prendergast, Thomas A. "Canon Formation." In *A Handbook of Middle English Studies*, ed. Marion Turner. Hoboken: John Wiley and Sons, 2013.

Radulescu, Raluca, and Alison Truelove, eds. *Gentry Culture in Late Medieval England*. Manchester: Manchester University Press, 2005.

Raybin, David. "'Wommen, of Kynde, Desiren Libertee': Rereading Dorigen, Rereading Marriage." *The Chaucer Review* 27 (1992): 65–86.

Reale, Nancy M. "A Marchant Was Ther With a Forked Berd." In *Chaucer's Pilgrims*, ed. Lambdin and Lambdin.

Riddy, Felicity. "Engendering Pity in the *Franklin's Tale*." In *Feminist Readings in Middle English Literature: The Wife of Bath and All Her Sect*, ed. Leslie Johnson and Ruth Evans. London: Routledge, 1994.

Rigby, Stephen H., ed., with the assistance of Alistair J. Minnis. *Historians on Chaucer: The* General Prologue *to the* Canterbury Tales. Oxford: Oxford University Press, 2014.

Robertson, D. W., Jr. "Chaucer's Franklin and His Tale." *Costerus* 1 (1974): 1–26.

Rossiter, William T. *Chaucer and Petrarch*. Cambridge: D.S. Brewer, 2010.

"Chaucer Joins the *Schiera: The House of Fame*, Italy and the Determination of Posterity." In *Chaucer and Fame: Reputation and Reception*, ed. Isabel Davis and Catherine Nall. Cambridge: D.S. Brewer, 2015.

Salisbury, John of. *Ioannis Saresberiensis episcopi Carnotensis Policratici: sive, De nugis curialium et vestigiis philosophorum libri VIII*, ed. Clemens C. I. Webb. 2 vols. Oxford: Clarendon Press, 1909.

Salter, Elizabeth. *Chaucer: The* Knight's Tale *and the* Clerk's Tale. London: Edward Arnold, 1962.

Saul, Nigel. "The Social Status of Chaucer's Franklin: A Reconsideration." *Medium Ævum* 52 (1983): 10–26.

"Chaucer and Gentility." In *Chaucer's England: Literature in Historical Context*, ed. Barbara A. Hanawalt. Minneapolis: University of Minnesota Press, 1992.

Scala, Elizabeth. "The Deconstructure of the *Canterbury Tales*." *Journal x* 4 (2000): 171–90.

Absent Narratives, Manuscript Textuality, and Literary Structure in Late Medieval England. New York: Palgrave Macmillan, 2002.

"The Women in Chaucer's 'Marriage Group.'" *Medieval Feminist Forum* 45 (2009): 50–56.

Desire in the Canterbury Tales. Columbus: The Ohio State University Press, 2015.

Schleusener, Jay. "The Conduct of the *Merchant's Tale*." *The Chaucer Review* 14 (1980): 237–50.

Schotland, Sara Deutch. "Avian Hybridity in '*The Squire's Tale*': Uses of Anthropomorphism." In *Rethinking Chaucerian Beasts*, ed. Van Dyke.

Schwebel, Leah. "Redressing Griselda: Restoration through Translation in the *Clerk's Tale*." *The Chaucer Review* 47 (2013): 274–99.

Scott, Kathleen L. "Past Ownership: Evidence of Book Ownership by English Merchants in the Later Middle Ages." In *Makers and Users of Medieval Books: Essays in Honour of A. S. G. Edwards*, ed. Carol M. Meale and Derek Pearsall. Cambridge: D.S. Brewer, 2014.

Seaman, David M. "'The Wordes of the Frankeleyn to the Squier': An Interruption?" *English Language Notes* 24 (1986): 12–18.

"'As thynketh yow': Conflicting Evidence and the Interpretation of *The Franklin's Tale*." *Medievalia et Humanistica* n. s. 17 (1991): 41–58.

Sembler, Elizabeth Mauer. "A Frankeleyn Was In His Compaignye." In *Chaucer's Pilgrims*, ed. Lambdin and Lambdin.

Severs, J. Burke. "Did Chaucer Rearrange the Clerk's Envoy?" *Modern Language Notes* 69 (1954): 472–78.

The Literary Relationships of Chaucer's Clerkes Tale. Hamden: Archon Books, 1972.

Shoaf, R. A. *Dante, Chaucer, and the Currency of the Word: Money, Images, and Reference in Late Medieval Poetry*. Norman: Pilgrim Books, 1983.

"The *Franklin's Tale*: Chaucer and Medusa." *The Chaucer Review* 21 (1986): 274–90.

Simmel, Georg. *The Philosophy of Money*. Trans. Tom Bottomore and David Frisby. London: Routledge & Kegan Paul, 1978.

Simpson, James. *Reform and Cultural Revolution*. Oxford: Oxford University Press, 2002.

Smith, Barbara Hernstein. *Contingencies of Value: Alternative Perspectives for Critical Theory*. Cambridge: Harvard University Press, 1988.

Smith, D. Vance. *Arts of Possession: The Middle English Household Imaginary*. Minneapolis: University of Minnesota Press, 2003.

Sobecki, Sebastian. "A Southwark Tale: Gower, the 1381 Poll Tax, and Chaucer's *The Canterbury Tales*." *Speculum* 92 (2017): 630–60.

Spearing, A. C. *Textual Subjectivity: The Encoding of Subjectivity in Medieval Narratives and Lyrics*. Oxford: Oxford University Press, 2005.

Medieval Autographies: The "I" of the Text. Notre Dame: University of Notre Dame Press, 2012.

Specht, Henrik. *Chaucer's Franklin in the* Canterbury Tales*: The Social and Literary Background of a Chaucerian Character*. Publications of the Department of English, University of Copenhagen. Copenhagen: Akademisk Forlag, 1981.

Stelten, Leo F. *Dictionary of Ecclesiastical Latin*. Peabody: Hendrickson Publishers, 1995.

Stock, Lorraine Kochanske. "Foiled by Fowl: The Squire's Peregrine Falcoln and the Franklin's Dorigen." In *Rethinking Chaucerian Beasts*, ed. Van Dyke.

Storm, Melvin. "Chaucer's Franklin and Distraint of Knighthood." *The Chaucer Review* 19 (1984): 162–68.

Straus, Barrie Ruth. "'Truth' and 'Woman' in Chaucer's *Franklin's Tale*." *Exemplaria* 4 (1992): 135–68.

Strohm, Paul. *Social Chaucer*. Cambridge: Harvard University Press, 1989.

Chaucer's Tale: 1386 and the Road to Canterbury. New York: Penguin, 2014.

Swanson, Heather. *Medieval Artisans: An Urban Class in Late Medieval England*. Oxford: Basil Blackwell, 1989.

Swanson, R. N. "Learnings and Livings: University Study and Clerical Careers in Late Medieval England." *History of the Universities* 6 (1987): 81–103.

Sweeney, Michelle. *Magic in Medieval Romance from Chrétien de Troyes to Geoffrey Chaucer*. Dublin: Four Courts Press, 2000.

Tatlock, John S. P., and Arthur G. Kennedy. *A Concordance to the Complete Works of Geoffrey Chaucer*. Gloucester, MA: Peter Smith, 1963.

Taylor, Craig. "The Squire." In *Historians on Chaucer*, ed. Rigby.

Taylor, Karla. "Chaucer's Reticent Merchant." In *The Idea of Medieval Literature: New Essays on Chaucer and Medieval Culture in Honor of Donald R. Howard*, ed. James M. Dean and Christian K. Zacher. Newark: University of Delaware Press, 1992.

Thormann, Janet. "Networks of Exchange in *The Franklin's Tale.*" *Postmedieval: A Journal of Medieval Cultural Studies* 3 (2012): 212–26.

Thrupp, Sylvia L. *The Merchant Class of Medieval London.* Ann Arbor: University of Michigan Press, 1948.

Travis, Peter W. *Disseminal Chaucer: Rereading* The Nun's Priest's Tale. Notre Dame: University of Notre Dame Press, 2010.

Trigg, Stephanie. *Congenial Souls: Reading Chaucer from Medieval to Postmodern.* Minneapolis: University of Minnesota Press, 2002.

Turner, Joseph. "Speaking 'Amys' in the *Franklin's Tale*: Rhetoric, Truth, and the *Poetria nova.*" *The Chaucer Review* 52 (2017): 217–36.

Van Dyke, Carolynn, ed. *Rethinking Chaucerian Beasts.* New York: Palgrave Macmillan, 2012.

Vaughan, Míċeál F. "Creating Comfortable Boundaries: Scribes, Editors, and the Invention of the *Parson's Tale.*" In *Rewriting Chaucer: Culture, Authority, and the Idea of the Authentic Text, 1400–1602*, ed. Thomas A. Prendergast and Barbara Kline. Columbus: The Ohio State University Press, 1999.

Wallace, David. *Chaucerian Polity: Absolutist Lineages and Associational Forms in England and Italy.* Stanford: Stanford University Press, 1997.

"Chaucer's Italian Inheritance." In *The Cambridge Companion to Chaucer*, ed. Piero Boitani and Jill Mann. Cambridge: Cambridge University Press, 2003.

Warner, Lawrence. *Chaucer's Scribes: London Textual Production, 1384–1432.* Cambridge: Cambridge University Press, 2018.

Warton, Thomas. *The History of English Poetry, from the Close of the Eleventh to the Commencement of the Eighteenth Century.* 4 vols. London: J. Dodsley, 1774.

Watts, William. "Verray Felicitee Parfit and the Development of Chaucer's Philosophical Language." *The Chaucer Review* 43 (2009): 260–81.

Wheeler, Bonnie. "*Trouthe* without Consequences: Rhetoric and Gender in the *Franklin's Tale.*" In *Feminea Medievalia I: Representations of the Feminine in the Middle Ages*, ed. Bonnie Wheeler. Cambridge: Academia Press, 1993.

Williams, Tara. "The Host, His Wife, and Their Communities in the *Canterbury Tales.*" *Studies in the Age of Chaucer* 42 (2008): 383–408.

"Magic, Spectacle, and Morality in the Fourteenth Century." *New Medieval Literatures* 12 (2010): 179–208.

Wood-Legh, K. L. *Perpetual Chantries in Britain.* Cambridge: Cambridge University Press, 1965.

Wood, Chauncey. *Chaucer and the Country of Stars: Poetic Uses of Astrological Imagery.* Princeton: Princeton University Press, 1970.

Wright, Edmond. "Faith and Narrative: A Reading of *The Franklin's Tale.*" *Partial Answers: Journal of the Literature and the History of Ideas* 3 (2005): 19–42.

Wurtele, Douglas. "The Blasphemy of Chaucer's Merchant." *Annuale Mediaevale* 21 (1981): 91–110.

Zieman, Katherine. *Singing the New Song: Literacy and Liturgy in Late Medieval England.* Philadelphia: University of Pennsylvania Press, 2008.

"Escaping the Whirling Wicker: Ricardian Poetics and Narrative Voice in *The Canterbury Tales.*" In *Answerable Style*, ed. Grady and Galloway.

Index

CAMBRIDGE STUDIES IN MEDIEVAL LITERATURE

1 Robin Kirkpatrick *Dante's Inferno: Difficulty and Dead Poetry*
2 Jeremy Tambling *Dante and Difference: Writing in the "Commedia"*
3 Simon Gaunt *Troubadours and Irony*
4 Wendy Scase *"Piers Plowman" and the New Anticlericalism*
5 Joseph J. Duggan *The "Cantar de mio Cid": Poetic Creation in its Economic and Social Contexts*
6 Roderick Beaton *The Medieval Greek Romance*
7 Kathryn Kerby-Fulton *Reformist Apocalypticism and "Piers Plowman"*
8 Alison Morgan *Dante and the Medieval Other World*
9 Eckehard Simon (ed.) *The Theatre of Medieval Europe: New Research in Early Drama*
10 Mary Carruthers *The Book of Memory: A Study of Memory in Medieval Culture*
11 Rita Copeland *Rhetoric, Hermeneutics, and Translation in the Middle Ages: Academic Traditions and Vernacular Texts*
12 Donald Maddox *The Arthurian Romances of Chrétien de Troyes: Once and Future Fictions*
13 Nicholas Watson *Richard Rolle and the Invention of Authority*
14 Steven F. Kruger *Dreaming in the Middle Ages*
15 Barbara Nolan *Chaucer and the Tradition of the "Roman Antique"*
16 Sylvia Huot *The "Romance of the Rose" and its Medieval Readers: Interpretation, Reception, Manuscript Transmission*
17 Carol M. Meale (ed.) *Women and Literature in Britain, 1150–1500*
18 Henry Ansgar Kelly *Ideas and Forms of Tragedy from Aristotle to the Middle Ages*
19 Martin Irvine *The Making of Textual Culture: "Grammatica" and Literary Theory, 350–1100*
20 Larry Scanlon *Narrative, Authority, and Power: The Medieval Exemplum and the Chaucerian Tradition*
21 Erik Kooper (ed.) *Medieval Dutch Literature in its European Context*
22 Steven Botterill *Dante and the Mystical Tradition: Bernard of Clairvaux in the "Commedia"*
23 Peter Biller and Anne Hudson (eds.) *Heresy and Literacy, 1000–1530*
24 Christopher Baswell *Virgil in Medieval England: Figuring the "Aeneid" from the Twelfth Century to Chaucer*
25 James Simpson *Sciences and the Self in Medieval Poetry: Alan of Lille's "Anticlaudianus" and John Gower's "Confessio Amantis"*
26 Joyce Coleman *Public Reading and the Reading Public in Late Medieval England and France*
27 Suzanne Reynolds *Medieval Reading: Grammar, Rhetoric and the Classical Text*
28 Charlotte Brewer *Editing "Piers Plowman": The Evolution of the Text*

29 Walter Haug *Vernacular Literary Theory in the Middle Ages: The German Tradition, 800–1300, in its European Context*
30 Sarah Spence *Texts and the Self in the Twelfth Century*
31 Edwin D. Craun *Lies, Slander and Obscenity in Medieval English Literature: Pastoral Rhetoric and the Deviant Speaker*
32 Patricia E. Grieve *"Floire and Blancheflor" and the European Romance*
33 Huw Pryce (ed.) *Literacy in Medieval Celtic Societies*
34 Mary Carruthers *The Craft of Thought: Meditation, Rhetoric, and the Making of Images, 400–1200*
35 Beate Schmolke-Hasselmann *The Evolution of Arthurian Romance: The Verse Tradition from Chrétien to Froissart*
36 Siân Echard *Arthurian Narrative in the Latin Tradition*
37 Fiona Somerset *Clerical Discourse and Lay Audience in Late Medieval England*
38 Florence Percival *Chaucer's Legendary Good Women*
39 Christopher Cannon *The Making of Chaucer's English: A Study of Words*
40 Rosalind Brown-Grant *Christine de Pizan and the Moral Defence of Women: Reading Beyond Gender*
41 Richard Newhauser *The Early History of Greed: The Sin of Avarice in Early Medieval Thought and Literature*
42 Margaret Clunies Ross (ed.) *Old Icelandic Literature and Society*
43 Donald Maddox *Fictions of Identity in Medieval France*
44 Rita Copeland *Pedagogy, Intellectuals, and Dissent in the Later Middle Ages: Lollardy and Ideas of Learning*
45 Kantik Ghosh *The Wycliffite Heresy: Authority and the Interpretation of Texts*
46 Mary C. Erler *Women, Reading, and Piety in Late Medieval England*
47 D. H. Green *The Beginnings of Medieval Romance: Fact and Fiction, 1150–1220*
48 J. A. Burrow *Gestures and Looks in Medieval Narrative*
49 Ardis Butterfield *Poetry and Music in Medieval France: From Jean Renart to Guillaume de Machaut*
50 Emily Steiner *Documentary Culture and the Making of Medieval English Literature*
51 William E. Burgwinkle *Sodomy, Masculinity, and Law in Medieval Literature: France and England, 1050–1230*
52 Nick Havely *Dante and the Franciscans: Poverty and the Papacy in the "Commedia"*
53 Siegfried Wenzel *Latin Sermon Collections from Later Medieval England: Orthodox Preaching in the Age of Wyclif*
54 Ananya Jahanara Kabir and Deanne Williams (eds.) *Postcolonial Approaches to the European Middle Ages: Translating Cultures*
55 Mark Miller *Philosophical Chaucer: Love, Sex, and Agency in the "Canterbury Tales"*
56 Simon A. Gilson *Dante and Renaissance Florence*
57 Ralph Hanna *London Literature, 1300–1380*
58 Maura Nolan *John Lydgate and the Making of Public Culture*
59 Nicolette Zeeman *"Piers Plowman" and the Medieval Discourse of Desire*

60 Anthony Bale *The Jew in the Medieval Book: English Antisemitisms, 1350–1500*
61 Robert J. Meyer-Lee *Poets and Power from Chaucer to Wyatt*
62 Isabel Davis *Writing Masculinity in the Later Middle Ages*
63 John M. Fyler *Language and the Declining World in Chaucer, Dante, and Jean de Meun*
64 Matthew Giancarlo *Parliament and Literature in Late Medieval England*
65 D. H. Green *Women Readers in the Middle Ages*
66 Mary Dove *The First English Bible: The Text and Context of the Wycliffite Versions*
67 Jenni Nuttall *The Creation of Lancastrian Kingship: Literature, Language and Politics in Late Medieval England*
68 Laura Ashe *Fiction and History in England, 1066–1200*
69 J. A. Burrow *The Poetry of Praise*
70 Mary Carruthers *The Book of Memory: A Study of Memory in Medieval Culture (Second Edition)*
71 Andrew Cole *Literature and Heresy in the Age of Chaucer*
72 Suzanne M. Yeager *Jerusalem in Medieval Narrative*
73 Nicole R. Rice *Lay Piety and Religious Discipline in Middle English Literature*
74 D. H. Green *Women and Marriage in German Medieval Romance*
75 Peter Godman *Paradoxes of Conscience in the High Middle Ages: Abelard, Heloise, and the Archpoet*
76 Edwin D. Craun *Ethics and Power in Medieval English Reformist Writing*
77 David Matthews *Writing to the King: Nation, Kingship, and Literature in England, 1250–1350*
78 Mary Carruthers (ed.) *Rhetoric Beyond Words: Delight and Persuasion in the Arts of the Middle Ages*
79 Katharine Breen *Imagining an English Reading Public, 1150–1400*
80 Antony J. Hasler *Court Poetry in Late Medieval England and Scotland: Allegories of Authority*
81 Shannon Gayk *Image, Text, and Religious Reform in Fifteenth-Century England*
82 Lisa H. Cooper *Artisans and Narrative Craft in Late Medieval England*
83 Alison Cornish *Vernacular Translation in Dante's Italy: Illiterate Literature*
84 Jane Gilbert *Living Death in Medieval French and English Literature*
85 Jessica Rosenfeld *Ethics and Enjoyment in Late Medieval Poetry: Love after Aristotle*
86 Michael Van Dussen *From England to Bohemia: Heresy and Communication in the Later Middle Ages*
87 Martin Eisner *Boccaccio and the Invention of Italian Literature: Dante, Petrarch, Cavalcanti, and the Authority of the Vernacular*
88 Emily V. Thornbury *Becoming a Poet in Anglo-Saxon England*
89 Lawrence Warner *The Myth of "Piers Plowman": Constructing a Medieval Literary Archive*
90 Lee Manion *Narrating the Crusades: Loss and Recovery in Medieval and Early Modern English Literature*

91 Daniel Wakelin *Scribal Correction and Literary Craft: English Manuscripts 1375–1510*
92 Jon Whitman (ed.) *Romance and History: Imagining Time from the Medieval to the Early Modern Period*
93 Virginie Greene *Logical Fictions in Medieval Literature and Philosophy*
94 Michael Johnston and Michael Van Dussen (eds.) *The Medieval Manuscript Book: Cultural Approaches*
95 Tim William Machan (ed.) *Imagining Medieval English: Language Structures and Theories, 500–1500*
96 Eric Weiskott *English Alliterative Verse: Poetic Tradition and Literary History*
97 Sarah Elliott Novacich *Shaping the Archive in Late Medieval England: History, Poetry, and Performance*
98 Geoffrey Russom *The Evolution of Verse Structure in Old and Middle English Poetry: From the Earliest Alliterative Poems to Iambic Pentameter*
99 Ian Cornelius *Reconstructing Alliterative Verse: The Pursuit of a Medieval Meter*
100 Sara Harris *The Linguistic Past in Twelfth-Century Britain*
101 Eric Kwakkel and Rodney Thomson (eds.) *The European Book in the Twelfth Century*
102 Irina Dumitrescu *The Experience of Education in Anglo-Saxon Literature*
103 Jonas Wellendorf *Gods and Humans in Medieval Scandinavia: Retying the Bonds*
104 Thomas A. Prendergast and Jessica Rosenfeld (eds.) *Chaucer and the Subversion of Form*
105 Katie L. Walter *Middle English Mouths*
106 Lawrence Warner *Chaucer's Scribes*
107 Glenn D. Burger and Holly A. Crocker (eds.) *Medieval Affect, Feeling, and Emotion*
108 Robert J. Meyer-Lee *Literary Value and Social Identity in the "Canterbury Tales"*

CPSIA information can be obtained
at www.ICGtesting.com
Printed in the USA
BVHW051003220921
617257BV00015B/305

9 781108 707435